Irrepressible Adventures with Britannia

IRREPRESSIBLE ADVENTURES WITH

BRITANNIA

Personalities, Politics and Culture in Britain

Edited by Wm. Roger Louis

I.B.Tauris
London · New York

Harry Ransom Center
Austin

Published in 2013 by I.B. Tauris & Co Ltd
6 Salem Road, London W2 4BU
Distributed in the United States and Canada
Exclusively by Palgrave Macmillan
175 Fifth Avenue, New York NY 10010
www.ibtauris.com

Harry Ransom Center
University of Texas at Austin
P.O. Drawer 7219
Austin, Texas 78713-7219

The paper used in this publication meets the minimum requirements of
American National Standard for Information Sciences—
Permanence of Paper for Printed Library Materials

ISBN 978-1-78076-797-0 hardcover
ISBN 978-1-78076-798-7 paperback

Library of Congress Control Number: 2013948588

Print production by Studio Azul, Inc., Austin, Texas

Table of Contents

List of Authors

Jad Adams has specialized in work on radicals and nationalists in the nineteenth and twentieth centuries, including the biography *Tony Benn* (1992), which he has recently updated to include the intervening twenty years. He has also written the biographies *Emmeline Pankhurst* (2004) and *Gandhi: Naked Ambition* (2011). His *World History of Women and the Vote* is due to be published in 2014.

Aram Bakshian, Jr., describes himself as a lifelong wordsmith. His articles on politics, history, gastronomy and the arts have been widely published in the United States and overseas. An aide to presidents Nixon, Ford and Reagan, he has been a Resident Fellow at Harvard's Institute of Politics, was the founding editor of the *American Speaker*, and is a contributing editor to the *National Interest*.

Christopher Benfey is Andrew W. Mellon Professor of English at Mount Holyoke College. His books include *Love, Art, and Scandal in the Intersecting Worlds of Emily Dickinson* (2008), *The Double Life of Stephen Crane* (1992), and *Degas in New Orleans* (1997). His most recent work is a family memoir, *Red Brick, Black Mountain, White Clay* (2012). His poems have appeared in the *New Yorker* and the *Paris Review*.

George Bernard is Professor of Early Modern History at the University of Southampton and Leverhulme Major Research Fellow. His books include *The King's Reformation: Henry VIII and the Remaking of the English Church* (2005), *Anne Boleyn: Fatal Attractions* (2010), and *The Late Medieval English Church: Vitality and Vulnerability before the Break with Rome* (2012). He was editor of the *English Historical Review*, 2001–11.

Albert J. Beveridge III has been a Washington lawyer for almost fifty years. He cofounded one of the oldest and best-known environmental law firms in the country, now Beveridge & Diamond. He has served as President of the George C. Marshall Foundation and is presently general counsel to the American Historical Association, a member of the National Council on the Humanities, and a doctoral candidate in history at Johns Hopkins University.

Anne Chisholm, biographer and critic, chairs the Royal Society of Literature. Her books include the biographies *Nancy Cunard* (1979), *Lord*

Beaverbrook (with Michael Davie, 1992), and *Frances Partridge* (2009). She reviews widely and has been a judge for the Booker and the Duff Cooper prizes. She is currently working on a new edition of the letters of Dora Carrington, painter and companion of Lytton Strachey.

Linda Colley is Shelby M. C. Davis 1958 Professor of History at Princeton University. Her books include *Britons: Forging the Nation 1707–1837* (1992), which won the Wolfson Prize; *Captives: Britain, Empire, and the World, 1600–1850* (2002); and *The Ordeal of Elizabeth Marsh: A Woman in World History*, named one of the ten best books of 2007 by the *New York Times*. Colley is a Fellow of the British Academy and Academia Europea.

Richard Davenport-Hines is a past winner of the Wolfson Prize for History and Biography. His biographical subjects include W.H. Auden, Marcel Proust, and Lady Desborough. He is the editor of Hugh Trevor-Roper's *Wartime Journals*, and Trevor-Roper's correspondence with Bernard Berenson. He has written histories of syphilis and sexual oppression, drug taking, the Gothic Revival, the sinking of the *Titanic*, and the Profumo Affair.

Geoffrey V. Davis recently retired from the Chair of English Literature at the University of Aachen, Germany. He is currently head of the European Association for Commonwealth Literature and Language Studies. He is co-editor of the series Cross-Cultures: Readings in the Post-Colonial Literatures in English. His most recent publication is a co-edited volume entitled *Voice and Memory: Indigenous Imagination and Expression* (2011).

Sheldon Garon is the Nissan Professor of History and East Asian Studies at Princeton University. A specialist in modern Japanese history, he also writes transnational history with a focus on the flow of ideas and institutions among the United States, Japan, and European and Asian countries. His latest book is *Beyond Our Means: Why America Spends While the World Saves* (2011). His other books include *Molding Japanese Minds* (1997).

Brian Harrison, after publishing books on British reform movements, Oxford University's history, and the evolution of British political institutions, edited the *Oxford Dictionary of National Biography* (2000–4), and was knighted in 2005 for "services to scholarship." His latest books, in the New Oxford History of England, are *Seeking a Role: The United Kingdom, 1951–1970* (2009) and *Finding a Role? The United Kingdom, 1970–1990* (2010)

Max Hastings was the first journalist to enter the liberated Port Stanley during the 1982 Falklands War. He then served for ten years as Editor-in-Chief of the *Daily Telegraph*. His military histories include *Nemesis: The Battle for Japan, 1944–1945* (2007) and *All Hell Let Loose: The World at War, 1939–1945* (2011). His biographical studies include *Finest Years: Churchill as Warlord, 1940–1945* (2009).

Rosemary Hill is a writer and historian. Her biography of A. W. N. Pugin, *God's Architect* (2007), won the Wolfson History Prize, and her *Stonehenge* (2008) received the Historians of British Art Prize. A contributing editor to the *London Review of Books*, a trustee of the Victorian Society, and a Quondam Fellow of All Souls College, Oxford, she is currently completing a book on antiquarianism in the Romantic period.

Steven Isenberg was Visiting Professor of Humanities at the University of Texas at Austin from 2002 to 2009, until becoming the Executive Director of the PEN American Center. He was formerly Chief of Staff to New York Mayor John V. Lindsay, President of Adelphi University, Executive Vice President of the *Los Angeles Times*, and publisher of *New York Newsday*. He is an Honorary Fellow of Worcester College, Oxford.

David L. Leal is Associate Professor of Government and Director of the Irma Rangel Public Policy Institute at the University of Texas. His research interests include Latino, Mexican, and Canadian politics as well as immigration, religion, and politics. His works include three dozen journal articles and the co-edited volumes *Immigration and the Border* (2013), *Immigration and Public Opinion in Liberal Democracies* (2013), and *Latinos and the Economy* (2010).

Paul Levy was food and wine editor for the *Observer* in the 1980s and subsequently, to the present, arts correspondent for the *Wall Street Journal*. He is co–literary executor of Lytton Strachey's estate and trustee of the Strachey Trust. His books include, as editor, *Eminent Victorians: The Definitive Edition* (2002); he has also edited *The Letters of Lytton Strachey* (2005). His autobiography is *Finger-Lickin' Good: A Kentucky Childhood* (1990).

Jeremy Lewis spent much of his working life as a London publisher, but has been a freelance writer and editor since 1989. The author of three volumes of autobiography, he has also published *Cyril Connolly* (1998), *Tobias Smollett* (2003), *Penguin Special: The Life and Times of Allen Lane* (2005), and *Shades of Greene* (2010). The Editor-at-Large of the *Literary Review,* he is currently writing a book about David Astor.

Ferdinand Mount's novels include a six-volume sequence, *Chronicle of Modern Twilight.* (The title alludes to the sequence *A Chronicle of Ancient Sunlight* by Henry Williamson.) He was editor of the *Times Literary Supplement* from 1991 to 2002. He is a regular contributor to the *Spectator* and the *London Review of Books.* His latest book is *The New Few, or A Very British Oligarchy* (2012).

Susan Napier is formerly the Mitsubishi Professor of Japanese Studies at the University of Texas. She is now Professor of Japanese Studies at Tufts University, where she also teaches courses on science fiction, film, and fantasy. She is the author of four books, the two most recent of which are on Japanese animation. She is currently working on a book on Hayao Miyazaki, Japan's greatest fantasy animation director.

Tom Palaima is the Robert M. Armstrong Centennial Professor of Classics and Director of the Program in Aegean Scripts and Prehistory. The recipient of a MacArthur Fellowship and three Fulbright awards, he has lectured widely and has long been a regular contributor to the *Austin American-Statesman* and the *Times Higher Education.* He co-authored, with Larry Tritle, "The Legacy of War in the Classical World" in *The Oxford Handbook of Warfare in the Classical World* (2013).

Andrew Roberts has done extensive research in Uganda, Zambia, and Tanzania while spending his scholarly career at the School of Oriental and African Studies at the University of London. He is a past editor of the *Journal of African History.* His publications include *A History of Zambia* (1976) and *The Colonial Moment in Africa* (1990). He is the editor of the *Cambridge History of Africa, 1905–1940* (1986).

Adam Sisman's first book was the biography *A. J. P. Taylor* (1994). He then wrote *Boswell's Presumptuous Task: The Making of the Life of Dr. Johnson* (2001), which was awarded the National Book Critics Circle Award for biography, and *The Friendship: Wordsworth and Coleridge* (2007). His most recent book is *An Honourable Englishman: The Life of Hugh Trevor-Roper* (2011).

John Spurling is a playwright, critic, and novelist. After graduating from St. John's College, Oxford, he helped administer a UN Plebiscite in the Southern Cameroons. His first novel, *The Ragged End* (1989), was partly based on this experience, while his thirty-odd plays include a trilogy on the British Empire. His other novels include *A Book of Liszts* (2011) and *The Ten Thousand Things* (2014), set in fourteenth-century China.

Brian Urquhart was a member of the UN Secretariat from the time of its creation, and eventually succeeded Ralph Bunche as Undersecretary General for Special Political Affairs. His books include *Hammarskjold* (1972), *A Life in Peace and War* (1987), and *Ralph Bunche: An American Life* (1993). His father was the English painter Murray Urquhart.

Philip Waller is a past Editor of the *English Historical Review* and a Fellow of Merton College, Oxford. His principal book is *Writers, Readers, and Reputations: Literary Life, 1870–1918* (2006). His other books include *Town, City, and Nation: England, 1850–1914* (1983); *Democracy and Sectarianism: A Political and Social History of Liverpool, 1868–1939* (1981); and, as editor, *The English Urban Landscape* (2000).

David Washbrook studied at Trinity College, Cambridge, and taught at the University of Warwick, 1974–93. He was subsequently Reader in South Asian History at Oxford University and a Fellow of St. Antony's College before returning to Cambridge in 2007. His publications include *The Emergence of Provincial Politics: The Madras Presidency, 1870–1920* (1976). He is the author of "The Two Faces of Colonialism" in the *Oxford History of the British Empire*.

Geoffrey Wheatcroft is a journalist and historian. He studied Modern History at New College, Oxford, and joined the *Spectator* in 1975. He writes regularly for the *Spectator*, the *New York Times*, the *Wall Street Journal*, and the *New York Review of Books*. His books include *The Randlords* (1995), *The Controversy of Zion* (1996), *The Strange Death of Tory England* (2005), *Le Tour* (2007), and *Yo, Blair!* (2007).

The editor, Wm. Roger Louis, is Kerr Professor of English History and Culture and Distinguished Teaching Professor at the University of Texas at Austin, an Honorary Fellow of St. Antony's College, Oxford, and a past President of the American Historical Association. His books include *Imperialism at Bay* (1976), *The British Empire in the Middle East* (1984), and *Ends of British Imperialism* (2006). He is the Editor-in-Chief of the *Oxford History of the British Empire*. In 2013, he was awarded the Benson Medal of the Royal Society of Literature.

Introduction

WM. ROGER LOUIS

T his volume begins, as have its predecessors, by endorsing G. H. Hardy's belief that the agony of having to repeat oneself is so excruciating that it is best to end the agony by offering no apology for doing so. In the spirit of the adventurous refrain—more, still more, yet more, penultimate, ultimate, resurgent, and now irrepressible—I again follow his example. This book consists of a representative selection of lectures given to the British Studies seminar at the University of Texas at Austin. Most of the present lectures were delivered in the years 2011–13.

Lectures are different from essays or scholarly articles. A lecture presumes an audience rather than a reader and usually has a more conversational tone. It allows greater freedom in the expression of personal or subjective views. It permits and invites greater candor. It is sometimes informally entertaining as well as anecdotally instructive. In this volume, the lecture sometimes takes the form of intellectual autobiography—an account of how the speaker has come to grips with a significant topic in the field of British Studies, which, broadly defined, means things British throughout the world as well as things that happen to be English, Irish, Scottish, or Welsh. The scope of British Studies includes all disciplines in the social sciences and humanities as well as music, architecture, and the visual arts. Most of the lectures in this collection fall within the fields of history, politics, and literature, though the dominant themes, here as previously, are literary and historical—even more specifically, in this volume, the rise and fall of literary and historical reputations. Occasionally, though rarely, the lectures have to be given in absentia. In such cases the lectures or at least substantial parts of them are read and then critically discussed. The full sweep of the lectures will be apparent from the list at the end of the book, which is reproduced in its entirety to give a comprehensive idea of the seminar's evolution and substance.

In 2013, the British Studies seminar celebrated its thirty-eighth year. The circumstances for its creation were favorable because of the existence of the Humanities Research Center, now known as the Harry Ransom Center, at the University of Texas. Harry Ransom was the founder of the HRC, a Professor of English and later Chancellor of the University, a collector of rare books, and a man of humane vision. Through the administrative and financial creativity of Ransom and subsequent directors, the HRC has developed into a renowned literary archive with substantial collections, especially in English literature. Ransom thought a weekly seminar might provide the opportunity to learn of the original research being conducted at the HRC as well as to create common bonds of intellectual interest in a congenial setting of overstuffed armchairs, Persian carpets, and generous libations of sherry. The seminar was launched in the fall semester of 1975. It has remained consistent in its dual purpose of providing a forum for visiting scholars engaged in research at the HRC and of enabling the members of the seminar to discuss their own work.

The sherry at the Friday seminar sessions symbolizes the attitude. The seminar meets to discuss whatever happens to be on the agenda, Scottish or Indian, Canadian or Jamaican, English or Australian. George Bernard Shaw once said that England and America were two great countries divided by a common language, but he understated the case by several countries. The interaction of British and other societies is an endlessly fascinating subject on which points of view do not often converge. Diverse preconceptions, which are tempered by different disciplines, help initiate and then sustain controversy, not end it. The ongoing discussions in British Studies are engaging because of the clash of different perspectives as well as the nuance of cultural interpretation. Though the printed page cannot capture the atmosphere of engaged discussion, the lectures do offer the opportunity to savor the result of wide-ranging research and reflection.

I am grateful above all to Philippa Levine, the Co-Director of British Studies, for help in sustaining the program. The seminar has two University sponsors, the College of Liberal Arts and the Harry Ransom Center. We are indebted to the Dean of Liberal Arts, Randy

Diehl, for his support and especially for allocating resources for the program of Junior Fellows—a few assistant professors appointed each year to bring fresh blood, brash ideas, and new commitment to the program. We are equally grateful to the Director of the HRC for providing a home for the seminar. I wish also to thank Frances Terry, who has handled the week-by-week administrative detail from early on in the seminar's history. I am indebted to Kip Keller and Holly McCarthy for their steadfast assistance in many ways.

The seminar benefits especially from the support of the Creekmore and Adele Fath Foundation. When Creekmore Fath was an undergraduate at the University of Texas in the 1930s, he valued especially the chance to exchange ideas and become friends with faculty members. The Fath Foundation now enables the seminar to offer undergraduate and graduate scholarships and generally to advance the cause of the liberal arts. The students appointed to scholarships are known as Churchill Scholars. The Churchill Scholars, like the Junior Fellows, not only contribute to the vitality of the seminar but also extend its age range from those in their late teens to their late eighties.

For vital support we continue to thank Mildred Kerr and the late Baine Kerr of Houston, John and Susan Kerr of San Antonio, Becky Gale and the late Edwin Gale of Beaumont, Custis Wright and the late Charles Alan Wright of Austin, Tex Moncrief of Fort Worth, Althea Osborn and the late Robert Osborn, and the two dozen stouthearted members of the seminar who have contributed to its endowment. We are indebted to Dean Robert D. King for his help over many years. I again extend special thanks to Sam Jamot Brown and Sherry Brown of Durango, Colorado.

THE CHAPTERS—MORE PRECISELY, THE LECTURES—are clustered together more or less chronologically and thematically. The first deals with Victorian England. Despite recent full and scholarly accounts, Prince Albert's reputation has never fully recovered from Lytton Strachey's remark that he was a piece of "impeccable waxwork." **Rosemary Hill**'s lecture reassesses Albert's achievements as well as his working relationship with the Queen. There is no question about Victoria's love for Albert, but she was less well educated as well as impetuous, physically strong, overbearing, and "too hasty and too passionate." Albert himself was in many ways the opposite. When he married Victoria in 1840, he had had no job other than consort. He had a well-trained mind and gradually acquired a knowledge of British politics, though he never was quite able to adapt to the ways of English society. The monarchy was relatively popular, but he believed that dynastic rule could not be taken for granted. His quizzical attitude proved to be an invaluable asset. One of his achievements was the creation of the public image of the Royal Family, a monarchy in which uniqueness is counterbalanced, at least until recent times, by complete normality. Not least, Albert worked relentlessly behind the scenes, content to let Victoria take the credit for his ideas and decisions. After his death in 1861, the Queen without Albert became a political liability, at least to those involved in governmental decisions. Albert's own reputation diminished. In the days of Bloomsbury and beyond, Albert perhaps suffered more than anyone else from the reaction against Victorianism.

In India before independence there were 562 Princely States, roughly half of the Raj, that possessed sovereignty but were ruled indirectly by the British. The range of British control or influence varied widely, but usually the principal function was to guarantee tax collection and the functioning of public services. This system of indirect political control was managed by an administrative part of the Raj called the Political Service, which was responsible directly to the Viceroy. **John Spurling**'s great-uncle, Sir Edmund Gibson, was one of the residents, or advisers, to several of the princes. His diaries and letters provide historical insight into a relatively obscure but vital part of the Raj. Gibson passed the Indian Civil Service examination in 1910 and subsequently spent three and a half decades in the service of Princes. His first significant assignment was with the fifteen-year-old Maharaja of Bharatpur in Rajasthan, in the northwest of India, in 1915. Gibson was eventually involved in alleviating communal violence between Hindus and Muslims. He tried also to persuade the Princes to support to a new and, as it turned out, abortive federal constitution for India. An attempt was made to assassinate him in 1932. He took it in stride, nonchalantly continuing to play bridge that evening as usual. "One Man's Raj" is a rare account that illuminates the everyday life of a Resident in the lost world of the Princes before 1947.

Founded in 1843, *The Economist* now has 1.5 million subscribers, half of them in the United States. Such is its density that there are probably few readers who concentrate on it from cover to cover. Yet **Aram Bakshian** decided in 2012 to concentrate on the magazine page by page in its entirety each week. For the sake of intellectual curiosity, he aimed to assess its history, its quality, and its influence. One thing became immediately clear. It has maintained a consistency of style since the time of the editorship of Walter Bagehot in the nineteenth century. The writing is succinct, precise, usually void of polysyllables, and usually characterized by dry, understated wit. The emphasis is on analysis rather than original reporting. Its comment on contemporary affairs is often unwelcome in much of Asia and Africa. The quirky obituaries are probably read as much as any other part of the magazine—it once ran an obituary on God. All in all, Bakshian concludes, *The Economist* sustains its historic status and has dramatically succeeded in expanding its circulation because of the quality of its coverage. Geographically, politically, economically, scientifically, intellectually, and artistically, *The Economist* is in a class by itself.

The *English Historical Review* was founded in 1886. It is the oldest historical journal in the English language. It is characterized by empirical research and is anti-jargon in tone. It insists on each article having an argument or dominant theme, though the argument might be implicit rather than explicit. **George Bernard** was its twentieth editor, serving for an entire decade (2001–11). He candidly describes what he believes to be the reason for its stable and consistent quality. In the system called peer review, each submitted article is sent by the editor to at least two anonymous readers, sometimes more, who respond with confidential advice on rejection or acceptance, or, in the case of the latter, acceptance with the provision that the author submit a rewritten version taking into account the criticism made by the readers. Despite anonymity, it is well know that many of those associated with the journal have been based in Oxford. To some of those excluded from this elite circle of historians, the *English Historical Review* has traditionally appeared to be "the voice of the History Establishment." Myths die hard. Recognizing wryly that the legend of effortless superiority contributes to the mystique of the journal, Bernard believes, like previous and subsequent editors, that the best response is simply to continue accepting and perfecting closely reasoned articles based on original research.

Before the Second World War, Michael Roberts was an editor, poet, critic, and teacher in mathematics and physics. In 1936, T. S. Eliot published Roberts's *The Faber Book of Modern Verse*. According to **Andrew Roberts** (one of the sons of Michael Roberts), another of his noteworthy books was *The Recovery of the West* (1941), which dissented from the then-popular view that the West was in decay. When Michael Roberts began his wartime career at the BBC, the overseas broadcasts were small, mainly Arabic and Spanish (aimed at Latin America) but followed soon by French, German, and Italian. By mid-1941, the BBC was broadcasting in at least fifteen languages. Roberts's own work is historically significant. In mid-1942, he became

Clandestine Press Editor, an assignment involving contact with the editors of underground newspapers in occupied Europe. The clandestine press department became a planning catalyst that helped shape postwar Europe. Roberts's career at the broadcaster thus reveals an obscure but vital prelude to the reconstruction of Europe as well as a critical part of the history of the BBC during the war.

David Astor was editor of the *Observer* for over a quarter of a century, from 1948 until 1975. Apart from the editorials, there was one part of the paper to which he paid especially close attention: the Profiles, or full-page character sketches of prominent personalities. Astor tried to make the profiles fair and accurate, to describe beliefs or the "soul" of a person as well as provide biographical detail. **Jeremy Lewis**'s lecture resembles an extended version of one of Astor's profiles. It reveals a person at such odds with his mother, Nancy Astor, that his failure to reconcile himself to her harsh and pointed demands contributed to his mental breakdown in the early 1930s while at Balliol, which he left without a degree. He later said that the *Observer* became the Oxford he never had. Astor himself did not much like writing from scratch, and curiously enough he read few books. He was a brilliant line editor, writing and rewriting editorials and other parts of the paper in such detail that it gave the impression of indecision ("the editor's indecision is final" was the office motto). Yet in 1956 he penned in his own hand one of the sharpest and most decisive lines in the history of British journalism. At the time of the British invasion of Suez in 1956, he denounced the British government as crooked and dishonest. That brave stand alienated many of his middle-aged and affluent readers. Circulation fell off, and the *Observer* never again commanded the same prestige and authority.

Ferdinand Mount pays tribute to John Keats, whom he believes to be the poet who, perhaps more than any other, lives on intensely with us to the present. Keats had high spirits, his mental and physical energies were prodigious, and he was generous as well as intellectually tough. The collection including *Endymion* is among the most important works of English poetry ever published. Yet can it and other poems such as "Ode to a Nightingale" be attributed to drug-inspired visions? Was Keats high on laudanum when he wrote his best poetry, as seems commonly to be believed? In the nineteenth century, many people took laudanum as a painkiller or simply to get high. Whatever Keats's intake, it is an insult to his intelligence to believe that he needed it as a stimulant. Keats endured snobbish abuse in this own time, and for posterity to believe that his gift for brilliant conversation, letter writing, and generosity had its source in drugs is another patronizing insult. It denigrates both Keats's poetry and his reputation to think that his work was drug inspired.

Albert J. Beveridge III asks the question, why do the reputations of some musicians, artists, and writers decline, only to revive at a later time? Anthony Trollope's peak of popularity was in the 1860s and early 1870s. Within a quarter of century he had written more than twenty-five novels plus travel books, short stories, and a biography of Palmerston. After his death his readership diminished. Part of the reason for the immediate decline was the sheer volume of his work. How could one person write so much? The critical period of revival was the Second World War. Many of the books in London warehouses were destroyed during the Blitz, and fewer new novels were published because of scarcity of paper. Readers turned to libraries, where they found Trollope in abundance. The BBC gave him a wide audience in the 1940s. At the same time his fame increased in America. The Boston Public Library ranked him close to the top of favorite nineteenth-century writers. His popularity has held up since then to the present, for good reason. Trollope gives the reader insight into character, or what Trollope himself called "pathos and comedy" in common behavior. Whether common people, dukes, or archbishops, his readers could recognize human beings like themselves at all levels of society.

The behemoth of a book by **Philip Waller,** *Readers, Writers, and Reputations*—not easy to read in bed because of its 1,198 pages—covers the period 1870–1918. The book's aim is to draw readers into the actual lives of authors who were then writing for an ever-increasing mass audience. How did an author's book become a best seller? The answer is complicated but includes lecture tours, letters to newspapers, exchanges with critics, and not least the propaganda of literary agents. The implicit theme is the cult of the author. A peak of measureable success seemed to be membership in the Athenaeum (while the reader may infer that membership in the Reform Club was an indication of a more rackety and rowdier way of life). With this lecture in hand, Waller's themes and arguments can be more readily understood. The book itself deserves reading as a coherent and comprehensive treatment of a distinctive theme as well as a work of reference. It is invaluable for understanding the authors and the massive reading public of the period.

Robert Graves acquired early recognition as one of the poets of the First World War. Yet he refused to republish any of his war poetry for over half a century. Though his bitter feelings became apparent in his autobiography, *Good-bye to All That* (1929), Graves per-

sisted in suppressing his wartime poetry. **Tom Palaima** provides the
explanation. Graves had his own austere definition of poetry and
his own view of himself as a poet. During the war he suffered from
shellshock and more than once came close to mental and physical
breakdown. In contrast to the work of his fellow war poets, his poems written during the war therefore strike the reader as detached
and unemotional, whereas it was his deliberate belief that wartime
poetry, his own at least, would be futile. Trying to tell the truth of
the war would serve no purpose. Simply put, those who had not experienced war, who had not witnessed what he called its "suicidal
sacrament," would not understand it. Tom Palaima does a great service in explaining the reasons why Graves wished to suppress his
wartime poetry.

   "Bloomsbury Reassessed" by **Paul Levy** pursues a dual theme.
One is autobiographical: how a member of Harlan "Colonel" Sand-
ers's family, of Kentucky Fried Chicken fame, became co-executor
of the Lytton Strachey Trust. Together with Michael Holroyd, Levy
established the Strachey Trust to safeguard the Strachey papers and
to pursue a more general aim of registering the location of British
literary archives. The other theme is an explanation of the connection between the Bloomsbury set of intellectuals in the early twentieth century and the activists of the 1960s. He made clear in his book
on Strachey published in 1972, *The Most Interesting Question,* that collectively the members of Bloomsbury anticipated the problems of
the 1960s. It may seem obvious now, but it was a brilliant insight at
the time, to conclude that Strachey and his fellow Bloomsberries
would have favored gay rights, women's liberation, the legalization
of marijuana, and the opposition to the Vietnam draft.

   Dora Carrington was born in 1893 and committed suicide at the
age of thirty-nine in 1932. In her early life she studied art at the
Slade School of Fine Art. **Anne Chisholm** explains that her skill as
a letter writer may make her correspondence her greatest achievement. During her own lifetime she was neglected as a painter, in
part because she refused to have her art displayed or sold. She fell
in love with Lytton Strachey in 1915. After a brief experimental period, they decided that they would not, or could not, have sex. Carrington's relationships with other men did not compensate for the
longing she had for Strachey. She was not beautiful, but she was al-
luring and striking, in part because of the apple-like color of her
face. She enjoyed the jokes and games as well as the fun and laughter
she brought to the Bloomsbury circle. Though some of her Bloomsbury companions took a rather patronizing attitude, her surviving
paintings establish her as an artist of distinction. Her uninhibited

letters reveal her love for Strachey as a remarkable and durable loving relationship.

In his lecture on fathers and sons, **Steven Isenberg** presents two quite different examples in different eras but with a common theme. Edmund Gosse's *Father and Son* was published anonymously in 1907. J. R. Ackerley's *My Father and Myself* was published posthumously in 1968. The connecting theme is the influence of father on son. Gosse fils responded to warmth and rigid encouragement, while Joe Ackerley regarded his father "more as a piece of furniture than as a human being." Ackerley found it difficult to confide in his father and knew nothing of his father's secret life until after his death. Both sons, Ackerley no less than Gosse, wanted fatherly love and approval. Gosse's son found it through a combination of temperament and conscience. Joe Ackerley never managed to crack the secrecy of his detached father. The two sons had in common the working out of their own identities by grappling with the lives of their fathers.

Brian Urquhart's early memories are of a primitive farm cottage without electricity or running water. His father was a painter, a gifted watercolorist especially of landscapes and portraits. He had an intense, consuming dislike of war and went to any length to avoid conscription—assuming false names, hiding. When Brian was six, his father abandoned the family. Brian and his brother never forgave his father for deserting their mother, who nevertheless managed to give her sons an excellent education and continued as a teacher until age eighty. At the outbreak of the Second World War, Brian feared that his news of enlisting in the British Army would upset her because of his father's pacifist beliefs. In fact, she was greatly relieved at Brian's becoming a soldier. Brian's memory of his father remained prejudiced—so much so that it later came as a surprise to discover the freshness, spontaneity, and skill of his father's paintings.

Ivy Compton-Burnett published nineteen novels between 1925 and 1963. **Richard Davenport-Hines** traces her career as well as her novels and their underlying theme of what he calls emotional cannibalism. The setting is usually a large domestic household, which at any point might be riven by incest, suicide, parricide, and infanticide. After the First World War, she lived with Margaret Jourdain, an authority on Regency furniture. They shared a large flat with linoleum floors in Kensington. During the Second World War, soldiers and civilians under aerial bombardment read her novels about human desires and animosities against the background of their own fear of impending destruction. Her themes of cruelty, vindictiveness, jealousy, and a general sense of moral turpitude remained

constant. Her wartime audience was in fact reading of the same dys-
functional relationships that existed in Hitler's bunker and Stalin's
Kremlin—for that matter in Churchill's war cabinet and Roosevelt's
White House. Yet despite the misanthropic refrain, her novels have
an emotional resilience. There is no nostalgia. In illuminating human cruelty, she also demonstrates bravery and suffering, and an
originality of ironic despair—in the words of one of her critics, her
novels possess "a spirited, unpardoning sense of justice."

Dan Jacobson was never an overtly political writer, but in the judgment of **Geoffrey V. Davis** his literary distinction can be traced to
his consciousness of the social and economic as well as the political
consequences of apartheid. Born in South Africa in 1929, Jacobson
spent most of his childhood in Kimberley. During his early years,
he became aware of the way in which race, religion, social status,
and wealth were all intertwined in a system in which Africans lived
among themselves, colored people of mixed blood in their own
parts of town, Indians and Chinese among the nonwhites, Greeks
and Jews among the whites. In later years, especially during a trip
to Lithuania to explore his family's antecedents, it came almost
as an epiphany that he was, in his own phrase, once and forever
more a South African. Though he was alienated from South Africa,
much of his later work, for example, the travelogue *The Electronic
Elephant,* returns to themes of race, religion, and social status. He
probes consistently into human nature and problems of complicity
and betrayal—yet his buoyant good nature offsets the darker side of
his work and helps make him a compelling modern writer.

The reasons for Sherlock Holmes's enduring popularity can be
traced to the first of the stories written by Arthur Conan Doyle. By
the time of his death in 1930 there were some fifty-six stories and
other works that formed the "Canon," as it is called by those dedicated to the Holmes literature. Conan Doyle was trained in medicine and served as a ship's doctor on a whaling ship and later as
surgeon on a steamer in West Africa. As **David L. Leal** explains, the
medical background enabled Conan Doyle to apply forensic science
to the routine of Holmes's life. Above all, the stories are important
as studies in the psychology of the criminal. Capable of abductive
reasoning, Holmes has a strong character and a capacity for inge-
nious disguises. The stories have intricate but logical plots as well as
radical criticism of official incompetence. No one at the time would
have believed—certainly not Conan Doyle himself—that a Holmes
fan club would develop its own corpus of essays and books that are
often well written, copiously documented, and sometimes hilari-
ously funny. The requirement for membership in the club is the

willingness to believe in Holmes as a genuine human being. Holmes is a real detective who faces bizarre episodes of everyday life. He suffers from depression, occasionally uses cocaine, and possesses the stamina and skill of a prizefighter. His knowledge embraces the law as well as well as the geography of London. From small pieces of evidence he draws large conclusions. His discoveries in chemistry help him analyze bloodstains, and his experiments with fingerprinting and ballistics were well ahead of his time. Holmes is a legendary figure who adjusts to later periods of time, sometimes with different caps and pipes—but whatever the era, the character of this slightly arrogant master of deduction remains constant. Succeeding generations claim him as a hero, sometimes adjusting him to their own times in movies as well as further stories in scientific detection.

The one-hundredth anniversary of Tarzan, created by the American writer Edgar Rice Burroughs in 1912, caused considerable comment, not all of it favorable, on the significance of a white Englishman growing up as an ape. Tarzan discovered eventually that he was not only a human being but in fact an aristocrat, Lord Greystoke. Tarzan (meaning "white skin") was raised by an ape mother Kala (meaning "beautiful"). **Christopher Benfey** explains that the legendary Tarzan is more complicated and engaging than is commonly assumed, yet also simplistic. Tarzan always rescues Africans in encounters with exploitative whites, though he does not have a high opinion of the Africans themselves. He held stereotyped views of Arab as well as black Africans, regarding both as subhuman. He had also a condescending attitude toward women despite his obvious love for the American woman whom he eventually marries, Jane. What then are we to make of Tarzan's continuing popular appeal? Tarzan emerges as a consistent and chivalrous opponent of colonial oppression. He embodies the strand of American opinion that despised the hypocrisy of European colonialism. But he changes over time. Tarzan's later symbolic significance becomes clear when he fights against the Mau Mau in Kenya and takes Israel's side against the Arabs, especially the arch-villain Gamal Abdel Nasser.

If it is true that each generation gets the fantasy novels it deserves, then **Susan Napier** believes we are lucky to have Harry Potter. The seven novels have received considerable critical disdain. Yet the Harry Potter books have a consistence and coherence within the realm of fantasy fiction. The stories draw on adventure, detective work, and sports, all of which are enhanced by magic. There are witches, dragons, and a secret castle or school, Hogwarts. Yet despite camaraderie and likable individual quirks, there is a dark side to many of the characters. Harry seems to be in search of a father figure to replace his own father killed by the villain of the series, Voldemort, but Harry's father himself was rebellious, rule breaking, and bullying. The wizard headmaster of Hogwarts, Dumbledore, appears at first to be wise, generous, and farseeing but the reader later learns that he might have betrayed his family and friends. Sirius, Harry's godfather, is reckless to a fault. Young readers learn skeptically to explore their own identities in relation to family and friends. Harry and his companions are alone in a parentless world where authority cannot help them. Nor, ultimately, does magic or technology. The young heroes of the series find their own sources of strength in hope, imagination, love, and humor.

THE BLACK HOLE OF CALCUTTA is a legendary episode in the history of the British Empire. After the fall of Calcutta in 1756, the Nawab of Bengal incarcerated 122 British soldiers and civilians, one of which was a woman, in a small dungeon with no ventilation and only two barred windows. The next day, only twenty-three had survived. Retaliation came quickly. Robert Clive marched on Calcutta and set in motion, in the traditional British view, the events leading to the rise of the British Empire in India. **David Washbrook** reassesses the myth from an Indian as well as a British vantage point. Traditionally in British accounts, the Black Hole incident exposed Asiatic moral depravity and the need to bring Indians under the civilizing influence of British law and education. But there may never have been a real Black Hole incident at all. It may have been propaganda for the East India Company. The interesting question is how Calcutta society reacted to the legend of its own barbarity, and how Indian historians have subsequently dealt with it.

Sheldon Garon emphasizes how the German-Japanese alliance of the Second World War has distorted historical understanding of the similarities of the two island empires. The British and the Japanese held in common the belief that saving money was a key element in building a stable society. The Japanese responded to the idea that character and prosperity could be built on virtues of perseverance, honesty, diligence, and self-denial. Self-cultivation and self-discipline in Japan became an ethical code parallel to the belief in both Britain and America that diligence and thrift would improve the nation as well as the individual. During the Second World War, the Japanese continued to observe the British and admired their fortitude during the Blitz as well as their stoical acceptance of food rationing, the same as in Japan. After the war, austerity remained common to both countries. Yet in later decades the Japanese viewed the British as a people enfeebled by the 'English disease'. They now detected a loss of traditional British vitality and national efficiency.

"The Breakup of Britain" is a reasoned historical explanation by **Linda Colley** of the uneven rise of Scottish nationalism and the equally uneven and ambiguous English response. With the weakening after 1945 of the joint Scottish and English experience of global empire, there was a loss of a common identity. England became more culturally diverse while Scotland retained a legal, educational, ecclesiastical, and intellectual distinction of its own. Scottish nationalism thus reflects a widespread decline of what it once meant to be "British." There may be further momentous developments. We are witnessing what Colley describes as "nationalist academic apartheid," in which students in England and Wales will pay £9,000 a year for a university education while students in Scotland (and incoming students from European Union countries) will receive a free university education. One general solution, put forward by, among others, Churchill, might be to create regional assemblies. But even creative initiatives will probably be affected by recent reactions to Scottish nationalism in England and the related issue of the north-south divide not only in England but also in Wales and Ireland.

Two of **Adam Sisman**'s biographies deal with closely linked historians, A. J. P. Taylor and H. R. Trevor-Roper. The biographies were published sixteen years apart: *A. J. P. Taylor: A Biography,* appeared in 1994, the other, *An Honourable Englishman: The Life of Hugh Trevor-Roper,* in 2010. Taylor was a man of the Left and Trevor-Roper of the Right; but they had more in common than was usually assumed at the time. Both were independent thinkers, both were combative, and both were more than willing to express unorthodox opinions. The issue of Hitler brought them into collision. In the *Origins of the Second World War* (1961), Taylor portrayed Hitler as little more than an average German blown large: the real enemy was the German people. Trevor-Roper published a devastating attack, arguing that Taylor had distorted the historical evidence, and that Hitler and the Nazis were the principal cause of the war. Yet Taylor and Trevor-Roper were not enemies but friends (despite public disagreement); "totally untrue" about mutual animosity, said Trevor-Roper, much later, with tears welling up in his eyes. Sisman concludes that Taylor remains a great historian and Trevor-Roper holds equal rank in a different way as an historical essayist.

The relative decline of labor history in Britain since the 1960s leads **Brian Harrison** to investigate the recent energy shown by the historians of Conservatism. He argues that Thatcher's robust leadership caused soul-searching within the ranks. The electoral success from 1979 onward inspired more vigorous study of the Party's past. Thatcher's impact on British society was so wide-ranging that it encouraged a similar broadening within historical writing in general. Her emphasis on the moral case for capitalism made the Party seem less reactionary, less obstructive. It became a party of radical change that could throw Labour and Liberals on the defensive, and eventually forced both after 1990 to move to the right. The moralistic "Victorian" dimensions of her strategy, which she worked out late in her premiership, failed to reconcile the problem of how to safeguard morality without religion. Her ideas reflected her Methodist upbringing and the belief that churches were integral to families, neighbors, communities, and the nation. But her views also had overtones of a Dickensian Britain, and it had little to offer a party compelled to survive in a secularized society of the late twentieth century. If she had retained power after 1990, Thatcher would have faced serious difficulties.

The pen portrait of Tony Benn by **Jad Adams** delineates Benn's prominent features as a famous British Radical. Especially in Benn's speeches there are shades of consistent honesty, disconcerting candor, and a self-depreciating sense of humor. He regarded the Suez invasion as an act of illegal aggression; he was active in the Movement for Colonial Freedom; and he became increasingly hostile to the European Union as bureaucratic and centralized with no democratic representation and no accountability. He believed that the Falklands dispute with Argentina should have been resolved through the United Nations. He has recently urged the use of referendums on major issues. He believes in the transfer of power from institutions to the people through devolution, as happened in Scotland and Wales in 1998. On the present war in the Middle East, it represents to Benn a colonial liberation movement by the Muslim world against the West. His radical or unorthodox views have not diminished his popularity, especially among younger generations. He personifies protest against the Establishment and is often referred to as the conscience of the British people.

After the death of Margaret Thatcher, **Geoffrey Wheatcroft** reflected on her life and career, her improbable background as a grocer's daughter, and her fame as one of the significant political figures of the twentieth century. Despite her reputation as divisive and arrogant, she remained in many ways an ordinary woman, sexually attractive but with the preoccupations of everyday life. Her husband, Denis, irreverent and amiable, was an indispensable consort. One obvious reason for her overall political success was the close relationship she forged with President Reagan, who helped her immeasurably in emerging triumphant from the Falklands War. Yet in private she was critical of the "shilly-shallying" of those within the American government, including the president himself, for failing to hold a strong and consistent line. Another point is less well known but significant in the Middle East as well as in Anglo-American relations. Mrs. Thatcher refused to shake hands with Menachem Begin because he was a terrorist. She demanded to know from the U.S. secretary of state: were the Israelis ever going to leave the West Bank, or did they regard it as a permanent part of Israel? This insight into her views on the Palestine question will certainly have to be taken fully into account by future historians.

Respect for the Queen has never been higher. The monarchy survived a tempestuous period before and after the death of Diana, Princess of Wales, in 1997, when sympathy for the institution significantly diminished. In fact her family problems seem to increase compassion for the Queen herself. Her reign has been marked by discipline, discretion, and, in the view of **Max Hastings**, dutiful dullness. But present popularity should not be mistaken for unassailable or permanent support of the monarchy. Hostility could suddenly erupt by members of the family acting indiscreetly and thereby suddenly placing the royal family in jeopardy, even if few people seem to want radical constitutional change. For the present, what is remarkable is that even in a period of relative economic decline, public enthusiasm for the Queen is unprecedented. There is a simple reason: her popularity or respect over six decades on the British throne can be explained not only by her common sense and caution but above all because she has changed with the times yet has managed entirely to stay out of controversy.

Prince Albert, 1842. Painting by Franz Xaver Winterhalter.

1

Prince Albert

ROSEMARY HILL

Prince Albert is perhaps the most famous Victorian after Victoria herself, but he is, for the same reason, difficult to see within the aura that time and his wife have cast around him. There were at least three Victorian ages, one of which, from around 1845 to 1861, might better be called Albertine. These were the years when the Queen's husband, Albert of Saxe-Coburg and Gotha, was largely responsible for setting the tone, pace, and scope of the monarchy, and so to some extent of the reign. Despite which, he remained obscure as a personality. He was caricatured in his lifetime by an alternately sycophantic and satirical press, while in death the immense shadow that Victoria's mourning cast over him—and, indeed, the whole of the later part of the century—blotted the Prince Consort out again. The gilded figure enshrined in the Hyde Park memorial gradually congealed into Lytton Strachey's "impeccable waxwork," and Albert, as an individual, was for some time lost to history.[1]

He had started life at a disadvantage that he never entirely lost. Albert Francis Charles Augustus Emmanuel, Prince of Saxe-Coburg-Gotha, was born at Schloss Rosenau just outside Coburg in Thuringia on 26 August 1819, the younger son of a minor Saxon duke of extravagantly philandering habits. Albert's parents' marriage ended on such acrimonious terms that after the age of five he never saw his mother again, and the engagingly candid journals of

his youth record that he cried a great deal. Not surprisingly he disliked his father and avoided him when possible.

His grandmother and his uncle Leopold meanwhile had plans for
him. Leopold was the widower of Charlotte, Princess of Wales, and
he intended that Albert should fulfill the ambition of which Leopold himself had been cheated by the death of his wife, namely, that
he should rule England as consort. He was to marry his first cousin,
Victoria, a few months his senior, and then as de facto King to work
for the creation of a united Germany under Prussia. To fit him for
this role, his tutor imposed a harsh discipline, and there were more
tears. But Albert was studious, intelligent, and good-natured. He
put his shoulder to the dynastic wheel. By the age of sixteen, he was
writing an essay on German national character.

Victoria, meanwhile, having lost her father as a baby, was growing
up as heir presumptive to her uncle William IV under the increasingly resented regime of her mother, Albert's aunt, the Duchess
of Kent. First cousins—indeed, delivered by the same midwife—
already they had much in common, but their childhoods, equally
rooted in an unusual combination of private insecurity and the im-
minence of public destiny, must account to some extent for the personal success of a marriage planned so far in advance and with so
little regard for the feelings of the parties involved.

Not that it was love at first sight. On Albert's initial exploratory
visit to meet his cousin, before her accession, under a thinly contrived pretext that fooled nobody, he thought her "not beautiful
by any means," and Strachey's blunt assertion that "he was not in
love with her" is no more than the truth.[2] A youth of fragile health
and regular habits, he found the relentless "entertainments" of the
English court far from entertaining, unlike Victoria, who enjoyed
dancing all night and watching, from Buckingham Palace, as the
sun rose behind Westminster Abbey. When she was eighteen in 1837,
her uncle died. She became Queen, and Albert returned to England two years later at her somewhat peremptory invitation to press
his suit. He came with his elder brother, the pair arriving at court
haggard and underdressed after a violently seasick journey during
which they lost their luggage.

Victoria, however, was charmed. "It was with some emotion," she
wrote in her diary that night, that she beheld the bedraggled Albert, who, despite it all, she could see was "beautiful."[3] Soon she was
violently in love, and it was she who made most of the running. She
was obliged by protocol, as Queen, to put the proposal. Albert duly
accepted and they married in 1840. If he had already tasted something of the potential humiliations of his situation, he was soon fully

aware of the fact that while her accession had set his wife free from her mother's domination and brought her power and recognition, the fulfillment of his own long-foreseen destiny had merely ushered him into an elegantly appointed cul-de-sac. His well-trained mind was aghast at the vagueness of Britain's unwritten constitution, which, he noted, "is silent as to the Consort of the Queen."[4] Indeed, "a very considerable section of the nation had never given itself the trouble to consider what really is [his] position."[5]

As the Queen's husband, he had no job and no authority, and there were many who were anxious that he never should. The title "Prince Consort" was not granted him until 1857, and he never received a peerage, which would have allowed him to sit in the House of Lords and thus play a part in the legislature. He was known personally to hardly anyone in the country except Victoria, and public opinion was initially wary of him, both as a German and as a consort in a nation that had had few happy experiences of royal husbands. They tended, it was felt, either to do too much or too little. Philip of Spain's marriage to Mary Tudor had brought unwelcome foreign influence, while Queen Anne's union with the "dull-brained, wine-bibing" George of Denmark had inspired little enthusiasm.[6] Neither marriage was in living memory, but Albert had arrived at a moment when the British were much preoccupied with reconsidering their past.

In particular, in the wake of Catholic Emancipation and with the Oxford Movement gathering momentum, they enjoyed refighting the Reformation. Plays, paintings (famously, Delaroche's *Execution of Lady Jane Grey*), new editions of John Lingard's revisionist *History of England,* as well as A. W. N. Pugin's architectural manifesto *Contrasts,* all treated it as the determining event in national history. The facts were fiercely argued, and at a popular level there was much debate about whether it was a Good Thing. For Protestants, England's savior was Elizabeth, the Virgin Queen who had reigned alone and made her reluctance to marry an instrument of foreign policy. Hence, on top of everything else, the devoutly Lutheran Albert had to contend with persistent rumors that he was a Roman Catholic. He was still only twenty-one, and it was understandable, perhaps, that when Benjamin Haydon saw him at a court ball, he thought he looked like a "cowed and kept pet, frightened to sit, frightened to stand."[7]

That he managed to make a success of his marriage and to find a role in public life speaks powerfully of Albert's sense of duty, his patience, and his precociously sophisticated grasp of that relationship between the personal and the political that had been instilled in him from birth. This was the area, that constitutionally shadowy corner in which he had been at first dismayed to find himself, where he was, in time, to make his greatest contribution. Albert clearly came to love Victoria, but she was always the more besotted, and he used his hold over her, including the powerful sexual excitement that, as Victoria confided eagerly to her diary, had characterized the relationship from the beginning, to transform both the appearance and the reality of the monarchy. It was not easy. The early years of the marriage saw him not infrequently playing the stoical Petruchio to her bad-tempered Katherine.

Victoria was less intelligent and less well educated than her husband. She was fond of her own way and saw no reason not to have it in matters of state as well as at home. All in all, the young queen had more in common with her unpopular and self-indulgent uncles George IV and William IV than the fresh-faced appearance and her famous promise at her accession to "be good" suggested. Courtiers and Victoria herself recorded tearful scenes and door slamming on her part, and implacable calm, or the appearance of it, on Albert's. Once he locked himself in his study while the furious Victoria bellowed outside that she was the Queen and she commanded him to let her in. He refused to open up until she asked nicely.

Albert imposed order on a chaotic and wasteful royal household in which responsibilities had become divided along lines of protocol long since lost to memory. Thus the outsides of the windows at Buckingham Palace were cleaned by the Lord Chamberlain's department, while the insides were the responsibility of the Office of Woods and Forests. The Queen could never have a fire in her dining room because one department was responsible for laying it and another for lighting it. Albert's rationalization saved enough money for the couple to buy an estate on the Isle of Wight and to build Osborne House on it—a large villa, mostly designed by Albert and reminiscent of the houses in which he grew up.

Closer to home, he imposed regular bedtimes on his wife. He also explained her constitutional position to her, for he understood, unlike Victoria, that although the monarchy had received a boost in popularity when she came to the throne, it could take nothing for granted. It was less than a decade since Robert Peel had predicted that it would not last another five years. The years immediately before her accession saw the worst civil disorder in British history. At Nottingham, the castle was destroyed; in Bristol, the bishop's palace was set on fire and millenarianism was preached from many pulpits. By 1837 the disturbances had abated, but they had imparted a more critical, more overtly censorious flavor to public opinion. The high taste and low morals of the Georgians were actively despised. It was indicative of the change of mood that 1841 saw the closure of the Vauxhall Pleasure Gardens and the first appearance of the satirical magazine *Punch*. *Punch* cast a cool, appraising eye on public institutions, and it did not spare the monarchy. From its earliest issues, it entertained readers with regular jokes about court protocol and the cost of this new and useless foreign prince, with his "tooth-brush in ordinary, and Shaving-pot in waiting." Once he produced the male heir in 1841, he became, to *Punch's* mind, redundant.

IT WAS PEEL WHO CAME TO ALBERT'S RESCUE by finding him a job. This first independent undertaking was the chairmanship of the royal commission established to oversee the decoration of the new Palace of Westminster, and it suited Albert perfectly while underlining the difficulties of his position. The old Palace of Westminster, a medieval building much extended over the centuries, had been destroyed by fire in 1835. Its destruction brought the turbulence of the 1830s to a climax. Something rotten, it was widely felt, had been cauterized at the heart of the nation, and the new palace was to symbolize a better Britain. The shell of the building was up by 1840, and the commission was a response to increasing public pressure for state funding of the arts. This was still a relatively novel idea in Britain, where the National Gallery had opened only in 1838. Albert saw an opportunity to do for his adopted country what King Ludwig was doing for Bavaria. He had taste as well as a knowledge of contemporary art, he was the only one of the commissioners who collected modern art, and he threw himself into the task with a will.

Competitions were organized for artists. Information about fresco, the most obviously suitable, though technically difficult, way to decorate a Gothic building was obtained from the German painter Peter Cornelius. Hugely popular exhibitions of potential schemes were held in Westminster Hall and much discussed, for the public expected a lot for their money. The scheme was supposed to encourage artists, educate visitors, stimulate the members of the Lords and Commons, and tell the national story from its misty Arthurian origins to the field of Waterloo.

The result was inevitably a mixed success. Fresco proved all but impossible to bring off amid the fog and soot of 1840s London. The subject matter was frequently changed, the architect quarreled with the sculptors, and some critics, including Anna Jameson, questioned the desirability of the whole endeavor, suggesting that to encourage "mere liking" for the arts among all classes would lead to them being "essentially vulgarized."[8] German influence was suspected, blamed on Albert, and denounced in the press, while the artists themselves were not always as grateful for royal patronage as might have been hoped. William Dyce, one of the few painters to make a success of fresco in his murals for the Robing Room, warned Charles Cope, who was just starting work on the House of Lords, that "when you are about to paint a sky seventeen feet long by some four or five broad, I don't advise you to have a Prince looking in upon you every ten minutes or so—or when you are going to trace an outline, to obtain the assistance of the said Prince . . . to hold up your tracing to the wall . . . It is very polite . . . but rather embarrassing."[9]

Albert couldn't win. If he did nothing, he was a parasite, yet anything he did do was interference. His attempts at army reform, and later his Chancellorship of Cambridge University, brought much criticism and only partial success. Victoria was not unjustified in feeling that he never got enough credit for his achievements.

The one project in which he was unequivocally successful with the public, the area in which even *Punch* did not like to criticize him, was in the creation of the royal family, the institution that was to fill that awkward space between the monarch's private life and her constitutional role. After the unedifying spectacle of George IV and Queen Caroline's divorce and the late marriage of convenience between William and Adelaide, which produced no surviving child, it was gratifying to Britain's increasingly powerful and opinionated middle classes to see their own ideal of respectable family life reflected at the top of society. A cheerful vision of hearth, home, and a burgeoning brood of healthy children was purveyed in dozens of popular engravings and chromolithographs. They showed Victoria and Albert among the toys in the nursery or the Queen playing the piano as her husband turned the music. For its Christmas supplement of 1848, the *Illustrated London News* produced an engaging colored print of the whole family at Windsor, gathered round the candlelit tree. Albert was essential to this version of the myth of royalty, which continues to serve the monarchy well today, in which uniqueness is counterbalanced by normality, a combination that ensures that the most banal remark or the ability to perform the simplest domestic task ensures outpourings of excited loyalty.

By 1848, the couple had seven children and Albert had gained some degree of acceptance. As the British looked anxiously across the Channel, where revolution after revolution convulsed the Continent, there was a feeling that they could do worse. Republican agitation all but died away.

Albert's next major venture, the Great Exhibition of the Works of Industry of All Nations, in 1851, ever after known as the Great

Exhibition, was perhaps the high-water mark of his career, a popular success and a personal one for which the Prince did for once get the public appreciation he deserved. It was he who provided the impetus, addressing meetings of mayors and industrialists to whip up enthusiasm while Henry Cole got on with the practicalities of presenting what the Prince envisaged as a "living encyclopaedia" of international production.

The resulting display in the Crystal Palace in Hyde Park was a kind of Benthamite panopticon, a rational arrangement of all of human knowledge at a glance, or at least in a day's visit. More than six million people came to inspect more than one hundred thousand objects arranged by nationality and materials. Albert hoped that it would persuade the British to introduce some scientific and technical elements to their narrowly academic education system. It didn't, but it did pave the way for the design reform movement and, later, Arts and Crafts. It provided funds for the museum complex at South Kensington, just opposite Hyde Park, which was popularly known as Albertopolis and at the center of which is now the Victoria and Albert Museum. And the Exhibition ushered in a new, High Victorian way of interpreting the world and of ordering public life.

Meanwhile, Albert, realizing that he could be most effective where least suspected of involvement, had been gradually getting his hands on the levers of such political power as remained with the monarch. His wife trusted him more, needed him more, and after a decade of constant childbearing was often simply too tired to attend to as much business as she once had. Mindful of public opinion and not personally vain, her husband was discreet about his role, content to let Victoria take the credit for his ideas and decisions. Behind the scenes, he worked relentlessly. His greatest strength was in foreign affairs. A torrent of letters, memoranda, and state papers flooded from the desk beside Victoria's, where he worked long hours beginning, in winter, some time before dawn. Between 1853 and 1857, his comments on the Eastern Question filled fifty folio volumes, and if ministers sometimes quailed or rolled their eyes, they often found that the advice was sound; in due course, with no public acknowledgment, they followed it.

And so as before, public image and the reality were at odds, but while there was more to him as a politician than was generally supposed, there was also somewhat less of the happy family man. It was not surprising, perhaps, given their own upbringings and their mutual self-absorption, that Victoria and Albert were not notably successful parents. She made no secret of the fact that she disliked being pregnant and was not overly fond of the babies when they arrived. Albert liked his children and was especially close to his eldest daughter, Vicky. But he expected to mold them as he himself had been molded. Neither parent could get on with their eldest son, Bertie, the future Edward VII, who was not moldable. He tried hard, but as his mother put it unsentimentally, he was a "stupid boy" with a "small empty brain"; persistent discouragement and criticism made him unhappy and rebellious.[10] He was growing up to be a worry and a disappointment.

Between Victoria and Albert themselves, relations were not, perhaps, entirely happy, or at least not as smooth as Victoria imagined. Strachey, whose contempt for the age never over-rode his insight into character, is surely right to point out that while Victoria, physically strong and intellectually weak, adored her husband, she did not fully appreciate a man who was the exact opposite. "Victoria idolised him," Strachey writes, "but it was understanding that he craved for, not idolatry; and how much did Victoria, filled to the brim though she was with him, understand him? How much does the bucket understand the well? He was lonely . . . full of energy and stress (sturm und drang) and torment."[11]

Toward the end of the 1850s, Albert seems to have lost heart and begun to give up the unequal struggle that had been his life's work. His health, never strong, began to fail, and Victoria's torrential devotion did not extend to ensuring his physical comfort. Her neurotic dislike of overheated houses meant that at Windsor Castle she had thermometers in ivory cases in every room to ensure that the temperature never rose above 60. Poor Albert was so cold that he had to wear a wig to breakfast. By 1861, body and spirit had been fatally undermined. His feelings for Victoria were not, as he told her, enough to make him "cling to life" as she did.[12] He spoke openly about expecting to die and not minding much. Whether too selfish or too terrified to understand the true state of affairs, Victoria managed to protect herself from much anxiety until it was too late. She told herself that it was masculine malingering. At the end of November, she wrote to reassure Vicky that her Papa was "in reality much better," just rather depressed, "as men really only are—when unwell."[13] Two weeks later he was dead.

THE SHOCK TO THE NATION WAS IMMENSE at every level, out of proportion, it might seem at first, to the very mixed feelings Albert had inspired in life. The process of reassessment, reinvention, and sanctification began almost at once, but for a while—indeed for the next few years—the place that he had in reality occupied in public and private life was laid open. A vast chasm yawned, for in his absence

there was no need and indeed no opportunity to conceal or mini-
mize the Consort's role. "With Prince Albert we have buried our sovereign," wrote Disraeli not, for once, overstating the case. "This German Prince," he continued, saying what could not be said in Albert's
lifetime, "has governed England for twenty-one years with a wisdom
and energy such as none of our kings has ever shown."[14] When he
died, Albert had been working, to some effect, to avert a crisis in
diplomatic relations with the United States, which had become so
strained that many people expected war. His last intervention in
state affairs, made when he was already gravely ill, was a reword-
ing of a rebarbative dispatch from Lord John Russell, the Foreign
Secretary, which Albert rewrote in such a way as to allow room for
diplomatic maneuver. War was averted, and the American ambassador predicted accurately that "the English will value him better now
he is gone."[15] *The Times* talked of losing "the most important man in
the country," "the very centre of our social system, the pillar of our
state."[16] The stock market plummeted, and as church bells rang out
across the countryside, a blanket of black crape descended on all respectable citizens, including, as the news spread slowly through the
empire, Indians, Africans, and Maoris.

Palmerston if anything understated matters when he said, "The
Queen would be a less national loss."[17] In fact the Queen without
Albert was something of a liability. Victoria had never been alone
before. First her mother and then her husband had centered their
own existence entirely on hers, and ambivalent as her feelings for
the Duchess of Kent had been in life, her death, nine months before
Albert's and much more foreseeable, had plunged Victoria into ago-
nies of flamboyant distress that only her husband had been able to
get her to curb. Some commentators have since perhaps been rather
harsh about this, seeing it as an overreaction, an "orgy of grief."[18]
Yet Victoria had lost her father as a baby, and who can say what long-
suppressed anxieties resurfaced with the death of her other parent
or to what extent the "morbid melancholy" to which she was always
inclined might be better understood as clinical depression.[19] What
is certain is that love had, in her experience, always been intimately
associated with control. Without Albert and her mother there was
nobody to provide either on the scale required to restrain a temperament always inclined to self-indulgence and by now, as the Queen
of the Netherlands tartly observed, thoroughly used to "the *habit* of
power."[20]

With the passage of time, as she clung to her grief as if it were Albert himself, Victoria's state of mind lapsed increasingly into solip-
sism, her mourning spreading unconstrained like her figure, for she

soon left off her corsets. She did exactly what she wanted and nothing else, spending as much time as possible at Balmoral, the home she and Albert had built in the Scottish Highlands, avoiding public engagements, refusing to entertain visiting heads of state, and, to the dismay of the court and her family, allowing the servant John Brown increasing liberties, including lighting his pipe in her presence and taking frequent swigs from the whisky flask. Whether or not they became lovers, they were certainly intimate. Brown's character resembled Albert's in only one way, but it was the one that mattered most to the Queen: he offered total devotion laced with just enough lèse-majesté to suit her need for love to be combined with dominance.

The implications of all this for Victoria and for Britain were widely felt. At Whitby on the Yorkshire coast, where jet occurs naturally, trade boomed as the demand for tasteful and affordable mourning jewelry spread across the classes. Dickens felt obliged to cancel a lucrative reading tour, and did so with ill grace. Republicans sustained a severe setback, and ladies in waiting wrote gloomily in their journals of having to wear relentless mourning at Court. When Princess Alice, Victoria and Albert's third child, married Louis of Hesse in 1861, her trousseau was entirely black.

Albert's absence was felt almost everywhere for the next two years. Then, as the country moved on through grief and sympathy to acceptance, and lightened its royalism with an enthusiastic welcome for Alexandra, Bertie's wife, the beautiful new Princess of Wales, Queen and people began to fall out of step. After three years, mourning began to look like sulking, and Albert himself began the long fade from memory into mummified cult figure. Dickens, never Albert's greatest admirer, wrote to his friend the cartoonist John Leech, "If you should meet with an inaccessible cave anywhere to which a hermit could retire from the memory of Prince Albert and testimonials to the same pray let me know of it. We have nothing solitary and deep enough in England."[21]

Prince Humbert of Italy was not amused to find himself staying at the White Hart Inn in Windsor, having been told there was no room at the castle. A cartoon of Buckingham Palace with a To Let sign, rumors that Victoria had gone mad or was about to abdicate, and the *Saturday Review*'s pointed remarks about "seclusion" being "one of the few luxuries which Royal personages may not indulge" coincided with a new boom in republican clubs, which sprang up from Plymouth to Aberdeen.[22] For the rest of the decade, most of Albert's work in shoring up the monarchy was undone by the woman who claimed to have appreciated it most. As Gladstone put it, "The

Queen is invisible, and the Prince of Wales is not respected."[23] The whole "Royalty question," he regretted, was coming up for discussion once more.

Victoria's obliviousness of what the living Albert had thought and wished extended to her enthusiasm for memorials to him, the unveiling of which, all over the country, were among the few activities she could be persuaded to undertake. In his lifetime, he had dismissed the idea of a commemorative statue after the Great Exhibition, on the grounds that he did not want to be confronted by his own image in Hyde Park; and if, as he thought was "very likely," it became "an artistic monstrosity," he would be "permanently laughed at in effigy."[24] It had been one of the relatively few occasions on which *Punch* had been entirely in sympathy with him. Now he was not laughed at, but only because he was turning to stone in the public memory. There were indeed a number of monstrosities. The Manchester Albert Memorial is not a great work, and there are several much less distinguished tributes. That the grandest monument of all, George Gilbert Scott's Albert Memorial in Hyde Park, designed in 1862, was also a great work of High Victorian art was the result of good luck rather than judgment, which the Queen entirely lacked in matters of art. Nevertheless, it would have embarrassed its subject horribly.

Just when it seemed that the nation's patience might run out, in 1871 the hapless Bertie inadvertently came to the rescue by nearly dying of typhoid, the same disease that was thought to have killed his father exactly a decade before. Despite press skepticism about the long-term value of "typhoid loyalty," the service of thanksgiving for the Prince of Wales's recovery marked another turning point in the reign, a moment when, as in 1848, the British looked at the alternatives to hereditary monarchy and decided to stick with what they knew.[25] If Victoria had died in 1871, the last decades of the century would not be bracketed together historically with the previous three, for the Late Victorian age was different in character again from the early and the Albertine. Republicanism receded once more.

In the meantime, one of Victoria's few really original achievements was to publish a book, something that no English sovereign had done since James I. *Leaves from the Journal of Our Life in the Highlands,* recording some of the happiest moments of her marriage, appeared to rave reviews in 1868 and let a little cozy gaslight in on the monarchy, its pretty but unremarkable watercolors and the plain prose, from which an editor had tactfully removed the spelling mistakes and repetitions, reassured the public once again, as in Albert's day, that Victoria was just like them, a devoted wife who had become a respectable, grieving widow.

As the Queen aged into a bombazine silhouette, grandmother of the nation, and Empress of India, her people remained loyal, and after her death Albert faded still further from reality. For all Strachey's insights into character, he had no interest in an objective assessment of an age that had become to the children of the Victorians a byword for hypocrisy and bad taste. As Strachey's friend Virginia Woolf, to whom his life of Victoria is dedicated, characterized it, this was an age of "crystal palaces, bassinettes, military helmets, memorial wreaths, trousers, whiskers, wedding cakes"—nothing, for Bloomsbury, had ever been "at once so indecent, so hideous and so monumental."[26] Attitudes were slow to change. In 1961, with *Punch* well into its cozy dotage, a new satirical magazine, *Private Eye,* was born, and poor Albert and his by then rusty and much derided monument, the gilding having been removed during the First World War in case, it is said, it might attract zeppelins, were once again a source of mirth.

But as the 1960s wore on, both Prince and monument began to be reconsidered. In 1997, Stanley Weintraub's life of Albert, *Uncrowned King,* began but has surely not completed the process of reassessment, while a long campaign by the Victorian Society and others led to the restoration of the Hyde Park memorial in time for its unveiling in October 1998 by Victoria's great-granddaughter Elizabeth II. Queen Elizabeth is, after Victoria, the second-longest reigning British monarch. That she has reigned so long, that the monarchy has survived at all, owe more than is often suggested to the Queen's still somewhat underrated great-grandfather, Albert of Saxe-Coburg Gotha.

Fall Semester 2012

A version of this lecture appeared in the *London Review of Books,* 23 February 2012.

1. Lytton Strachey, *Queen Victoria* (London, 1921), p. 223.
2. Ibid., p. 104.
3. Diary of Queen Victoria, quoted in Robert Rhodes James, *Albert Prince Consort* (London, 1983), p. 81.
4. Albert to his tutor Baron Stockmar, 24 Jan. 1854.
5. Ibid.
6. *Glasgow Herald,* 17 Dec. 1861.
7. John Joliffe, ed., *Neglected Genius: The Diaries of Benjamin Robert Haydon, 1808–1846* (London, 1990), p. 203.
8. Anna [A. B.] Jameson, *Companion to the Most Celebrated Private Galleries of Art* (London, 1844), p. 387.
9. C. H. Cope, *Reminiscences of Charles West Cope, RA* (London, 1891), p. 258.
10. Roger Fulford, ed., *Dearest Mama: Letters between Queen Victoria and the Crown Princess of Prussia, 1861–1864* (London, 1968), p. 212.
11. Strachey, *Queen Victoria,* pp. 129, 233.
12. Quoted in Cecil Woodham-Smith, *Queen Victoria* (New York, 1972), I, p. 417.
13. Roger Fulford, ed., *Dearest Child: Letters between Queen Victoria and the Princess Royal, 1858–1861* (London, 1964), p. 370.
14. Benjamin Disraeli, *Letters: 1860–1864,* ed. Mel Weibe et al. (Toronto, 2009), p. 164.
15. Martin Duberman, *Charles Francis Adams* (Stanford, 1968), p. 286.
16. *The Times,* 16 Dec. 1861.
17. Quoted in Helen Rappaport, *Magnificent Obsession: Victoria, Albert, and the Death That Changed the Monarchy* (London, 2011), p. 72.
18. Ibid., p. 39.
19. Earl of Clarendon, quoted in ibid.
20. S. W. Jackman and Hella Haasse, eds., *Stranger in the House: Letters of Queen Sophie of the Netherlands to Lady Malet, 1842–1877* (London 1989), p. 227.
21. Madeline House and Graham Storey, eds., *The Letters of Charles Dickens* (Oxford 1998), X, p. 425.
22. *Saturday Review,* 26 Mar. 1864.
23. Agatha Ramm, ed., *The Gladstone–Granville Correspondence* (Cambridge, 1998), p. 170.
24. Quoted in Theodore Martin, *The Life of HRH the Prince Consort* (London 1882), II, p. 90.
25. *Reynolds's Newspaper,* 10 Dec. 1871.
26. Virginia Woolf, *Orlando* (1928; World's Classics edn., 1992), p. 222.

Sir Edward Gibson, 1921

2

One Man's Raj

JOHN SPURLING

Sir Edmund Gibson was my great-uncle: my grandmother was one of his two elder sisters. For over seventy years our family used to spend the summer at a seaside resort on the south coast of England, Bexhill-on-Sea, in a house built in 1898 by my great-grandfather. After the Second World War, that was where I encountered Uncle Ted every two years or so when he came back from his home in India to see the rest of the family and to buy new pairs of handmade shoes from his shoemaker, Lobb's, in London. He had retired at the end of the war and stayed on after Indian Independence, living on a small farm in the north of India, near Dehra Dun.

He was a tall and by then portly person, and I admired him greatly. My only relation with a title (KCIE, Knight Commander of the Indian Empire), he was friendly and kind, and always gave me a half crown when he left. He was also the only one of my numerous elderly relations who was slyly, drily humorous. I remember particularly one of the rare warm and sunny days when we were bathing: he emerged from our bathing hut in his old-fashioned bathing costume (whole torso, shoulder straps) wearing a panama hat, a cigarette stuck in his mouth—he was a heavy smoker. Walking carefully down the pebbles, he entered the sea and floated on his back, still wearing his panama hat and still smoking his cigarette.

After the death of Ted's youngest sister, my great-aunt Olivia, his diaries and letters covering the years 1907 to 1936 were found in her house, where Ted stayed when he was in London. What most surprised me when I first read them was the revelation that the slow-moving, almost stately old gentlemen I knew had once been such a hard-working and hard-playing one, even in such a fierce climate as India's.

His basic routine, even in late middle age, was to rise at six a.m., ride or walk for an hour or so before a light breakfast, work on files or cases in his office, judge cases in court from eleven to about three, take a siesta, then play games of polo, hockey, volleyball, tennis, squash, or golf, followed by dinner with friends or friends to dinner, a game of bridge, and so to bed at ten if he could, but sometimes at midnight or later. He was also a great reader of books and in his early years wrote articles and satirical verse for two papers published in India, the *Pioneer* and *Truth*. On Sundays, his walks or rides were longer, and as a practicing Christian, he frequently led church services in the absence of a visiting parson. Never married—perhaps in a sense he was married to India—he always had a dog or two and, whenever he could, a garden full of flowers.

He had many friends, both Indians and Europeans, and although he was often irritated by his cloud of domestic servants, the longer-serving ones, especially his majordomo, Merwaram, were evidently friends too and accompanied him on his walks or rides. One of them played chess with him. I believe that when he died, in India in 1974, at the age of eighty-eight, he left his farm and presumably its contents to his steward. That may be where the rest of his diaries went, for I think he continued to keep them.

Edmund Currey Gibson was born in London in 1886, the third child and eldest son in a large and closely knit family of three girls and six boys. Their parents were the Reverend Thomas Gibson and his wife, Frances, née Currey. She was the daughter of another Church of England clergyman, and both had clerical ancestors for several generations. Ted was educated, like his father, at Merchant Taylors' School in London and St. John's College, Oxford. His diaries begin when he was in his second year at Oxford, studying "Greats"—a four-year classics course.

In November 1910, after passing the Indian Civil Service exams, he left London by train, crossed the English Channel, boarded a ship at Marseilles, and sixteen days later reached Bombay. His first posting was to Sangor in the Central Provinces, as an Assistant Commissioner. His job was to inspect liquor, opium, and gunpowder shops, along with schools, public gardens, the jail, the treasury, and the slaughterhouses; he heard minor cases in court and settled the frequent disputes over fields. He was often out on tour, on horseback; his servants would go on ahead to make camp, bringing the tents and other equipment in bullock carts.

Life in Sangor could be exciting. On 4 April 4 1911, he wrote to his father about a local menace:

> I am at present engaged in arranging for the offer of £10 for the destruction of a man-eating panther near here which has already killed four men and mauled many more. The villagers who believe it to be a magician in disguise are quite terrorised by it as it walks up to their houses and carries them off as they sleep. You would have thought that with all the flower of England's youth at the Cavalry school here it would soon be accounted for, but people are very chary of meddling with man-eating panthers. They are far worse than tigers and when you are stalking them they are really stalking you, and they have a habit of climbing up the tree in which you are watching at night and pulling you down.

On Durbar Day, 12 December 1911, King George V was crowned Emperor of India in Delhi and the capital of India was moved from Calcutta to Delhi. Ted attended the more modest celebrations in Sangor, dressed in a tailcoat.

> In this I rode a sombre figure in the midst of a glittering cavalcade of Cavalry School Officers. The subaltern in a Native Cavalry Regiment is far more splendid than a Field Marshal. I should not have thought the whole of London could produce so much gold lace.

In 1913 he applied to join the Political Service. As a result of the piecemeal conquest of India in the eighteenth and nineteenth centuries, a large part of the subcontinent was governed directly by the government of India, headed by the Viceroy (also called the Governor-General), but another large part consisted of 693 Princely States (according to the *Imperial Gazetteer of India,* this figure was reduced in 1929 to 562). Some were very large, some tiny, and each was governed by its own raja, rana, maharaja, or nawab, under treaty with the British. These rulers were largely responsible for their own internal affairs, taxation, agriculture, roads, and so forth, and the larger states had their own armies. The British guaranteed their territories against incursion by other princes or by outside powers and, through the Political Service, kept watch over their finances and the treatment of their subjects. The service consisted of the Political Secretary, immediately under the Viceroy, and a corps of political officers assigned to the Princely States, either as Residents (in the larger states, such as Hyderabad, Kashmir, and Gwalior), Agents to the Governor-General (overseeing numerous small states), or

Political Agents (in charge of one or more medium-sized states). The assignment was somewhere between ambassador and governor. Ted spent much of the rest of his career in the Political Service, which was staffed partly by people from the Indian Civil Service but also by officers transferred from the Indian Army.

In 1913, Ted's application made its way very slowly through the bureaucracy, and in January he was posted first to a small town called Akola, and then to an even smaller one, Basim:

> Not a bad place except for its extreme isolation. It is pretty and has a good climate. The station consists of the police assistant and myself and an American lady missionary doctor, and an American missionary and his wife.

But he sometimes found his work distressing:

> Most of today I spent writing a Judgment in a theft case which has been going since January 1912. The accused stole a buffalo but the evidence on both sides is fabricated to such a degree that I must let him off though I am sure he is guilty. I am however very reluctant to do so. The complainant is a Rohilla [a tribe from Afghanistan] and must have spent hundreds of rupees on pleaders and witnesses, and now the poor man loses his buffalo worth 140 rupees into the bargain. There is no justice in India. About 99% of criminals get off.

In July 1914 he got his first leave and sailed home to England. It was not the best moment: the First World War began a month later.

If he kept diaries during the war years, they have disappeared, but his letters show that he was back in India by the beginning of 1915, in a completely new post, working for the Political Service as guardian and tutor to the fifteen-year-old Maharaja of Bharatpur.

Bharatpur, southeast of Delhi in Rajputana (Rajasthan), was a medium-sized state with a mainly agricultural population. It had been ruled by a Hindu Jat dynasty since the eighteenth century. Ted's pupil, His Highness Maharaja Shri Brijendra Sawai Kishan Singh Bahadur Jang—known as Kishan Singh or, to his intimates, as Kani—was born in 1899 and succeeded his father a year later. His father was not dead, but had been deposed by the British for murdering his barber, and then exiled to the city of Agra. In the meantime, until Kishan Singh came of age in 1918, Bharatpur was ruled by his mother, the Maji Sahiba, as regent. Both of them, mother and son, were in England, where the boy attended Wellington College, when the war broke out. They returned immediately to India, where Kishan Singh, married since the age of thirteen to the sister of another maharaja, continued his education at Mayo College, the school for ruling princes in the city of Ajmer.

At the end of the Mayo College term in July 1915, Ted wrote to his mother from the hill station of Mount Abu, south of Ajmer:

> I have to spend my whole time with the young Maharaja and to-day we shall have to begin lessons I suppose, though what I can teach him I don't know. However that is the least important part of his education. This is *the* ideal job. I am lucky to get such a nice charge. The Maharaja is a very good-looking boy of 15, very keen on everything with very nice manners and very friendly. In most ways he is just like an English boy. In about a fortnight we are going up to Kashmir. I am looking forward to it very much, though I feel I ought to be in the trenches with Geoff and Robert.

These were two of his younger brothers. Robert, age twenty-one, the brightest of the family, a scholar of Winchester and Cambridge, was killed in action in the Battle of the Somme the following year.

By the autumn of 1916, Ted was becoming disillusioned with his job. The frequent letters and notes he received from Kishan Singh, addressed to "Dear Sab," show that Ted's attempts to keep the young prince's mind focused on his studies rather than on polo ponies, cars, hunting, and amusements were met with charming excuses and evasions. In the new year, Ted registered for military training as a reservist, although his boss, the Political Agent, Colonel Bannerman, wanted him exempted on the grounds that he was indispensable. Ted was having none of it:

> I strongly protest against this. My work here is, as it always has been, the merest farce, owing to State intrigues, the jealousy of the Mother, and the weakness (almost amounting to imbecility) of the Agent to the Governor-General (Sir Elliot Colvin) and Colonel Bannerman.

In 1918 he was transferred to Ajmer as Assistant Commissioner. Ajmer-Merwara, a large enclave in among the Princely States of Rajasthan, was governed directly by the government of India, meaning Ted was again working for the Indian Civil Service.

THE WAR ENDED LATER THAT YEAR, but 1919 was a terrible year for India. The worldwide influenza epidemic killed at least twelve million Indians. Mohandas Gandhi started his satyagraha movement—civil disobedience and nonviolent noncooperation—to which the government of India responded with repressive legislation against the press and political troublemakers. Ted and other British officials, with the help of the police and, on occasion, soldiers from the cantonment at Nasirabad, managed to keep Ajmer relatively peaceful, but to the north, in the Punjab, there were murderous riots. On 13 April came the notorious Jallianwala Bagh massacre in Amritsar,

when troops commanded by Brigadier Dyer fired on a mass meeting in an enclosed space, killing 379 people and wounding many
more. Some people believed that Dyer had averted another Indian
Mutiny, but the reputation of the Raj was severely damaged. From
then on, with many ups and downs, Indian independence became
gradually inevitable.

Ted's former pupil, meanwhile, had reached his majority and
been formally invested as maharaja. Ted spent the Christmas holiday as Kani's guest in his palace in Bharatpur. He saw a Hindi version of *King Lear* and another of *Hamlet;* had Christmas dinner with
presents round a Christmas tree and charades afterward; played
tennis, squash, bridge, hockey, polo, and croquet; and went hawk-
ing, pigsticking, and duck shooting.

In October 1921 he was once more posted to Bharatpur, as tem-
porary Political Agent, just in time for a visit by the Prince of Wales.
The future King Edward VIII was touring India, sent by the British
government in the hope that he might counteract India's growing
disaffection with British rule. Ted played polo against him.

> I played "back" and therefore had to mark the Prince who was
> playing "one" and had the honour of being hit on the head with
> his polo stick.

After a duck shoot and just before a state banquet in the Bharatpur
palace, Ted met the future King privately.

> I was summoned to the Prince's room . . . and had a tete-a-tete
> with him at the close of which he pressed into my hand a pair of
> sleeve links with his monogram and crest in blue enamel on them.
> He has the most wonderful charm and being perfectly natural is
> very easy to talk to.

But the Prince's visit did little to calm things down in India, as Ted
remarked in February 1922:

> I believe that more than 500 people were killed during the riots
> that coincided with his visit to Bombay.

In 1922, at Kani's request, Ted was posted as a member of the
Bharatpur State Council. These were Kani's palmiest days, and
perhaps Ted's too. From April to July he accompanied the maharaja and a large retinue on a trip to southern India. They stayed
for some time in the hill station of Ooty (Ootacamund). There they
played in a polo tournament, traveled about in one or another of
Kani's several Rolls-Royces (including a Rolls truck) or in his two-
seater Pierce Arrow (imported from the United States), took part in

a gymkhana, and went out with the local hunt, for which Kani and Ted equipped themselves with pukka "pink" (that is, red) coats. The maharaja was spending money recklessly:

> He bought 7 elephants a few days ago and his expenditure on odds and ends (horses, jewellery, clothes, etc.) is stupendous.

From Ooty, they traveled to the coast, crossed the sea for a quick tour of Ceylon, and, back in India, visited the French enclave of Pondicherry.

Early in the next year, 1923, the maharaja became very ill with paratyphoid and was ordered by his doctor to go up to the Himalayan hill station of Simla. Kani had always had delicate health, but this was the first of many serious episodes of fever. In fact, he only had another six years to live. After making several visits to Simla, where Kani was buying a house and had ordered special uniforms for the bearers of his rickshaw, Ted went on leave in July 1923. While in England, he had the use of a new silver Rolls-Royce ordered by the maharaja.

When he returned in October, he was met at Bombay by a young aide-de-camp, Kishen Singh, in full uniform, and accompanied to a reserved compartment on the train. At Bharatpur, they were met by the maharaja himself with a red carpet and a guard of honor. The other people on the train, Ted told his parents, most of them his fellow passengers on the *Caledonia,* "must have thought they had been entertaining a new Viceroy unawares." During Ted's absence, his whole house had been fitted with electric light. That evening there was a banquet in the palace, followed by dancing girls.

In 1924, Ted was posted back to Ajmer as Commissioner, to Kani's dismay. He appealed to the Viceroy to send Ted back to Bharatpur, and even asked Ted to leave government service and work permanently for Bharatpur. As indicated in a letter to Ted, Kani seemed to have got his way with the Viceroy:

> I have now been asked by the Political Department to put in Officially re your return and so I think you will return HOME now very soon. I need hardly tell you how Bharatpur is looking forward to your return . . . WITH LOVE FROM ALL OF US, EVER YOURS, KANI.

In 1925, Ted was back in Bharatpur, now as Political Agent, with responsibility also for the neighboring Princely States of Dholpur, Alwar, and Kotah.

In June, Kani and his retinue, including Ted, migrated to the hill station of Mount Abu for "Abu Week." Ted did not much care for hill stations and their social whirl:

> There are fancy dress dances, gymkhanas, dinners, polo, tennis
> and golf tournaments, garden parties etc. I hope we shall have
> some heavy rain to damp this forced hilarity.

One of the events was a costume party given by the Maharaja of
Bikaner:

> When the time came to put on my dress I found that the breeches
> supplied by Ranken's were small beyond hope of enlargement.
> Went to consult Mrs Wingate. Came back and got a pair of black
> leather breeches off one of Kani's Bodyguard. Struggled into
> these and the rest of my Mexican Brigand's costume and went to
> Mrs W's who corked my face and put on the beard and mous-
> tache . . . Kani fetched me after dinner. He was also a Mexican
> brigand and rode into the Reception room on his pony.

Back in the state of Bharatpur, Ted's thirty-ninth birthday, on
6 July 1925, was celebrated at the maharaja's fabulous palace of
500 fountains in Deeg, "a wonderful scene with the fountains playing, coloured electric lights and everyone in zareen achhkans [gold-
colored knee-length jackets]." Kani's attachment to Ted is perhaps
most directly and sweetly expressed in a letter from that October,
when Kani turned twenty-six and Ted gave him a birthday present,
a pencil:

> Ordinary pencils I may have—but none which represent such kind
> sentiments from someone who has been and I am thankful is and
> ever will be such a true and genuine friend. I must apologise for
> using the word friend . . . but I know of no other, chiefly because
> you who have been all in all to me did not teach me another more
> adequate phrase by which I could have addressed you. Ever yours
> Kani.

But Bharatpur was in financial difficulties, and Kani applied for
a loan from the government. Ted discussed the problem with superior officials and with Kani, but he himself was going on leave, and
would be transferred back to Ajmer upon his return. There was a
farewell dinner for Ted at the palace, and the next day Kani drove
him to the railway station.

> There was a Guard of Honour there and all the State officers. Said
> goodbye to them and received innumerable garlands. The Maha-
> rani came on to the platform in her motor. Kani came down with
> me to Bombay (with Kishen, Balbir and Amar Singh). I travelled
> in his saloon. A salute was fired and Auld Lang Syne played as the
> train left.

Kani and his officials even accompanied Ted onto his ship, and as it
left Bombay they followed it out in a steam launch.

Toward the end of 1927, Ted was posted as Political Agent for the Princely States of Western Kathiawar, on the west coast of India. He was based at Rajkot, where he presided over a visit from the new Viceroy, Lord Irwin:

> I had lunch with the Viceregal party one day and had a long talk with HE [His Excellency]. He has great charm and is very natural and pleasant. Lady Irwin too is very nice. Rajkot is a hideous place and the country round it dreary, flat and monotonous. I have never seen a less attractive spot. The roads are so vile that I have decided not to use my Armstrong Siddeley and have today bought a Chevrolet to do my touring in.

Indeed he spent much of his six-month stint in Kathiawar touring the district and visiting as many as possible of the eighty or so local rulers. In January 1928, Ted sent an account of one such visit:

> Last week I camped at a place called Khirasra, an isolated and in-significant village surmounted by a dilapidated fort in which the ruler lives. His total revenues amount to between two thousand and three thousand pounds per annum. He does his best for his State but is despondent and discontented. In the past he had a glimpse of Paradise and is now a prey to regret that he can never enter it again. His Paradise was Bexhill where he spent two years 1912 and 1913.

Bexhill, of course, was where Ted's family always spent their summer holidays. It seems to have been particularly popular with both Anglo-Indians and Indian rulers. Later on in his diaries, when he was on leave in the 1930s, Ted mentions visiting Kani's four sons, who were staying with their guardian in Bexhill.

Soon after his visit to the disconsolate ruler of Khirasra, Ted motored to Jalia to interview the mother of the boy-ruler:

> I was ushered into a room where the interview was to take place. Being a purdah lady she could not of course appear and I looked in vain for a curtained door or window behind which she might be lurking. There was no sign of any possible place of retreat but presently a voice came up through a hole in the floor and I found that the lady was there and conversed with her through the floor.

Finally, shortly before leaving his post in Kathiawar, Ted visited the large, prosperous, and progressive state of Jamnagar, whose ruler was the Jam Sahib.

> The house I am staying in is on a princely scale, furnished throughout by Maples [the London furniture store] regardless of expense and the walls adorned by originals of modern artists of repute. There are two nice Burne Jones among them.

Back in Ajmer as Commissioner, Ted was told toward the end of 1928 that Kani had been prohibited from going within a hundred miles of his state and was living in Delhi. At the end of January 1929, he heard from his former pupil:

> Your kind letter cheered me considerably—for it showed that you had not forgotten me . . . We have had a fine go of luck, apart from every other happiness I have been very seriously ill—even now I can't get out of bed, while Her Highness has also been laid up with Pleurisy—and is still unable to leave her bed . . . I do hope you will come, as you threatened to do in your letter, for it will do us good.

Early in March, Ted was able to visit what he called "this terribly tragic household":

> Found Kani extremely ill—terribly emaciated and only able to speak in whispers. The Maharani who has also been ill for nine weeks is lying in a room on the upper storey. Sat with them both. Shyama—the dancing girl—is looking after Kani.

Kani died less than a month later, age twenty-nine. Ted's always laconic diary simply notes the fact of Kani's death, with a line drawn underneath, before recording the events of an ordinary day—a committee meeting, office work, and in the evening a walk with his majordomo. The maharani died five months after her husband, in August 1929, leaving four young sons and three daughters.

Ted remained Commissioner of Ajmer-Mewara from 1929 to 1933. This period coincided with an increase in nationalist agitation, dangerous riots in the Punjab, Gandhi's famous march to break the Salt Act, his subsequent imprisonment, and the outlawing of the Congress party. In early 1931, following an agreement between the Viceroy and Gandhi, Ted arranged for the release of forty-three political prisoners. But Ted's difficulties that year were caused less by Congress and the nationalists than by the constant threat of communal violence between Hindus and Muslims and by the huge cuts in Ajmer's budget demanded by the government after the financial crisis caused by Britain going off the gold standard.

On 26 December 1931, he thanked his parents for their Christmas presents, adding:

> The political atmosphere in Ajmer is very electric. We shall see what happens when Mr Gandhi returns to India.

When Gandhi got back from London in January 1932, he and eighty thousand other Indians were arrested and jailed, and Congress was outlawed. There was no serious trouble in Ajmer, though the enmity

between Hindus and Muslims was simmering. Here is Ted's diary
entry for 25 April:

> Went . . . to see Robertson [the Police Superintendent]. As I was
> leaving his office and talking to the City Inspector, one Ramchan-
> dra Bapat, a revolutionary, came up, drew out a revolver and tried
> to shoot me. The City Inspector tackled him at once and after I
> had got over the first panic I and others helped to secure him. It
> was found that four cartridges (.450) had misfired! There was a
> fifth which when tested went off!

The would-be assassin was apparently a failed student, acting on his
own, and was later sentenced to ten years in jail, which Ted thought
too much. The courageous inspector was promoted, and Ted was in-
undated with visitors, garlands, and congratulations. One of the Indian papers reported on a public meeting at which citizens of Ajmer
thanked "the Almighty for His having saved such a valuable life for
this city and the province where he has rendered unparalleled service." Four days later in Midnapore, near Calcutta, a British district
magistrate was shot and killed in his office by two revolutionaries.

Early in the next year, the Political Service offered Ted the post
of Agent to the Governor-General for the Princely States of Bihar,
Orissa, and the Central Provinces—an important promotion. After
going to Bharatpur for the wedding of Kani's eldest daughter, he
began attending farewell parties in Ajmer. There were at least fifteen, some private, some public, some given by Indians, some by Europeans. On 25 March he was seen off at the station by a guard of
honor with a bagpipe band, a huge crowd of people, and "garlands
innumerable."

His main task in his new post was to persuade the princes in the
area—of whom there were forty—to agree to a federation consisting of eleven self-governing provinces and the Princely States. The
Government of India Act, incorporating this idea, was passed in
1935, but because the princes were suspicious of it and Congress
disliked the idea of sharing power with them, it never took effect.
In the meantime, Ted, based in the city of Ranchi in Bihar, spent
1933–1934 quartering his new territory of sixty thousand square
miles by train and car, visiting most of the Princely States and discussing federation with them.

In November 1934, after his long-postponed leave, he was posted
as Resident in Gwalior, one of the five largest Princely States, not far
south of Delhi, famous for its almost impregnable fortress and its
huge nineteenth-century palace, which was modeled on Versailles
and contained the largest chandelier in the world. The maharaja,

from the famous Maratha dynasty of the Scindias, was a minor—"a
very nice boy with an excellent disposition but completely dominated
by his mother who is an ignorant, obstinate and scheming woman
and a prey to superstition"—surrounded by a powerful court. Ted
spent the next couple of years, until the maharaja was invested with
his full powers, by coping with the complexities of affairs in Gwalior and with the aftermath of the Government of India Act and the
idea of federation:

> The Princes of India, being now face to face with grim realities
> instead of vague abstractions appear to be shying off Federation.
> Their hesitation is not unnatural but I suppose that they will ulti-
> mately resign themselves to the inevitable.

They never did, and instead had to resign themselves after independence to being swept away altogether.

Gwalior is one of the hottest places in India, but Ted was soon
regularly playing volleyball, usually with Indian cavalry regiments
and after a while with his own Residency team. He was also again
leading church services, including one celebrating King George V's
Silver Jubilee, which was attended by the maharaja and the members of the Council of Residency. In October, Ted took part in a
Hindu religious procession with the maharaja:

> We mounted our elephants and went side by side in the Dasehra
> procession through the town . . . The procession was imposing
> but my dizzy perch in a silver howdah on a very tall elephant was
> rather trying.

In November, Ted presented the cups and medals for the All-India
Hockey Tournament. It was won by Gwalior, whose most famous
player, Roop Singh, was on the Indian hockey team that took the
gold medal in the 1932 and 1936 Olympic Games, defeating Germany in Berlin in the final of the latter. King George V died at the
beginning of 1936, and Ted led the Memorial Service in Gwalior's
Anglican church. In June he visited the new Viceroy, the Marquess
of Linlithgow, six feet five inches tall, who was tasked mainly with
the ultimately hopeless job of making federation work. Ted was to
meet him again at the maharaja's investiture with his full powers.

In October, Ted was given responsibility for two more Princely
States, Rampur and Benares, but could not visit them until after the
Maharaja of Gwalior's investiture. The Viceroy and his wife arrived
by train on 1 November. The maharaja was enthroned the next day,
followed by a state banquet at the palace. Ted entertained at the
Residency on 3 November:

> The dinner was in a tent on the terrace behind the house—51 diners at 3 tables: band on the lawn: grounds flood-lit. The catering was done by Grand Hotel.

In December the new King-Emperor—the man who had once hit Ted on the head with a polo stick—abdicated.

In the last days of that year Ted was touring again:

> I spent Christmas Day in Benares. There is a nice church there to which I repaired at 8 am. The Chaplain who took the service did it deplorably badly . . . The rest of the day was spent discussing Federation until the evening when we went to see a Tarzan picture at the Cinema.

He returned on 31 December after an eight-hour drive from Benares to Gwalior, where he changed, played hockey, and opened "innumerable Christmas cards."

There the extant diaries end.

After his return from leave, Ted became Agent to the Governor-General for the States of West India. Then, from 1944 until his retirement in 1946 at the age of fifty-eight, he was based in Calcutta as China Relations Officer. He lived the rest of his life in Independent India.

I never visited him there, but my friend J. G. Farrell did, in 1971, when he was researching his Booker Prize–winning novel, *The Siege of Krishnapur.* I was afraid they might not get on, since Jim Farrell had left-wing views and Uncle Ted was certainly no socialist. But they shared an ironic view of life, and Jim was impressed by how open-minded and un-blimp-like his host was. They were sitting on his veranda after lunch when Jim, noticing a plume of smoke down by the river, asked what it was. Uncle Ted, the lifelong bachelor—as was Jim—replied that it was his driver's wife. She had made a pyre and set light to herself the night before after a row with her husband.

Spring Semester 2013

The Economist

3

The Economist

ARAM BAKSHIAN, JR.

Twenty-five years ago, if you had asked a typical senior American corporate type or public official what his or her weekly reading consisted of, the answer would usually have run something like this: "*Time, Newsweek,* and maybe *U.S. News & World Report* . . . oh, yes, and *The Economist.*" Today, instead of being an afterthought, *The Economist* probably would head the list. It might even be the only publication mentioned. *U.S. News & World Report* ceased being a full-scale newsmagazine years ago. *Newsweek,* since 2010 the feeble foster child of Tina Brown's flamboyant *Daily Beast* website, has lost much of its influence and most of its original staffers and subscribers. Even mighty *Time,* once the educated American middle class's undisputed arbiter of all things political, economic, social, and cultural, has suffered massive staff and circulation hemorrhaging and is in the throes of a seemingly endless search for a new identity. *Time* knows that it isn't what it used to be, but still can't make up its mind what it should become.

All this would seem to be conclusive evidence that the era of the weekly newsmagazine is over, rendered obsolete by burgeoning electronic media and 24–7 cable-news coverage and commentary. But if the once-great redwoods of American weekly journalism are all dead, dying, or seriously ill, a smaller, older English oak survives and flourishes, possibly because it has never tried to be anything other than itself: a literate, informed (and occasionally smug) publication aimed at a literate, informed (and occasionally smug) readership.

First published in 1843, which makes it eighty years older than *Time* and ninety years older than *Newsweek, The Economist* remains true to the statement of purpose printed in its first issue, still proudly run each week at the foot of its contents page: a pledge of commitment to the "severe contest between intelligence, which presses forward, and an unworthy, timid ignorance obstructing our progress."

The age of Victorian optimism is long gone, and the sun has forever set on the British Empire. But *The Economist* goes on, exemplar of that old Victorian determination to get things done and do them right. Today it is arguably more influential, more widely read, and more prestigious than at any time in its 169-year history, and in a way that is unlike any other magazine. Why is this so? And how well does the quality of its content live up to *The Economist*'s lofty status?

Answering the first question is easier than answering the second. More than any other serious news journal since the invention of the Gutenberg press in the fifteenth century, *The Economist* is the beneficiary of a unique global-linguistic confluence: the universal dominance of the English language. This triumph was made possible by an event unprecedented in world history: one language being shared by two successive global superpowers that, between them, have led the shaping of the modern world from the dawn of parliamentary politics and the Industrial Revolution all the way to the present day. Power has shifted from one country to the other, and may do so again, but the English language remains paramount. Starting in Great Britain, it began a triumphant march that saw it become the mother tongue of countries such as the United States, Canada, Australia, and New Zealand, all originally colonized and populated by people of Anglo-Saxon heritage. But it didn't end there. English also is the language of the educated elite in Asian, African, Pacific, and West Indian countries once part of the vast British Empire. To cite one small piece of evidence, many of today's best-written (and best-selling) English-language novels are written by English-speaking Indians, Pakistanis, Caribbeans, and Africans, all linguistic beneficiaries of a now-defunct British Empire and a still-expanding global market for English-language fiction.

Meanwhile, even as England—first overextended and then exhausted by two world wars—ceased to be a superpower, a new English-speaking colossus, the United States, filled the void, not just because of its military and economic might but also because of its scientific and technological supremacy. Around the world, English (now with an American inflection) expanded ever farther as the international language of science, commerce, academia, sea and air transport, diplomacy, and, thanks to globalized media, popular culture. At the same time, millions of foreign students, promising or privileged ones in particular, completed their educations at prestigious American and English universities after having learned English at home as a second language.

One result is a growing worldwide elite audience of English speakers and readers—about 1.5 million subscribers—for whom *The Economist* is the perfect fit, comprehensively covering both the United States and the United Kingdom and offering more thorough coverage of the rest of the world than any rival English-language periodical. *The Economist* has become the premiere worldwide newsweekly for the new global elite.

Not everyone is happy about this, especially those who view the world from a more leftward angle. Thus the *Observer,* a soft-Left and possibly envious English weekly newspaper with little influence or impact outside the British Isles, grumbles that *The Economist*'s writers "rarely see a political or economic problem that cannot be solved by the trusted three-card trick of privatization, deregulation and liberalization." There is some truth to this. At heart, *The Economist* remains what it began as, an advocate of the classic nineteenth-century English strain of liberalism that favored social reform, open markets, and a representative form of government with a franchise that expanded in tandem with better, increasingly accessible education and resultant economic progress. There is nothing new here, but these qualities remain the key to progress in functioning democracies—and will have to evolve in lawless, corrupt police states in much of the developing world and many parts of the former Soviet Union if they are to become stable, free societies.

The problem in countries such as Russia is not that ailing state industries and underdeveloped state natural resources were truly, lawfully privatized. It is that they were grabbed up by Kremlin insiders, transforming a handful of crooks, fixers, and members of the old nomenklatura into a corrupt and entrenched new oligarchy while leaving most ordinary Russians out in the cold. The same applies to "free elections" held before the emergence of a literate, informed electorate and freely competitive political institutions in countries without strong rule-of-law traditions. When the results turn ugly, the reason is not a failure of liberalization but the use of superficially "liberal" labels as cover for replacing an old set of oppressors with a new one through violence, intimidation, corruption, and the lack of a "liberal" foundation of individual rights and protections. In such cases, while the economic and political remedies advocated by *The Economist* may seem passé to trendy left-wingers in the West, they remain the best—and possibly the only—cure for what ails most of the nations and people of the developing world and much of the former Soviet Union (not to mention overextended, overregulated European welfare states tottering on the brink of bankruptcy).

Thus, by consistently championing basic values such as reform, social improvement, free trade, and individual rights, *The Economist* stands for values that are timeless, proven, and certainly not outdated. Indeed, on many of today's hot-button issues, *The Economist*'s brand of what might be called liberal libertarianism is, depending on your perspective, "politically correct" in the best or worst sense of the term. For example, it has emerged as a leading voice—critics might call it an alarmist one—in the global-warming debate. It also strongly advocates national gun control in the United States, favors abolition of capital punishment, and has "come out" in favor of gay marriage.

While he must have found *The Economist*'s endorsement of gay marriage gratifying, Andrew Sullivan, a longtime gay-rights activist and former editor of the *New Republic,* had another ax to grind. Sullivan, who happens to be of working-class British origins, was more driven by class than gender considerations when, in the pages of the *New Republic,* he denounced *The Economist*'s staff for being dominated by graduates of Oxford University's elite Magdalen College.

Sullivan's class animosity already may have been out of date when he wrote about it. To cite one human statistic, at that time the late Peter David, a graduate of the University of London rather than even one of Oxford's less prestigious colleges, already had been a member of *The Economist*'s staff for fifteen years and eventually would earn distinction for his nuanced analysis of Middle Eastern complexities. He once wrote that "it is necessary to remember that what people call 'the Arab world' is a big and amorphous thing, and arguably not one thing at all," a central fact that seems to have eluded ideologically driven Arabists and Israeli partisans alike. More recently, as the magazine's Washington bureau chief and author of the "Lexington" column on American life and politics, David was just hitting his stride before his premature death in a motoring accident in Virginia this May. The son of Lithuanian Jews who immigrated to England from South Africa, Peter David represented the kind of educated, informed intelligence that characterizes *The Economist* at its best and has nothing whatsoever to do with one's ethnicity or old school tie.

Another kind of criticism comes from intellectually pretentious, slightly envious Yanks rather than class-embittered Brits. James Fallows, who wrote speeches for President Jimmy Carter in the 1970s, complained in a 1991 *Washington Post* piece that *The Economist* "un-

wholesomely purveys smarty-pants English attitudes on our shores."
This is about as valid—or invalid—as accusing the American-run
International Herald Tribune or the European edition of the *Wall Street
Journal* of "unwholesomely" purveying "smarty-pants" American at-
titudes on the shores of Europe and Britain.

Admittedly, there are times when *The Economist* leans a little heavily on plummy English props and mannerisms. Michael Lewis, the
popular American financial writer and author of *Liar's Poker,* once
attributed the magazine's sometimes laboriously polished prose and
tone to the fact that *The Economist* "is written by young people pre-
tending to be old people," adding that if American readers "got a
look at the pimply complexions of their economic gurus, they would
cancel their subscriptions." This may be the reason almost all the
publication's articles still lack bylines, much less accompanying pho-
tos of the writers. Besides, that hint of pseudo-Dickensian creakiness
in its prose is part of *The Economist*'s charm and its distinctive brand.
It also helps explain its success among readers who prize good writing that exhibits a modicum of sophistication and literary ground-
ing instead of pandering to the lowest common denominator. As
for Fallows, someone should remind him that, for the most part,
"smarty-pants" tend to be much better writers than sansculottes.

The American journalist who has come closest to pinning down
The Economist's winning formula is Michael Hirschorn, in a perceptive essay in the July–August 2009 issue of the *Atlantic*. He suggests
that the secret of *The Economist*'s success

> is not its brilliance, or its hauteur, or its typeface. The writing in
> *Time* and *Newsweek* may be every bit as smart, as assured, as the
> writing in *The Economist*. But neither one feels like the only maga-
> zine you *need* to read. You may like the new *Time* and *Newsweek*.
> But you must—or at least, brilliant marketing has convinced you
> that you must—subscribe to *The Economist*.

This may explain how an idiosyncratic publication produced by an
allegedly pimply writing staff of about seventy-five from a cramped
space in London's St. James's quarter has proved to be David to rival
American Goliaths such as *Time* and *Newsweek*.

So much for *The Economist*'s success. What about the quality
of its content? Is it worthy of the pedestal on which it now perches?
One way to find out is to look at how well *The Economist*'s running
coverage and commentary stand up over time and after the fact. To
do, this I engaged in a twenty-two-week monitoring of the magazine,
encompassing all issues from 18 February through 14 July 2012.

Although I have followed *The Economist* for most of my adult life, this meant immersing myself in each issue in a way I never had before. Twenty years ago, Microsoft's Bill Gates said that one reason he didn't have a television set was that watching it wouldn't leave him enough time to read each issue of *The Economist* from cover to cover. For the first—and probably the last—time in my life, I found myself emulating Bill Gates. Trudging through *The Economist* week after week, I found I was watching less and less television, especially television news and documentaries of the "serious" sort, which, even at their best, cannot convey as much information as a really well-written article.

Looking back on it now, in the very first issue I monitored there were several items that held up very well and that addressed serious subjects ignored or oversimplified by most American media. The lead editorial (or if you are English, the leading leader) was entitled "Over-regulated America: The home of laissez-faire is being suffocated by excessive and badly written regulation." It proved to be a compact, compelling condemnation of the ill-considered Dodd-Frank law that Congress passed in 2010, concluding that it is

> far too complex, and becoming more so. At 848 pages, it is 23 times longer than Glass-Steagall, the reform that followed the Wall Street crash of 1929. Worse, every other page demands that regulators fill in further detail. Some of these clarifications are hundreds of pages long. Just one bit, the "Volcker rule", which aims to curb risky proprietary trading banks, includes 383 questions that break down into 1,420 subquestions.

This is likely one reason why "hardly anyone has actually read Dodd-Frank, besides the Chinese government and our correspondent in New York."

Here, in a single page, *The Economist* addressed the overarching problem of runaway federal regulation and the legitimate concerns that can lead to bad legislation, providing strong supporting examples and powerful statistical data to back up its position. It wasn't just interesting or convincing. It was useful: most readers would come away better informed on the subject than they had been before, even if they didn't agree with *The Economist*'s opinion on all points.

The second leader in the same issue, subtitled "The euro may survive brinkmanship over Greece, but the road to recovery will be long and hard," was a prescient warning of the crisis to come within the euro zone due to stagnating economies and ruinous debt levels in Greece, Portugal, Italy, and Spain. *The Economist* definitely saw that one coming.

Less pressing but equally prescient was a third leader, dealing with India's often meddlesome, hectoring attitude toward weaker neighbors such as Nepal, Sri Lanka, Bangladesh, and even Pakistan. At a time when India's diplomatic charm offensive was winning uncritical praise from Washington and most American media, *The Economist* took a more informed look at the country's increasingly imperious attitude toward its South Asian neighbors and the problems it could lead to.

Not so clear-sighted was the following week's "Lexington" column on the Republican race for the presidential nomination. Although Peter David, author of the column, was a gifted journalist and had been based in Washington since 2009, this was his first full-time, on-the-ground experience of an American presidential campaign. Like most foreign journalists dropped into that surreal world for the first time, he seemed to be unduly influenced by the groupthink of the predominantly liberal Washington press corps. In his 25 February column, David unrolled a scenario that dramatically overestimated the influence of fringe elements in the Tea Party and the Christian Right while ignoring the essentially moderate conservative alignment of rank-and-file Republican voters. So it came as no surprise that he bought into the widely held but mistaken view of liberal inside-the-Beltway pundits:

> It is now clear . . . that a large share of the party's conservatives just do not like Mr. Romney. This traps the party in a fratricidal exercise that could continue for months, if not all the way to the party convention in Tampa in August. Even if he loses next week in Michigan, Mr. Santorum should pick up enough delegates to keep his hope alive . . . There is new talk of an "open" convention, where no candidate has a majority and the call goes out for a white knight, if one can be found. Mr. Obama is a lucky man.

Is that so?

The Economist's lead editorial the next week demonstrated a clearer, more farsighted understanding of a very different kind of presidential election. Headlined "The beginning of the end of Putin: Vladimir Putin will once again become Russia's president. Even so, his time is running out," it foresaw the victory that Putin's brass-knuckle tactics would win at the polls. But it also foresaw its hollowness: "Everybody in Russia knows that Vladimir Putin . . . will be elected president on March 4th. This is not because he is overwhelmingly popular, but because his support will be supplemented by a potent mixture of vote-rigging and the debarring of all plausible alternative candidates. The uncertainty will come after the election, not before."

The *Economist* of 17 March sported a cartoon cover suggesting that the recovery had finally arrived. A featured briefing on the American economy agreed, concluding that "economic recovery doesn't have to wait for all of America's imbalances to be corrected. It only needs the process to advance far enough for the normal cyclical forces of employment, income and spending to take hold . . . It now seems that, at last, they have." Call it irrational exuberance, premature miscalculation, or whatever. *The Economist* clearly jumped the gun on this one. In fairness, it was not alone in doing so. The conventional wisdom on Wall Street and among Washington movers and shakers at the time was that happy days were, indeed, here again. It is not very surprising that the conventional wisdom proved wrong yet again; it is, however, a little disappointing to find *The Economist* joining the errant chorus.

On a more positive note, by 24 March *The Economist* had finally sobered up about the race for the Republican presidential nomination. No more pipe dreams about a Tea Party rebellion derailing the Romney candidacy and leading to a brokered convention. Instead: "Mr. Romney has won over half of the delegates awarded so far. That pace, if sustained, will be more than enough to secure him the nomination outright." Better late than never.

One of the signature virtues of *The Economist* is its ability to spot and put into perspective quiet but important developments ignored by most of the mass media. A small but striking example of this was a brief boxed item in "The Americas" section of the 5 May issue. Headlined "Gendercide in Canada? A study shows more boys than girls are being born to some ethnic groups," this disturbing story reported on data that indicated growing numbers of Asian-born mothers in Canada are deliberately aborting female embryos purely on the basis of their sex, especially in the case of a second or third expected child. Thus, in Ontario, a study revealed that Indian-born mothers giving birth to a third child had "1,883 sons and 1,385 daughters, a hugely distorted ratio of 136 to 100" that could be explained only by parents deliberately targeting female fetuses for abortion. "In India and China," *The Economist* noted, "sex-selective abortions are seen as crimes against humanity. Why should Canada view them any differently?"

The Economist has always prided itself on not panicking and instead taking the long view. The "Lexington" column in its 12 May issue was an example of that approach at its best. It also turned out to be Peter David's posthumous valedictory, running two days after his death. He commented on the "binary illusion" in U.S. politics:

> People tend to think in black and white. America is either in decline or it is ordained to be for ever the world's greatest nation. Government is either paralyzed or it is running amok, stifling liberty and enterprise and snuffing out the American dream. The election campaign accentuates the negative and sharpens this binary illusion . . . On a variety of objective measures, [America] is in an awful mess right now. And yet America of all countries has plenty of grounds to hope for a better future, despite its underperforming politics, and no matter who triumphs in November.

THE ECONOMIST HAS A NUMBER OF GLARING IMPERFECTIONS. But it usually manages to sort things out and muddle through. Along the way, it also keeps its eye out for the exotic, amusing, and interesting subjects we enjoy reading about but are seldom served up by the mass media.

This is particularly true when it comes to the magazine's books-and-arts section and its highly selective, sometimes offbeat obituaries. Two noteworthy examples appeared in the 19 May issue, the first a detailed piece on the Turkish government's aggressive campaign to recover art and artifacts from foreign museums and reclaim them as part of Turkey's cultural heritage. *The Economist* takes a balanced approach, sympathizing with the Turkish desire to revive its neglected, multiethnic Ottoman past, which Kemal Ataturk, the founder of modern Turkey, deliberately disparaged in order to forge a new, ethnically unified nation-state. But it also points out that many of the "Turkish" treasures being sought were the work of other peoples and cultures—Greeks, Medes, Romans, Byzantines, and possibly even Trojans—who occupied what became the Ottoman Empire and parts of modern Turkey long before the first Turkic nomads migrated there from the Asian steppes.

The second piece, a perceptive and evenhanded obituary of Carlos Fuentes, Mexico's foremost modern man of letters, captured all the flamboyant, conflicting qualities that somehow managed to coexist in an elegant, self-professed Marxist with aristocratic tastes who spoke out against tyrannies of the Left as well as the Right and was equally at home in Paris, New York, and Mexico. The obituary managed to make a more coherent and likeable whole out of the bundle of contradictions that was Carlos Fuentes—whom I happened to know—in a way the man himself never quite did in either his books or his life.

The same mix of the good, the bad, and the uneven ran through my immersion reading of *The Economist* all the way to the 14 July issue. Particularly valuable was the running coverage of the ongoing crisis within the European Union and, more particularly, the euro zone. *The Economist,* from its offshore perch in London, exhibits both a detachment and a close-up understanding of Europe that is unique.

The first glimpse at my long-awaited 14 July last number reminded me of some of the things I most admire—and a few I most dislike—about *The Economist.* The cover story, which turned out to be a very good one, was headlined "Comeback kid: Rebuilding America's economy." But the cover art was a silly, campy figure of a flexing bodybuilder's torso topped with a somber "Uncle Sam Needs You" head glowering at the reader. The off-putting part was two red-white-and-blue tassels attached to Uncle Sam's nipples, as if he were working as a male stripper. Someone in authority at St. James's Street should keep a closer eye on the art department.

In sum, I came away from twenty-two weeks of monitoring *The Economist* convinced that it is, indeed, the very best magazine of its kind, a status made easier to attain by arguably being the only magazine of its kind. For all its flukes and flaws, its level of intelligent reporting and analysis and the breadth of its coverage—geographically, politically, economically, scientifically, intellectually and artistically—is simply unmatched. There are frustrating moments when I am tempted to dismiss it by paraphrasing a few lines Dean Swift penned about a drafty old Irish manor house he enjoyed visiting.

> It is just half a blessing and just half a curse—I
> wish, my dear sirs, it were better or worse.

Yet at the end of the day, I have to admit that it passes the Robinson Crusoe test with flying colors: if I were marooned on a desert isle and could receive only one magazine, it would have to be *The Economist.*

Fall Semester 2013

A version of this lecture appeared in the *National Interest,* 22 August 2012.

THE
ENGLISH
HISTORICAL
REVIEW

VOLUME CXXI NO. 493 SEPTEMBER 2006

Edited by

Philip Waller

&

G. W. Bernard

OXFORD JOURNALS
OXFORD UNIVERSITY PRESS

ISSN 0013-8266

English Historical Review

4

Editing the *English Historical Review*

GEORGE BERNARD

Peer review, like democracy (as characterized by Churchill), is the worst form of assessment—except for all those other forms that have been tried from time to time. In the selection of research for publication in scholarly journals, peer review is essential as a safeguard and as a means of realizing the potential of research, but it must not be used inappropriately as an index of value or truth. Nothing human is infallible, and peer review is no automatic guarantee of quality. But it is less bad than other options.

As editor of the *English Historical Review,* the oldest journal of historical scholarship in the English language and one of the most prestigious scholarly journals in any subject in the world, I relied on peer review. I read all submissions (around eighty a year). I then chose referees, usually two but frequently more. History as a subject is about particularities. It is essential to secure guidance about a paper from someone well versed in its particular field. I needed to be informed about the author's grasp of the sources on which the paper was based; that requires deep and specialized knowledge. I needed to be informed about the author's awareness of the existing literature on the broader field in which the paper falls. And I needed guidance on whether the paper makes a substantial contribution to our knowledge and our understanding. All that is vital. And at every point the process involves matters of judgment, often fine judgment.

Choosing referees is an art. I drew on long involvement in my subject as researcher, teacher, and active member of the Royal Historical Society. In effect I drew on a huge mental address book. Often I knew the work of those whom I approached, and quite often I knew them in person. Sometimes I asked scholars known to me personally or through their work to recommend potential referees. The Internet makes it much easier to find supporting information about scholars' research interests, including samples of their writings; and more prosaically, it is now much easier to elicit contact details. And that has led to a much wider range of scholars being approached.

I sent virtually all submissions out to referees. Very rarely I received hopelessly inadequate submissions—three pages on the general history of one country in the Second World War; a lengthy diatribe assuring me that Barack Obama would never be elected President of the United States—and these I rejected out of hand. But increasingly when, I suspect, an overeager undergraduate or a master's student submitted a course essay, often not bad as such but not a work of research, or an amateur historian, perhaps beginning by exploring the history of his or her family, sent in preliminary findings, I drafted a brief letter of rejection indicating what was lacking and then sent it, without asking permission, to an expert known to me in the field, asking to be informed if I was missing something. My chosen experts never complained at being imposed upon and often helpfully elaborated on my drafts. That procedure allowed me to sugar the pill of rejection by using the words "I have taken advice," without unduly burdening referees. Rejection by the editor alone is much less palatable.

Referees were offered brief guidance in a covering letter (originally drafted by Philip Waller): "Ideal is a separate report for forwarding to the author, giving reasons for acceptance/rejection." Referees often said more in a covering letter, or in person. But we left it to the judgment of referees to determine what constituted appropriate reasons. Since the *EHR* is not short of submissions (of the eighty a year, I had space to accept twenty to twenty-five), I added to the standard letter the sentence "It would be helpful to know if an article is outstanding or makes a substantial contribution to its field." Of course I accepted articles that fell short of that high standard, but I found it useful to read referees' calibrations. Apart from that, we noted that "it is rare that an article is accepted as it stands" and added the guidance that "if you report favourably, please advise about revisions, great (structure of argument, questionable judgements, omissions of relevant historiography, etc.) and small (you can decorate and return the typescript, correcting infelicities of style, punctuation, etc).” And we asked for suggestions of alternative homes for a paper deemed not suitable for publication in the *EHR*.

That is all that is required. Referees do not need training; it is difficult to know how one might set about that. Learning and experience are the qualities sought. I did approach some younger scholars, especially if a paper came up very close to their doctoral subject; typically, however, older scholars have cumulatively developed a larger range of expertise. Yet I was always making a personal choice: I had a mental blacklist of people I would never approach because I did not have confidence in their judgments.

I much valued closely argued evaluations. I did not find checklists or ticked boxes alone very helpful; they did not provide the subtle assessment required. Typical checklist categories such as “accept,” “minor revision,” “major revision,” and “reject” are not very helpful. It is very rare for a submission to be accepted without revision, so referees in favor but on condition of some minor revisions are at once confronted by an unclear choice. “Accept”? Perhaps better “minor revision”? But would that jeopardize acceptance? And once when I hastily checked the verdict on a paper, both referees had checked “major revision.” Since I had a ready supply of good submissions, such a recommendation seemed to point at best to “revise and resubmit” but more likely rejection. But when I returned to the paper and read the reports carefully, I realized that both referees were in fact strongly in favor of acceptance, but also believed that substantial changes were needed. It was their detailed guidance that gave me what I needed, not the ticks in the boxes.

Most scholars whom I approached to referee agreed to act. When they declined, it was usually because of personal reasons or because they guessed the identity of the author and felt that they were too close. And most referees produced remarkably engaged and constructive assessments of the article under consideration, often several pages long, even so stimulating that I often took notes for my own purposes. Sometimes I wished I could publish their reports. I often felt humbled when I saw how much trouble referees went to, traveling, for example, a long way to the British Library just to see a manuscript cited by the author.

It is integral to the process of peer review that the identities of referees were known to me but to no one else (since I left office, the assistant editor has been added to the inner circle). It may be that the modern fashion for transparency and openness will eventually undermine peer review, but that would, I think, be a real loss. Inadequate or incomplete work would end up being accepted and published more often. Of course, some referees, especially those recommending publication, were very ready for their anonymity to be waived, and a few then went to considerable lengths to perfect the paper.

The *EHR* asks authors not to reveal their identity (for example, in references to their own work). But in many cases it requires little imagination to guess correctly that the author is a well-published senior scholar. Often papers have been read at seminars and conferences before being sent to the *EHR*. So I did not unduly worry if a submission was not anonymous. I was often amused, nonetheless, by how often referees were mistaken in thinking they knew who an author was. "Clearly written by a novice" was a recent verdict on a submission by one of the most established figures in the discipline.

Quite a few submissions come from young scholars whose research is promising but not yet ready for publication. Receiving an engaged referee's critical report can sometimes come as quite a shock, I fear. Schoolteachers, undergraduate tutors, and indeed graduate supervisors do not nowadays always go at it hammer and tongs when correcting errors or improving structures; in an academic world in which low marks are seen not as a reflection of the shortcomings of the student but rather as evidence of bad teaching, it may well be that it is only when a young scholar submits a paper to a learned journal that he or she receives, in the referees' reports, for the first time, the kind of constructive criticism that an earlier generation of students would have already routinely received at school. Peer review, then, serves as a last bastion of scholarly standards.

It is worth adding here that I did not find any correlation between the age of authors and rate of acceptance. My early impression was that experienced scholars did better, but when I made a count, that proved to be not so. Quite a few papers by senior scholars were rejected—anyone rejected by the *EHR* is in excellent company, including mine—while several submissions by young scholars were successful, including one by an author who was just twenty-two at the moment of submission.

Usually, referees were in agreement and their judgments concurred with mine (though mine, like that of any editor, had in many cases to be an untutored judgment). But when referees disagreed—sometimes radically—then I sought further guidance. I on one occasion asked for opinions from as many as eight referees before ultimately accepting that paper, for which there were five voices in favor and three against. I would have accepted it at once had the choice been mine only. Another submission elicited one enthusiastic and another quite positive verdict, but also a damning critique from a third referee. Since that referee is someone I revere and the report was not just an extraordinarily subtle critique of the argument but also a most incisive reinterpretation of the whole subject, after much reading and rereading, and discussion with the quite positive referee, I finally decided on rejection, even though simply counting the number of referees would have led to acceptance: I made a qualitative, not a quantitative, judgment.

It is when referees are divided that an editor's judgment is most evident. But even when referees were agreed, I was always on the alert, reading their reports against the grain, straining to be as fair as possible to the author. Some submissions are manifestly weak, poorly documented, inconsistently argued, inattentive to existing knowledge. And I was grateful when referees clearly pointed out such shortcomings. But I always stood back and asked whether what the referee was condemning was not a shoddy paper but simply one with which he or she did not agree. In history there are claims that are simply wrong and not worth pursuing. But there is another category, that of plausible hypotheses, perhaps ultimately unpersuasive but nevertheless raising questions and provoking scholars into considering topics afresh, including those thought settled. Some referees are too quickly dismissive in such cases, lamentably unwilling to entertain alternative views. Others more generously report that although they find a claim unconvincing, nonetheless it deserves publication so that the questions raised receive widespread attention.

One of my most remarkable experiences as editor occurred when I sent a paper to a referee whom I suspected would not be sympathetic to the author's interpretation. The referee responded by saying that a conventional referee's report would be pointless: instead, the referee offered to write a full-length paper for the journal in response to the submission, which, in the referee's view, was certainly a highly professional piece of work and undoubtedly put forward an important case; publication was unhesitatingly recommended. But the referee insisted that it was nonetheless deeply flawed and that the best way of dealing with that would be not a lengthy critical report that the author could hardly accept without tearing up his submission, but a full-length paper presenting an alternative view. All that struck me as a model of scholarly integrity. And it came to pass as offered.

IT IS A CONTROVERSIAL SUBMISSION of this kind that especially demands the sensitive attention of an editor. And it is above all when there is a dominant orthodoxy that such editorial vigilance is most needed. Prejudiced referees may nonetheless still be worth consulting for the detailed comments they make—though their recommendation to reject must be taken cautiously. And while orthodoxies can become unreasonably entrenched, they too deserve their defenders. There is no intrinsic merit in questioning orthodoxy: an argument may have achieved the status of orthodoxy precisely because it is true.

All this inescapably makes peer review a rough-and-ready process, especially in the most hotly debated matters. There is every incentive for frustrated would-be authors to impugn peer review. Much of the criticism of the process reflects the disgruntlement, justified or not, of those whose submissions have been rejected. In my five years as articles editor, I think I had four complaints—which, given that I must have rejected 250–300, is not bad. Two were amateur historians aggrieved that referees did not attach the importance that they did to a particular individual.

One complaint came from Ian Mortimer, whom I name, since he has repeated it (though coyly referring to me as the editor of the *EHR* rather than by name) in a chapter entitled "Twelve Angry Scholars: Reactions to 'The Death of Edward II,'" in his collection of essays *Medieval Intrigue: Decoding Royal Conspiracies* (2010). Mortimer claims that Edward II, King of England, was not murdered in 1327, as is conventionally believed, but survived his deposition for over a decade. Mortimer impugns what he sees as the sole source stating that Edward died then, Lord Berkeley. And he makes use of reports by people claiming later to have seen Edward II or to have heard or met those who had seen him. Mortimer's essay making his case was accepted and published in the *EHR* by my predecessor; the referees were not persuaded by the argument, but one of them in particular felt that the case deserved an airing. The paper duly appeared in December 2005.

The following autumn, just after I took over as articles editor, Mortimer submitted a short paper on one of the sources saying that Edward II had not been murdered. I sent that paper to three referees, including the two who had assessed his published paper. Their verdict was to reject, largely on the grounds that it added little to the previous piece. So the decision was clear-cut. And my own sense was that the material and discussion in the latest piece were insufficiently new to take up precious space.

The *EHR* has an informal convention that no scholar may be published more than once every five years. Close readers of the *EHR* will know that on a couple of occasions I broke it. But in Mortimer's case I felt that his new piece was simply an addendum to his earlier paper, and so I invoked the convention. I also sent him summaries of the referees' reports—summaries because one of them was written as a personal letter to me, and because the other two were quite sharp in tone. I did not leave out anything I judged material. And in particular I included the criticisms that one of the referees made of Mortimer's overall claim, not just of the new paper, since I thought that might be useful to him. A year later, those criticisms appeared in print in much the same wording in an article published in the *Transactions of the Bristol and Gloucestershire Archaeological Journal,* allowing Mortimer to identify his critical referee, but of course I had no idea that the referee was going to do that. It is worth pausing to note that the critique I had been sent was itself a piece of scholarship of publishable quality.

Mortimer's conclusion was that his new article had been rejected because of the prejudice against him and his interpretation by "angry men," notably the sharply critical referee. Because he was mistaken, I wrote at some length informing him of how things had gone, though not naming names. It did no good. He repeated his complaints when we met by chance at a book launch, and then returned to the charge in his chapter "Twelve Angry Scholars." Mortimer believes that his argument is based on information, not interpretation or impressions of probability. The referees' negative comments were, Mortimer claims, based not on the author's failure to meet scholarly standards, but on "a refusal *in principle* to accept a revision to the common belief that Edward died in 1327" (p. 122).

And his particular complaint against me was that I had sent his new paper to one of the "angry men." He identified that referee, as I have already noted. If his identification were correct, Mortimer continued, "it would mean that the editor of *EHR* sent a highly contentious article about the later life of Edward II to a retired academic whom he *knew* to have a pre-formed judgement on the matter of his death" (p. 137).

Here Mortimer labors under a serious misapprehension, namely, that had I known that my potential referee did have firm views on the matter—whatever a "pre-formed judgement" might be—it would have been wrong for me to ask him to report on the submission. When there is scholarly contention, it is, on the contrary, vital for an editor to hear reasoned criticism on both sides.

I invoke Henry VIII's practice. Thomas Cranmer, Archbishop of Canterbury, informed the theologian Wolfgang Capito, probably in 1537, that Henry VIII had been very pleased to receive Capito's recent treatise. And he went on to say that the king, who is a most acute and vigilant observer, is wont to hand over books of this kind that have been presented to him, and those especially which he has not the patience to read himself, to one of his lords in waiting for perusal, from which he may afterwards learn their contents. He then takes them back, and presently gives them to be examined by some one else, *of an entirely opposite way of thinking to the former party.* Thus, when he has made himself master of their opinions, and sufficiently ascertained both what they commend and what they find fault with, he at length openly declares his own judgment.[1]

Henry VIII's practice is not a bad model for an editor of a learned journal.

Perhaps Mortimer was so upset because he has too high a view of peer review. Rejection, however disappointing, does not necessarily mean that a submission is damned: in this case, the most important consideration was that it was deemed not to add substantially to his earlier paper. And it is important to grasp that acceptance and publication of a paper in an historical journal does not constitute endorsement of its conclusions, only that, in the judgment of the editor, guided by the referees, the information and the reasoning it offers are worthy of the attention of other scholars in the field. Just because the *EHR* has published a paper questioning whether Edward II was murdered in 1327 does not mean that within the historical establishment that claim is now orthodoxy.

A practical consideration complicating rejections in such cases as Mortimer's was that the process of peer review inescapably became protracted. When referees are divided and more opinions are sought, months can go by before a decision is reached. If the ultimate decision is to reject, authors feel not just disappointment at the verdict but also understandable frustration at the time it has taken.

In my final two years as articles editor, I tried hard to reduce the time taken from submission to decision. When I took over as articles editor in 2006, the queue was long: it was taking two and a half years for an accepted article to appear in print. By 2008, I had cut the queue to around a year, often less, giving me scope to fast-track what struck me as important papers without imposing undue delays elsewhere. As editor, I was completely on my own, without support, and often fighting problems created by inadequate and ill-informed copyediting and typesetting in India. With six issues a year, there was a two-month cycle in which the day each week, usually Saturday or Sunday, that I gave to the *EHR* was for two weeks in each cycle given up to preparing copy for the next issue and for two weeks in each cycle given up to dealing with proofs and revisions. So it was only in the weeks that I wasn't pursuing those editorial duties that I could, crucially, go through the list of articles pending and chase referees or make decisions as appropriate. I was astonished to find how often letters or e-mails failed to reach referees or me.

SUBMISSIONS SUCH AS MORTIMER'S make colorful stories, so it is important to emphasize that they were rare and untypical. And the most heartening surprise of my years as editor was the number of authors whose papers had been rejected but who wrote to thank the referees and me for what they took as valuable and constructive criticism. It happened often. Was it politeness alone? I don't think so, since I could judge myself just how helpful comments often were.

Despite being rough-and-ready and sometimes protracted, peer review remains invaluable. The process is not just about acceptance and rejection—it is much more creative than that. It is important to highlight the contribution that referees' comments make both to the enhancement of a paper that has been accepted and to further work that may turn a rejected paper into an article worthy of publication. Most authors in their first footnote thanked the referees for their comments; having seen both the original and the revised version of articles, I am certain that such thanks were not mere form. It is, as I have already noted, rare for a paper to be accepted and published as originally submitted: indeed, one of the best papers published in my years as editor required some months of additional labor by the author to realize its very considerable potential. Even when a paper is accepted, in most cases there is work to be done.

And I came to recognize that an important part of an editor's job is to realize the potential of a paper that is not quite ready. One of my most common actions as editor was, often by adding a sentence here or there, to try to draw out and highlight the conclusions and significances and implications of what was already a good and deeply researched paper. On perhaps eight occasions when editing an already accepted paper that had reached the head of the queue, I felt that it was not yet publishable. And I then set to, switching on the Caps Lock button on my laptop and interjecting sentence by sentence in REBARBATIVE UPPERCASE throughout the article. No author complained. That has given me the secret satisfaction of knowing that significant parts of a paper are as much mine as they are the author's. And sometimes an author's gratitude is lasting, as when one whose paper required serious attention a couple of years ago e-mailed regrets at having to decline an invitation to our garden party, but adding, "Actually, what I would most like to do is to personally thank George for all the care and consideration he showed in editing my paper and seeing it through to publication. I would not have got there without his help. Please pass on my thanks and appreciation." Messages like that are a real consolation!

At a much lower level, peer review offers a basic safeguard against fraudulent work or a spoof or plagiarism. Referees are fallible scholars, but even so there is a good chance that they will spot mischief. One referee informed me that a paper submitted to me had already appeared in print word-for-word in a journal dealing with American military matters. The author had not thought to tell me that, complaining, disingenuously, about the time taken to reject the paper. But that delay could not have justified his submission elsewhere, since that journal published it just a month after it had been received by the *EHR*.

An editor wants informed assessments. But these may take time. If you say that preventing some malpractice means waiting for referees, some might respond by saying that it is a rare problem. Yet, crucially, the mere fact of peer review acts as deterrence. And as with all forms of deterrence, the more successful it is, the more it is open to shortsighted attacks on the time and resources it uses up. But I have an uneasy feeling that the author in this case was hoping I would not notice—and then that author could have had a go at the whole system of peer review as the practice of a corrupt and incompetent establishment.

I have been amused at how some historians see the *EHR* as somehow central to such an historical establishment. True, I was only the twentieth editor since the foundation of the *Review* in 1886, and I did feel, as my colleague and successor Martin Conway put it, that I was joining some kind of pantheon. On its centenary, the then editor, Angus Macintyre, thought the appropriate way to celebrate was to publish a list of editors. And until my appointment, being editor of the *EHR* was one of those offices that automatically conferred inclusion in *Who's Who*. What makes little sense, though, is to see the *Review* as exemplifying establishment or institutional views. Willie Lamont, noting that "the *English Historical Review* is the voice of the History Establishment," criticized the *EHR* for not carrying a review of the first edition of E. P. Thompson's *The Making of the English Working Class* and for not reviewing Keith Thomas's *Religion and the Decline of Magic* at all: he saw that as reflecting the prejudices of the historical establishment, presumably that these were not subjects or treatments worthy of serious historians. Indeed, immediately after I was appointed, Keith Thomas asked me whether I knew that his book had never been reviewed in the *EHR;* I did.

But it did not occur to me then to ask John Roberts what lay behind that. In my experience, the absence of a review reflects not some editorial or establishment prejudice but more prosaically the failure of an intended reviewer to send in the review. And I did try hard as review editor to secure reviews of paperback editions if the original hardback of an important book had not been reviewed. It is a nice conceit to imagine a gathering of senior historians, presumably including the editor, conspiring to publish an article by A and reject one by B, or to commission a hostile review of C's book and a favorable one of D's. But it just does not work like that. No one ever gave me any orders about the content of the journal.

True, appointment as editor of the *English Historical Review* is by patronage. But that patronage is largely exercised by the existing editors, and the judgments are eminently practical. Formally, the editor of the *EHR* is appointed by Oxford University Press; but in practice, the head of Humanities and Social Science journals relies on guidance. I owed my appointment to my immediate predecessor, John Rowett; and Philip Waller and Martin Conway, with whom I have shared the editorship, were my choices.

I have perhaps spent too long on the criticisms and awkwardness of peer review. Yet I wish to end by emphasizing that other options all seem much less helpful. As editor, I should not have wished to make decisions without expert guidance. And I cannot easily see how any alternative way of eliciting that expert guidance might function. At first sight, the commissioning of papers might seem an attractive option. And I was certainly open to the possibility. One colleague told me that he had just read a draft for one of his friends and would encourage a submission to the *EHR*, which duly came and, after peer review, was accepted. Another scholar, someone I know quite well, a very modest scholar, sent me a draft paper to read, insisting that this was not intended as a submission to the *EHR* but simply for me, as a Tudor specialist, to read and to say whether it was at all worthwhile. It was excellent. So without asking first, I sent it to two friends, both eminently suitable as referees on the subject, saying that this was not a submission to the *EHR* and that my letter was not a request for them to act as referees, but that I should be grateful to know whether they agreed with me that it had the quality of an *EHR* article. Of course they agreed; and so quickly did they respond that I was able to inform the author at once. But commissioning is generally not that helpful. Commissioning in the sense of "would you like to write a paper on" is not very appropriate for an academic journal. A scholarly paper, unlike a newspaper column, cannot be written quickly on demand. The generous referee who offered to write a paper rather than a critical referee's report took eighteen months to do so.

Academic journals are much more mirrors (the comparison is Mark Goldie's)—the submissions reflecting what scholars are doing and interested in—than the creations of editors. I could encourage or deter in response to queries about whether a proposed paper would be welcomed, but in practice that achieved little, since all depends on the quality of the reasoning in a paper. A narrowly focused study of a seemingly unimportant individual, for example, can in the right hands turn into a paper of lasting importance. I have been asked whether I could give preference to some topics or some treatments rather than others. Perhaps in theory, perhaps in unwitting practice, but not really. I could not conjure up large numbers of papers to my liking. I had to deal with what I received. An undergraduate who interviewed me recently asked whether I could reject postmodernist submissions. The difficulty with that line of questioning is that I never received any. Perhaps the reputation of the *EHR* as a journal of empirical scholarship deters submissions that are purely theoretical. But I am not quite sure what a postmodernist history article would be like. Most of the theorists—Keith Jenkins, Alun Munslow—either do not write historical monographs or articles at all, or when they do—I think of Patrick Joyce—it is hard to distinguish them from any others. Except, perhaps, for one feature, but this is much more common, namely, the use of theoretical language and fashionable abstractions. And here, yes, I did often wield my editor's pen, pressing authors to avoid terms such as *discourse* or *negotiation* or *construction* and instead to express their thought freshly in language that everyone would at once understand. In doing that, I was, however, acting as an editor, not as a censor, and I was editing papers already accepted for publication. My definition of the kind of historical writing published in the *EHR* is conceptually aware empirical scholarship.

A free-for-all would serve little purpose. Anyone can already publish anything on the Web, with no control of its quality whatsoever. That simply pushes the burden of judgment onto the reader. An academic journal relying on referees offer scholars the assurance that anything published in it has been carefully considered, and no doubt improved, both by referees specialist in the field and by an editor applying consistent standards across the range. For an author to be accepted by a journal is a mark of merit. Such acceptance constitutes success in a competition, since only a small proportion of papers submitted to the *English Historical Review*—perhaps 20–25 percent—can be accepted. Their success is greater still if it is reckoned that because the *English Historical Review*'s reputation for quality is so well known, only those who believe that they have a realistic chance of gaining acceptance will submit an article.

What publication in a journal such as the *EHR* offers is association. The *EHR* is, in a sense, a brand, and it seems to have acquired that status very quickly. Once acquired, such an aura can become self-perpetuating. Scholars have a sense of what the ideal *EHR* article looks like, perhaps based on the best papers they have read, especially when beginners. An ambitious young scholar will have read important papers in past issues: if he or she succeeds in getting a paper accepted, he or she may feel a sense of having arrived as a scholar. I can remember my astonishment and delight when my first paper appeared in the *EHR* immediately after one by Karl Leyser, Chichele Professor of Medieval History at Oxford and one of the most deeply learned scholars of his day; and when my second paper in the *EHR* appeared ten years later, I was no less astonished that it was followed by one by my tutor, Peter Dickson, an extraordinarily precise scholar whom I revered. What was I doing in such company? The *EHR* is thus a kind of academic community, and to be published in it is to be admitted, or to continue to be admitted, to that community. Yet that community is not confined just to those whose articles are accepted. It also embraces, invisibly, all those involved in peer review.

And it is far better to see historical research as a collective and cooperative endeavor in which each published paper adds its mite to the corpus of knowledge and understanding, and some papers turn out to add even more. Peer review plays an invaluable part in that endeavor. Indeed, since scholars selflessly give up their time to write engaged reports on submitted articles, an effort for which they receive the thanks of the editor but no pay and no public recognition, peer review ought to be seen as a prime example of just that cooperative endeavor, part of a civil and a civilized society. It should not lightly be jeopardized.

Spring Semester 2012

1. Thomas Cranmer, *Miscellaneous Writings and Letters,* ed. J. E. Cox (Cambridge, 1846), p. 341.

Michael Roberts, 1935

5

Michael Roberts and the BBC

ANDREW ROBERTS

From 1941 to 1945, my father, Michael Roberts (1902–48), a teacher, poet, and critic, worked in the European Service of the BBC. Meanwhile, my mother, Janet Adam Smith, was bringing up a young family in the north of England. My father's letters to her constitute a lively, almost daily chronicle of life in wartime London.[1] Collating these with his BBC papers offered an opportunity to throw light on one corner of a major British institution at a critical moment in its history.

Michael Roberts (M.R.) was raised in Hampshire. From Bournemouth School he went on to read chemistry at King's College, London, and mathematics at Trinity College, Cambridge. In 1925 he became senior physics master at the Royal Grammar School, Newcastle-on-Tyne. He enjoyed school life there, but after six years he was restive. He had literary ambitions, and London beckoned. So in 1931 he moved back south, to teach mathematics at Mercers' School, in the City of London.

From a flat in Fitzroy Square, M.R. made himself known at key points in the literary world. In 1932–33, he began contributing to T. S. Eliot's *Criterion* and compiled three anthologies: *New Signatures*, *New Country*, and *Elizabethan Prose*. Reviews were mostly respectful, and the BBC chose M.R. to broadcast in the series "Whither Britain?"; he was the youngest speaker, except for Quintin Hogg (the future Lord Hailsham), in a lineup that included Shaw, H. G. Wells, Lloyd George, and Winston Churchill. M.R.'s talk was broadcast

on 27 February 1934; he introduced himself as a schoolmaster concerned with the ideas of young people and also acquainted with
young poets and scientists. By then, however, he was a schoolmaster without pupils: on 1 February he had been dismissed by Mercers, whose governors took a dim view of lessons exploring the nature of religious and scientific belief. He applied to the BBC for a
job in schools broadcasting; he didn't get it, but the redoubtable
Mary Somerville (secretary to the Council for School Broadcasting)
hoped he "would get to the B.B.C. in another capacity."[2] Meanwhile,
M.R. had written the larger part of a book, *Newton and the Origin of
Colours* (1934), for a series called Classics of Scientific Method, and
in the autumn he returned to the Royal Grammar School, Newcastle. Early in 1935 he was invited by Eliot to compile what became the
Faber Book of Modern Verse (1936), which introduced British readers
to Hart Crane, Wallace Stevens, Allen Tate, and E. E. Cummings.

In June 1935 my father married. For four years, my mother had
been assistant editor of the *Listener,* a BBC weekly. She had organized
the book reviews and chosen the poetry. The *Listener* became the
platform of choice for several young writers in the 1930s. My parents
settled in Newcastle. They started a family, climbed mountains, continued to write for London periodicals, and also wrote books. Over
the next few years, Faber published four books by M.R.: *The Modern
Mind* (1937), about the influence of science on language; a study of
T. E. Hulme, the philosopher-poet killed in 1917; a book of poems,
Orion Marches (1939); and *The Recovery of the West* (1941), which confronted "the strong feeling that Western civilisation is in decay" and
sought a moral basis for social reconstruction. When war broke out
in September 1939, the Royal Grammar School was evacuated to
Penrith, Cumberland, on the edge of the Lake District; there M.R.
conceived and compiled the *Faber Book of Comic Verse*. In July 1941 he
was offered a job in the European Service of the BBC.

This part of the BBC was a recent growth, created in response to
the outbreak of war. Founded in 1922, the BBC had begun to broadcast overseas in 1932, when the Empire Service was inaugurated.
By 1938, international rivalry had caused the BBC to introduce
foreign-language services: at first the Arabic and Spanish (for Latin
America), followed by the French, German, and Italian. The advent
of war prompted further expansion and reorganization. In 1939–40
the Empire Service was enlarged to become the Overseas Service; a
North American Service was introduced to reach the United States;
and a consolidated European Service was created.

War portended closer control of the BBC by the government. As
German forces occupied more and more of Continental Europe,

the BBC became "a new armament of war."[3] The Treasury, via the Foreign Office, financed the European Service; in return, the Foreign Office expected to have rights of informal liaison. The possibility of censorship, or at least of governmental guidance, was confirmed by the creation of a Ministry of Information (MOI), which in turn, in 1941, spawned the Political Warfare Executive (PWE). This body soon caused trouble for the European Service. The BBC believed that the best propaganda was the truth; the PWE, on the other hand, was chiefly dedicated to "black" propaganda—the deliberate deception of the enemy; and it had its own radio stations. Each agency asserted superior claims to scarce public funds.

By mid-1941, the European Service was broadcasting in at least fifteen languages; by the end of 1942, twenty-two. Each language service was headed by an editor, who was normally a British national, and staffed by announcers and translators who were mostly refugees. At the center of operations was the director of European Broadcasts, Noel Newsome, who before the war had been foreign news editor for the *Daily Telegraph,* where he had strongly opposed appeasement. At the BBC, daily directives from Newsome inspired or infuriated the editors in charge of the language services. His position was underpinned by his close rapport with the controller of the European Service; from 1941 to 1944 this was Ivone Kirkpatrick, a career diplomat, who from 1942 also sat on the executive committee of the PWE. Alongside Newsome's Central News Desk there was the Central Talks staff, which included Alan Bullock, the future biographer of Hitler and Ernest Bevin.

One part of the European Service remains to be mentioned. Like the rest of the BBC, the service was concerned not only with producing "output" but also with assessing its impact. The service thus had its own Intelligence Department, which gathered information about the reception of BBC broadcasts in both German-occupied and neutral Europe. This was hugely important, since the Germans and their collaborators took increasingly severe measures to prevent people from listening to the BBC. To be caught doing so made one liable to harsh penalties, extending to summary execution. The mere ownership of radio sets was prohibited, and BBC transmissions were subject to jamming. Nevertheless, many people under enemy occupation or domination were brave enough not only to defy such intimidation but also to assist the BBC by reporting on conditions for listening. Their letters reached London by devious routes, usually through neutral countries, and a surprising number of people managed to escape from the Continent. To handle such sources of information, the Intelligence Department had eight intelligence officers, each covering a separate region, and sixteen assistants (some of them refugees), as well as clerical staff. Asa Briggs, in his magisterial survey of British broadcasting, observed in 1970: "There is no more fascinating aspect of the history of broadcasting during the war than that concerned with the efforts both of engineers and of producers to reach their audience and of specialists in listener research to assess their impact upon it."[4] The Danish section of the department had already been studied, but otherwise historians have been slow to take the hint.

It was the director of the Intelligence Department, Jonathan Griffin, who had sought out M.R. in Penrith. Griffin too was an author. Six months younger than M.R., he had written three books on military matters and a fourth based on a brief assignment in Prague in 1938—he had previously run the department's Eastern Europe section. He had been given M.R.'s name by W. O. Galbraith, European presentation manager (in charge of scheduling broadcasts), who had been a colleague of M.R. at the Royal Grammar School, Newcastle. Griffin interviewed M.R. in July 1941 and reported: "He is very much our man [with] a sense of evidence and a habit of really thinking problems through . . . He is at present teaching in an elementary school."[5] This startling error betrays inattention or plain ignorance. What Griffin thought of M.R.'s literary work is not clear, though he was probably unaware that *The Recovery of the West* had recently prompted a long editorial in the *Times Educational Supplement* for 12 July.

Be that as it may, M.R. moved to London in September and took up the post of general intelligence officer, working at first at Bedford College in Regent's Park and from December at Bush House, a massive stone building in Aldwych between the Strand and Kingsway. It was named for an American, Irving T. Bush—no relation to the presidents—who was also responsible for the enormous Bush Terminal in Brooklyn and Bush Tower, a Times Square skyscraper. Bush House, designed by New York architects, had opened in 1925 as a trading center. This is why the grandiose entrance is surmounted by figures representing England and America and framing the inscription "To the friendship of English speaking peoples."

By the end of 1941, M.R. had helped produce two major "Studies of European Audiences." These reports and others like them were based on letters from listeners and interviews with refugees. In 1942 the BBC received 1,200 letters from France and interviewed 700 Frenchmen, 140 Belgians, and 120 people from the Netherlands. M.R. later recalled that in 1941–42 he interviewed between 200 and 300 persons and read about 2,000 reports from occupied Europe.

One irksome task was to listen to records of enemy jamming: "a particularly nasty occupation for anyone with a taste for Mozart." In 1942, M.R. served as secretary to a subcommittee on jamming, making quarterly reports on radio reception in Europe. In March, he was made ready to fly to Lisbon to prepare the way for the possible appointment of a permanent BBC representative; it seems, however, that he did not go.

The editor of *Comic Verse* found some relief from office routine in concocting "Ruritania," a skit that by July was "in great demand" in Bush House. By then, the Ministry of Information wanted M.R.'s services for "foreign publicity," but his BBC superiors thought him "far too valuable to be spared."[6] Indeed, the survival of the Intelligence Department had been in question until April 1942 because of apparent "overlap" of functions with the PWE. That department had recently become a dangerously near neighbor: in February 1942, from a base at Woburn, north of London, it had begun to move into Bush House, occupying a floor significantly above the European Service. The PWE remained skeptical about the Intelligence Department and about other aspects of the European Service. M.R. had his own misgivings. In December he sent Griffin a searching critique of the department: "Our work is not always taken with due seriousness by our colleagues . . . Our function is to produce useful information, not interesting reading matter." Griffin's own "Europe Surveys" were superfluous. "Some of the dead wood in the Department might be cut out"—a job for Griffin, M.R., and Emile Delavenay, Griffin's deputy, who ran the French section.[7] A leaner, fitter department might save £2,000–£3,000 a year. (M.R.'s own salary was then £680.)

Griffin must have felt much like some feckless schoolboy taken to task by M.R. in classroom or camp. In any case, he took no effective action, and M.R.'s temper was further frayed by Griffin's absence, through illness, for over a month early in 1943—which meant that M.R. had to take over the completion of two major audience surveys for 1942.

In April, M.R. returned to the charge. There were still too many on staff: six could go, including one intelligence officer; some were doing work that should be done by the PWE. Griffin himself was severely rebuked: he had let a "ridiculous private war with P.W.E." drag on; he had failed to open up new channels for intelligence from beyond Europe, despite entertaining "high personalities"; and he was often out of his office for long periods.[8] Again, Griffin temporized; it was agreed that these matters should be considered in June. They were not; and meanwhile the Intelligence Department had come under renewed pressure from the PWE, and also from the French and German services. On 21 June, a clearly harassed Griffin went on the attack, accusing M.R. of nine errors in a report; he copied the memo to Kirkpatrick, controller of the European Service. M.R. went to see Griffin, who "completely crumbled up in his chair": "I've never seen anyone like it. I felt very sorry for him." The next day, M.R. wrote a point-by-point rebuttal, concluding:

> I realise that, as you have since told me, your memorandum was written whilst you were in a very natural state of exasperation resulting from recent events. I suggest that you should withdraw your criticisms so that we can part amicably.[9]

For M.R. was about to leave the Intelligence Department. He had in fact offered his resignation in April; now Kirkpatrick offered him the new post of clandestine press editor, within the Central News Department. M.R. demurred; he preferred a job offer from the Political Intelligence Department (PID) of the Foreign Office, but Kirkpatrick, unwilling to let him go, secured his assent on 28 June.

M.R.'s relations with Griffin had at best been correct rather than cordial. In 1942 he dined three times with Griffin and his wife, Joan, but their way of life was not his. They then lived—rather well—in Brown's Hotel, Mayfair. In July—when one of M.R.'s fellow guests was Violet Bonham-Carter, a BBC governor—Griffin had just had nearly three weeks' holiday; M.R, from a bedsit in Notting Hill, escaped to Cumberland for weekends with his family every three or four months. Emile Delavenay (father of the biographer Claire Tomalin) was impressed by the Griffins' literary and political connections; himself a teacher of literature, he admired Jonathan's "fastidious" prose as well as his "*farouche intégrité*." In contrast, M.R. is not mentioned in Delavenay's memoirs, nor by his interviewer, Martyn Cornick. Still, when Griffin wrote his annual report on M.R. in August 1943, he acknowledged his "marked gift for organisation," adding, "The department owes a good deal to him."[10]

M.R.'s new job indicated the BBC's response to a marked increase, by mid-1943, in the number, and circulation, of underground newspapers and leaflets in occupied Europe; that development in turn reflected the surge in popular support for resistance as the prospect of an Allied victory became clearer. The initiative was taken by Newsome. Once the BBC decided to make specific provision for the clandestine press, Belgium loomed large, since a clandestine press was strongly established there. Indeed, the idea may be traced back to *La Voix des Belges,* a clandestine paper that in February had urged "the broadcaster" to provide a range of material from which the underground press might make its selections. M.R. was chosen to start the new service, since as general intelligence officer he had had a remit for Belgium and the Netherlands. In the first transmission, on 12 July, M.R. explained,

> We are acting as your special correspondent in London, and we are under your instructions. Our intention is to help the editors of the clandestine press in Belgium, France, Luxembourg, and especially in those countries where radio sets have been confiscated: Poland, Norway, Holland. Here in London, we read your papers carefully. Print your instructions in your paper, and we shall do our best to serve you.[11]

At the end of the year, he wrote to a friend, Helen Sutherland:

> I am very glad indeed to be useful to such men . . . [they] redeem the character of *all* writing, by showing that in time of difficulty and danger it still has a real function. The kind of thing I broadcast is very straightforward—tables of facts and figures; leading articles from *The Times* or *The Economist;* notes about the clandestine press in other countries, so that the editors will feel that they are part of a European organisation, and so on.[12]

FROM THE FIRST, THERE WAS A KEEN APPETITE for material on questions of long-term concern: population trends, post-war economic prospects, British social policy (the Beveridge Report, the Butler White Paper on education). In January 1944, one program was largely devoted to the growth of the French Maquis; the next week, an item about a German shortage of tires was followed by one on education for Africans. Asa Briggs remarks, "The role of the BBC in providing information for Europe's extensive clandestine press can scarcely be overestimated," but this was a casual aside, and historians have not looked into the subject.[13] Besides, the service was more than a source of information; it became, in effect, a clearinghouse for ideas—almost, indeed, a debating chamber—for some of Europe's freest and bravest thinkers. In December 1943 it enabled French and Norwegian editors to exchange views about the likely shape of post-war political parties; it gave Continent-wide circulation to Danish insistence on adhering to the rule of law when dealing with collaborators. Yet not all editors wished to be entirely solemn. *La Voix des Belges* asked for a little humor. M.R. saw himself "haunting the Palladium and the Shepherd's Bush Empire" in search of jokes.

At first, the programs went out twice a week; in October they were increased to three a week. They were initially broadcast in French, Dutch, and English; German was added in October, and Italian and

Serbo-Croat in May 1944. Now and again M.R. had to read the English scripts himself: hearing one playback, he was pleased with his South Country accent: "The whole job was a co-operative effort of editor, translators, announcers, studio managers and engineers, all of whom took a special interest in these technically difficult transmissions and were proud to help their gallant colleagues of the clandestine press."[14] Communication with editors was reinforced by encounters in London. Soon after the service started, M.R. had lunch with a Dutch editor; this was probably J. C. S. Warendorf of *Het Parool,* who had reached England in June. As clandestine press editor, M.R was more or less his own master; he compiled the material himself, with help from Joan Pritchard, who had been his secretary in the Intelligence Department. Inevitably, there was occasional internal criticism of M.R.'s program content, but his work was highly appreciated by the Belgian government-in-exile and by Warendorf, who later wrote of M.R.'s "insight into the distress of occupied Europe."[15]

Alongside his principal duties, M.R. had for some time been involved in schemes for diversifying British propaganda. During the winter of 1942–43, he was called on to contribute ideas for the "Projection of Britain," an initiative of Newsome's deputy, Douglas Ritchie, but this was halted by both Kirkpatrick at the BBC and Bruce Lockhart at the PWE. Later in 1943, for the Joint PWE/MOI/BBC Re-occupation Committee, M.R. advised on the selection of films and books for Belgium and the Netherlands, but this committee—as the PWE's own historian, David Garnett, later pointed out—was based on the false assumption that the British would take charge of civil administration in liberated areas. M.R. complained in March 1944 about "these irrelevant committees from which I never succeed in resigning." In October 1943 he proposed the compilation of a popular illustrated record of the war that might be called *The Book of Liberation.* Six months later, the Ministry of Information wrote to J. B. Priestley, asking him to write a book about the British role in the liberation of Europe; Priestley declined. Nonetheless, a book that M.R. had finished three years earlier was much admired by John McMillan from the Political Intelligence Department. *The Recovery of the West* was enjoying a certain réclame. In June 1943, extracts appeared in *La Revue du Monde Libre* (printed in London but "apportée par la R.A.F."), which caused the book to be discussed in a German-controlled paper in Paris; and it was banned in Slovakia. By the end of 1943, 900 copies had been sold of a German translation published in Zurich; it was reviewed in the *Neue Zürcher Zeitung* (11 January 1944). McMillan wanted to offer M.R. "the opportunity of expressing himself extensively *in print*" and in January urged the PID to try to get him, without success.[16]

Instead, in April 1944, M.R. had to take over the Czech section of the European Service; A. J. Van Velden replaced him as clandestine press editor. The Czech section, especially at that stage in the war, embodied the tensions inherent in the European Service. While Newsome and Ritchie vigorously asserted the supremacy of "central" BBC control over news broadcasting, they had to reckon with the editors who headed the various regional sections; besides, broadcasts depended on non-British announcers, who had their own views about what should be heard by their compatriots, and who might be backed by governments-in-exile. In the Czech section, by mid-1944 broadcast content was being shaped by a British editorial staff of six; there were ten announcers, of whom two were Slovak. Tact was needed to allay fears of quasi-colonial subordination.

Hitherto, the editors of the Czech section, Shiela Grant Duff and then Professor R. R. Betts, had been given "a very free hand," which may have eased relations with their Czech colleagues; in any case, both had been acquainted with Czechoslovakia and its languages. Then Betts resigned in April "on grounds of ill-health" and M.R. took over.[17] Soon afterward, he went (for the second time) to see *The Bartered Bride* at the New Theatre instead of reading a book about Slovak problems. He wanted to sack a few people in the section, and the filing system needed overhauling. The language typists, bound to a round-the-clock schedule, objected to working five days a week. M.R. began to understand why Betts had wanted out. Then the attention that had to be given to President Benes's birthday marginalized the war news. In June, he described his troubles with the Czechs to his friend Kathleen Raine, who worked for the PID in Bush House; she said they were a novel by Kafka. (It is not clear whether M.R. knew that a recently appointed Czech announcer, George Steiner, was married to a niece of Kafka.)

In July, M.R. was called to discuss his section's problems with the controller (Kirkpatrick), Ritchie, and H. J. Dunkerley, director of organization for the European Service. M.R. admitted that he had been tactless, but Kirkpatrick thought his firmness "was absolutely justified."[18] There were further rumblings among the announcers: Steiner and one other declared that it was "impossible to work with Mr Roberts," but the prevailing view was "If Mr Roberts goes, who comes next? If it is Professor Betts, I prefer Mr Roberts."[19] In any case, M.R. had been heartened by the section's behavior on 30 June after a flying bomb had landed in Aldwych outside Bush House: "The whole racket of a disgruntled, scheming section standing up nobly to our local bomb, has been exhilarating, exasperating and enjoyable." And he was on his way out: early in August he handed the section over to V. Duckworth Barker and returned to the clandestine press.

By then, of course, the need for this specialized service was much reduced, thanks to the liberation of France; in September, M.R. submitted a new scheme of broadcasts. And by November, the European Service had decided to abolish the Clandestine Press Unit and transfer M.R. to the Talks Section. M.R. had already taken up a suggestion by Van Velden that the clandestine press would welcome summaries of important recent books. These helped meet a need identified by Newsome: people on the Continent, "cut off for years from the habit and opportunity of political thinking and intellectual activity of any kind, possessed nevertheless a consuming desire for it."[20] Alan Bullock was later to emphasize "the isolation and numbing effects of occupation."[21] The book summaries began on 17 September: M.R. himself summarized T. S. Eliot's *Four Quartets* and books by Harold Laski, Jacques Maritain, Lewis Mumford, and Erwin Schrödinger. But by the end of 1944, M.R. had become impatient to escape the interminable demands of work in Bush House. In March 1945, just before he left the BBC, he analyzed the needs of the European Talks section, in which long-term planning had become impossible:

> The conditions under which Bullock, van Velden and myself have worked for the past three months are lunatic. My usual position has been this. I am trying to write a summary of Niebuhr's book on democracy for next Tuesday. In the middle of a sentence I am told to write a piece on the Conservative Party conference . . . I am interrupted at least fifteen times by having to read the French Football Chronicle, a Bulgarian talk on the Fire Service, a Greek talk on Polish problems, and the Dutch programme for women.[22]

All the same, the prevailing ethos of the European Service had been congenial to M.R. A few years later, he reviewed the war memoirs of the head of the PWE. M.R. concluded, "In a free democracy, sound and consistent decisions can be taken by humble individuals who have never heard of the demi-gods 'in the Country' or 'on the eighth floor.'"[23] Six months after he had left the European Service, M.R. was moved to speak out in defense of former colleagues. Late in 1945, the BBC suspended the Spanish program organizer, dismissed his assistant, and suspended political commentaries in both the Spanish and Portuguese services. Writing to the *New Statesman*

(3 November 1945), M.R. observed that listeners "may infer that His Majesty's Government has made a bargain with General Franco": "The difficulty seems to be that today there is no official machinery for laying down policy in advance, and that the wartime organization for ascertaining the reactions of public opinion in Europe has been disbanded." The Intelligence Department had been abolished in December 1944, and meanwhile Britain was, in Noel Annan's useful phrase, "changing enemies." The BBC's post-war concessions to Spain and Portugal must be seen in the context of the perceived communist threat to western Europe, and it may be relevant that the key decisions were taken by the acting controller of the European Service, Harman Grisewood, a Roman Catholic.

Throughout his time at the BBC, M.R. was called on by other bodies to speak and write. In 1943–44 he took part in courses arranged by Chatham House (the Royal Institute of International Affairs), where he gave a talk in October 1944 titled "The New Forces in Western Europe." He spoke with authority, as one of the few people familiar with the currents of thought that had found outlets in the clandestine press. The talk was well received, and M.R. was nominated for the Council of Chatham House before it was realized that he was not a member. But apart from a few book reviews, he took no part in the literary life of wartime London; he was far too busy. In 1943, Nancy Cunard asked whether he had a recent poem about France for an anthology she was editing; he replied that he had "nothing in the locker."[24] There were a few notable encounters. One day in March 1944, M.R. lunched with Cyril Connolly, David Garnett, Moura Budberg—the Russian adventuress and translator—and Raymond Aron, who since 1940 had been in London editing the monthly *La France Libre*. M.R. occasionally saw literary friends: William Empson (in the BBC's Eastern Service, at Oxford Circus) and his wife were very hospitable, and it was at one of their parties, in December 1943, that M.R. first met George Orwell, after he had left the BBC to edit *Tribune*.

As M.R. LOOKED ROUND FOR ANOTHER JOB toward the end of 1944, he hoped for something that would allow him to write books again: "I sometimes wish that all my miscellaneous aptitudes added up." There were repeated approaches from Douglas McKie at University College, London, in the department of the history and philosophy of science, but there was no money for a new post there. In December, with many misgivings, M.R. agreed to become principal of a teacher-training college in Chelsea. This was the College of St. Mark and St. John; the first principal of St. Mark's had been Derwent Coleridge, son of the poet. The college had to be revived almost from nothing, and the buildings were in bad shape.

But the years at St Mark's—and there were to be less than four—are another story. I shall end this one with a poetry reading at the Empsons' on 31 May 1945, three weeks after VE Day and two months after M.R.'s departure from Bush House. The occasion was instigated by Kathleen Raine, then working for the British Council. The reading was to honor a French visitor, the "Maquis poet" Pierre Emmanuel. Among those who took part were Eliot, Dylan Thomas, George Barker, and Edgell Rickword. M.R. was chairman,

> banging on the floor with an empty beer bottle to call for order. On the whole, successfully. I thought all the boys read v. well and I enjoyed the evening.[25]

I hope that that the poet who had spent most of the war in Resistance work at Dieulefit (in the Drôme region) knew that the evening's chairman was the poet who in 1943 had introduced BBC broadcasts specifically for editors of the clandestine press in occupied Europe.

Spring Semester 2012

1. These letters are privately held, and I have not provided citations for them. BBC papers kept by Michael Roberts, together with his literary papers, are in the National Library of Scotland, Edinburgh (Acc. 13145; hereafter cited as NLS/MR).

2. M.R. to E. R. Thomas, 2 Feb. 1934; E. R. Thomas to M.R., 20 May 1934, NLS/MR, 49.

3. Asa Briggs, *The History of Broadcasting in the United Kingdom*, vol. III: *The War of Words* (London, 1970), p. 162.

4. Ibid., p. 71.

5. J. Griffin to Director, European Service, 25 July 1941, BBC Written Archives Centre, Caversham (WAC), LI/366.

6. H. J. Dunkerley to Director of Staff Administration, 24 July 24 1942, WAC, LI/366.

7. M.R. to Griffin, 12 Dec. 1942, NLS/MR, 76.

8. M.R. to Director of European Operations [Dunkerley], through European Intelligence Director [Griffin], 21 Apr. 1943, ibid.

9. M.R. to Griffin, 22 June 1943, ibid.

10. Griffin, annual report on M.R., 30 Aug. 1943, WAC, LI/366.

11. Script in NLS/MR, 92; folders 92–95 contain an almost complete set.

12. M.R. to Helen Sutherland, 18 Dec. 1943, NLS/MR, 50.

13. Briggs, *War of Words*, p. 421.

14. M.R. to A. Eur. Pres. D., 16 Feb. 1945, NLS/MR, 91.

15. *Het Parool,* 20 Dec. 1948.

16. J. H. McMillan to Chief Administrative Officer, PID, 24 Jan. 1944, NLS/MR, 72.

17. Briggs, *War of Words*, p. 470n.

18. Controller, European Service, to Director, European Operations, 13 July 1944, WAC LI/366.

19. M.R. to Controller, European Service, 2 Aug. 1944, NLS/MR, 90.

20. *BBC Yearbook, 1944,* p. 70.

21. "Broadcasting to Europe," Churchill Archives Centre, Cambridge, papers of Noel Newsome and Douglas Ritchie, 3/10, p. 16.

22. M.R. to A. R. Birley, 16 Mar. 1945, NLS/MR, 73.

23. *International Affairs*, 24, no. 4 (Oct. 1948): 579.

24. Nancy Cunard to M.R., 2 Oct. [1943], and M.R. to Nancy Cunard, 1 Nov. 1943, Nancy Cunard Collection, Harry Ransom Center, University of Texas at Austin.

25. Andrew Roberts, "A Date with the Empsons," *Times Literary Supplement*, 17 July 2009.

David Astor, 1964. Photograph by David N. Smith.

6

David Astor and the *Observer*

JEREMY LEWIS

Founded in 1791, the *Observer* is Britain's oldest Sunday newspaper; and its best-known and most widely admired editor was David Astor, who owned and edited the paper from 1948 to 1975. Famed for his liberal views, his internationalist sympathies, his gifts as a talent spotter, and his enthusiasm for good writing, Astor is best remembered for his denunciation of Anthony Eden's Suez policy in November 1956. This proved to be a mixed blessing and a turning point in the paper's fortunes, alienating advertisers and older readers and coinciding with a revival in the fortunes of its old rival, the *Sunday Times*. But Astor was never the most commercially minded of newspapermen, far preferring the elegant, ruminative essay to the rough-and-tumble of being first with the news, and painful as this particular episode must have been—he had known and liked Eden since before the war—he never expressed any editorial regrets about the stand he had taken.

Educated at Eton and Balliol College, Oxford, David Astor was, to all appearances, the quintessential upper-class Englishman: elegant and good-looking, with a thatch of fair hair, blue eyes, and a lopsided grin, he combined charm, modesty, and genuine diffidence with a steely center, kindness and exceptional generosity with clear-eyed determination. The generosity, though not the self-deprecation, was more American than English, and this most English-seeming of Astors was, in his origins at least, American through and through. His liking for America manifested itself professionally as well as personally: in the editorial welcome he gave to the Marshall Plan in 1947, at a time when dislike and resentment of America were widespread in Britain; in his lifelong "Atlanticism"; in his support for American policy in Vietnam (not shared by his younger colleagues on the paper); and in his disapproval of Graham Greene's anti-American opinions.

David Astor's ancestor John Jacob Astor, a butcher from the Rhineland village of Waldorf, came to the States in the late eighteenth century, made a fortune in the fur trade, and ended his days one of the richest men in the world and the owner of large swaths of Manhattan. In the last decade of the nineteenth century, his great-grandson, William Waldorf Astor, declared that America was no country for gentlemen—he had been spurned by the electorate—and settled in England. He bought Hever Castle in Kent, complete with moat and drawbridge, and Cliveden, a huge Italianate mansion on a spur of land overlooking the Thames near Maidenhead, between London and Oxford; his enormous wealth enabled him to mix with the grandest of the grand, and he was eventually made a viscount. His eldest son, Waldorf—David Astor's father—was given Cliveden, and in due course inherited both the *Observer,* which had been bought from Lord Northcliffe in 1911, and, to his intense annoyance, his father's seat in the House of Lords; the younger son, John Jacob, became the owner of Hever and went on to acquire *The Times.*

David Astor often claimed that the two great influences on his life were his Oxford friend Adam von Trott, who was executed for his part in the 20 July 1944 plot to assassinate Hitler, and George Orwell, whom he met through Cyril Connolly in the early years of the war, employed as a contributor to the *Observer,* and looked after when he was dying from tuberculosis. But the modest, self-effacing Waldorf was quite as important. "You are lucky enough to be rich," he told young David; "that gives you a profound responsibility towards all those who are not so lucky."[1] A gentle, liberal-minded man, he was educated at Eton and New College, Oxford; although he became a Tory MP, he not only supported the Liberal government's social reforms in the years before the First World War, but also served under Lloyd George during the war. He had to give up his seat in the Commons when his father died in 1919; his Plymouth constituency was thereafter represented by his American-born wife, Nancy, David's mother and the first woman to sit in the House of Commons.

One of a gaggle of beautiful and socially ambitious sisters, Nancy Langhorne was born and brought up in Virginia. When her first marriage ended in tears, she came to England to hunt for foxes and a husband, and ended up as the chatelaine of Cliveden. Tiny, fair haired, and with a firm nose and jaw, Nancy Astor was, by all accounts, a human whirlwind: clever but poorly educated, and a passionate Christian Scientist, she dominated the company in which she found herself, infuriating and entertaining in equal measure. She was overbearing, tactless, wonderfully sharp witted—most famously in her parliamentary exchanges with Winston Churchill, who couldn't stand her—and completely unafraid: she teased Stalin when they visited Moscow in 1931, together with Bernard Shaw and the young David Astor, and outraged Ribbentrop, then the German ambassador in London, and a lunch guest at the Astor's house in St. James's Square, by asking him why Hitler insisted on wearing that absurd Charlie Chaplin moustache. As a parent, she must have been fairly strong meat, embarrassing her children by showing off and singling them out for attention in grown-up company. She could not have been more different from her husband: David Astor once remarked that he often saw opposites as complementing each other, and that "perhaps because I admired two parents who had diametrically opposite characteristics . . . the theme of my journalism was often one of reconciliation."[2]

The Cliveden Astors had four sons and a daughter; born in 1912, David was the second son. Growing up in Cliveden must have been a curious business, and not simply on account of the grandeur of the house and grounds and the serried ranks of servants. The Astors were a social family: regular visitors included writers (Bernard Shaw, Sean O'Casey, H. G. Wells) and politicians (Neville Chamberlain, Lord Halifax, Churchill, Gandhi), and even Chaplin came to pay his respects. The Astor children were "brought up to admire not celebrities, but people of worth, and to admire celebrities for their worth only."[3] Having grown up surrounded by famous names, David as an editor treated politicians politely, but was never in awe of them; and when, in the 1960s, he visited John F. Kennedy at the White House, he came as an equal, as someone who had known young Jack in England before the war. On the other hand, the liberal-minded David had little experience of how the other half lived: a famous *Observer* story tells of how one of his colleagues had to explain what was meant by a mortgage ("Do you mean to tell me that members of my staff are living in debt?"), and another of how, never having traveled on the Tube, he asked his secretary to go out and book tickets for his children.

Among the frequent visitors to Cliveden were men who, as recent graduates from Oxford, had worked in South Africa after the Boer

War for Lord Milner, becoming known as Milner's "Kindergarten." They included Archibald Kerr, later Lord Lothian; Lionel Curtis; Bob Brand; and Geoffrey Dawson, the editor of *The Times,* later to achieve a certain notoriety as a supporter of appeasement at the time of the Munich Agreement. Members of the Kindergarten were enthusiastic advocates of well-meaning but windy ideas about international cooperation and a possible federation between Britain, its Dominions, and (at times) the United States. Although, as editor of the *Observer,* David Astor found himself having to pour cold water over Lionel Curtis's schemes for world government, the ideas of the Kindergarten permeated his thinking from an early age.

Cliveden achieved an undeserved notoriety from 1937 until the outbreak of war as a hotbed of appeasement: the "Cliveden Set," an invention of the left-wing journalist Claud Cockburn, was said to be peopled by anti-Semitic admirers of Hitler. Like many people at the time, of all political persuasions, the Astors felt that Germany had been shabbily (and foolishly) treated by the Treaty of Versailles, and—remembering the horrors of World War I—sought to avoid war at almost any price. But neither Waldorf nor Nancy had any illusions about the nature of Nazism, and after Hitler occupied what remained of Czechoslovakia in March 1939, they were all in favor of the "warmonger" Churchill being brought into government. David Astor spent little time in Cliveden at the time of its notoriety, but in later years he deeply resented the very notion of the "Cliveden Set."

Like many another upper-class Englishman, David Astor was sent away to prep school and then on to Eton. At Eton he proved an unexceptional student: he invited P. G. Wodehouse down to the school, won the hurdles in his last year, and spent the winter months beagling in the countryside round Windsor. Before going up to Oxford, he spent some time in Germany, attending Nazi rallies—Hitler had not yet come to power, but Astor hated what he saw—and visiting the ancestral (and run-down) village of Waldorf. Oxford proved a period of great unhappiness, so much so that he took time off to work in a factory in Glasgow and eventually left university without taking his degree, but it marked him in three very different ways. He met his great friend and hero Adam von Trott, a German Rhodes scholar at Balliol; he suffered debilitating bouts of depression so severe that he eventually sought help in the form of psychoanalysis, then in its infancy in Britain; and he took to visiting the magical house in Sutton Courtenay, south of Oxford, that he bought for his family after the war and came to use as his weekend retreat.

A tall, good-looking young aristocrat, von Trott was in Oxford when Hitler became the Chancellor of Germany in January 1933.

He immediately realized that a terrible thing had happened to the country he loved, and although Astor and other friends begged him to remain in exile, he insisted on returning home to qualify as a lawyer and work against the regime from within. A patriot but not a nationalist, von Trott shared—and encouraged—Astor's own internationalist sympathies: working against the regime involved a series of apparent compromises, including joining the German Foreign Office and, eventually, the Nazi Party. When, in the last months before the war, von Trott came to Britain on a series of secret missions to meet, among others, Halifax and Chamberlain on behalf of the German opposition, he was regarded with deep suspicion by many of his former friends from Oxford. David Astor had helped set up the meetings in the hope that war could be delayed, giving the opposition and the army time to mount a coup against Hitler, but the mood had changed in Britain by then. David Astor never forgave Maurice Bowra for showing von Trott the door when he came to see him in Wadham and for writing to Felix Frankfurter in Washington to warn against him. For the rest of his life, Astor fought a long and ultimately successful campaign to vindicate his friend.

David Astor's lifelong bouts of depression first manifested themselves while he was at Oxford. He loved the countryside, and birds in particular, but the woods and fields round Oxford seemed grey and lifeless; he was suffused by a sense of his own inadequacy and the pointlessness of life. Nor were matters helped by his embattled relations with his overpowering mother: he wrote her a series of agonized, angry letters, begging here to let him and his siblings lead their own lives, to stop telling them what to do. Psychoanalysis came to his rescue; he once declared that although he couldn't believe in any organized religion, he did believe in Sigmund Freud, and he never lost his faith. Years later as editor of the *Observer,* he had himself driven every morning from his home in St. John's Wood to Anna Freud's clinic in her father's old home in Hampstead, where he spent half an hour before going on to work. He founded and endowed a Freud Professorship at University College, London (Oxford had earlier declined the honor). He took a keen interest in the welfare of his staff at the *Observer,* recommending psychoanalysis to those who would listen. Nor was his interest restricted to individuals. Bearing in mind what had happened to the Jews in Nazi-occupied Europe, he was horrified by the ways in which groups could be demonized, and seemingly sane and civilized societies seized by irrational fears and hatreds. In the early 1960s, he founded a chair at Sussex University—first occupied by Norman Cohn—to investigate mass psychoses, from the witch hunts of the seventeenth century to the persecution of the Jews. His hatred of demonization led him, more controversially, to befriend the Moors murderer Myra Hindley, whose treatment at the hands of the tabloid press he deplored.

AFTER LEAVING OXFORD, ASTOR seemed unsure of what he should do. Something of a lost soul, he worked briefly at Lazards, the merchant bank; he took his first steps as a journalist on the *Yorkshire Post,* writing pen portraits of local huntsmen; he lived for a time at Whitby, on the Yorkshire coast, staging amateur theatricals and mixing with circus folk (later he would compare his role as an editor to that of a ringmaster). His father had always hoped that he, rather than his older brother, Bill, would eventually take on the *Observer* after the retirement of J. L. Garvin (editor, 1908–42), on the grounds that David shared his own liberal inclinations and was fascinated by the oddities of human behavior. But it was only in the months before the outbreak of war, when von Trott resurfaced in his life, that he gained a sense of direction and began to involve himself in the political world in which his parents had spent their lives. Dithering and indecision were replaced by a single-mindedness, a toughness, and a determination that remained with him for the rest of his life. Early in 1940 he joined the Royal Marines; he longed to see action, but found himself cooling his heels on the Kent coast. Acting as von Trott's English intermediary had given him an insight into political machinations and wire pulling, and his family background provided connections in high places—among them, Hilda Matheson, who had been his mother's political secretary in the 1920s before becoming a pioneering BBC producer and was by then running the Joint Broadcasting Committee, a short-lived body responsible for broadcasting to the Axis countries.

David Astor felt strongly that British propaganda directed at Germany was inadequate, and far too negative and defensive. He employed Willi Guttmann, a German émigré and future *Observer* colleague, to monitor German broadcasts to Britain. Over the next few months he bombarded the JBC, the Ministry of Information, J. L. Garvin, Ian Fleming at Naval Intelligence, and others with suggestions about how British propaganda to enemy and neutral countries could be improved. There were two key elements: eager to keep in touch with the opposition, and with von Trott in particular, he wanted German listeners to know that Britain's quarrel was with the Nazis rather than the German people as a whole; and he thought it essential to explain to the Axis powers, to neutral countries, and to the British themselves what Britain's war aims were, what values the country stood for, and what kind of society should emerge in Britain after the war was over. Hopes of dealing with the opposition faded with the end of the "phony war" in May 1940—von Trott's wartime efforts to liaise with the British were brusquely rebuffed—but Astor's ideas about post-war Britain found expression in the *Observer,* where they contributed to the climate of opinion that brought the Labour Party to power in 1945 and prepared the ground for the welfare state.

Although Churchill showed no interest in post-war reconstruction—or, for that matter, in dealing with German opposition groups—Astor both reflected and influenced a widespread belief that the war should be fought not just to defeat the Nazis but to introduce a fairer and more equal society at home. *The Times,* the *Daily Mirror,* Edward Hulton's *Picture Post,* Allen Lane's Penguin books, and think tanks such as Political and Economic Planning all displayed, from early in the war, positive enthusiasm for planning and full employment. Waldorf Astor declared that "unless we are bold in our post-war constructive policy we may be swept away by Communism when demobilization comes."[4] (David, for his part, never had any illusions then or later about Communist Russia or "Uncle Joe.") Stafford Cripps—Labour MP, member of the wartime coalition Cabinet, friend to both Astor and von Trott—was a central figure in this wartime shift to the left; as was William Beveridge, parts of whose report advocating a welfare state and a National Health Service appeared in the *Observer* before its publication in 1942. Astor joined Hulton's 1941 Committee—other members included H. G. Wells, Kingsley Martin, J. B. Priestley, Thomas Balogh, Victor Gollancz, Tom Hopkinson, and Ritchie Calder—and was active in other pressure groups urging the creation of a "New Jerusalem" once the war had ended.

Before long, Astor's belief that the war had to be fought on the political as well as the military front found expression in the *Observer.* An overpowering, oracular figure who ran the paper from his home in the Chilterns, Garvin, then in his seventies, was increasingly at odds with his proprietor over Churchill's handling of the war. Waldorf Astor was keen to involve David in the running of the paper, albeit part-time, given his military obligations; and when David suggested a series entitled "Forum," in which he and his young friends could ventilate their views about war aims and related subjects, his father urged a reluctant Garvin to agree to publish the pieces and to meet Astor's young contributors.

Disagreements over Churchill came to a head early in 1942, and Waldorf Astor, after much agonizing, gave Garvin his marching orders. David had neither the time nor the experience to take over the running of the paper, and Ivor Brown—an apolitical, old-fashioned literary gent who had been the drama critic since the 1920s—was, improbably and only temporarily, installed as editor. But the heir apparent had his foot in the door, and although he could work at the paper only part-time, David Astor began to make his presence felt, much to Ivor Brown's discomfiture. Cyril Connolly, whom David employed as the culture-cum-literary editor, quickly livened up the book pages. The experiment ended in tears, but Astor always claimed that he had been hugely influenced by *Horizon,* the literary magazine Connolly edited for ten years during and after the war, both in his instinctive preference for well-written, self-contained essays over journalistic reportage, and in his bias toward employing writers on the paper, even if they had little or no journalistic experience—as a result of which there was always a slight gulf between the gentlemen and the players, the gifted amateurs and the workmanlike professionals.

In the meantime, Astor had joined Mountbatten's Combined Ops as a publicity officer. His longing to see some action provoked a flurry of memoranda from Churchill, who wanted to know how and why Astor combined his military duties with work at the *Observer.* In September 1944, Astor saw action at last as a member of a nine-man inter-Allied mission dropped into eastern France to liaise with the Maquis; he was wounded in the shoulder on the second day out, flown to a hospital in Naples, and eventually rewarded with a Croix de Guerre.

In 1945, Astor joined the *Observer* full-time as its foreign editor. He soon made his mark, hiring George Orwell to write book reviews and to report from defeated Germany, and dispatching Hugh Trevor-Roper, George Weidenfeld, and von Trott's great friend Christabel Bielenberg to war-damaged Europe. He had already persuaded émigrés such as Sebastian Haffner, Arthur Koestler, Isaac Deutscher, and E. F. Schumacher (a protégé of Beveridge, best remembered as the author of *Small Is Beautiful*) to write for the paper. Paper rationing had reduced the *Observer* to six or eight pages—a quarter of its pre-war length—and poor Ivor Brown felt increasingly harried and out of his depth, never more so than when Eden, the Foreign Secretary, tore a strip off him for damaging Anglo-Russian relations by publishing a piece by Deutscher about Soviet plans for post-war Poland.

IN 1948, DAVID ASTOR CAME INTO HIS OWN at last, replacing Brown as editor. One of the problems with writing about newspapers is that even the best of them, like the *Observer,* are, by their very nature, ephemeral. With very few exceptions, those who write for them are soon forgotten, and even at the height of their reputations are seldom known outside their own countries. Nonetheless, one can get a sense of what Astor saw as the mission and editorial stance of the *Observer* from his ruminations on its "soul." "In the character of this paper," he once wrote,

> ethics matter more than politics. The particular ethics could be roughly defined as trying to do the opposite of what Hitler would have done. In fact, that may be their historic origin, as the paper's present personality was established in and just after the last war by people drawn together more by being "anti-fascist" than by anything else. Personally I admit to being haunted by what Hitler showed to exist in all us ordinary people, and therefore to being specially interested in antidotes to the kind of thinking he stimulated in people, and that he so readily adopted.[5]

Whereas Garvin's *Observer* was a Conservative paper, David Astor's was, with his father's full approval, liberal-minded but strictly non-party: in the campaigning for the 1945 elections, he made a point of printing statements by representatives of the Tory, Labour, and Liberal parties, a habit he continued in later years. In economics (a subject about which he professed to know nothing), the paper favored a mixed economy in which both government and the private sector played their parts, and in which a fair distribution of wealth was combined with rewards for enterprise. The *Observer's* politics were, in essence, those of the consensus that prevailed in Britain from the end of the war until the arrival of Mrs. Thatcher in 1979, coinciding pretty closely with those of the liberal wing of the Conservative Party and the rightward-leaning side of the Labour Party. On social matters, the paper took a liberal line: Astor favored homosexual law reform and, with Victor Gollancz and Arthur Koestler, led the campaign for the abolition of capital punishment. On the international scene, Astor favored European unity (a by-product of his friendship with von Trott) and the Atlantic alliance, but his particular enthusiasm, encouraged by George Orwell, was for the decolonization of black Africa. Apartheid was introduced into South Africa after the 1948 election—in which Malan's National Party came to power—and was fiercely opposed thereafter by the *Observer.*

"I always resisted the pressure in our left-inclined office from those who felt that left meant virtue and right meant vice," Astor once declared, and these and a host of other issues were fiercely debated at editorial conferences that, given the elevated level of debate, were sometimes likened to Oxford seminars.[6] (Astor himself once said that the *Observer* provided him with the education that Balliol had failed to deliver.) One of Astor's colleagues—it has never been clear which—remarked, apropos the seemingly interminable meetings, that "the editor's indecision is final," but more often than not Astor had a clear idea of what line he wanted the paper to take. A brilliant and inspiring editor both in his ideas and in his line-by-line editing, he was a great listener rather than an avid reader, and although his own writing was clear and trenchant, he found the whole business of putting words down on paper wearisome. His mother, in the meantime, took a dim view of the liberal-minded, leftward-leaning *Observer*. It was, she pronounced, a paper written by Jews for blacks, and was all the worse for it.

The years between 1948 and 1957 came to be seen, in retrospect, as a golden age at the *Observer*. Its writers included such admired figures as Patrick O'Donovan, Edward Crankshaw, Alistair Buchan, and John Gale (whose *Clean Young Englishman* is one of the great autobiographies of its time). Terence Kilmartin quickly proved himself to be the finest literary editor of his day, counting Harold Nicolson, Philip Toynbee, A. J. P. Taylor, and Malcolm Muggeridge among his regular reviewers. The enfant terrible Kenneth Tynan replaced a bruised Ivor Brown as the theatre critic, and the arts pages in general were widely admired. The poet Alan Ross wrote on cricket, while John Sparrow, A. J. Ayer, and other intellectual luminaries reported from soccer matches. Although Astor himself was abstemious—his parents were teetotalers, and for many years advertisements for alcoholic drinks were banned from the paper—a slurred and slumped figure encountered in the warren-like offices in Tudor Street might well turn out to be one of the paper's most distinguished journalists. Somehow, in between bouts of carousing in the pub and the endless editorial conferences, the paper began to take shape on Friday afternoon, when the Eastern European intellectuals departed the scene and the professional journalists, many of them veterans of the *Yorkshire Post,* moved in to convert reams of brilliant but overlong handwritten copy into a Sunday paper.

By the time of Suez, the *Observer* was regarded as the cleverest and best-written paper in Fleet Street, with a worldwide reputation, and its circulation was poised to overtake that of its long-standing but somnolent rival, Lord Kemsley's *Sunday Times*. But then, quite suddenly, its supremacy ebbed away. Astor's denunciation of Eden did not, as was sometimes claimed, slash circulation, but it appealed to the young, the impecunious, and the idealistic rather than the middle aged and well heeled, many of whom canceled their subscriptions. Younger, poorer readers were less attractive to advertis-

ers, many of whom—Jewish firms in particular—refused to do business with the paper. Two years later, the Canadian Roy Thomson
acquired the *Sunday Times*. David Astor and Roy Thomson liked
each other well enough, but in the years to come the *Sunday Times*
would both outsell and outwit its old rival, setting the pace with new
developments and leaving the *Observer* puffing in its wake.

In 1957 paper rationing ended, coinciding with the end of post-
war austerity and the consumer boom famously celebrated by Harold Macmillan ("You've never had it so good"). Newspapers became
bulkier; advertisements flooded in. The *Sunday Times* pioneered sections and supplements aimed at specific markets—women, businessmen, car owners, culture vultures, gardeners, and home improv-
ers—and David Astor reluctantly felt obliged to follow its example.
The *Sunday Times* boosted its circulation by serializing the memoirs
of wartime leaders, starting with those of Field Marshal Montgom-
ery; the *Observer*—a freestanding newspaper owned by a trust, un-
subsidized by regional newspapers or television stations—had neither the money nor the inclination to compete. Life became harder
still when the *Sunday Telegraph* was launched in 1960, a competi-
tor for sales and advertisements. Two years later the *Sunday Times*
launched its color supplement; the *Observer* followed on in 1964, serializing the wartime memoirs of Astor's old boss at Combined Ops,
Lord Mountbatten. In 1967, the energetic and innovative Harry Evans was made editor of the *Sunday Times,* and the competition grew
fiercer still.

But through all these changes Astor remained very much in
charge. A keen believer in "the scoop by interpretation," he concentrated his attention on the leader page and the editorial articles. He
took a particular interest in the paper's profiles, insisting that they
should be both fair and accurate, far removed from the character
assassinations associated with the down-market press. Although he
occasionally refused to publish a particular article, usually on the
grounds of his friendship with its subject, he allowed his journalists
a free hand, even if he disagreed with their conclusions. "My aim
has been to be militant in fighting for tolerance, freedom of expression, non-prejudice, here and abroad," he declared, adding, "What's
wrong with moderates is that they lack militancy."[7] At home, he
helped launch Amnesty International with a long *Observer* article.
When Nelson Mandela began his long imprisonment on Robben
Island in 1964, Astor sent him law books so that he could study in
prison, and Mandela later claimed that had it not been for the *Observer*'s support, he might well have been condemned to death. He
fought a long—and some thought quixotic—campaign on behalf

of the Naga people of northeast India, helped by the Reverend
Michael Scott, an austere Anglican clergyman whose main energies were focused on the campaign against apartheid. Summoned
to Number 10, Astor stoutly defended his political correspondent,
Nora Beloff, against charges of bias and inaccuracy leveled against
her by Harold Wilson. And he retained his rare gifts as a talent spotter. Kim Philby proved an embarrassment, but more often than not
Astor's hunches proved correct—and never more so than when, in
in the early 1950s, he asked Michael Davie, then an undergraduate
at Oxford, to become the diplomatic correspondent on the strength
of a letter Davie had written on holiday in Kent. Davie went on to
become, with Anthony Sampson, one of the most influential figures
on Astor's *Observer* as it moved into uncharted waters in the wake of
the *Sunday Times.*

By the 1970s, however, David Astor found himself increasingly
embattled. The paper's finances were ever more worrying, particularly after *The Times,* which had printed the paper for many years,
moved out of Printing House Square, leaving the *Observer* paying for
presses and printers that were used only one day a week. Astor found
himself digging into his own pockets to keep the paper afloat. Much
to the annoyance of his younger, more left-wing colleagues, he supported Edward Heath when the miners went on strike, followed by
the three-day week. He was out of sympathy with feminism, modish
Marxism, and aspects of the permissive society. Relations worsened
when, as an editor who prided himself on employing writers who
then became journalists, he found himself doing battle not just with
Fleet Street's overmighty print unions, but also with the National
Union of Journalists and his old friend Michael Foot, who wanted to
impose a closed shop on those working for national newspapers. Circulation was sliding—by now it was half that of the *Sunday Times*—
and the paper was losing money year after year. In September 1975,
David Astor announced his resignation as editor. He was succeeded
by his deputy, Donald Trelford, and the *Observer* was put up for sale.
Rupert Murdoch almost acquired it, but at the last moment it was
snatched from under his nose by Atlantic Richfield, an American
oil company, which paid one pound for the privilege of acquiring
Britain's oldest Sunday paper.

David Astor remained a director of the *Observer* until 1981, when
the paper was sold to the buccaneering entrepreneur Tiny Rowland, whose interests in black Africa seemed to run counter to all
that Astor had campaigned for over the years. But although he was
no longer a newspaperman, David Astor remained as active as ever.
His family had a long philanthropic tradition, and he was no ex-

ception. He helped found the Index on Censorship, along with Stephen Spender, Stuart Hampshire, and Dan Jacobson; he was actively involved with prison reform, the Koestler Awards, the British-Irish Association, the Minority Rights Group, Amnesty International, the Anna Freud Centre, Erin Pizzey's hostels for battered women, and organic farming, combining them all with a happy family life with his wife and children.

David Astor was loved and admired by almost all who knew him (Isaiah Berlin was an exception, albeit behind the scenes). He had his weak points: he was credulous at times—he was taken in by Uri Geller, and was prevented from buying the serial rights to his book only by his old friend and business manager Tristan Jones—and his dislikes could become obsessive, as in the long guerrilla campaign he waged against Christopher Sykes, whom he had recommended as a biographer of von Trott and welcomed as the biographer of Nancy Astor, but then turned against. Like any editor, he could be ruthless when dealing with colleagues whose faces didn't fit, and from misplaced kindness he sometimes left them to perish from neglect rather than firing them on the spot. But he was a good and brave man, an outstanding editor who made the *Observer* a byword for fine writing and high ideals, and one of the éminences grises who shaped the world of the 1950s through the 1970s.

Peregrine Worsthorne, a Tory journalist who spent most of his career with the *Telegraph* newspapers, once wrote of David Astor's time at the *Observer:*

> In my view his paper was wrong on most of the major issues—absurdly unrealistic about the prospects for democracy in black Africa, about the blessings of permissiveness, about Suez and so on. But it was wrong with such intelligence, and such an abundance of seriousness and knowledge, that even those who disagreed preferred its freshly minted arguments on the wrong side to a routine repetition of truisms on their own.[8]

It is a tribute that David Astor—that most tolerant and liberal-minded of men, who liked to see every side of an argument—would surely have appreciated.

Spring Semester 2012

1. Waldorf Astor to David Astor, n.d, Astor Papers, Reading University.

2. David Astor to Richard Cockett, 7 Mar. 1991, David Astor Papers, private collection.

3. Norman Rose, *The Cliveden Set: Portrait of an Exclusive Fraternity* (London, 2000), p. 39.

4. Waldorf Astor to Arthur Mann, 13 June 1942, Arthur Mann Papers, Bodleian Library, Oxford.

5. David Astor, "Memo on the Soul of the Paper," David Astor Papers.

6. David Astor to Richard Cockett, 7 Mar. 1991, David Astor Papers.

7. David Astor, "Memo on the Soul of the Paper."

8. *Sunday Telegraph,* 6 Oct. 1991.

John Keats, c. 1822. Painting by William Hilton; © National Portrait Gallery, London.

7

John Keats

FERDINAND MOUNT

W hat porridge had John Keats?" Browning offers this as the crass sort of question that stupid people ask. But in fact the first person to answer it would have been John Keats himself. He loved to talk about food, good and bad. He wrote to his dying brother Tom from Kirkcudbright, "We dined yesterday on dirty bacon, dirtier eggs and dirtiest potatoes with a slice of salmon." As Keats and his Hampstead friend Charles Brown tramped round Loch Fyne, he complained that all they had to live off were eggs, oatcake, and whisky: "I lean rather languishingly on a rock, and long for some famous beauty to get down from her Palfrey in passing; approach me with her saddle bags—and give me a dozen or two capital roast beef sandwiches." He bathed in the loch, at Cairndow, "quite pat and fresh," until a gadfly bit him. The inn at Cairndow is still there. So is the Burford Bridge Inn under Box Hill, where he finished *Endymion*. You can still follow the path through Winchester that he describes taking while thinking of the "Ode to Autumn."

No other dead poet is, I think, quite as intensely present to us still, somehow in the flesh. In his review of Keats's first published volume, Leigh Hunt fastened on the essential thing about him, that he had "a strong sense of what really exists and occurs." In a beguiling new biography, Nicholas Roe, the foremost Keatsian around, seeks to wipe away any lingering image of a sickly, moony dreamer and to show us the "edgy, streetwise" live wire who rejoiced in the material world for all the short time he was in it.

He was only five foot and three-quarters of an inch, but he always filled the room. When he recited poetry—his own or anybody's—he "hoisted himself up and looked burly and dominant." Hunt remembered his appearance when they first met: very broad shouldered for his size, with a face that was "delicately alive," something pugnacious about the mouth, and large, dark, glowing eyes. Which is just how he looks in Joseph Severn's picture of him listening to the nightingales, painted a quarter of a century after his death. Nobody forgot Keats or what it was like to be with him.

To his friends, Keats sometimes signed himself "Junkets," and when his restless spirit sent him off on a new excursion, the disappointed cry would go up, "What's become of Junkets?" At a noisy supper party given by the man who supplied the scalpels he used as a medical student, he and his friends argued about the correct derivation of a vulgar word for vagina. That evening he won ten shillings and sixpence from cutting cards for half-guineas, high stakes for struggling City clerks. Such episodes of "delicious diligent indolence" (characteristic of all the Keatses, according to their fussy trustee, Mr. Abbey) remind one of Bertie Wooster spending a restful afternoon at the Drones, throwing cards into a top hat with some of the better element.

Yet his energies were prodigious, physically and mentally. In Scotland, he and Brown walked twenty or thirty miles a day. He had translated the whole of the *Aeneid* by the time he was fifteen. His collected poems, mostly written over only five years, between the "Imitation of Spenser" in 1814 and the "Ode to Autumn" in 1819, fill 437 pages in the old Oxford edition. He could compose with remarkable rapidity. A cricket chirped in the hearth of Leigh Hunt's home in the Vale of Health, and Hunt challenged him to write a sonnet about it inside fifteen minutes. Keats met the challenge with the sonnet that begins "The poetry of earth is never dead."

There have been many fine biographies of Keats since the war, notably by Aileen Ward, Robert Gittings, and Andrew Motion. But none, I think, conveys quite so well as this one the sense of Keats as a poet of the London suburbs. Roe reconstructs beautifully the milieu from which he and his friends all came, on the northern edge of the City, where they had their day jobs and dreamed of fame.

Keats himself was probably born at the Swan and Hoop at Moorgate, the inn that his father, Thomas, had taken over from his prosperous father-in-law, John Jennings, and turned into Keats's Livery Stables. Thomas Keats had been brought up in the workhouse at Lower Bockhampton—Hardy country—and had come to town and married the boss's daughter Frances. Their three young sons were sent up to Clarke's Academy at Enfield, a school for Dissenters that had a far wider and more up-to-date curriculum than Harrow, where Frances had thought of sending them. Roe describes it, with justice, as "the most extraordinary school in the country." The idea that Keats, because of his modest background, was undereducated could not be further from the truth. But his happy start in life came to an abrupt end when, in April 1804, Thomas Keats fell from his horse to the pavement outside Bunhill Fields and smashed his skull only a few yards from home.

From this fatal accident, all Keats's troubles flowed. The substantial legacy from his grandfather was tied up in Chancery, where it remained for years—his sister, Fanny, was still trying to extricate herself from the muddle in the 1880s. Only two months later, Frances remarried, to a no-good called William Rawlings, whom she deserted almost as swiftly. (Roe deduces fairly enough that she was having an affair with Rawlings before she was widowed.) Frances was already addicted to opium and brandy, and the children were shuffled off to their grandmother's in Edmonton, never living with their mother again until she came up to Edmonton to die.

John nursed her, prepared her meals, read novels to her, and sat up with her at night, listening to the rattle of her breathing. Though she had more or less deserted them, his devotion was total, as it was to be to his brother Tom when he was dying of consumption. Looking back on his life, Keats reflected that he had "never known any unalloy'd happiness for many days together: the death or sickness of some one has always spoilt my hours."

Roe takes trouble to show how diligent Keats was in pursuing his medical training, first as apprentice to a disagreeable Edmonton surgeon, then at Guy's Hospital. When Keats complained that Newton had destroyed the magic of the rainbow, he was doing so not as a fretful dilettante but as someone with as rigorous a scientific training as was then available. Nor was he in the least soppy about nature. Thirty years before Tennyson's outburst against "Nature red in tooth and claw," Keats lamented the process of "eternal fierce destruction." Beneath the beautiful surface of the sea, "the greater on the less feeds evermore," and in Highgate Woods while he was gathering periwinkles and wild strawberries, the hawk was pouncing on the smaller birds, and the robin was "ravening a worm."

Roe does not spend much time on Keats's views of politics and religion, merely labeling them as unorthodox. Certainly, he never ceased to revere the republican heroes of the Civil War or to be hostile to the "pious frauds" of the Established Church. In his "Sonnet written in Disgust of Vulgar Superstition," Keats says how much he hates gloomy church bells, which would have made him

> feel a damp—
> A chill as from a tomb, did I not know
> That they are dying like an outburnt lamp.

Yet his description of life as "a vale of soul-making" and his insistence on "how necessary a world of Pains and Troubles is to school an intelligence and make it a soul" would certainly appeal to Christians then and now. When he was dying, Severn read aloud to him from *Don Quixote* and the novels of Maria Edgeworth, but Keats asked instead for Plato, *The Pilgrim's Progress,* and Jeremy Taylor's *Holy Living and Holy Dying,* not the likely choices of a committed atheist such as Shelley.

In his eagerness to show us the streetwise Keats, Roe sometimes slides past the more serious resonances. Especially destructive is Roe's itch to return to two themes that are found in other accounts of Keats's life but seem overplayed here. These are that Keats was dosed to the gills with laudanum when he wrote his last great odes, and that from 1816 onward he was taking mercury, no longer to cure his gonorrhea but to fend off his emerging syphilis.

The evidence is shaky. Dr. Sawrey could well have gone on prescribing mercury as a precaution against a return of the clap or as a remedy against an ulcerated throat, a first symptom of tuberculosis taking hold. There really isn't much license for Roe to assert that "some aspects of his distorted behaviour and perceptions towards the end of his life may be attributed to an awareness of this 'secret core of disease' rather than to tuberculosis." Even in full health, Keats was, well, mercurial, and tuberculosis is classically depicted—for example, by Thomas Mann—as inclined to bring on manic behavior.

The argument about the laudanum is reductive too. Yes, Keats took laudanum. When he was nursing Tom, they both did when they couldn't sleep. So did thousands of other people throughout the nineteenth century, as a painkiller or just to get high. But does this really make the "Ode to a Nightingale" into "one of the greatest re-creations of a drug-inspired dream-vision in English literature"? The poet tells us explicitly that neither the "dull opiate emptied to the lees" nor a beaker of blushful Hippocrene is assisting the flight of his fancy. To insist that laudanum was a necessary stimulant is to insult an intelligence that great critics such as T. S. Eliot have regarded as the keenest of any poet.

John Keats had enough trouble in his lifetime with his first publishers, who said that they regretted ever taking on his verses: "We
have in many cases offered to take the book back rather than be
annoyed with the ridicule which has, time after time, been show-
ered upon it." He could not help being wounded too by the gibes of
Blackwood's Magazine, where the venomous John Lockhart, under the
pseudonym "Z," declared that his poems were "drivelling idiocy" and
that this "wavering apprentice" was no better than a farm servant or
footman with ideas above his station. This kind of snobbish abuse
persisted long after Keats's death. In patting him on the head for the
"luxuriance" of his verse, W. B. Yeats described him in 1915 as "poor,
ailing and ignorant . . . the coarse-bred son of a livery stable keeper."

So Keats stands accused of being underbred, undersized, and under the influence. Reductive too, I think, is Roe's insistence that any
description of death and suffering in Keats's verse must be drawn
directly from the poet's own family life, as though he couldn't make
it up for himself.

Yet all has to be forgiven when we come to Roe's description of
Keats's last days, which is impossible to read without coming close
to tears. His last letters to Fanny Brawne remain as heartbreaking
as ever. When they were first published, Fanny was denounced as
a heartless flirt by the poet's more hysterical admirers. It was only
when her own letters to Keats's sister, also known as Fanny, were
published that readers slowly came to understand how warm and
touching and loyal she was.

There is none of this after-history in Roe's book. He ends rather
abruptly, almost as though he is too moved to carry on, with Keats
being buried in the English cemetery in Rome under the epitaph
he had requested of Severn: "Here lies one whose name is writ in
water." Which is, I think, a pity. We need to know how life moved on;
how Fanny Brawne mourned him for years, then married and had
three children; how Severn lived on in Rome until 1879, becoming
a local celebrity not for his painting but for being the only friend
who had stayed with Keats to the end.

And we need to survey the later history of Keats's reputation, to
see how the sad romance of his life made him a hero to the Victorians, and how he fell out of favor among a generation that preferred
battery acid to honeydew. The reaction against luxuriance has continued. A distinguished poet said to me not so long ago: "I can't see
how anyone could think Keats is any good."

Rereading Keats, though, I am still inclined to echo the judgment
of that acute and implacable critic Samuel Beckett:

I like him the best of them all, because he doesn't beat his fists on the table. I like that awful sweetness and thick soft damp green richness. And weariness: "Take into the air my quiet breath."

There is something irresistible too in the way Keats suddenly breaks out of the mossy glooms and speaks to us with a high clarity that makes me shiver, for example, in *Endymion:*

> But this is human life: the war, the deeds,
> The disappointment, the anxiety,
> Imagination's struggles, far and nigh,
> All human; bearing in themselves this good,
> That they are still the air, the subtle food,
> To make us feel existence, and to show
> How quiet death is.

And there is always an instinctive tenderness in his poetry, and in his letters too, which you won't find much of in chilly Wordsworth or sardonic Byron. I cannot stop thinking of the few lines he scribbled down right at the end, just after he had become secretly engaged to Fanny:

> This living hand, now warm and capable
> Of earnest grasping, would, if it were cold
> And in the icy silence of the tomb,
> So haunt thy days and chill thy dreaming nights
> That thou wouldst wish thine own heart dry of blood
> So in my veins red life might stream again,
> And thou be conscience-calm'd—see here it is—
> I hold it towards you.

Fall Semester 2012

A version of this lecture appeared in the *Spectator,* 20 October 2012.

Anthony Trollope, 1861. Photograph by Napoleon Sarony.

8

Anthony Trollope

ALBERT J. BEVERIDGE III

Why do some artists, referring broadly to musicians, painters, and authors, who were once very popular and at the top of their professions in their lifetimes decline in popularity, only to have their reputations and public esteem restored, in many cases long after their deaths? Probably the best-known example of this phenomenon is Johann Sebastian Bach. Before his death in 1750, Bach was one of the most widely respected and performed composers in Europe. His music was played everywhere—in churches, at court, and at public performances. By the time of his death, however, his reputation had declined and he was considered merely a "mathematical musician." A few years after his death, he was virtually unknown to the musical public. Ironically, the name "Bach" was widely recognized, but it referred to his sons C. P. E and J. C. Bach.

All that changed dramatically, however, in the period 1832–82, and it can be attributed to a concert produced and conducted by the twenty-year-old Felix Mendelssohn. Mendelssohn came from a thoroughly musical family. His great-aunt Sarah Levy was an accomplished amateur musician who supported her own music salon in Berlin and sang in the Berliner Singakademie, which performed German choral repertoire under the direction of Carl Friederic Zelter, who happened to be young Felix's principal music instructor. Felix's grandfather, an admirer of J. S. Bach, had purchased at auction in 1805 a number of Bach manuscripts, forty-three of which had been sent for safekeeping to the Singakademie. When Felix was fifteen, his grandmother had the manuscript of the great *St. Matthew Passion* in the Singakademie copied and given to him as a gift. When he saw the copied manuscript, Felix (a musical prodigy) recognized what an extraordinary work it was and resolved to have it performed. He was able to produce and conduct a public performance of the work when he was twenty. The concert was a huge success, and virtually overnight Johann Sebastian Bach was restored to the musical pantheon.

The main purpose of this lecture is to consider the decline and subsequent revival of the reputation and popularity of Anthony Trollope. The story is not nearly as dramatic as Johann Sebastian Bach's, since Trollope's reputation never approached those heights, nor was his eclipse as great. Although Trollope scholars such as his biographer N. John Hall argue that Trollope's popularity has never really declined to any significant extent, there is ample evidence that his readership shrank after his death and revived only during and after the Second World War.

Anthony Trollope was unquestionably one of the most popular Victorian novelists. It is not easy to determine the popularity of authors in Victorian England. There is no doubt that Dickens was first, but thereafter the rankings are less certain. There were no best-seller lists, and the most objective standard of popular acceptance, book sales, is usually inapplicable. Many popular novels of the period were initially published in literary magazines such as the *Cornhill Magazine,* the *Fortnightly Review,* and *Pall Mall Magazine,* thus diminishing substantially the market for the final product. Second, books were very expensive. A new three-decker (three-volume novel), the format that Trollope and many others frequently used, cost 31*s.* 6*d.* It is tricky to convert prices from more than a hundred years ago to today's equivalents, but for purposes of comparison, 31 shillings was about 1.5 percent of a teacher's annual salary, and 0.5 percent of a clergyman's salary, in 1870. That means in present terms that a book would cost well over $400. Accordingly, except for proven writers like Dickens, publishers usually printed relatively few copies for sale to the general public—750 to 1,000 copies for many authors.

That created the perfect opportunity for circulating libraries, the most prominent of which was Mudie's. Mudie's charged a guinea (21 shillings) annually for a ticket, and a ticket entitled a borrower to take out one volume at a time. There was a reduced rate for an annual subscription of up to three tickets, which would entitle one to check out a three-decker. It was a big business. Mudie's ordered up to 180,000 volumes a year (about half of which were fiction), and it negotiated the prices it paid. It had awesome market power. *The Times* called Charles Mudie, "the mighty monarch of books whom authors worship, and readers court," adding, "For Mudies, one writer in England is paramount above all others, and his name is Trollope." Mudie's was the key to Trollope's popularity.

Trollope's run lasted about eighteen years, from his first big success, *Barchester Towers* (1857), to *The Way We Live Now* (1875), for which he received his largest book fee, £3,200. After 1873, his popularity went into a gentle decline, at least if one judges from the prices he was paid for his novels. The amounts he received were gradually but consistently reduced, and there is evidence that the same was true for the payments he received for serialization. He wrote fifteen novels after 1875, including some very good ones—*The Prime Minister, The American Senator,* and *The Duke's Children*—but none of them sold as well as *The Eustace Diamonds* (1873).

His biographer Victoria Glendinning writes that the decline was to be expected.

> Like an entrepreneur, every artist successful in his lifetime has a set span—whether 20 minutes or 20 years—during which his gift and the historical moment are in magic sympathy. . . . By the mid-1870s, Anthony Trollope's significance for the mass of contemporaries was waning. His historical moment was passing. He knew it.[1]

Glendinning may have a point about an author's historical moment, although Trollope's was—and indeed is—not yet over. But the general public seemed to be losing interest in him, perhaps because of the sheer volume of his output rather than from any absence of "magic sympathy." It wasn't a reflection of declining artistic powers or a change in the public's taste. *The Times* complained that "Mr. Trollope writes faster than we can read," and Henry James criticized what he called his "gross fertility." When one considers that by 1873 he had produced twenty-five novels, plus travel books and essays, in twenty-six years of writing, it is understandable that the public and critics might not have been snapping up his latest productions.

Trollope died in 1882 at the age of sixty-seven. He was treated kindly by the press. The *Times* obituary generally praised his works, as did many other newspapers and periodicals. But the *Times* editors, rather perversely, printed on the same day an unsigned article by the novelist Mrs. Humphrey Ward, which stated: "Anthony Trollope would not rank with the great novelists of the Century—[like] Scott, Balzac, Dickens, George Eliot, George Sand, Thackeray or

Turgenev, but among the second rank with Austen and Gaskell."
Her list certainly includes some heavyweights, but Walter Scott and
George Sand? And grouping Trollope and Austen with Elizabeth
Gaskell?

    How different it is today. Trollope is one of the most widely read
nineteenth-century British authors, along with Austen, Dickens,
and Eliot. All his novels are in print. The best of his work, the Palliser and Barchester series, six novels each, plus *The Way We Live
Now,* amounts to thirteen novels. There are many more worth reading. But even by limiting him to those thirteen works, only Dickens wrote a comparable number; Austen has only six, and Eliot and
Thackeray, seven each.

    There are additional signs of continuing interest. Three major
Trollope biographies were published between 1990 and 1992. The
Folio Society, beginning in 1987, published all forty-seven novels in
deluxe editions, and they sold very well. Oxford University Press issued a new edition of the Palliser series in 2011 and 2012. Several
of Trollope's novels have been produced on television by *Masterpiece
Theatre,* and institutions such as the Metropolitan Club in Washington and the Century Association in New York hold regular Trollope
lunches.

    THE STANDARD NARRATIVE, at least up to about a decade ago, was
that Trollope remained more or less unread after the publication
of his autobiography a year after he died until Michael Sadleir published *Trollope: A Commentary* (1927). In his foreword, Sadleir argued
that Trollope's novels "had virtually faded from the consciousness of
British fiction readers, the middle generation had learnt from their
parents to despise him, and the younger generation barely knew his
name."[2] This refrain was repeated as late as 1945, when the *Trollo-
pian,* a short-lived journal published by the University of California
Press and dedicated to Trollope and his works, argued that "he was
widely admired during his lifetime and consistently disparaged for a
quarter of a century thereafter."

    Thanks to the researches of recent biographers, it has become
clear that Sadleir's argument was an exaggeration and that Trollope always had a group of admirers in Great Britain and especially
in the United States. There is no question that his prominence declined substantially after his death, had a brief revival during the
First World War, receded during the inter-war years—though his
reputation was kept alive by admirers such as Ford Maddox Ford,
Hugh Walpole, Hilaire Belloc, and Compton McKenzie—received a

major boost during the Second World War, and continues to climb today.

War was a big help to Trollope's popularity. Soldiers during the First World War carried copies of Trollope with them to read in the trenches, but it was during the Second World War that he experienced his greatest rise in popularity. Two factors were principally responsible: the unavailability of books by contemporary authors, and a scarcity of paper for printing. One casualty of the war that has received little attention is what the London Blitz (fifty-seven days and nights of continuous bombing from 7 September 1940) did to the book trade. It destroyed over twenty million unissued volumes, virtually wiping out the market for contemporary authors. Readers turned to libraries or other sources for reading material. In late 1940, Christine Foyle, the director of London's largest bookshop, noted the huge demand for books, classic works in particular. Unfortunately, the scarcity of paper so limited printing that, as Angus Calder wrote in *The People's War,* "new copies of novels by Trollope and Jane Austen were eventually quite unobtainable."[3]

One consequence of the scarcity of paper was that the BBC began broadcasting radio plays adapted from the works of popular classic authors, including Trollope, which earned him a wide audience. The radio plays not only filled a gap but also increased demand for the original texts. Eventually, the radio dramas developed into a new genre called the radio feature. A radio feature might include an imaginary conversation between a current writer and a literary figure from the past or, in a spinoff called the *New Judgement* series, an analysis by a contemporary author of the work of a notable literary figure from the past. These programs were part of a larger British propaganda effort, which included support for films such as *That Hamilton Woman,* to demonstrate England's superior and enduring history and culture.

This series of radio programs ran from 19 November 1941 through December 1951. Elizabeth Bowen, a frequent contributor, wrote a memorable one on Trollope, in which a young soldier takes leave of his uncle on the way to the front. His uncle gives him a copy of Trollope's autobiography, which he begins to read on the train. The soldier soon falls asleep to the rhythm of the rocking carriage. When he awakes, the seat opposite him is occupied by none other than Trollope, and the two of them begin to talk about his life and work. The program was a big hit and even prompted Oxford University Press to print a small edition for distribution by Bowen to her friends.

The war increased Trollope's popularity in the United States too. *Time* magazine wrote on 20 August 1945:

> Last week, it seemed that Trollope was making a popular come-back in the U.S. "I am asked for anything by Trollope five times a day," reported the owner of one of Manhattan's largest second-hand bookshops. The San Francisco Public Library reported Trollope withdrawals to be 76% greater than last year. Boston book-sellers simply can't supply the demand.

Additionally, the Boston Public Library reported that it placed Trollope as high as third on its list of the eighteen most popular writers of the previous century.

Why was war so significant for Trollope? Undoubtedly, there was nostalgia for the idyllic country life that he wrote about. Siegfried Sassoon, a poet of the First World War, described the comfort that Trollope gave him during his time in the trenches: "If only I could wake up and find myself living among the parsons and squires of Trollope's Barchestershire, jogging easily from Christmas to Christmas and hunting three days a week with the Duke of Omnium's hounds."[4] But there was likely something more profound at work than mere nostalgia. In a story on National Public Radio in 2004, a judge on the International Criminal Court described his reaction to the evidence of the massacres that took place during the Balkan conflicts of the early 1990s. He was so appalled by the barbarity and the gruesome descriptions that he became disoriented—virtually unmoored, so to speak. He found that the best way to regain his equilibrium was to go to the Mauritshuis, a mile or so from the court, and stand for several minutes in front of Vermeer's *View of Delft*. The picture calmed him and brought him a measure of tranquility. Reading Trollope in times of war may have had some of the same effect.

But evocations of serenity cannot explain why Trollope's popularity has been maintained in the sixty-five years since the end of the Second World War.

Perhaps his attitude toward women might provide a clue; perhaps an enterprising graduate student might provide an insight. After all, many of the most memorable characters in Trollope's fiction are women, including, in the Palliser novels, Lady Laura Kennedy, Violet Ephriham, Lady Glencora, and Mme. Max Goesler. Trollope portrays them as equal, even superior to their husbands and indeed to male society in general. He is extremely sympathetic to their frustrations at the restrictions placed on them by reason of their sex.

And he is no less sympathetic toward young women like Ayala Dormer, whose overriding need was to find a suitable husband.

Trollope was no advocate for women's liberation. He disliked what he referred to as female agitators, such as Elizabeth Peabody of Boston, whom he met on one of his trips to the United States. He parodied her in *Is He Popenjoy?* as Olivia Q. Fleabody and ridiculed the audiences she addressed as being "made up of strongly-visaged spinsters and mutinous wives, who twice a week [are] worked up . . . to a full belief that women would be chosen by constituencies; would wag their heads in courts of law . . . and have balances in their banks."[5] This tension—a favorite academic word—between his fictional portrayals of women and his personal attitudes seems like grist for a graduate student's mill. But although there were eighty dissertations written in the first decade of the twentieth century in which Trollope was a principal subject, as compared with seventeen in the 1970s, they provided no help. Titles such as "Male Moral Inadequacy in the Novels of Anthony Trollope" did not shed any light.

Perhaps some clues might be uncovered by considering the subject matter of his most popular novels: religion, politics, and sex. The English clergy read his novels and probably discussed them in their sermons and with their parishioners. It is doubtful that Trollope is mentioned in many sermons today.

It is not the same with politicians. There is evidence that modern politicians and political commentators read Trollope. *Time* reported on 1 August 1960 that John F. Kennedy was browsing through Anthony Trollope's *The American Senator* after he won the nomination in Los Angeles in 1960. That report is considerably more credible than one from Stewart Alsop and Charlie Bartlett in the *Saturday Evening Post* of 8 December 1962. The article purported to describe discussions that had taken place in the middle of the Cuban missile crisis in October 1962. According to the authors:

> It was Bobby Kennedy who suggested what has since been dubbed the "Trollope ploy." The Victorian novelist, Anthony Trollope had a standard scene: a young man with no marital intentions makes some . . . gesture toward a marriage-hungry maiden—he squeezes her hand, even kisses her. The lady instantly seizes the opportunity by slyly accepting what she chooses to interpret as a proposal of marriage. Robert Kennedy suggested that the President simply interpret the . . . [Soviet] letter as a proposal for an acceptable deal.

But it was not a "standard scene" in Trollope. It occurs only in *The American Senator.* So perhaps JFK was reading Trollope after all and perhaps, as Robert Polhemus writes, "Arabella Trefoil's fate was to be one of the great peacemakers of all time."[6]

There is also at least one political commentator today, David Brooks of the *New York Times*, who reads Trollope. In a column on 9 June 2011, he compared current political leaders to the political leaders that Trollope admired.

> Trollope's ideal politicians share certain traits. They are reserved, prudent and scrupulous. They immerse themselves in dull, practical questions like, say, converting the currency system.
>
> They are not sweeping thinkers but they make sensitive discriminations about the people and the circumstances around them. They learn to operate within the constraints imposed by their idiom, and they don't whine or complain about those constraints. They develop delicate understandings of what is required at a given place and time.
>
> Trollope's ideal leaders are not glamorous celebrities of the sort we have come to long for since J.F.K. They are more like seaman or carpenters. They are judged by their professional craftsmanship.

A good deal of nostalgia seems to be reflected in Brooks' observations. What would the Duke of Omnium do in the face of a worldwide debt crisis? Brooks mentions JFK but not FDR. Maybe we do not need celebrity, but we do need leadership.

Professor Amanda Anderson of Johns Hopkins University, a specialist in the Victorian novel, suggested a couple of reasons for Trollope's continuing popularity. First is his "deceptively readable" style. Trollope has been accused of having no style, and he appeared to trivialize its importance by arguing that "style to the writer is not the wares which he takes to the market, but the vehicle in which they may be carried." In actuality, he developed a distinctive style, as his biographers Richard Mullen and C. P. Snow argue, by copying, summarizing, and writing hundreds, perhaps thousands of reports in his job with the post office. He learned to write quickly and clearly. Bureaucracy might seem like a strange place to develop a clear, precise writing style, but Trollope had a model, Henry Taylor. Taylor was one of those men who could have flourished only in Victorian England. He rose to the number three spot in the Colonial Office. It was not for his public service, however, that he was revered, but for his verse dramas, which were the rage in the period. He had a passion for a clear writing style, which he argued in his influential little book *The Statesman* (1836), was a "pillar of good government." It should be noted that on the connection between clear writing and good government, George Orwell's essay "Politics and the English Language" (1946) cannot be bettered.

Finally, Professor Anderson suggested that more than any other Victorian novelist, Trollope was interested in the psychological makeup and development of his characters. He was very "modern" in this respect. C. P. Snow echoes this thought: Trollope was endowed "with the specific insight, the delicate fluid empathy, which made him the finest natural psychologist of all nineteenth-century novelists." Snow goes on to argue that Trollope had the gift of what he calls "percipience":

> He could see each human being he was attending to from the outside as well as the inside . . . That is, he could see a person as others saw him: he could also see him as he saw himself. He had both insight and empathy, working together in exceptional harmony. Further, and this may be even more uncommon, he could not only see a person in the here-and-now, with immediate impact, but also in the past and in the future.[7]

Snow's description brings to mind the assessment that Trollope "sees his characters as strange sheep more in need of understanding than judgment. His flawless heroes are few and few of his villains lack their small virtues."

This lecture has not fully explained Trollope's continuing popularity, which in fact may defy complete explication. But it is worth noting that respected authors, like legions of ordinary readers, appreciated his gifts. Nathanial Hawthorne commented in 1860:

> My own individual taste [in books] is for quite another class of works than those which I myself am able to write . . . Have you heard of Anthony Trollope? They precisely suit my taste—solid and substantial, written on the strength of beef and through the inspiration of ale and just as real as if some giant had hewn a great lump out of the earth, put it under a glass case, with all its inhabitants going about their daily business and not suspecting they were being made a show of.[8]

And here is Henry James, who early on reviewed several of Trollope's novels harshly, in 1883:

> If he [Trollope] was in any degree a man of genius (and I hold that he was), it was in virtue of this happy, instinctive perception of human varieties. His knowledge of the stuff we are made of, his observation of common behaviour of men and women, was not reasoned or acquired, not even particularly studied. All human beings deeply interested him, human life, to his mind was a perpetual story . . . He had no airs of being able to tell you *why* people

in a given situation would conduct themselves in a particular way; it was enough for him that he felt their feelings and struck the right note, because he had, as it were, a good ear.[9]

And James's observations on Trollope's love of the ordinary chime with one made by the biographer N. John Hall: "Trollope did not write for posterity; he wrote for the day and the moment, but these are just the writers whom posterity is apt to put in its pocket."[10]

Fall Semester 2012

1. Victoria Glendinning, *Anthony Trollope* (London, 1992), p. 443.

2. Michael Sadleir, *Trollope: A Commentary* (London, 1927).

3. Angus Calder, *The People's War: Britain, 1939–1945* (London, 1969), p. 511.

4. Quoted in Philip J. Waller, *Writers, Readers, and Reputations: Literary Life in Britain, 1870–1918* (Oxford, 2006).

5. Quoted in N. John Hall, *Trollope: A Biography* (Oxford, 1993), p. 343.

6. Robert M. Polhemus, *The Changing World of Anthony Trollope* (Berkeley and Los Angeles, 1966), p. 210.

7. C. P. Snow, *Trollope: An Illustrated Biography* (London, 1975), pp. 9, 112.

8. Quoted in ibid., pp. 110.

9. Henry James, "Anthony Trollope," *Century Magazine,* July 1883.

10. N. John Hall, ed.,*The Trollope Critics* (London, 1981), p. 19.

Readers, Writers, and Reputations

Writers, Readers, and Reputations

PHILIP WALLER

My purpose in this lecture is to reflect on *Writers, Readers, and Reputations: Literary Life in Britain, 1870–1918* (Oxford University Press, 2006): the difficulties and surprises I encountered while writing it, others' responses to it, and an estimate of its enduring significance—always supposing that it will have some.

This is a tall order. Most writers, academics included, have had the feeling, when returning to something after a long interval, of its having been perpetrated by someone else who just happens to have the same name. Academics are frequently engaged in projects that stretch over many years and can be attended to only intermittently, between undergraduate tutorials and graduate supervisions, between seminars and lectures, between examining at all levels from university entrance to doctoral theses, between interviewing every scholarly sort from admissions applicants to professorial candidates, and being mired in administration—in my case, serving first as Senior Tutor and then as Sub-Warden of Merton, which, for those blessedly unfamiliar with the statecraft of Oxford colleges, I can identify as two of the more onerous offices. In addition, for about twenty years I was head of faculty for the Boston University program in Oxford, and for three years before the publication of the book I was editor of the *English Historical Review.* As well as all this, I both edited and contributed to *The English Urban Landscape* (2000) and wrote nine lives for the *Oxford Dictionary of National Biography.* Being married with children, I also felt it sensible from time to time to reintroduce myself to my wife and family. When I started out on the book, our children were small; by its end, they were all through university, married, and beginning their own families.

The purpose of this unblushing autobiography is to give some impression of the climate in which the book was conceived; above all, to recapitulate that strange sensation of having repeatedly to pick up the rhythm of thought belonging to that other person who was once me, who had scribbled down mysterious notes after reading this and that, and who had periodically composed some disjointed slices of prose, but all too long ago. You must spend a great deal of time rereading in order to attain some partial recovery, during which you reflect to yourself quite impartially, hmm, that is really quite interesting, how did I come to think of that? Or, much more frequently, hmm, that is bilge—and you must begin all over again. That the book was written at all is a tribute to insomnia, because you can turn things over in your head instead of sleeping, which is quite a waste of time really. I can also recommend a dog. I am a serial springer spaniel man myself. Springers insist on at least two walks a day, and that is salutary duty for an academic otherwise padlocked to his desk. Moreover, you can bounce ideas off a dog as you walk along, for a canine provides just the right amount of uncritical adoration to persuade you to carry on with a book that any rational person would abandon.

The fundamental question is how I chose the topic I did. Historians like to unpick the different strands of forethought and fortuitousness that, amid the confusion of life, combine to deliver a particular consequence. *Writers, Readers, and Reputations* is decidedly to be classified as an unanticipated consequence, and since it hits the scales at almost six pounds, and comprises over half a million words (570,642 to be exact) on almost 1,200 pages, such a major accident merits a little explanation. Its origin lies some thirty years ago when that sublime author of a history of the world John Roberts became general editor of the New Oxford History of England series. John invited me to contribute a volume embracing 1885 to 1918, an era covered in the original Oxford History of England by the masterly Robert Ensor, who in 1936 issued *England, 1870–1914,* and completed almost thirty years later by the maverick A. J. P. Taylor with *English History, 1914–1945* (1965). Here was a stiff challenge.

It was essential to consider how best to get into shape. The party-political side of the story had to an extent been mapped out by signposts erected in my regular teaching. Moreover, I had already adventured beyond the Westminster village in *Democracy and Sectarianism: A Political and Social History of Liverpool, 1868–1939* (1981), a 575-page trifle that details the ethnic and religious underpinnings of party-political strife in Liverpool, which for much of the late Victorian period and the early twentieth century was heralded as the second city in the empire, after London. Then in 1983, in *Town, City, and Nation: England, 1850–1914,* a book of a paltry 350 pages, I had essayed a social history of the country through an urban perspective, looking at life in those forms of habitation that, even if not strictly speaking new, had been newly developed to a unimagined and unprecedented magnitude and influence: conurbations and suburbs, garden cities and seaside resorts, manufacturing and commercial centers, the great provincial cities and the capital itself. The book also examined central-local government relations and analyzed the character and quality of public services.

Rather than start by dilating on aspects with which I was most familiar, it seemed refreshing to begin by reading for a chapter on the imaginative literature of the period. This reading was neither strict nor systematic, but it was immensely pleasurable to rediscover authors I hadn't encountered since childhood or youth and to try to situate them in historical context. It was also intriguing to meet authors of whom I knew nothing and to ask where they fitted in. So I read some more, then more again, and continued to read, all the while recognizing that I had a problem. The parting of the ways came when I composed a chapter on the topic, as if for the New Oxford History volume. I was thoroughly unsatisfied rather than dissatisfied, because far deeper than any feeling of failure was the conviction of how much I had enjoyed thinking and writing about these matters. I was hooked, and formally resigned the New Oxford History commission. Alternatively, I can now claim that *Writers, Readers, and Reputations* constitutes the longest chapter ever written in the Oxford History of England, old or new series.

THE COVER DESIGN of *Writers, Readers, and Reputations* depicts a popular engraving of Charles Dickens's study, *The Empty Chair, Gad's Hill, 9 June 1870.* Invited to Dickens's home to illustrate *The Mystery of Edwin Drood,* the artist Luke Fildes instead found himself fashioning a commemorative icon of the great writer's demise that moved Dickensians everywhere, including Vincent Van Gogh, whose own empty *Chair* painting of 1888 was conceived in tribute. Fildes's image indicates one theme of the book: how writers' reputations were made (and as often unmade and remade) in the half century after 1870, when, coincidentally with Dickens's death, the introduction of universal elementary education in Britain generated an unprecedented phenomenon, a mass reading public, and the neologism "best seller." Distributed in cheap editions, Dickens sold more copies in the fifty years after his death than during his lifetime, and was himself outsold by newcomers such as Hall Caine and Marie Corelli, Charles Garvice and Nat Gould.

Their names are nowadays little known. That matters were different then may be instanced by Hall Caine. A furious and jealous Joseph Conrad judged Caine a "megalomaniac" who cultivated a facial resemblance to Shakespeare crossed with Christ; but Caine had cause for conceit as the author of the first million-selling novels in Britain, *The Christian* (1897) and *The Eternal City* (1901). He was so famous that a brand of cigarettes bore his name; he featured too in an advertisement for Beecham's Pills. In 1908, in an autobiography published when he was fifty-five, he boasted of having made more money by his pen than any previous author. His two homes were Greeba Castle on the Isle of Man and Heath Brow, Hampstead, not bad going for a Merseyside shipwright's son. Nor was his stardom confined to Britain. When Maxim Gorky was fêted at a reception in London before the First World War, he scanned the assembled mountain range of literary eminences, whose peaks included Arnold Bennett, Thomas Hardy, George Bernard Shaw, and H. G. Wells, and was grievously disappointed. "*Where* is Hall Caine?" he thundered.

Caine aspired to be Britain's Tolstoy and constructed his work on a scale to match that of the epic Russian novelist and sage, who admired him in turn. The devotion that Caine gave to his writing was impressive, and was meant to be so: he would feed the press supposed exclusives about how he painstakingly researched the background for his stories, agonized over characters and plotting, and revised his prose time after time. Here was an author who, according to his self-image at least, polished his work not just as a craftsman but also as a perfectionist. The Bible was a great source for his stories, as he freely admitted. He intended that his work too would be read for all eternity.

Reflecting this attention to detail, the Hall Caine oeuvre was small. By comparison, Henry James turned out the stuff at industrial rates, and not one novel sold more than 10,000 copies during his lifetime. James's moment came posthumously, when professors in English literature faculties across Britain and North America prescribed him as a necessary punishment for students; such professors also determined that Hall Caine should be ignored. On top of being a best seller, Caine enjoyed the stage success that had unhappily eluded James when *Guy Domville* flopped in 1895. Indeed, dramatized—and early cinematic—versions of Caine's stories brought him greater remuneration than his book royalties. (As an aside, it can be noted that Alfred Hitchcock's silent movie version of Caine's novel *The Manxman*, with the leads taken by foreign stars, who presumably had little clue what was going on, has strong claims to be considered Hitch's worst film.) By contrast, Henry James never won popular acclaim, in spite of well-placed acolytes who referred reverentially to him as the Master. This neglect deserved sympathy—or else demanded satire. *Lives of the 'Lustrious* (1901) duly delivered the second. Its authors were a dubious duet, "Sidney Stephen" and "Leslie Lee," no doubt the mixed-up offspring of the parent editors of the *Dictionary of National Biography*, Leslie Stephen and Sidney Lee. In the same style as that adopted for building the nation's literary Valhalla, they summarized James's life and achievements thus:

> James, Henry: Six-shilling Sensationalist . . . born at Hangman's Gulch, Arizona, in 1843. This favourite author, whose works are famous for their blunt, almost brutal directness of style and naked realism, . . . under a variety of pseudonyms produced in rapid succession a large number of exciting stories, the most popular of which are probably *The Master-Christian, The Red Rat's Daughter, The Mystery of a Hansom Cab, The Eternal City,* and *The Visits of Elizabeth.*

With meticulous scholarship, *Lives of the 'Lustrious* completed James's biography by citing archival sources, which included the "Jacobite Papers; Daisy and Maisie or The Two Mad Chicks." The counterfeit is obvious; unobvious now is that the best-seller titles attributed to James were genuine, albeit penned by others—respectively by Marie Corelli, Guy Boothby, Fergus Hume, Hall Caine, and Elinor Glyn. *Lives of the 'Lustrious* thus poked fun both at James's lust for popularity and at the best sellers' lust for immortality.

Not every best seller shared Caine's ambition, although Marie Corelli—born plain Mary ("Minnie") Mackay—had every confidence that she would surpass him. *Punch* mockingly composed this doggerel, "Tips for Critics," in 1909:

> If you want a great *casus belli,*
> If you would be thumped to a jelly,
> Just *dare* to suggest
> That the greatest and best
> In the world is *not* Marie Corelli!

In pomp, she resided in Stratford-on-Avon, where she took to being piloted in her own gondola, specially imported from Venice along with "a swart and muscle-bound gondolier" to navigate the vessel; so she described her pleasure until the Latin helmsman spoiled the

romance by picking fights following an overenthusiastic consumption of the local beer. Still, Stratford natives upheld a proper peck-
ing order. When Sir Horace Plunkett found himself marooned there,
his motorcar having broken down, he hired a guide whose "first and
chief object submitted for my devotion was Marie Corelli's house."
No doubt, Plunkett pondered, Shakespeare had succeeded in his
own small way, but on nothing like this scale. Corelli was courted
by royalty at home and abroad—or so she let it be rumored—and
she was in great demand as a lecturer, and not just to unsophisticated peasants: she was the first woman to address the Royal Society of Literature. In these lectures, she fulminated against modern
immoralities, blasting science and secular education, Ibsenism and
aestheticism, new manners and New Women. Here was a seeming
paradox: a self-made woman herself, and most assuredly not a self-
effacing one, she yet campaigned against female suffrage.

There were many less noisy best sellers. I was delighted to come
across Nat Gould, who by the 1920s had amassed sales of some
twenty-four million copies from horse-racing fiction, mostly flogged
in cheap "yellowback" format. Nowadays, Gould's eradication has
been almost total, including the village where he lived, because it
now lies beneath London Heathrow airport. Gould's proclaimed
philosophy was to produce nothing more than "a story that will
hold the reader from start to finish." "We can't all write classics,"
he added cheerily. This bluff manner was in part a facade, because
Gould was not at all neutral: "If readers are in search of sexual problems, or suchlike nastiness, they will not find them in my writings. I
have no desire to wallow in filth." That he appeared unvarnished in
attitude was important; still, what mattered most was that he wrote
exciting stories. Consider, by contrast, Beatrice Harraden, who had
but one best seller to her name, the deeply miserable *Ships That Pass
in the Night* (1893). During the First World War, she was librarian in
a military hospital, of which she recollected: "We had to invest in
any amount of Nat Gould's sporting stories." In fact, she said, the
wounded soldiers asked for nothing else.

These contrasts between one best seller and another, and between authors who made a splash and those who created scarcely a
ripple, pervade *Writers, Readers, and Reputations;* but it is authors' relations with the reading public that give the book its unifying character. In surveying the literary marketplace, it assesses the influence
of reviews and the partiality of reviewers, and the anxious invention of a classical canon to counter the corruption of public taste
supposedly abetted by the best seller, as if a literary Gresham's Law
operated in which bad books drove out good. Debates about falling

standards may appear perennial; yet each period involves many a distinctive twist. Most of the properties we now associate with literary boosterism took off between 1870 and 1914. These constitute a pattern threading through the book, showing, for instance, how authors projected themselves by product advertising—J. M. Barrie for a fee puffing the Craven tobacco mixture—or else profited from spin-off merchandise—Beatrix Potter licensing Peter Rabbit dolls, board games, wallpaper, and cards. Here was the world of the celebrity author, who exploited pinup photography and carefully contrived interviews, flattering profiles and feature articles, plus stage-managed public appearances on both sides of the Atlantic. In 1879, the publisher James T. Fields tried to beguile Tennyson into touring North America by saying that he could make £20,000 (the equivalent of around $1 million today). "By lecturing? By reading?" asked the amazed poet laureate. "No," said Fields, "By standing in a room and shaking hands with 20,000 people." Literary agents, members of a new profession, promoted authors the more. The leading scribblers were lionized by high society, and they swanned about clubland and scooped up knighthoods, honorary degrees, and prestigious prizes, many with cash jackpots attached. They aimed to sway national opinion by lending their names to campaigns and even seeking election to Parliament. During the First World War, authors were enrolled as propagandists, a natural development from their previous pronouncing on all manner of issues, including religious belief and unbelief, feminism and women's rights, and questions of censorship and personal freedom.

ALL THIS IS BY WAY OF A SKETCH to convey some of the fascination of the material and to explain why the subject seized me; but now it is appropriate to say something about how the book has struck others. In a crass throwaway remark in my preface, dashed off when I was fed up, having been working too many late nights to get the index done and send the whole lot off to OUP, I observed that when I began the research in the early 1980s, "the subject was eccentric to most concerns, certainly in history faculties, largely in literature faculties too, both seized with sundry '-isms'. Since then it has stealthily become fashionable. It is now enveloped as 'Life Writing', characteristically sonorous jargon that signifies a new academic specialism (a.k.a. a professional job creation scheme), though it risks simultaneously throttling public interest." Ouch! I still blush to read that, and true to form, there is now a Centre for Life-Writing in Oxford itself, as well as in many other universities. I very much regret using insulting language, though I do indeed deplore jargon and think that academics' ideological turf wars are largely incomprehensible and off-putting to the general public.

Worse than a crime, my ill-tempered throwaway lines in the preface were a blunder, an open invitation to reviewers in academic journals to take potshots before forming a lynching party. Notwithstanding, most turned out to be surprisingly kind. Chris Hilliard, whose generally appreciative review appeared in *Twentieth Century British History*, began by saying about my title that, "'authors' would have been more accurate than 'writers.'" This puzzles me, and I still for the life of me can't see what difference between the two words justifies making such a fuss. Where Hilliard was accurate was to say that I was "more concerned with writers' careers and public personae, and with the profession of authorship, than . . . with content and style." Although I demonstrate a concern both with what was written and how it was written, it is true that I am no literary scholar, still less trained in textual analysis. What I am is an historian, and historians tend to be relatively uncomplicated creatures, thinking, for instance, that some important things to know about books are how many copies were sold, which writers struggled and which made money, how authors conducted themselves, and what public influence they wielded—in other words, as the subtitle has it: literary life in Britain, 1870 to 1918. Accordingly, the compass I covered in that pursuit was extremely wide, as the chapter headings and contents indicate.

Once literary scholars understood what I was attempting, they were often generous in their applause. I shall cite only two opinions from that side, although it is inescapably immodest to make a display of any. The *Review of English Studies* pronounced it a "magnificent study, one that will be recognized as a defining literary history of the period"; and Professor John Carey ended his encomium by saying, "I haven't read a historical work that has given me [such] a sense of mastery and freshness since Keith Thomas's *Religion and the Decline of Magic* [1971], and I believe that your book will become—and deservedly—as celebrated as his." It was very nice of him to say that; and although undoubtedly excessive praise, it naturally leads into the question, what makes a book last?

Here we should reflect for a moment on the broad division observable in contemporary publishing between academic and trade books. What characterizes the trade book, aimed at the wider public, is a general absence of historiography and footnotes; if there are citations and explications, these are confined to a few endnotes. My book is a very odd hybrid, therefore. It contains almost no historiography, and other scholars' works are principally cited for information rather than to incorporate or dispute their arguments. These omissions have been criticized; and not only do I plead guilty, I confess to premeditation. So why did I design my book without these features? The first reason relates to the aspiration of aiming, vainglorious though it is, to write something that may endure. There is a provincialism of time as well as of place; that is, there are certain characteristics and certain fashions, of the intellect as well as of appearance, that stamp a particular period and are limited to that age, as opposed to universal and timeless concerns. That was one cause of Marie Corelli's rise to best-seller status and equally one cause of her eclipse, that she stridently ventilated her opinions about this and that current controversy via her novels. This made her the sensation of the hour; yet that hour would pass and those passions cool, and they struck a later generation of readers as dated obsessions detracting from the story.

In the same way, an elderly historical monograph that harps on about some long-ago scholarly spat will seem of little interest and even less importance because it has been distorted by a parochial argumentative frame. I am not counseling historians to disregard overarching theories, but it is always the loose ends, the things that don't square, the exceptions to the rule, that seem to me the most fascinating. This is especially the case with literary life. Certainly, I was interested in authors as a group; but on the occasions when they tried to act together—even in areas where they apparently had shared interests, such as copyright, book pricing, and public-library lending rights—they didn't prove very clubbable; and my book is invariably an assertion of how different from one another authors were, in spite of being exposed to common trends. By stripping out historiography and literary theory, I might just possibly have increased the book's longevity and staying power.

In other respects, my book could not be classified as a trade book, because it is of a length and weight that tests the endurance and biceps of the reader; it also contains vast numbers of footnotes, frequently over 200 per chapter, and these often include additional information as well as simple references. Aside from fulfilling a footnote fetishist's wildest dreams, this action cannot be considered general-reader friendly. Nor is it student-friendly either. There are twenty-eight chapters, which most students will count twenty-seven too many; and while each chapter is marked by distinctive themes and ideas, there are no summaries by way of introductions and conclusions. This again was deliberate, and for two reasons. I have always found dreary and patronizing the modern fashion for first spelling out what you are going to do and later spelling out what you have done, as if students are incapable of understanding for themselves. And if you do spoon-feed students like this, then they are inclined to skip the in-between and just read the chapter introductions and conclusions. As a tutor, I had usually worked out a position on this or that question; but I didn't like to insist on it, because I never wanted students to act as a mere chorus, antiphonally chanting back to me what I already thought. Especially, I had no wish to reproduce in students pale echoes and servile imitations of myself. Doing so would be the antithesis of higher education and, to include a selfish motive, would make tutorials inordinately boring, as if in a dialogue with a parrot. Far more interesting is to provide students with an array of stimulating suggestions in order to get them to think for themselves or to rethink their initial interpretation. Most reviewers, however regretful that I did not supply more navigational aids, remarked on the richness of the book and its myriad insights, ensuring that, as Dinah Birch remarked in the *Times Literary Supplement,* "every reader, no matter how familiar with the literature of the period, will learn from the range of its excavations."

But remember again the subtitle: literary life. Though it was an indulgent ambition, I aimed to draw readers into experiencing the lives of authors in their different aspects. To do this, it was necessary sometimes to seem almost flippant, because a good many authors were quite unabashed about the artifice and pose involved in authorship and were much inclined to classify their occupation on the droll side of the human comedy. So I was particularly pleased when John Carey declared himself impressed not simply by what he grandly called the "matchless range of knowledge" on display in the book, but by the "imaginative agility in finding avenues along which to approach . . . [this] challenging subject . . . [Your] chapter on the dress and get-up adopted by writers, for example, which is one of my favourites, is surely one that would not have occurred to anyone else yet it proves remarkably illuminating as well as very funny." It was my intention throughout to approach literary life from unexpected and original angles, and thereby imbue even familiar things with freshness because they had been placed in unusual settings.

How do the experiences that I depict compare to those of authors in our own day, and have contemporary authors been at all interested in making comparisons? I had always hoped that present-day writers would somehow come across my book, because—setting aside the historical peculiar—I reckoned that they might be among the best judges of the authenticity of its account of literary life. And as it happens, some of the most gratifying reaction has come from current writers. In the *Spectator* (14 June 2006), the novelist A. N. Wilson began by musing about those occasional questionnaires that ask famous people to nominate the books that changed their lives. Wilson cited John Gross's *The Rise and Fall of the Man of Letters;* when it was first published in 1969, he was a bookish teenager and it "determined for me the direction I wanted my life to take." "Gross's book became my Bible," he added. He reckoned that he had read it about fifteen times before he himself became a writer and had to face up to its disappointments, although "the vision Gross conjured up for me remains the ideal of human life." Still, Wilson went on to say, "there undoubtedly was room for a bigger, more academic study of the literary scene" than Gross had been able to provide, and he now declared that this "truly mammoth and encyclopaedic work" to be it. He concluded that, alas, "it is slightly too large to read in bed, otherwise I'd say it would be my bedside book for the next ten years. I shall certainly go on reading, and rereading, and enjoying its multifarious details, its deep learning, its humour and its love for every aspect of English literary life in what was, after all, the heyday."

I was further gratified by Philip Pullman's reaction. With the exception of J. K. Rowling, Pullman is currently England's most successful fantasy writer for children, best known for the trilogy *His Dark Materials,* comprising *Northern Lights* (1995; U.S. title, *The Golden Compass*), *The Subtle Knife* (1997), and *The Amber Spyglass* (2000). In 2012, he retold the Brothers Grimm's fairy tales; but from my point of view he is most to be remembered for his selections in the *Guardian* (29 November 2008) when he was among the celebrities invited to nominate their books of the year. Normally, the chief interest of this annual log-rolling exercise is to work out the connection between nominator and nominee: were they at school or college together; do they share the same literary agent or publisher; are they sleeping with each other or want to sleep with each other? You can imagine my shock, therefore, to find Philip Pullman, a person whom I have never met or had any dealings with, nominating *Writers, Readers, and Reputations* as one of his books of the year, together with Stieg Larsson's *The Girl with the Dragon Tattoo,* surely the only time these two books will ever be twinned together. So what explanation did Pullman give? Mine was "a book I read slowly," he declared not unexpectedly, while adding that he did so "with continuing pleasure and fascination." What stood out for him was this: "The vulgar brutality of the bestseller lists, the profitable misery of lecture tours, the iniquity of reviewers, the knife-in-the-back competitiveness—nothing has changed." My picture of literary life between 1870 and 1918 struck Pullman as very real, indeed containing notable resemblances to today. That verdict was then echoed by other professional writers; for instance, by D. J. Taylor in the *Literary Review* (December 2009–January 2010), who incidentally conveyed via a former pupil the ultimate compliment that I had written so well about novelists that even he hadn't heard of. Likewise, there was Ian Jack, whose interest was sufficiently stirred by Pullman's commendation to announce, "Now I might go and buy a copy." Whether Jack actually did so and inspired imitators I can't say, although a stampede to the bookstores was not obviously registered in royalties. The American Library Association included it among its Outstanding Academic Books in 2007, also without any discernible impact on sales. As most authors of monographs are aware, we shall never compete with best sellers such as *Cactus Cultivation for Nudists,* and my film deal has yet to be confirmed. The uplift for the writer in these circumstances is not financial.

At this point, you may reasonably ask whether any unpleasant note was struck in this otherwise flattering reception. There was one, and naturally it issued from the University of Cambridge, where Stefan Collini decided that *Writers, Readers, and Reputations* epitomized the Oxford History Faculty, being practically devoid of analysis and argument. Why he should be so ill disposed toward the Oxford History Faculty is quite mysterious, and I have never come across him personally or reviewed him. His rebuke was offset by faint praise, administered with extreme condescension; but the extraordinary thing about Collini's performance in the *London Review of Books* was that not only every piece of historical evidence contained in his review but also all the analysis and arguments in it were taken from my book and then paraded as if he had thought of them for himself. More curious still, as another Oxford history tutor, unprompted, pointed out in a letter to the *LRB,* Collini even exhumed a stale jibe from a previous review of his in 1995, in which he had sneered at Raphael Samuel's *Theatres of Memory,* saying that it brought to mind "the old joke about Oxford history as the 'home of lost causality.'" Recycling is plainly Collini's forte, because he then reissued his review, with only cosmetic changes, in *Common Reading: Critics, Historians, Publics* (2008).

It is not right to end on a fractious note. Does my book matter and will it last? These days there are all sorts of quantitative measurements of an academic's alleged effectiveness: citation indices, impact assessment exercises, and other foolometers imported from business studies. These are forthwith adopted by bean counters in university administration to determine to two or three decimal points the exact influence any book has. Such fatuous arithmetization will become increasingly easier if the often-prophesied decline of the physical book ever occurs. Indeed, since 2009, *Writers, Readers, and Reputations* has been included in *Oxford Scholarship Online,* the cross-searchable electronic library of key academic titles published by Oxford University Press, which has become a leading vehicle for the widest possible dissemination of work, allowing users to click through the free abstracts and keywords and then onto the full text of the book itself if a library has a subscription. Now it is a persistent fallacy, archly advanced by Gibbon in his *Decline and Fall of the Roman Empire* (1776–88), that history comprises "little more than the register of the crimes, follies, and misfortunes of mankind." I beg to differ from the great historian, because my particular patch has involved a great deal of fun too; and if I had to choose an invitation for people to sample *Writers, Readers, and Reputations,* I should take it from *The Idle Thoughts of an Idle Fellow* (1886). This its author, Jerome K. Jerome, dedicated to his pipe:

> What readers ask now-a-days in a book is that it should improve, instruct, and elevate. This book wouldn't elevate a cow. I cannot conscientiously recommend it for any useful purposes whatever. All I can suggest is, that when you get tired of reading 'the best hundred books', you may take this up for half an hour. It will be a change.

Spring Semester 2013

A version of this lecture appeared in the *Oxford Historian,* June 2007.

Robert Graves, 1915. This item is from the First World War Poetry Digital Archive, University of Oxford (www.oucs.ox.ac.uk/wwllit); © The Robert Graves Literary Estate.

10

Robert Graves's War Poems

TOM PALAIMA

In 1941, Robert Graves was asked, as a "poet of the last war," to comment on the poetry that was already being written during the Second World War. He rightly pointed out that the terms *war poet* and *war poetry* were "first used in World War I and perhaps peculiar to it." He then spent almost his entire essay explaining how war poems came to be "published by the thousand" during the First World War and why, when he was publishing his own *Collected Poems* in 1938, he "could not conscientiously reprint any of my 'war poems'—they were too obviously written in the war-poetry boom."[1] There was indeed a great poetry boom during the Great War. Depending on how British war poets are specified, their number exceeds 2,000.

This choice by Graves has made his war poetry less well known than similar works by his contemporaries. The editor of a recent anthology of the "essential" poetry of the First World War considers it a significant achievement "to include some of the war poetry of Robert Graves which he suppressed for over half a century."[2]

Graves's decision is puzzling. What did he think a First World War war poem was? Why did he think that writing war poems during what he calls a war-poetry boom made them unfit to be included among other poems he had written? Would he have applied the same criteria, in 1941 or at any time, to the poems of, say, Siegfried Sassoon? Was Graves trying to dissociate his war poems from those of hundreds of soldier-poets who, despite the morally unjustifiable statistics of suffering (65,000,000 soldiers mobilized; 8,500,000 killed and died; over 21,000,000 wounded), "continued to write in unironic terms about duty, glory and honour" and to "accept the righteousness of the war and the nobility of the soldiers' sacrifices"? Did Graves view his own war poems as somehow different from those of canonical war poets such as Sassoon and Wilfred Owen, who "reacted against the war with bitterness, outrage, and a burning desire to enlighten an indifferent and ignorant public"?[3]

Graves may have suppressed his war poems and limited their original publication because he felt ambivalent about how well they conveyed his own attitudes toward a war in which he fought and was wounded so severely that he was officially declared dead. He may also have doubted how well his war poems reflected his post-war thinking about war as a social phenomenon.

Graves was a well-trained classicist, and some of his war poems have clear classical themes. "Escape," a *katabasis* (an account of a trip to the underworld), first privately printed in 1916 and inspired by Graves's own near-death experience, and "The Legion," first printed in 1917, have drawn the fullest recent critical attention. An idiosyncratic feature that both share with other of Graves's war poems is the distance he puts between what soldiers experienced during the war and the themes of the poems. It is worth asking why Graves writes this way about the trauma of war. He has peculiar qualities as a war poet that can best be understood in relation to other writers of war myths, ancient and modern.

Of Siegfried Sassoon, Wilfred Owen, and Robert Graves, the famous triad of First World War soldier-poets associated directly or indirectly with Craiglockhart War Hospital and the Freudian ideas of Dr. W. H. R. Rivers, Graves strikes me as both the easiest to pigeonhole, as Paul Fussell did, and the hardest to place in the right pigeonholes. If Graves is to be understood as a war poet, he has to be understood in relationship to his memoir *Good-bye to All That*. Fussell considers *Good-bye to All That* a work of fiction, an interpretation that brings up the thorny problem of truth in war writing. To help sort all this out, it will be useful to look into the state of mind, spirit, and temperament Graves was in when he wrote his war poems and later when he produced *Good-bye to All That* in a remarkable, furious, eight-week frenzy from May into July 1929.[4]

I think that the rhetorical stances Graves adopts in some of his war poems are conditioned by symptoms of post-traumatic stress that he developed before he suffered the shocks of war. His symptoms were related to a strict, un-nurturing, unplayful childhood that lacked strong parental or other humanly vital attachments. Graves takes up the same subjects that other war writers, both poets and non-poets, deal with directly, seriously, and with intensely communicated emotions. But Graves's rhetorical strategies put him and his readers at a distance from the strong feelings war evokes. The narrative voice in his war poems is detached and unemotional. Ironically, that psychological distance helps us take in traumatic scenes and events without being too troubled or disturbed by them. This may be partly, too, because we are not among those whom trench warfare caused to be, as Graves later puts it, "bound to one another by a suicidal sacrament."[5]

Graves wrote his war poems in the clean and spare style that the experiences of war imposed on classic war writers like Ernest Hemingway, Tim O'Brien, and George Orwell. Their efforts thereby to capture what is concrete and real can make non-initiates feel left out. With some soldier-poets, including Graves, this may be purposeful. A war story in a poem by Graves may be told, as Bill Broyles remarks generally about stories soldiers are likely to tell, "not to enlighten but to exclude": "Its message is not its content but putting the listener in his place. I suffered, I was there. You were not. Only those facts matter. Everything else is beyond words to tell."[6]

Graves as a war poet keeps his own feelings at a remove. This is very different from what Sassoon and Owen do in their classic poems. Graves's stance is even different from his own unremittingly satirical take on Homer's *Iliad,* as he explains it in the introduction to his translation *The Anger of Achilles: Homer's "Iliad"* (1959). Because of my own feelings about the loss of a former student, good friend, and scholarly collaborator to suicide in Iraq on June 5, 2005, I cannot write about the war poetry of Robert Graves in a purely academic way. Or, to put it another way, I marvel at Graves's own self-willed detachment.

Like most modern readers, I am more comfortable with the canonical war poets Owen and Sassoon because they are not detached. They offer graphic portraits of the senseless waste of human lives caused by the stupidity of those in charge and their indifference to human suffering. The extreme anger they show in trying to get readers on the home front to feel what they and their fellow soldiers have gone through, mostly for senseless reasons, feels modern. Sassoon is angry with civilians who do not share in or even acknowledge the suffering of soldiers in the field, and who support, passively or actively, the governmental decisions that cause deaths and wounding, physical and psychological, on a scale never seen before. These poets use irony to inflict trauma—wound their readers, humiliate their targets—in an effort to make readers feel what the soldiers suffered and to provide some release of their own frustration and anger.

Graves generally veers away from irony and descriptions of violence, and not just because of his neurasthenia or post-traumatic stress. He grasped the danger in casting pearls of trauma before swine. He may have questioned whether war poems of any sort could produce sympathetic suffering. He may have wondered what purpose would be served if readers were in fact made to feel the cathartic pity and fear of tragedy, and not just suffering per se.

For reasons like these, I think, Graves was horrified at what Sassoon was doing in summer 1917 when he wrote his *non serviam.* Graves took steps to rescue Sassoon from what he saw as a kind of pointless social or political suicide. The staff officers at headquarters and the people back home, as Fussell and many war writers and veterans have documented, were not ever going to "get it." Despite clear and available facts about the scale of carnage and violence wrought upon children, women, and men during wars, modern societies can and will deny the obvious.

Despite his belief that poetry was an act of faith and that poems could "move mountains" short distances, Graves believed firmly in the futility of trying to get the realities of war experiences across to those who have not been through them.[7] So even in his occasional antiwar preaching, Graves lacks conviction. A poem like "The Next War" is without intensity, zeal, or belief, even in its punch lines. We see this when we compare Wilfred Owen's "Dulce et Decorum Est" with Graves's poem.

Owen addresses his famous plea directly to his adult readers: do not inspire impressionable young men to desire the false glory of war. His vivid images immerse us in the horror of "men cursing through sludge." Most of these men, before going to war, were in their physical prime. They now are "drunk with fatigue," "knock-kneed," "coughing like hags," "limping," "blood-shod." All of them, Owen asserts hyperbolically, have gone "blind" and "lame." One unfortunate soldier is "guttering," "choking," and "drowning" in what looks to other soldiers through the eye covers of their gas masks like a "green sea." The helpless, suffering soldier "plunges at" the narrator and at us. We feel every jolt of the wagon upon which his dying body has been flung.

In contrast, Graves's poem is addressed to young children themselves—as if they can understand what he is getting at—and secondarily to his readers. He offers a general description of "Kaisers and Czars" tritely strutting the stage and "young friskies" jumping and fighting with "bows and arrows and wooden spears" while "playing at Royal Welch Fusiliers."

> You young friskies who today
> Jump and fight in Father's hay
> With bows and arrows and wooden spears,
> Playing at Royal Welch Fusiliers,
> Happy though these hours you spend,
> Have they warned you how games end?
> Boys, from the first time you prod
> And thrust with spears of curtain-rod,
> From the first time you tear and slash
> Your long-bows from the garden ash,
> Or fit your shaft with a blue jay feather,
> Binding the split tops together,
> From that same hour by fate you're bound
> As champions of this stony ground,
> Loyal and true in everything,
> To serve your Army and your King,
> Prepared to starve and sweat and die
> Under some fierce foreign sky,
> If only to keep safe those joys
> That belong to British boys,
> To keep young Prussians from the soft
> Scented hay of father's loft,
> And stop young Slavs from cutting bows
> And bendy spears from Welsh hedgerows.
>   Another War soon gets begun,
> A dirtier, a more glorious one;
> Then, boys, you'll have to play, all in;
> It's the cruellest team will win.
> So hold your nose against the stink
> And never stop too long to think.
> Wars don't change except in name;
> The next one must go just the same,
> And new foul tricks unguessed before
> Will win and justify this War.
> Kaisers and Czars will strut the stage
> Once more with pomp and greed and rage;
> Courtly ministers will stop
> At home and fight to the last drop;
> By the million men will die
> In some new horrible agony;
> And children here will thrust and poke,
> Shoot and die, and laugh at the joke,
> With bows and arrows and wooden spears,
> Playing at Royal Welch Fusiliers.

"The Next War" shows flashes of Graves's below-the-surface, Sassoon-like anger at governmental ministers who, comfortably at home, "fight to the last drop" of the blood of millions of other men dying "in some new horrible agony." But he does not provide any close-up looks at the agony of soldiers bleeding out those last drops.

Graves's anger likewise shows when he tells the boys that notions of fair play will not prevail when "you'll have to play, all in; / It's the cruelest team will win." But he does not put us in his scenes. Nor does he give us a narrator who provides personalized observations of battle. His most graphic words are tame in comparison with Owen's rich vocabulary of war's horrors. Graves is content with "starve," "sweat," "die" (three times), and "stink." "The Next War" lacks the kind of literal enthusiasm that Graves, as a well-trained scholar of Greek and Latin, deeply believed was necessary to create good poetry.

Graves saw that depictions of trauma and cruelly ironic twists, if imbedded in poetic content that conveyed too much genuine human feeling and if described in vivid and beautiful language, could be used as a kind of sentimental entertainment. Sincere emotions can too easily be philistinely misused, desecrated. And I think he knew and felt this deeply well before he set foot in France.

If we read Graves's descriptions of his early life attentively and with human sympathy, we see that his childhood was not happy or nurturing. He felt anger and dislike toward, and distance from, his father, Alfred, a school inspector. Alfred, father of ten children by two wives, was absorbed in his own educational reform work (having to do in part with sports, which Graves detested) and had no time or inclination to take Graves's youthful writing seriously. The money-obsessed Alfred placed Graves in a succession of preparatory schools that were below his level of intellectual attainment and were not suited to his temperament and spirit. His lack of pocket money, his ready-made clothes, and his disinclination to participate in the sports that his father's reforms promoted marked him out. At home, he lived in an atmosphere of extreme discipline, austerity, strict rules of moral conduct—the biographer Bruce King says that Graves lived in "moral terror"—coldness of disposition, rigid class separation, lack of companionship, Puritanism, prudery, and emotional repression.[8]

Graves describes his parents, home life, the several schools before Charterhouse that his father placed him in, and his years at Charterhouse, where "from my first moment . . . I suffered an oppression of spirit that I hesitate to recall in its full intensity." Graves says that as the eighth of ten children, he related to his mother and father as if they were grandparents—they were forty and forty-nine years old when he was born: "We had a nurse, and one another, and found that companionship sufficient." Moreover, at the age of four and a half, Graves suffered the detachment trauma of being sent off to a public fever hospital, where he first began to grasp the implications of class distinctions.[9]

ONE PLACE WHERE GRAVES permits himself the use of irony is worth singling out: his poem "The Persian Version," published in *Collected Poems, 1938–1945* (1946), because it is the exception that proves the rule, as he sees it. The poem operates within the sphere of central or civilian command, a vast distance away from the front lines. It never gets to the suffering of the Persian soldiers who lost their lives on the plains of Marathon in 490 BC.

In fact, Graves classifies the poem not as a poem but as one of his satires or grotesques. And I think that we must take literally the short clarification that he writes in the foreword to *Collected Poems, 1938–1945:* "I write poems for poets and satires and grotesques for wits. For people in general I write prose, and I am content that they should be unaware that I do anything else. To write poems for other than poets is wasteful."[10] Graves has a nearly infinite capacity to be coy, but this statement, at least as it applies to his war writing, strikes me as meant to be taken straight. And it is telling.

> Truth-loving Persians do not dwell upon
> The trivial skirmish fought near Marathon.
> As for the Greek theatrical tradition
> Which represents that summer's expedition
> Not as a mere reconnaissance in force
> By three brigades of foot and one of horse
> (Their left flank covered by some obsolete
> Light craft detached from the main Persian fleet)
> But as a grandiose, ill-starred attempt
> To conquer Greece—they treat it with contempt;
> And only incidentally refute
> Major Greek claims, by stressing what repute
> The Persian monarch and the Persian nation
> Won by this salutary demonstration:
> Despite a strong defence and adverse weather
> All arms combined magnificently together.

Randall Jarrell takes Graves at his word. For Jarrell, Graves is "first and last a poet: in between he is a Graves."[11] But even as a poet, Graves is sui generis.

"The Persian Version" appeals to intellects that are refined enough to appreciate pure irony, not irony in the service of social causes, least of all social reform. Its witticism is not even designed to bring home an intellectual point. True wits already see the lies, charade, and cruel misfortunes many suffer in life and surely suffer in war. They take delight when one of their kind points out another instance in good literary style. But as Graves, with his deep knowledge of classical texts, would be well aware, they do not feel obliged to do anything about human behaviors that have been manifest in the Western tradition ever since the god-sanctioned suffering brought on by Agamemnon's high-command egotism in the first book of Homer's *Iliad*.

Paul Fussell, in his many critical studies of war, comes close to sharing Graves's attitude and perspectives. But like Sassoon and Owen, Fussell has a different sensibility. All three stand in contrast to Graves because they think what they write can make a difference. Most telling is that Graves says he writes his poems for poets because it is stupid to do otherwise. This implies that his poems do not have general social aims. They are only for special people. Readers like me, and perhaps you, are uninvited guests at an exclusive party.

According to the antagonist Judge Holden in Cormac McCarthy's novel *Blood Meridian,* grasping the realities of war offers insight into the human condition: "Only that man who has offered up himself entire to the blood of war, who has been to the floor of the pit and seen the horror in the round and learned at last that it speaks to his inmost heart, only that man can dance."[12] It is when such insight is falsified or not widely shared within an individual's defining cultural group that psychological wounding, disillusionment, and feelings of alienation and betrayal arise that can explain many of the distinctive symptoms of post-traumatic stress.

Tim O'Brien gives some advice on how to tell whether a war story is true or not. In so doing, he is pushing into the territory explored, mapped out, sketched, and painted by McCarthy:

> A true war story is never moral. It does not instruct, nor encourage virtue, nor suggest models of proper human behavior, nor restrain men from doing the things men have always done. If a story seems moral, do not believe it. If at the end of a war story you feel uplifted, or if you feel that some small bit of rectitude has been salvaged from the larger waste, then you have been made the victim of a very old and terrible lie. There is no rectitude whatsoever. There is no virtue.[13]

O'Brien swears allegiance to obscenity and evil in the same way that Owen in "Dulce et Decorum Est" runs a word camera over the face of the gassed soldier, "a devil's sick of sin." Graves never wants to go where they go, even in his poems.

"The Persian Version" is both a satire and a grotesque. Graves relies on our understanding, from Herodotus's description of Thermopylae and the Persian Empire, that there was one free person among all the human beings in all the different cultures King Darius ruled. Fussell singles out the two ironic concluding lines of the poem as characteristic of Graves's "unsoftened views of the Staff and institutions like it.[14] They are, in my opinion, characteristic of a different kind of irony, one used only when Graves can be sure that it will have the intended effect.

Here the effect is worked on wits who can appreciate that Darius, 1,750 miles away in what we now call Iran (whether Persepolis or Susa), will accept the distant battle at Marathon, a small strip of beach and plain in northeastern Attica, a battle we view as a turning point in Western history, as a minor skirmish in which the officers on the spot report that the troops acquitted themselves well. The mild sarcasm here cuts into the flesh of Western intellectuals who make more of the battle of Marathon than it can bear.

Graves's "The Adventure" (1916) treats how false reports from the field are processed on the front by fighting soldiers and field officers. As in the companion poem "The First Funeral" (1916), Graves taps into nursery memories as he explores experiences that require close observation of the grotesque. In "The Adventure," the German wire party that British machine gunners said they wiped out becomes a fearsome tiger killed in a child's imagination. Inspection of the terrain—impressing what horrors on the imaginations of the soldiers, Graves does not say—reveals no corpses. But if we want a corpse, Graves has already given us one.

In "The First Funeral," a bloated corpse decaying on barbed wire in no-man's-land is a dead dog that Graves and his older sister come upon in 1899, when he was four years old, at the end of Sandy Road where it crosses the golf course. She prods it with a stick. She takes charge of burying it, sprinkling it with wild mint; Graves finds the mint. They give it a burial. Graves and his reader are on the safer terrain of memory, in which he can and does take the action he cannot take in France, at the front. There he has no older sister to tell him what to do, or to do it with him or for him. The dead soldier he finds is hung up on the German wires and couldn't be buried, Graves writes. He never tells us whether the soldier is British or German. The young brother and sister in Graves's memory declaim the kind of short funeral rites that soldiers could take time safely to utter while standing exposed to danger: "Poor dog, Amen!"

Soldiers will self-censor what they know others cannot grasp without distortion or some degree of trivialization, but their own self-imposed silence has a cost. Graves does this, too. There are other examples: the suicide in the trenches that he reports matter-of-factly in *Good-bye to All That* and his vision of a dead enemy soldier in "A Dead Boche" are different strategies of indirection from the one he uses in "The First Funeral." The indifference and incomprehension of noncombatants can be emotionally traumatizing, leading some soldiers to keep inside those things that they consider most personally meaningful, thereby preventing others from committing sacrilege upon their sacred knowledge.

Sometimes soldiers cannot interpret clearly the mysteries of events. Hence, two of the most meaningful commentaries on anything that has happened or been experienced in war are "there it is" and "don't mean nuthin'." Compare Kurt Vonnegut's repeated "And so it goes" in *Slaughterhouse-Five*. This is the tone that Graves strikes in "A Dead Boche."

> To you who'd read my songs of War
>   And only hear of blood and fame,
> I'll say (you've heard it said before)
>   "War's Hell!" and if you doubt the same,
> To-day I found in Mametz Wood
> A certain cure for lust of blood:
>
> Where, propped against a shattered trunk,
>   In a great mess of things unclean,
> Sat a dead Boche; he scowled and stunk
>   With clothes and face a sodden green,
> Big-bellied, spectacled, crop-haired,
> Dribbling black blood from nose and beard.
>   13 July 1915

The poem starts out ready to preach that war is truly hell, but Graves has no heart to be Owen or Sassoon, O'Brien or McCarthy, or Homer. He checks himself. He leaves off. He never drives the moral home. He leaves the German corpse "dribbling black blood from nose and beard." He forces us to walk away from the scene of this single accident of war, just as he had to.

Like rubberneckers driving by a fatal auto accident, we never learn who this dead German is. Graves does not speculate, as O'Brien did in "The Man I Killed," or finally investigate, like Paul Bäumer in Remarque's *All Quiet on the Western Front*. The German corpse remains a dead Boche. He is not *the* dead Boche. He is not Graves's dead German, so he is not ours. And Graves doesn't fantasize or tap into nursery memories of performing shorthand rites. He cannot bring himself to write something like "Poor Boche, Amen," because he never spoke the words "Poor dog, Amen!" His sister did. Four syllables that might be set alongside "there it is" and "don't mean nuthin'" and "and so it goes" are not even murmured in prayer here.

In his short story "The Man I Killed," Tim O'Brien reconstructs an entire imaginary personal life history for an "almost dainty young man of about twenty," a Vietcong soldier he is forced to shoot along a trail, where the enemy's head lay "not quite facing . . . small blue flowers shaped like bells." In contrast, we see how much Graves suppresses in "A Dead Boche" and "The First Funeral." They are Graves poems, singular within the genre of soldiers, of whatever literary talent, expressing their thoughts on a single enemy dead.

GRAVES HAS HIS OWN WAY of reading the *Iliad* of Homer, the earliest and still arguably the greatest war poem in Western literature. His version of it, *The Anger of Achilles,* is unsettling. It is what moves Fussell to characterize Graves as a farceur who has never met a lie he didn't like and wouldn't tell.

But this may simply prove that most of us are not ready to accept what Tim O'Brien claims: a true war story has no point, truth does not exist in factual reality, truth does not even exist in a vivid description of a dead corpse. After all, the Greeks knew that what is true is what is unforgettable, the literal meaning of the Greek adjective *a-lēthēs*. And what is unforgettable about a dead soldier on a wire may be that when you came upon it, you wanted to do what your sister helped you do for a dead dog sixteen years before. Graves's devastating takes on all the heroes in the *Iliad* and his championing of the ugly, irritating, ignoble smart aleck Thersites get across what Homer's Trojan War meant to him: the *Iliad* is *Catch-22.*

Why not? Other Greek city-states must have had what Athens had, their own Aristophanes to make them laugh at war's horror. Joseph Heller admitted that he was obsessed with the *Iliad* when young, and that Achilles was the constant model for his central character, Yossarian.

I cannot come completely to terms with Graves's translation of the *Iliad* except as an idiosyncratic modern reading derived from his peculiar psychological background and his war experiences. Given who he was, Graves could not see what one sort of ancient reading must have been. To me, there is one true answer to the question why Homer is so graphically accurate about combat deaths and about the whole futile experience of war. He had to be. His audience knew what war was. They had lived war. The Homeric poems served as acculturating instruments, in the same way Remarque's *All Quiet on the Western Front* and O'Brien's *Things They Carried* are now used in schools, becoming something Graves never intended any of his works to be.

The *Iliad* gives an honest picture of almost all aspects of warfare. The catalogue includes those in command betraying what is right, failing again and again in planning strategies, and having little regard for the well-being of the common troops. The *Iliad* shows us cowardice and courage; the tragedy of war for men, women, and children in a city under attack; combat rage; soldiers having greater sympathies for enemy soldiers than for their own officers or civilian leaders; war fought for dishonorable purposes; prayers to the gods going unanswered; men deriving deep pleasure from violent acts; death and destruction; blind luck and bad luck.

Graves goes through the contents of the *Iliad* and makes it his kind of war poem. He puts a satirical spin on every item. In so doing, he is, in Tim O'Brien's words, "heating up the story," but in his own way. Graves is doing what a Thersites instinctively has to do, but unlike Thersites, Graves aims at producing bitter and intellectualized laughter. Graves's translation of the *Iliad* is a hybrid: part prose—like *Good-bye to All That,* written for the rest of us—and part grotesque, a Graves poem written for wits who could savor the joke.

True war stories reveal truths about our very natures and about the formative and driving principles of our culture. Graves, knowing that these crucial truths were being ignored, decided—who can say he did so wrongly?—that these truths would always be ignored, or at least that his telling of his own truths would serve no purpose.

Graves knew that those who rise to power will never internalize the psychological disturbance of the narrator in O'Brien's "The Man I Killed," or of Remarque's Paul Bäumer as he watches a French soldier die slowly in a shell hole with him, or of the two American GIs, one in the European theater, one in the Pacific, whose thoughts are recorded in Studs Terkel's oral history *The Good War:*

> It was sunshine and quiet. We were passing the Germans we killed. Looking at the individual German dead, each took on a personality. These were no longer an abstraction. They were no longer the Germans of the brutish faces and the helmets we saw in the newsreels. They were exactly our age. These boys were like us.

> In Guam, I saw my first dead Japanese. He looked pitiful, with his thick glasses. He had a sheaf of letters in his pocket. He looked like an awkward kid who'd been taken right out of his home to this miserable place.[15]

Graves uses rhetorical distancing to handle the first corpse that he sees. He never places us with him on the field of battle. We never confront a dead body with him. He presents us with what his first sight of a corpse called forth: childhood memories of the dead dog his sister and he came across on a walk and of the make-believe funeral rites they enacted. Even children know you bury dead people, Graves's poem tells us. It is a time-honored custom we have known since the last line of the *Iliad* (24.804) was written:

> Thus they conducted the funeral rites of horse-taming
>   Hector.

Fall Semester 2012

1. Robert Graves, *Collected Writings on Poetry,* ed. Paul O'Prey (Manchester, 1995), p. 79.
2. David Roberts, *Minds at War: The Poetry and Experience of the First World War* (Burgess Hill, West Sussex, 1996) p. 11.
3. Elizabeth Vandiver, *Stand in the Trench, Achilles: Classical Receptions in British Poetry of the Great War* (New York, 2010), pp. 2–3.
4. Paul Fussell, *The Great War and Modern Memory* (New York, 1975), p. 208.
5. Graves, *Collected Writings on Poetry,* p. 467.
6. William D. Broyles, Jr., "Why Men Love War," *Esquire,* Nov. 1984, p. 61.
7. Graves, *Collected Writings on Poetry,* p. 6.
8. Bruce King, *Robert Graves: A Biography* (London, 2009), pp. 17–19.
9. Graves, *Good-bye to All That* (2nd edn., New York, 1957), pp. 41, 13.
10. Robert Graves, *Collected Poems, 1938–1945* (New York, 1946).
11. Randall Jarrell, *Third Book of Criticism* (New York, 1969), p. 78.
12. Cormac McCarthy, *Blood Meridian* (New York, 1985), p. 331.
13. Tim O'Brien, *The Things They Carried* (New York, 1998), pp. 68–69.
14. Fussell, *Great War and Modern Memory,* p. 85.
15. Studs Terkel, *The Good War* (New York, 1985), p. 5.

Lytton Strachey, c. 1920. E. O. Hoppe and Edward Gooch-Hulton Archive / Getty Images.

11

Bloomsbury Reassessed

PAUL LEVY

In Britain, few educated people younger than forty have heard of the Bloomsbury Group; hardly anyone can name any of its members apart from Virginia Woolf. Yet in 1968, when I was a PhD student in Britain on a Harvard Traveling Fellowship, it was a rare week that went by without a reference in newspapers or magazines—or on even radio or television—to this intellectual magic circle.

Why were they so celebrated then? And why so little known now?

Though Bloomsbury members' pictures and decorative schemes, as well as their books, journalism, and *affaires*, were relished by bohemians and left-wing readers from the 1920s through the 1960s, they became household names thanks in large part to the biography of Lytton Strachey published by my friend and Strachey Estate co-executor Sir Michael Holroyd in 1967–68. Strachey, who died in 1932, had been mildly interesting to the Anglo-American recreational reading classes, but Holroyd's volumes brought the entire subject of homosexuality out of the intellectual closet, whence it has never returned. This example helps explain why Bloomsbury has temporarily dropped out of the headlines. It seems less relevant, or even uninteresting, because we have accepted its values as our own—exactly as I had predicted in the introduction to my first book, *Lytton Strachey: The Really Interesting Question* (1972).

In early September 1957, the Wolfenden Report recommended that "homosexual behaviour between consenting adults in private should no longer be a criminal offence." At the time, there were more than a thousand men in prison in England and Wales for homosexuality, and their mean age was thirty-seven. The provisions of the Wolfenden Report became law as part of the decriminalizing Sexual Offences Bill in July 1967, whose passage almost coincided with the publication of the first volume of Holroyd's life of Strachey that September.

The revelation in that volume that caused the most upset was of the youthful homosexuality of Lord Keynes. John Maynard Keynes (1883–1946) was widely thought of as the savior of the British economy during the slump of the 1930s, and therefore as one of the architects of the Allied victory in the Second World War. More importantly in 1967, Keynesian policies having been adopted by most successful Western economies, the capitalist world was thought to have a great stake in maintaining Keynes's personal reputation. Or so economists such as Keynes's biographer Sir Roy Harrod felt. He told me that he was distressed and worried that in the unsophisticated United States, revealing Keynes's sexual predilections would undermine support for Keynesian economic policies and give succor to the enemy on the right—meaning the free-market followers of Milton Friedman.

Also troubled by the book was Maynard Keynes's younger brother, the eminent surgeon and Blake scholar Sir Geoffrey Keynes (1887–1982). He sent Holroyd a succession of discouraging cards and letters, written in his elegant handwriting, but in disturbing brown ink. He remained convinced almost to the end of his very long life that he could somehow persuade this unwelcome genie to return voluntarily to his bottle. James Strachey (1887–1967), the youngest of the thirteen Strachey siblings, was Holroyd's most important critic—for it was James who owned his brother's copyright (the executorship of which was later passed along to Holroyd and me by James's widow, Alix). James, the editor and translator of much of the Standard Edition of Freud, had been gay in his youth. He was famously in love with Rupert Brooke, had an affair with Maynard Keynes, was pursued by the Everest mountaineer George Mallory, and married Alix in 1920. James resumed his love affair with Noël Olivier (whom Rupert had also loved when she was still a schoolgirl) after her own marriage. James and Noël's relationship seems to have endured almost until James's death.

James read the drafts of both volumes of Michael's life of Lytton, annotating them copiously, forcefully asking for cuts and changes. Sometimes Michael felt the demands were justified, as in the case of some people still living. At others he demurred, finally reaching an agreement with James that his objections would be noted (and often quoted) in footnotes. These notes are one of the tremendous pleasures of reading those graceful, pioneering volumes. James's final verdict was that readers would be shocked by the homosexual revelations of volume I, but moved by volume II, which recounts the love between Lytton and Carrington, and the strange story of their deaths.

A digression into autobiography will, I hope, throw some light on the survival of the people and values of Bloomsbury from the late 1960s to the present day. I first met Michael Holroyd in 1968 when he was visiting Harvard in the course of launching the handsome American edition of his book. Before I became a dropout from academia—which happened in 1971, when I was attending Oxford, where I had been elected to the all-graduate Nuffield College—I had been researching my book on G. E. Moore and the Cambridge Apostles. Harvard, its patience surprisingly not exhausted by the ten years I took over it, waived the dissertation requirement and mailed a PhD diploma to me in 1979 in exchange for two copies of the printed volume.

I very nearly did not meet Holroyd. A young history professor, whom I knew was giving a party for him after his lecture, sponsored his visit. I asked directly for an invitation, which was just as directly refused. Fortunately for me, the other guest of honor at the party was Lord David Cecil, the father of Hugh Cecil, my best friend at Harvard. So at Michael Holroyd's talk I was seated between Lord and Lady David Cecil. Lady David was the Bloomsbury-born Rachel MacCarthy, daughter of Desmond and Mollie. Desmond MacCarthy, one of Britain's most celebrated literary critics, was the best friend of G. E. Moore; Moore was Rachel's godfather.

When I arrived back in England in August 1968 and went to the large Regent's Park flat where I had arranged to rent a room, I sat down for a cup of nasty instant coffee with my landlord-cum-flatmate, a philosopher I had known during my year in his department at University College London. "As you will surely discover eventually," he said. "I think I had better tell you straightaway that I am a member of the Cambridge Apostles." This was a stunning piece of luck. "So," he went on, "I have arranged for you to meet someone at Cambridge who has agreed to act as an intermediary with the current members." Telescoping a couple of years here, at one of their annual meetings the Apostles conferred about helping me, but decided to make their records, called "the Ark" in Apostolic jargon, available only to other Apostles. Whereupon, I am told, my supporters nominated me for membership. This, however, was a step too preposterous, since by then I not only had no formal connection with Cambridge, but also had matriculated at Oxford. One of the Apostolic Young Turks disapproved so strongly of the ban on letting me see the Ark that he purloined it and gave me the contents to copy—which is why my book on Moore and the Apostles contained the sole accurate list of its members from its founding in 1820 to 1916.

Hugh Cecil had been to Kentucky and met my family (which was still living there), and Rachel and David viewed themselves as in loco parentis to me. They invited me to Red Lion House at Cranborne, Dorset, for the first weekend of my return. Frances Partridge was among the houseguests that weekend; she rebuked me for being "intolerant" when I said I couldn't understand drinking tea instead of coffee at breakfast. Though she wasn't certain she liked—or even trusted—me at first, we ended up having a long, affectionate friendship that ended only on her death in February 2004, a month or so short of her 104th birthday.

When, in August 1968, I first approached Dorothy Moore (1892–1977), the widow of G. E. Moore, she was still living in their house at 86 Chesterton Road in Cambridge. Unbeknown to me, I was only one suitor among several for access to Moore's papers, which she kept in the cupboard of a bureau in her bedroom. She greeted me, along with her forty-six-year-old son, Timothy, with, I thought, wry amusement. In fact, she was impressed by my Harvard credentials, and even more by my American directness and my Cecil connection. At the end of our first meeting, she sent me off with a file of letters to Moore. Innocent to the last, I did not know this was the prize sought by tens of graduate students and full professors alike. These are now in the Cambridge University Library, along with the other papers she eventually gave me to work on.

Not until after her death was I allowed by Tim to have a good rummage in the cupboard, which produced the material I had needed for years: evidence that Moore had attended the initial meeting of a Cambridge organization opposed to conscription during the period leading up to the First World War. I was convinced that the former Apostles who had opposed the war, and their Bloomsbury friends, must have taken their lead from Moore in this matter. But Mrs. Moore told me that she thought her husband (whom she hadn't yet met—they married in 1916) would not have supported such a group and had in fact supported the war lukewarmly. At the back of the cupboard was a carefully kept copy of a Cambridge University newsletter that gave me the dates confirming that Moore had influenced the Bloomsbury opponents of the war and conscription. My eureka moment came a couple of years after the conclusion of the American debacle in Vietnam, and it was hard not to draw parallels between the two unpopular wars and the hatred of the draft among my own generation of Americans.

Though she had married into an offshoot of the Quaker branch of what Noel Annan called the "Intellectual Aristocracy," Mrs. Moore had a soft spot for more conventional aristocrats. She would not have admitted this, I think, to the high-minded Cambridge intellectual ladies who made up most of the circle of her friends. But she was beguiled by my tales one New Year's Eve of Christmas with the Cecils. Christmas dinner at Cranborne Manor was at a long table made from boxes that had contained (or maybe still did) shotgun cartridges, covered in an endless white tablecloth and adorned with silver and crystal. I seem to recall that there were footmen.

Dorothy Moore was in her late seventies when we met. She had refused to call her husband "George," and said that if he had to have a "plain name," she would call him "Bill," and she always did. She smoked a pipe, and her right thumb was often blackened from tamping the bowl of it. She liked Madeira and an obscure Portuguese red wine called Periquita, which she bought from the Wine Society. With her aperitif, she often served a strange English snack food called "cheese footballs," spheres of cheesy wafers filled with runny cheese. Though she was not very mobile, in the late 1960s it was still possible for me to take her out to lunch at Grantchester—I knew she was keen on food and wine.

Similarly, Alix Strachey (1892–1973), the American-born, British-educated widow of James Strachey (who, along with him, had been psychoanalyzed by Freud in Vienna), loved her grub. She used to say to me, however, that she applied good socialist principles to her food. This meant that she preferred that meals be assembled and prepared with a minimum of human labor. As she liked to point out, the best French *petit pois* came in jars—and even good socialists had to admit that the very best came from Fortnum & Mason and were delicious spooned from the jar and eaten with bottled mayonnaise. For Christmas one year I gave both Mrs. Moore and Mrs. Strachey carefully chosen hampers from Fortnum's. Mrs. Strachey was delighted. Mrs. Moore said, "I see you didn't have time to shop yourself."

Alix lived alone at Lord's Wood, near Marlow, Berkshire, the house that had belonged to her mother, the painter Mary Sargant-Florence, whose murals decorated the building. When Michael Holroyd finished using the Strachey papers housed there, he returned all of them to an outbuilding, except those thought to be so important that they had been sorted and labeled by the psychologist W. J. H. "Jack" Sprott in an accordion folder kept in the upstairs "schoolroom." The rest were in old, moldering suitcases and tea chests in what Alix called "the studio wilderness," which was reached across a stone courtyard. There, mice nibbled at portfolios of old photographs, unbound numbers a variety of journals—including *Simplicissimus,* the German weekly satirical magazine that began publication in 1896—and exquisite Japanese woodblock prints, along with boxes and boxes of correspondence, Apostles papers, and typescripts and manuscripts of published and unpublished work by Lytton and James.

Alix Strachey entrusted some of her papers to me at our first meeting. At Nuffield College, I had excellent conditions for storing and looking after documents, and Mrs. Strachey was keen that Lytton's and James's papers should join Moore's in Oxford. The Strachey Trust was founded in 1972 when Alix Strachey, realizing she was the widow of the last of the issue of General Sir Richard and Lady Strachey, being childless and feeling that there were no relations to whom she wished to leave the archive or the estate's royalties from literary copyrights, decided to form a charity to be the beneficiary. She made a will leaving these to the charity, with the British Psychoanalytic Society named as residuary legatee. This meant the "psychos," as she always called them, inherited the house and their share of the rights to the translation of the Standard Edition of Freud, for which she and James famously did many of the translations, and to all of James's psychoanalytic copyrights. In some ways this was an unhappy arrangement, since after Alix's death in 1973, the psychos were in a hurry to get their loot and sell the house. In addition, the country solicitor who had drawn up Alix's will was not competent to deal with a literary estate—as was proved by his abandoning the case and the county about halfway through probate. Somehow we untangled it all. There was no difficulty about the charity: one of the founding trustees worked for Lord Goodman, the outstanding lawyer in this field.

The other trustees included Lucy Norton, the distinguished translator of the *Memoirs of the Duc de Saint-Simon,* an older lady whose well-intentioned maneuvering made many more problems than it solved for Holroyd and me. We also counted Lord Annan and Quentin Bell among the original trustees, and they smoothed many a stony path for us. One of the aims of the Strachey Trust was to preserve Britain's literary heritage. The trustees, like many academics, viewed with alarm the buying policies of the great American collections. In the 1970s, with photocopying in its infancy, impoverished British researchers feared having to pay the cost of airfare to Manhattan, Princeton, or Austin in order to work with original documents. The Strachey Trust knew that such trade could not be halted. British institutions lacked the buying power to compete with American libraries, so the Strachey Trust's aim was simply to keep legible copies behind when important documents were exported.

MANY CHOICE BRITISH LITERARY TROVES were crossing the Atlantic in the suitcases of a firm called Hamill and Barker, run by Frances Hamill and Margery Barker, two charming old Chicago ladies from socially prominent midwestern families. They had splendid Bloomsbury connections. They had met Leonard Woolf in 1950 and quickly persuaded him to sell them the letters and diaries of Virginia Woolf that are now in the Berg Collection of the New York Public Library. It was just after the war, food rationing was still in place in Britain, and Hamill and Barker paid cash. The tax position on literary estates was a question few had considered—paying cash made it unnecessary even to raise the subject. Leonard was not alone: Alix, for a similar consideration, had parted with the letters of James and Rupert Brooke—which also ended up at the Berg; she gave the agents the Carthaginian portmanteau nickname "Hamilcar Barca."

Probably the Strachey Trust's greatest coup was to fund its aims by selling its own archive to the nation. I had become a friend of the head of Sotheby's Manuscripts Department, Roy Davids. The keeper of manuscripts at the British Library, Daniel Waley, who had fringe Bloomsbury connections himself, had approached us about the purchase; I was able to commission Davids to arrange the sale by private treaty.

One of the problems that both Holroyd and I encountered was simply to try to find the location of papers we needed to use in our research. His tales of pursuing the papers of his subjects—Lytton, Augustus John, George Bernard Shaw—would be hilarious had they not been so expensive and consumed so much of his vaunted, world-record advance for *Bernard Shaw*. Hamilcar sometimes placed an embargo on the buyer's revealing the deal—in more than one case even though the vendor had not requested it. Years later I had an impossible task in trying to track down Lytton's letters to David ("Bunny") Garnett. Though Angelica, Bunny's wife, as well as her stepchildren, tried to help, no one remembered the sale of them—though now a cursory Internet search reveals that they are in the Robert H. Taylor Collection at Princeton.

So a big aim of the Strachey Trust, as Michael and I wrote in a letter published in the *Times Literary Supplement* in 1972, was to establish a register of the whereabouts of modern British literary manuscripts. Daniel Waley tipped us off that Philip Larkin was to address a meeting of the Standing Conference of National and University Libraries at Reading in 1979, proposing just such a project. I was delegated to attend and to intervene during the question period by waving the Strachey checkbook and urging someone present to take up the challenge. Our host, the Reading University library team, accepted the challenge and the check—and the Strachey Trust has now provided the seed money for the original location register, for its expansion backward in time from 1900 to 1700, for its updating, and for the WATCH (Writers and Their Copyright Holders) register.

Holroyd brought a combination of high intelligence and common sense to the way he restored the Strachey papers after he had used them in his biography, returning them exactly as he found them, wrapped in yellowing pages of *The Times,* tied into bundles with legal red tape. When I came along, I could guess from the date of the newspaper who had made up the packets and, presumably, read their contents. I could also detect from the sharp, never-unfolded creases in *The Times* wrappings of one box of letters, that Michael had not unwrapped them. These, in fact, would not have been of much interest to him, but to me they were pure gold.

The box contained letters from Alfred Richard Ainsworth (1879–1959), an undergraduate at King's College who was elected to the Apostles in 1899, nominated by Moore. His claim on posterity is that he is the original of Ansell, the philosopher in E. M. Forster's *The Longest Journey.* In 1904, when Moore's Fellowship at his own college, Trinity, expired, he went to Edinburgh to live with Fred Ainsworth, who taught Greek there until 1907. The next year, Ainsworth married Moore's youngest sister, Sarah.

I couldn't say to Mrs. Moore that this arrangement sounded to me like the oldest dodge in the book, but as in the case of conscription during the First World War, I had a strong hunch that Moore had had more than a mere bond of sympathy with the largely homosexual Apostles of the generation younger than he. And in Ainsworth's letters to Lytton, I found some support for that view. Though Mrs. Moore occasionally chided me for slowness, I think that my subconscious knew that I couldn't publish the whole story until after her death. Two years after the publication of my book (and four years after Dorothy's Moore's death), I met Dame Rebecca West (1892–1983) at a party. She had read my book (and, she said, reviewed it enthusiastically for the *Sunday Telegraph,* though the notice was never published). She told me that as a girl of twelve or thirteen, she and her family lived in Edinburgh near "a couple of odd-looking gents who appeared to be inseparable," and she realized when reading the book that they were Moore and Ainsworth. When I said to her that Moore was so stunningly good-looking as to be unforgettable, she replied that "he must have lost his looks by then"—and she was probably right. Photographs taken in 1914, only nine or ten years later, show a distinctly paunchy middle-aged man. But Dame Rebecca found no difficulty in entertaining the idea that Moore and the physically unprepossessing Ainsworth had been lovers.

When, thanks to an introduction from Frances Partridge, I was invited in 1969 to stay at Cobbe Place in Sussex by Quentin and Olivier Bell, I had tea with Leonard Woolf at Monks House, the seventeenth-century cottage at Rodmell where Virginia had drowned herself in the River Ouse in 1941. The eighty-nine-year-old former Apostle assured me that Moore and Ainsworth were gay; he was just as adamant that he himself was the only person he had ever known who had never experienced homosexual desire.

It was during that same visit to Cobbe Place that I was introduced to my host's sister, Angelica Garnett (1918–2012), who was a very beautiful, elegant, youthful fifty-one. The world thought she was Quentin Bell's sister, the daughter of Vanessa and Clive Bell. The secret, which Angelica wasn't let in on until she was seventeen, was that she was the daughter of the painter Duncan Grant (1885–1978), with whom Vanessa (1879–1961) lived for forty years or so. Vanessa had married Clive Bell (1881–1964) in 1907, but their marriage was well over by 1916 when Duncan and his lover, David Garnett (1892–1981, always known as "Bunny"), came to work with Vanessa as fruit farmers in Sussex. This was their alternate service as conscientious objectors to the war.

Indeed, the bisexual Duncan made Vanessa pregnant while they were both living with his lover, Bunny; and Bunny was present at the birth of Angelica. He famously wrote to Lytton on the occasion: "I think of marrying it. When she is 20, I shall be 46—will it be scandalous?" To the chagrin of Vanessa, Duncan, and nearly everyone else in Bloomsbury, he did just that in May 1942, when Angelica was twenty-four. Though all this is common knowledge now, it wasn't really made public until Angelica published her memoir, *Deceived with Kindness* (1985).

Duncan had invited me, while I was at Cobbe Place, to lunch at Charleston, the farmhouse they all shared. It was along a track from Tilton, the Georgian country house that had been home to Maynard Keynes, and was still occupied by his widow, the former Russian ballerina Lydia Lopokova. Duncan was in his late eighties then, but still working and still possessed of a playful energy that kept him young in spirit. Since he had not been at Cambridge with the other Bloomsbury men, he had relatively little to tell me about Moore's influence. Instead, he showed me around Charleston and his studio. I especially remember a little Derain painting on the wall near the dining room. I think it hung above the telephone, which he used to ring up Lady Keynes. The conversation went something like this. Duncan: "Hello, Lydia. I have a nice young man having lunch with me. He is writing about G. E. Moore and would like to talk to you about Maynard." I could hear the other part of the conversation amplified through the earpiece of the old-fashioned Bakelite telephone: "Duncan, oh Duncan. You know I am old woman now. I see nobody." "It's true," said Duncan, by way of consoling me. "She lives in one room, like an old Russian peasant woman, with strings of onions hanging from the chimney." In fact, she was seven years younger than Duncan.

By the time Bunny Garnett decided, about 1969, to edit and publish some of the letters and diaries of the painter Dora Carrington (1893–1932), I was already the custodian of the Strachey papers. I remember taking the original of the famous journal and commonplace book "Carrington, Her Book" to Bunny. He was then living on a houseboat, moored off Cheyne Walk, London, which I remember grimly, since it was where one of his four children by Angelica drowned. But there were a good many happier times with Bunny. Once, at lunch at our farmhouse in Oxfordshire, my wife introduced him to one of the large number of part-Burmese cats to whom we had given Bloomsbury names. This one was called "Duncan." "I don't know whether to be pleased or annoyed," said Bunny, "that you have called a cat after my best friend."

In the late 1970s, the *Observer* sent me to interview him at his cottage on the grounds of the Château de Charry, near the wonderfully named town of Montcuq in southwestern France. The eighty-plus-year-old Bunny buzzed around the local towns in his Deux Chevaux with the pistol-grip gearshift. He, his daughter Fanny, and I drank lots of the local black wine of Cahors. I was sitting on the riverbank at twilight when Bunny first told me that he and Duncan had been lovers—but I don't think I took it in, certainly not to the extent of realizing the complications this entailed for his second marriage, to Angelica.

Bunny's first marriage had been to Ray Marshall (1891–1940), the sister of Frances Partridge. In 1962, Bunny and Angelica's seventeen-year-old daughter Henrietta married Frances and Ralph Partridge's only child, Burgo (1935–63). Burgo and Henrietta's daughter Sophie was born three weeks before Burgo died. So Angelica and Frances were the maternal and paternal grandmothers, while Bunny was both grandfather and, by marriage, great-uncle to the infant Sophie.

THERE WAS ONE EXCEPTION TO MY GOOD LUCK in meeting those who had known Moore, and it was the most important exception. Despite the pleas of Dorothy Moore, who addressed him in her letters as "Dear Bertie" ("I cannot bring myself to call him Lord Russell," she told me), Bertrand Russell (1872–1970) simply refused to see me. Even when his neighbor in Wales, Rupert Crawshay-Williams, interceded on my behalf, the answer was no. This was at a time when the ancient philosopher was firing off weekly letters about the wickedness of the American administration and Vietnam, and despite what he knew to be my agreement with him on this particular matter, he rebuffed me several times. Following his death, I discovered why he did not wish to be interviewed about Moore: though the episode may appear almost trivial to modern sensibilities, Russell had behaved very badly, even a bit dishonorably to Moore, and simply did not want it raked up. When on holiday with Moore, Russell had encouraged a stranger they encountered to speak coarsely and at length about his sexual exploits. In a letter to his fiancée, Alys, Russell boasted he had done this in order to corrupt and destroy Moore's famous "innocence."

Noel Annan was one of my chief benefactors. It was an open secret that he was an Apostle, as he had mentioned the Cambridge Conversazione Society (its actual name) from time to time when writing about nineteenth- and twentieth-century cultural history. To maintain the official fiction that I was doing an Oxford DPhil, whereas everyone knew I was finishing up a PhD for Harvard, it was suggested that Isaiah Berlin should be my supervisor. He could not see the point of having an Oxford man doing a Cambridge man's job, and so introduced me to Noel. A nice Bloomsbury-related Berlin anecdote: one evening at a recital at the Holywell Music Rooms, Isaiah, seeing me in the front row of the circle, leaned up from the floor and said in a stage whisper: "When younger, I used to meet Virginia Woolf from time to time; and she always began the conversation by saying, 'You know, Isaiah, we Jews . . .'"

It was Noel who smoothed my path at Cambridge and saw to it that I not only met E. M. Forster at his old college, King's, and was befriended by the college librarian, the great bibliographer A. N. L. (Tim) Munby, but also that I was received by F. A. Simpson (1883–1974) of Trinity, whom the *Oxford Dictionary of National*

Biography identifies as an "historian and eccentric." The Master of Trinity, Lord Butler, seated me next to Simpson at dinner at High Table. When the ninety-year-old author of *The Rise of Louis Napoleon* at last understood that I wanted to know about G. E. Moore, he began a story: "The worst thing Moore ever did was . . ." Just then the waiter brought in the serving platter; the scent of hot food diverted Simpson's attention to his plate; and he spoke not another word all evening.

Plenty of people included in Noel Annan's "intellectual aristocracy" had kinship ties to Bloomsbury but disregarded or even disapproved of the group. Ursula Vaughan Williams (1911–2007), whom I met because her late husband, the composer Ralph, had been one of Moore's lifelong close friends, seemed to me to frown on the Bloomsberries for being a little racy. Dorothy Moore, who had met Virginia Woolf, and knew and liked Desmond MacCarthy (another of her husband's bosom friends), was more comfortable with her many more sober acquaintances than with the giddy Stracheys or Stephenses. In this she was representative of the educated, liberal opinion of older people in the late 1960s and 1970s. The young were attracted to Bloomsbury because of the success of those artists and writers in upsetting the bourgeois order. Those who were middle-aged or older, while they might have admired the lack of sexual and social inhibition they detected in Bloomsbury, were often a little nervous about it.

For a while, almost into the 1960s, it was said that the culture section of the *New Statesman* was the house organ of Bloomsbury. Desmond MacCarthy was the original literary editor, Cyril Connolly had been in the staff, Maynard Keynes was a big influence as chairman of the board of the *Nation* (with which it amalgamated in 1931), Leonard Woolf was a regular contributor, his friend Janet Adam Smith was literary editor (1952–1960), and she was replaced by Karl Miller, another Apostle. This example is emblematic of the cultural establishment's relation to Bloomsbury; its influence was felt in art criticism (Roger Fry and Clive Bell), theatre criticism (Desmond MacCarthy), the Arts Council (founded by Keynes), the BBC, and the two main Sunday papers, the *Observer* and the *Sunday Times*. The Bloomsbury attitudes represented by this part of the national press, though considered a little edgy, were close to the cultural norms of the educated majority.

In the late 1960s, young people thought they were discovering social stances and mores that, in fact, Bloomsbury members had held and practiced two generations earlier. In *Lytton Strachey: The Really Interesting Question,* I showed, tongue in cheek, that Lytton had been in favor of gay rights, women's rights, and the legalization of marijuana, and opposed to the Vietnam draft. Light-hearted anachronism aside, as Angus Wilson and Michael Foot recognized in their reviews of the book, Lytton and his lot really did anticipate the causes and the social ferment of later times.

Strachey came back to public attention for a brief moment when Christopher Hampton's film *Carrington* was released in 1995. Before that there had been no translations at all of Holroyd's *Strachey;* suddenly there were French, German, Italian, Spanish, Swedish, and Japanese versions, and in France Holroyd even won a prize, which his epoch-making, taboo-breaking book never did in Britain.

My children's generation is now taking over the cultural shop, and I regret to say that I have yet to meet a thirty-year-old who has read *Eminent Victorians* or, really, even heard of Lytton, though the Saturday and Sunday book sections of the British national newspapers still refer to him with only minimal description. Economists still cite and argue about Keynes, and readers still love Virginia Woolf and E. M. Forster. Virginia and Frances Partridge might also be remembered as diarists. Would-be philosophers have to engage with the arguments of those Bloomsbury-fringe figures Moore, Russell, and Wittgenstein. Duncan Grant, Vanessa Bell, Roger Fry, and Clive Bell, and the feminist heroine Carrington will be discussed, though maybe not appreciated, by specialist art historians. But all in all it seems as though the Bloomsbury moment has passed.

Fall Semester 2012

Dora Carrington, 1912

12

Carrington Revisited

ANNE CHISHOLM

Not long after my biography of Frances Partridge was published, in 2009, I was asked whether I would edit a new selection of Dora Carrington's letters. Frances's and Carrington's lives had been intimately intertwined; they married the same man, Ralph Partridge, and in the 1920s were part of one of Bloomsbury's most renowned ménages when Frances squared the triangle established by Carrington, Ralph, and the man who, in his fashion, loved them both: Lytton Strachey, author of *Eminent Victorians* and subverter of social and sexual convention. Frances and Carrington could not have been more different. Their relationship was complicated and sometimes troubled. Even while I was focused on Frances as her biographer, I was aware of Carrington's curious power, her ability, often remarked on by those she beguiled, to make other women seem tame and ordinary.

Even so, I hesitated. It was not as if Carrington's letters were unknown. In 1970, a substantial selection was published, edited by David Garnett, and Gretchen Gerzina's thorough biography, based largely on the letters, had appeared in 1989. Were there enough unpublished letters, either omitted by Garnett or not then available to him, to justify a new edition? Equally, were there aspects of her life and character hitherto ignored or underemphasized that a new selection from her correspondence could illuminate?

In due course, after deciding that the answer to these questions was yes, I was commissioned to take a new look, through her letters, at Carrington, known today, if at all, as a minor artist who on her suicide in 1932, at age thirty-nine, left behind a handful of under-rated paintings and a sad story of unfulfilled love.

The letters are exceptionally good. Gerald Brenan, the hispano-phile writer who loved her to distraction and corresponded with her copiously, told her they were like

> the rustling of leaves, the voices of birds, the arrangements of natural form. Education has not deadened in you this mode of expression, has not, as it has for nearly all of us, reduced speech and writing to the level of a vulgar formula.[1]

Lytton Strachey, the highly critical literary man whom she revered, wrote to her: "Your letters are a great pleasure. I lap them down with breakfast and they do me more good than tonics, blood cap-sules or iron jelloids . . . I consider your letters perfect." Virginia Woolf, who was not always kind about her, described them as "tear-ing like a mayfly up and down the pages" and praised their original-ity as "completely unlike anything else in the habitable globe."[2] For Michael Holroyd, Strachey's biographer and the founding father of contemporary Bloomsbury studies, the great appeal of Carrington's letters lies in their timeless emotional power: "Love, loneliness, beauty, elation and harrowing despair—these are what she wrote about with such freshness and immediacy that, fifty years later [he was writing in 1970], the ink seems only just to have dried."[3]

Some have considered her letters her greatest achievement. While Sir John Rothenstein, a director of the Tate Gallery, called her "the most neglected serious painter of her time," Richard Shone, an art historian and the author of *Bloomsbury Portraits*, says, "I myself would give away all her paintings to hold on to her deceptively simple and often hilarious letters."[4] Alan Hollinghurst, the award-winning nov-elist, calls her letters "wonderful . . . vivid, funny, impulsive and moving."[5]

Working on her letters, I have come to feel that our existing im-pression of Carrington is incomplete and to some extent distorted. Significant omissions in the Garnett edition have affected not only biographers' view of her but also, and much more strongly, the film version of her life that appeared in 1995. *Carrington*, the well-made, prize-winning film based on the revised edition of Holroyd's Strachey biography, scripted by the distinguished playwright Chris-topher Hampton, and brilliantly acted by Emma Thompson and Jonathan Pryce, has helped fix a certain image of its protagonist in our minds. A new edition of her letters should shift and expand that image.

Carrington was in Bloomsbury but not altogether of Bloomsbury. Her uninhibited, unstudied letters were personal, never literary, and she was regarded as ignorant and uneducated by the seriously literary Bloomsberries. Many of them were puzzled by her and could be patronizing about her. David Garnett put it like this in his introduction to her letters: "When famous hostesses . . . invited the literary lion Lytton Strachey to their houses they would no more have thought of including Carrington than of asking him to bring his housekeeper or his cook."[6]

She mesmerized her contemporaries at the Slade School of Art, where she was a prize-winning student, but afterward could hardly bear to exhibit or sell her paintings. Her painting was vital to her, but she had little confidence in it. Needing to make money, she illustrated books, designed dust jackets for the Hogarth Press, made bookplates and tiles, painted inn signs, decorated rooms, and adorned fireplaces and furniture. She was part of the Omega Workshop, but her first one-woman show was not held until 1970, in the year the letters were published. In 1995, when the film *Carrington* came out, she finally had a major retrospective show at the Barbican. Since then her paintings and drawings have soared in value. So have her letters: a single-page unillustrated note of no special significance sold last year at auction for over £700.

In fact, many of Carrington's letters are themselves works of art. All her life she was a natural, easy, and copious correspondent. Words and pictures flowed seamlessly onto the page; she scattered drawings into the text and along the margins—visual puns on names, birds, flowers, faces, cats, naked girls, the occasional phallus—and sometimes paused for a more considered study: Lytton Strachey reading by the fire, or herself scribbling in her four-poster bed. Her letters reveal an emotionally complicated young woman with a gift for intimacy, a taste for intrigue, and a need for independence, with an unusual originality of mind. Far from depicting her as a victim or a slave of Strachey's, a minor character in his story, they show her as central, even powerful, someone who drew both men and women to her, who was much loved.

Bloomsbury continues to interest us today not just because of the individual talents within the group but because of the way its members chose to live. Carrington played a key part in establishing two of the group ménages, as Virginia Woolf recognized when she wrote in her diary of the household at Tidmarsh Mill where Strachey, Carrington, and Ralph Partridge set up house together: "Lytton's way of life, in so far as it is unconventional, is so by the desire and determination of Carrington." Unconventional though she was in some ways, Carrington was practical, energetic, and determined to make Lytton comfortable and happy. Their correspondence is full of domestic details—dealing with servants, furnishing fabrics, choosing menus—in all of which he took more than a polite interest. And her presence was essential to him as an active homosexual, both as cover for what was illegal and shocking and as a young woman who attracted young men. Her letters make it clear that she knew and understood this.

From her Slade days on, Carrington was someone who made an impression. She was not a beauty, but her appearance and coloring were striking; the painter Paul Nash admired her fine blue eyes and the "heavy golden bell" of her hair; to Virginia Woolf, she was "apple red and firm in the cheeks" with "a fat decided clever face."[7] David Garnett, who had been attracted to her in their youth, wrote of her: "Her complexion was delicate, like a white heart cherry; a curious crooked nose gave character to her face and pure blue eyes made her seem simple and childlike when she was in fact the very opposite." The famed hostess Ottoline Morrell likened her to a moorland pony or "some strange wild beast"; Julia Strachey thought her "a modern witch." Glimpses of her, mostly unflattering, can be found in novels by her contemporaries. D. H. Lawrence put her into *Women in Love* as Minette Darrington, a lisping fair-haired artist model who torments her love, and then into "None of That" as Ethel Cane, a middle-aged woman with artistic pretensions who ends up in Mexico (as did Carrington's and Lawrence's close friend Dorothy Brett, another possible Ethel), where she commits suicide after being gang-raped. Aldous Huxley, who made unsuccessful advances to her, put her into *Crome Yellow* as silly Mary Bracegirdle, tiresomely obsessed with her virginity. Her traces can also be found in works by Gilbert Cannan and Katharine Mansfield, and she is certainly behind the diminutive sex therapist in Wyndham Lewis's satire *The Apes of God*. The encounters and relationships behind these fictions are all reflected in her letters.

CARRINGTON WAS BORN IN 1893, one of five children of a solid, undistinguished, middle-class family. She would later (in a long, unpublished letter about her early years) describe her childhood as "awful." She adored her elderly father, who had spent most of his life in India before marrying a governess and retiring to respectable Bedford. There Carrington grew up disliking both her prudish mother, whose suspicious scrutiny, she maintained, drove her toward concealment and lies, and the prevailing dullness of provincial life. Her artistic talents were spotted while she was still at school, and she arrived to study at the Slade in London in 1910 at the age of seventeen.

At the Slade, she and her close women friends Barbara Hiles (later Bagenal), Dorothy Brett, and Ruth Humphries were dubbed the "cropheads" after they cut their hair short and declined to dress or behave in a conventionally feminine manner. Soon she was the focus of competitive attentions from three of the outstanding male students—Paul Nash, C. R. Nevinson, and, most dramatically, the East End prodigy Mark Gertler, the first Jew to attend the Slade. Carrington had grown up afflicted by painful periods and a fear of sex; secretive by nature, she was inclined to play her admirers off against each other. The "triangular trinity of happiness" in which she became involved with Strachey and Partridge was by no means the first; from the Slade on, she evaded commitment to one relationship by cultivating another alongside it, preferring the tension and unhappiness this caused to feeling trapped and labeled as lover, partner, or, worst of all, wife. Panic-stricken at the thought of belonging, physically or emotionally, to anyone, she was destructive of more than one male friendship. These recurring triangles are exposed in a torrent of letters that reveal much about her devious, elusive, but always beguiling nature. Often considered a Bloomsbury specialty but coming naturally to Carrington, such behavior involved her over the years with Nash, Nevinson, Gertler, Strachey, Ralph Partridge, Frances Marshall, Gerald Brenan, Henrietta Bingham, Bernard Penrose, Stephen Tomlin, and Julia Strachey.

Carrington needed male attention, but her letters indicate that she never really enjoyed sex with men. Her friendships with women were often intense and usually erotically charged; the only acknowledgment of sexual pleasure in her correspondence occurs when she is writing of making love with a woman (Henrietta Bingham, the bisexual daughter of the American ambassador to London). Carrington's conflicts over her love life, which permeate her letters, can now be looked at more frankly than before, not least because matters such as lesbianism and abortion no longer need to be evaded or muted. Garnett's selection underplays her feelings for women, as did Holroyd's biography, and the film omits them entirely. Carrington was not consciously a pioneer bisexual, nor a feminist, but in her determination to live life according to her own nature, and in her constant struggle to have time and space to develop as a painter, she fought battles that remain familiar and urgent for women today.

By 1915, Carrington had left the Slade and fallen in love with Lytton Strachey. At the time, she was still painfully involved with

Mark Gertler, exchanging intense letters with him about painting, assuring him of her love but driving him mad by refusing to
sleep with him. Her letters to Lytton, however, strike a very different note. They are almost always humorous but, though deeply loving, seldom intense. She aimed to please and amuse him, and she
succeeded. Their correspondence flourished and they became very
close; although there was, at the beginning, attraction and sexual
experiment between them, it soon ceased. There are hints that she
regretted this, but also that it released her from her fear of being
owned or dominated. Her letters show that she understood how her
capacity to attract handsome young men increased her value to Lytton, who had been drawn to Gertler before they met and was to fall
much more seriously for Ralph Partridge.

Carrington's torrent of letters to Strachey, with their teasing references to beautiful boys and well-endowed men, show her complete
acceptance of his nature.[8] She had many private nicknames for both
of them: he was her *grand-père,* her uncle; she was his *grosse bébé,* she
was Mopsa; he was Count Lytoff, she longed only—could the symbolism really have been unconscious?—to be his pen wiper.

During the seventeen years (1915–1932) when Lytton Strachey was
the center of her life, their correspondence was constant, like their
affection, but they both pursued other relationships. Carrington
married Ralph Partridge in 1921 under duress, fearing that if he
left her she would lose Lytton and their life together; her letters to
him around this time are among the saddest in the history of love.
Within months, in reaction, she had started a secret romance with
Ralph's friend Gerald Brenan, an affair conducted with much more
passion and conviction on paper than when they were together. She
wrote at length to him on his remote hillside in Spain about her
past life and her passion for art, and it was to him that she confessed
most openly her dislike of marriage, her fear of sex, her dread of
maternity, and her brief, ecstatic love for Henrietta Bingham. Their
correspondence was all the more intense for being kept secret from
Ralph; there was a great deal of slightly farcical writing of secret
postscripts and smuggling of letters. While she and Ralph were married (although after the autumn of 1925, when he started to sleep
with Frances Marshall, sex between them stopped), she kept the unhappy Gerald on a string; she went to bed with him occasionally,
but her letters indicate that her orientation, emotional and physical, was increasingly toward women. She wrote admiring, suggestive letters to Alix Strachey, Rosamund Lehmann, Diana (Mitford)
Guinness, Julia Strachey, and even to Frances, her rival; her letters
to Poppet John, Augustus John's pretty daughter, though playful,

have a touch of infatuation about them. She also developed teasing, joking correspondences with several of Lytton's young men, in particular Sebastian Sprott and George (Dadie) Rylands. Carrington played emotional games with both men and women, especially on the page. Increasingly, as the years went by, such games compensated her for what she could never have with Lytton—full emotional and physical intimacy—and for the fact that she eventually lost both Ralph and Gerald to other women. When one of the games turned serious and she embarked on an affair in her midthirties with the younger and bluntly heterosexual Bernard (Beakus) Penrose, it was a disaster. He made her wretched by his lukewarm love, and then pregnant. Lytton and Ralph picked up the pieces.

Some matters were too private and too painful for letters. Her feelings for Bernard Penrose, her dread of loneliness as she saw both Lytton and Ralph drawn elsewhere, her fear of aging, are described not in her letters—or at any rate not in those that have survived—but in the journal she kept from 1927 to the end of her life. The letters she wrote after Lytton died are deeply sad, but it was into her journal that she poured her grief and her utter distaste for life without him.

TO A GREAT EXTENT, DAVID GARNETT's selection of Carrington's letters was conditioned, not surprisingly, by his own close connection with her world, first as a lover of Duncan Grant and then as husband of Frances Marshall's sister. To him, some of the material was too sensitive to use; he cut out any slighting references to Frances or Ralph, not least during the time when Lytton and Ralph were closest. He also exercised an editor's privilege of cutting a number of uncomplimentary references to himself and his first wife, Ray. As significantly, Garnett's attitude to Carrington was affected by his slightly patronizing view of her as an outsider. As he put it, "Carrington did not quite fit in to this group and entered it more as an appendage of Lytton Strachey's than in her own right."[9]

I have come to think that this remark misrepresents Carrington's role in Lytton's life and in their circle, and that in general Garnett's choice of letters was overly influenced by his veneration for Strachey and Bloomsbury. His edition starts in the year Carrington and Lytton met; important letters concerning her early life and especially her time at the Slade were omitted, and the intensity and variety of some of her other loves were underplayed.

Moreover, by encouraging a fresh look at Carrington through her letters, a rather different version of her may emerge from the one given in Christopher Hampton's film. Because films are so effective

at fixing an image and a story in public consciousness, it seems to
me important to point out where this one misleads. The dramatic
art is, of course, not bound by the same rules as the biographer's;
the film succeeds largely because it simplifies Carrington's story and
reduces the number of themes and characters. A film, like a novel,
makes up a story; the story can be more or less truthful, while a
biographer—or an editor—must remain true to known facts and to
the material, even while selecting and shaping it.

   In the film, the first time that Lytton sees Carrington, he mistakes
her for a boy. Apart from the fact that there is no evidence for this,
there is also no doubt that the young Emma Thompson, who played
Carrington, was much more boyish than Carrington ever was. Frances Partridge, who had known Lytton and Carrington intimately
and was consulted while the film was being made, left notes on her
reactions. Emma Thompson, she felt, took on some of Carrington's
mannerisms very effectively—her pigeon toes and her way of tossing
her hair out of her eyes—but was less successful at capturing her
voice and personality. Frances described Carrington as

> a combination of near genius and neurosis: the former shown by
> her letter writing, her art, her poetic attitude to life and nature,
> the latter in her sense of guilt, frightful nightmares, and lying her
> way out of difficulties. I doubt if she was ever the tomboy you de-
> pict at first.[10]

More crucially, Frances felt that the film, structured as it is around
Carrington's romantic and sexual involvement with Strachey,
Gertler, Partridge, Brenan, and Penrose, gave a false idea of her na-
ture. Too much of the film, she wrote, depicted

> relentless, jealous and insensitive sexual badgering of Carrington
> by her heterosexual admirers. I have it on good authority that she
> was not highly sexed but took it all mainly as something of a lark,
> and her favourite objects were lesbian.

The complete absence of Carrington's women friends from the film
is a serious omission. It was not just that she found women attractive;
she valued and depended on their support and affection, perhaps
partly because she claimed to dislike her conventional mother and
sisters. She admired and was drawn to some older women—Dorelia
John in particular—but her life was full of happy, easy, comforting,
and admiring relationships with women her own age or younger.

   With a story line essentially of a doomed love affair in which, after
some early happiness, Carrington's love for Lytton leads to frustration, despair, and suicide, the film's portrait of her tends toward the

melancholy. In fact, as I learned from Frances Partridge, Blooms-berries loved jokes, fun, games, and laughter, and Carrington was no exception. A handful of surviving home movies show her and her friends at play in the garden of Ham Spray or by the river. In these fragments, which incontrovertibly show us the real Carrington, are glimpses of an energetic, spirited young woman galloping off bareback on her white pony, Belle, or splashing frantically as she tries to clamber onto an inflated rubber swan. Although Blooms-bury thrived on intense emotions, intellectual seriousness, and ar-tistic aspirations, the group was made up of people who were not always intense or serious and who had much happiness together. As her letters show, Carrington shared, and indeed helped build, that happiness. Previous accounts of her have underplayed the positive, life-enhancing, energetic aspects of her nature; my hope is that by revisiting her letters, the balance may be redressed.

Spring Semester 2013

1. Gerald Brenan to Carrington, 29 Sept. 1921, Ransom Center, University of Texas at Austin.

2. Strachey and Woolf quoted in David Garnett, introduction to *Carrington: Letters and Extracts from Her Diaries* (London, 1970).

3. Michael Holroyd, review of *Carrington: Letters and Extracts from Her Diaries*, *The Times*, 1970.

4. Rothenstein and Stone, personal communication with the author.

5. Alan Hollinghurst, review of Paul Levy, ed., *The Letters of Lytton Strachey* (New York, 2005), *New York Review of Books*, 9 Mar. 2006.

6. Garnett, introduction to *Carrington*.

7. All quotations in this paragraph are taken from Gretchen Gerzina, *Carrington: A Life* (London, 1989).

8. Carrington's letters to Strachey are held by the British Library.

9. Garnett, introduction to *Carrington*.

10. Frances Partridge, notes on the film *Carrington* (1995), Frances Partridge Papers, King's College, Cambridge.

Sir Edmund William Gosse (early 1890s) and Joe Randolph Ackerley (1939). Gosse photograph by Eveleen Myers; Ackerley photograph by Howard Coster; both images © National Portrait Gallery, London.

13

Edmund Gosse and J. R. Ackerley

STEVEN ISENBERG

As a touchstone of explanation and emotion, seed and sorrow, emulation and escape, the business of fathers and sons never runs out of stock. Yet not that long ago the literary conventions against making familial reckonings public came of deeply held convictions about respect for the privacy and lives of parents, so much so that extra measures of courage were required to disclose and deliberate a story of father and son. Indeed, for all their authors' bravery and determination, Edmund Gosse's *Father and Son* was initially published anonymously, and J. R. Ackerley's *My Father and Myself* posthumously.

These memoirs address the power of the father, religious belief, sex, the quest for a self of one's own, and the shaping of identity. Contemporary themes all, yet the books bear marks of the British character forged in Victorian and Edwardian England—another time, another soil, another idiom. Edmund Gosse (1849–1928) was a large and ubiquitous figure in his literary world, an exemplary man of letters. Nothing is so lasting of his work as *Father and Son* (1907). Gosse set out the book's drama: "This book is the record of a struggle between two temperaments, two consciences and two epochs."

Gosse's parents were "lonely, each was poor, each was accustomed to a strenuous intellectual self-support." His father was a "zoologist, and a writer of books on natural history; [his] mother also was a writer, author of two slender volumes of religious verse." For both parents, "the various forms of imaginative and scientific literature were merely means of improvement and profit, which kept the student 'out of the world'"; what mattered was religious belief: "Pleasure was found nowhere but in the Word of God, and to the endless discussion of the scriptures each hurried when the day's work was over."

The emphasis on "strenuous intellectual self-support" and the confinement of pleasure set the tone for his birth: "In this strange household the advent of a child was not welcomed, but was borne with resignation." But that parental resignation seemed more grounded in enduring the pain of childbirth and accepting the baby's near death at birth. The initial difficulties, once past, ushered in the "dedication" by which Gosse was given to the Lord, entirely, in purpose and service: "Around my tender and unconscious spirit was flung the luminous web, the light and elastic but impermeable veil, which it was hoped would keep me 'unspotted from the world.'" He became the full recipient of his mother's solicitude, which brought not only the usual force of maternal love, but also "certain spiritual determinations which can but be rare," even if "vaguely common to many religious mothers." It was his mother's will, and the memory of it after her death, that kept his father obedient to her "unswerving purpose."

Gosse set himself the task of carrying on "a different inspection," "a study of . . . the record of a state of soul once not uncommon in Protestant Europe, of which [his] parents were perhaps the latest consistent exemplars among people of light and leading." Those principles, which shaped "the peculiarities of a family life," were the dominant forces of parental belief and action in Gosse's childhood.

> Here was perfect purity, perfect intrepidity, perfect abnegation, yet there was always narrowness, isolation, an absence of perspective, let it be boldly admitted, an absence of humanity. And there was a curious mixture of humbleness and arrogance; entire resignation to the will of God and not less entire disdain of the judgment and opinion of man. My parents founded every action, every attitude, upon the interpretation of the Scriptures, and upon the guidance of the Divine Will as revealed to them by direct answer to prayer. Their ejaculation in the face of any dilemma was "Let us cast it before the Lord!"
>
> So confident were they of the reality of their intercourse with God that they asked for no other guide.

Gosse said that in the early days of his childhood, "we were always cheerful and often gay," adding, "What I have since been told of the guileless mirth of nuns in a convent has reminded me of the gaiety of my parents." And so he noted of his life when he was "a mere part of them, without individual existence":

> I was mirthful when they were mirthful, and grave when they were grave. The mere fact that I had no young companions, no story books, no outdoor amusements, none of the thousand and one employments provided for other children in more conventional surroundings, did not make me discontented or fretful, because I did not know of the existence of such entertainments.

Gosse recalls from his youngest years a turn of precocity and the first rent in the fabric of obedience. Told to put before God "whatever you need . . . and He will grant it, if it is his will," Gosse prayed for a large painted humming top, "carefully adding the words: If it is Thy will." He is overheard and told by his father not to "pray for 'things like that.'" Gosse reminded his father that "he said we ought to pray for things we needed": "I needed a humming-top a great deal more than I did the conversions of the heathens or the restitution of Jerusalem to the Jews, two objects of nightly supplication which left me very cold."

Small incidents were the foundation for steps into doubt. Gosse's father told him that God would be very angry "if any one, in a Christian country, bowed down to wood and stone." Testing the injunction, Gosse, out of sight, put a small chair on a table and "said his daily prayer in a loud voice, only substituting the address 'O Chair' for the habitual one." Nothing happened, and so Gosse concluded that "God did not care."

The epistemological outcome was "not to question the existence and power of God; those were forces which I did not dream of ignoring, but what it did was to lessen still further my confidence in my father's knowledge of the Divine Mind." Another incident provided further evidence. A leaking pipe was attributed to workmen who were working on it, when in fact Edmund had made a hole in it. Waiting to be denounced and questioned, he remained frightened but silent. Blame fell elsewhere. Two extraordinary conclusions were made by the six-year-old boy. First, the idea that his father was "omniscient or infallible was now dead and buried": "My father, as a deity, as a natural force of universal prestige, fell in my eyes to a human level." The second was deeper, especially for a boy who had no children as companions. It was the discovery of "a companion and confidant" in himself: "There was a secret in this world and it belonged to me and somebody who lived in the same body with me."

These tales had special meaning in a childhood where imaginative literature was strictly prohibited. Gosse's mother believed fiction was a form of lying. He never heard "Once upon a time," and his reading joy came from the *Penny Cyclopedia*. He read works of theology, natural history, travel in a scientific vein, geography, and astronomy, subjects whose meaning nearly always eluded their young reader.

What sealed his closeness to his mother was living with her during her treatment for cancer. She had to stay in town, not being able to travel back and forth from their home. And so began the days when he read to his mother, plumped up her pillows, and ministered to her as a childish companion in hours of her isolation and suffering. Before her return home to die, he was "all important, her only companion, her friend, her confidant." It was during this time that his mother many times "tenderly and closely" urged his father "to watch with unceasing care over [Edmund's] spiritual welfare." Her prayers and hopes reconciled her to the belief that he would be "in the hands of her loving Lord."

Of this period of her faith, "so strong and single," Gosse said there was no mysticism—"she never pretended to any visionary gifts." To understand her, one must "accept the view that she had formed a definite concept of the absolute, unmodified and historical veracity, in its direct and obvious sense, of every statement within the covers of the Bible." There was nothing "symbolic, nothing allegorical or allusive" in Scripture. His parents' version of Protestantism seemed almost exotic: "Although their faith was so strenuous that many persons might have called it fanatical, there was no mysticism about them. They went rather to the opposite extreme, to the cultivation of a rigid and iconoclastic literalness." He twice says his parents were "devoid of a sympathetic imagination."

After the death of his wife, Philip Gosse, "tired out with anxiety and sorrow" and in a "melancholy state," became "great friends" with his son. Edmund was allowed a visit to his cousins, which awoke in him feelings that overcame his "old solitary discipline," through which his "intelligence had grown at the expense of [his] sentiment." He pronounced himself "innocent, but inhuman." After "having enjoyed a little of the common experience of childhood," he went beyond a "mental life that was all interior" and became "taken with a curiosity about human life." It was often viewed through a window of his house or by getting his father to take walks down the main road, where they even took to song. Those became "happy hours when the specter of Religion ceased to overshadow us for a little while."

His father's religious teaching was "almost exclusively doctrinal" and often "signally unfitted for the comprehension of a child." When Edmund said, "O how I hate the law," his father suddenly understood that his son "took the law to be a person of malignant temper," and that some of the biblical stories and injunctions, such as the arguments from the book of Hebrews, were bewildering, beyond Edmund's reach. Nonetheless, Edmund absorbed fully "the turpitude of Rome."

On their walks, father and son looked at sea anemones, starfishes, and ducks. They moved to Devonshire, where a "fresh rival rose to compete" with his father's "dogmatic theology." It was the sea, which Gosse describes by summoning Wordsworth's *The Prelude* and "drinking in a pure organic pleasure" from the connection to nature. For Gosse, "no other form of natural scenery than sea had any effect" on him for a long while. Moving passages in *Father and Son* illustrate the intimacy in the boy and his parent's shared silence of study and drawing, as well as in their collecting, discovery, and identification—the apprentice, with a "passion for imitation," hovering at the side of the master.

The year 1857, Edmund's eighth, was a crucible for his father because the evidence mustered by Charles Darwin and others in deducing the processes of evolution brought society and Philip to a "scientific crisis" in which "there rushed two kinds of thoughts, each absorbing, each convincing, each of them indisputable." Philip was shaken by the clash between geology and theology, so much so that "he took one step in the service of truth, and then he drew back in an agony, and accepted the servitude of error." Gosse emphasizes how his father's "attitude towards the theory of natural selection was critical in his career, and, oddly enough, it exercised an immense influence on [his] own experience as a child." One wonders at "oddly enough," because Gosse apprehended the anguish of his father and the embarrassment that came when Philip's attempt at reconciliation—a theory that God had created certain things as mistakes in order to test faith—was met with scorn on all sides. Gosse was aware that his father's "friendships" with Darwin, Joseph Hooker, and others of note, built on respect and admiration for his father's scientific ability and knowledge, were lost. The judgments rendered by Gosse are in an adult voice; he speaks of the loss of his father's friendships with "men of scientific leaning at the British Museum and Royal Society," laying the fault at his father's feet: "By a strange act of willfulness, he closed the doors upon himself for ever."

Because of Philip's "morbid delicacy of conscience," "he considered the failure of his attempt at the reconciliation of science with religion to have been intended by God as a punishment for something he had done or left undone." And so it boiled down to "geology *seems* to be true, but the Bible, which was God's word, *was* true."

It is no surprise that Philip Gosse's religious resoluteness was turned even more fully upon his son, mirroring his oft-repeated description that "our God is a jealous god." He used *jealous* in an "antiquated sense" to mean "total solicitude, a careful watchfulness." Edmund describes screaming when a beetle crawled on his face. To his scientific father, an insect did not merit fright or a scream. He said, "You, the child of a naturalist . . . *you* pretend to feel terror at the advance of an insect." He scolded Edmund for his behavior because it had interrupted nightly prayer, reminding him that God "consumes them in wrath who make a noise like a dog."

Philip's reaction to the beetle episode derived from his conviction that Edmund was not to be treated as a "commonplace child," but rather "an *âme d'elite* . . . to whom the mysteries of salvation had been divinely revealed and . . . accepted . . . one in whom the Holy Ghost had already performed a real and permanent work." And so from Philip's concern over Edmund's "spiritual condition," and from promises made to his dying mother, a plan was formed to secure Edmund's "maintenance in grace."

Philip, the leader of the congregation, succeeded in bringing his ten-year-old son into the company of the elect through baptism and conversion, by which one who was "a child of wrath" became forever a "child of God." To do this as and for a child was rare, and the politics of urging the saints to admit his son show Philip, in this case, wise and worldly in choosing judges from two of the leading objectors. Later they fell over themselves in astounded admiration after Edmund's oral examination. Edmund's feelings about the ceremony seemed in line with his father's: "My public baptism was the cultural event of my whole childhood. Everything since the earliest dawn of consciousness seemed to be leading up to it." But then he added, perhaps ominously, "Everything, afterwards, seemed to be leading down and away from it."

After the conversion ceremony, Edmund, "puffed out" with self-importance, would stick out his tongue in mockery at other boys. Although warning him against spiritual pride, his father was jubilant at his son's new status:

> My Father's happiness during the next few weeks is now pathetic to me to look upon. His sternness melted into a universal complaisance. He laughed and smiled, he paid to my opinions the tribute of the gravest consideration, he indulged,—utterly unlike his wont,—in shy and furtive caresses. I could express no wish he did not attempt to fulfil.

His father's reaction raises questions about self-tribute, ways in which a father takes (here, engineers) his son's accomplishments to be his own or to result from his endowment. The self-referential quality of his father's happiness comes of Edmund being wrapped in his religion, his congregation, his access to God's will and grace, and his carrying out what would have been the highest of Edmund's mother's hopes. And it is plausible to surmise that it was a balm to Philip to have his son come to his side after the bruising rejection by the scientific community for having chosen biblical literalness.

MRS. BRIGHTWEN, THE WOMAN WHO became Edmund's stepmother, brought to his life fresh air, literally by removing heavy bedclothes and opening his windows, and figuratively by exposing him to literature, which opened his imagination and heart. She never subtracted from Philip's authority, and so even with the oddments of his censorship (no to Sir Walter Scott, yes to Dickens), Mrs. Brightwen became Edmund's "great ally" in enlarging his life. Literature began to create and awaken sensibilities that were neither fostered nor encouraged by his father's religious tracts and tomes.

When his schooling away from home began, and with it the "extension of [his] intellectual powers," there was no push against faith but rather "a considerable quickening of fervor" and a new sympathy for and interest in scripture. Yet he soon found himself, without "animosity," recognizing "the strange narrowness of [his] father's system." He found that his father's convictions, "pushed to their logical extremity," resulted in the admission that not a single Unitarian or any inhabitant of a Catholic county could find "eternal life." That "rigid conception of the Divine mercy," along with the ideas "that a secret of such stupendous importance should have been entrusted to a little group of Plymouth brethren" and that leaders of Christianity in Europe, while "sincere," "were all of them wrong," set more cracks in his faith. He could not reconcile the tenderhearted qualities of his father with his belief "that God would punish human beings, in millions, forever, for a purely intellectual error of comprehension."

Living with a man who daily awaited the momentous arrival of the Lord to take away to "everlasting glory" all who were "sealed for immortality" made a final test for Edmund. One evening while he was a teenager, lying on a sofa in his schoolhouse and looking into the garden and then at the sea, the sunset light and air led to "an immense wave of emotion" that he believed meant "the final change was coming." He summoned "Lord Jesus" with prayerful readiness to take him before he was to leave home for London, feeling that his "heart [was] purged from sin." He said, "This was the highest moment of my religious life, the apex of my striving after holiness." But nothing happened, and he found that "the Lord has not come,

the Lord will never come." And so "the artificial edifices of extrava-
gant faith" began to totter and crumble.

> From that moment forth my Father and I, though the fact was long
> mercifully concealed from him and even from myself, walked in
> opposite hemispheres of the soul, with "the thick o' the world"
> between us.

Father and Son's epilogue takes "the unique and noble figure" of
Philip Gosse into years when his "characteristics became more severely outlined, more rigorously defined within settled limits." And
the fervor of his inquiry into the state of Edmund's faith resulted
in daily letters to London, which, unlike most parental inquiries,
were not about "conduct" but faith. In quoting from the letters, Edmund says he seeks "to call out sympathy, and perhaps wonder" at
the spectacle of his father's firmness. But for most readers this will
be hard-won sympathy because of the grinding assault of inquiry
and accusation that came from his father's reluctant recognition
"that holiness was not hereditary . . . but it might be compulsive."
As Edmund discovers Ruskin and Carlyle, a new translation of the
Greek New Testament arrives, with a prescription for daily readings.
By then, the Bible had become difficult for Edmund to read because
of its familiarity—"it had the colourless triteness of a story retold a
hundred times." His father's reckoning of Edmund's waning faith
compared him to a son of Job; he saw Edmund as a victim of the
"infidelity of the age."

When Edmund recalls his father's other interests—the watercolors, his study of botany—reminding readers that some of his own
mental acuity and agility came from his having been taught to pay
a respectful and informed attention to the natural world, the intellectual debt he owes his father is clear. But whereas Edmund finds a
way to extend some charity to his father, he can only cry out against
his father's faith,

> against the untruth . . . that evangelical religion, or any religion
> in a violent form, is a wholesome or valuable or desirable adjunct
> to human life. It divides heart from head . . . It invents virtues
> which are sterile and cruel; it invents sins which are no sins at all,
> but which darken the heaven of innocent joy with futile clouds of
> remorse.

Coming to the long letter from Philip that ends the book and feeling the full weight of its accusations and the adamant force of his
saying, "If the written word is not absolutely authoritative, what do
we know of God?" it is impossible not to feel at one with Edmund

when he speaks of his conscience having thrown off the "yoke of his dedication," and of his decision, made as respectfully as he could, without "parade or remonstrance," to take "a human being's privilege to fashion his inner life for himself."

WHAT DISTINGUISHES J. R. ACKERLEY's tale from Edmund Gosse's is how much of the former's autobiographical puzzling is circumscribed because so much of his father's life lay beyond his knowledge. Thus it is a book (and a life) as much about the limits of what Ackerley knew as it is about the unspoken, unrequited yearning for an opening of heart and mind. The door that Joe Ackerley wished to open on his father's life is the one he wished to open for his father, explicitly, on his own life.

His father, Roger, once spoke to him and his brother about sex:

> There was nothing he had not done, nothing he had not tasted, no scrape he had not got into or out of, so that if we should ever be in want of help or advice we need never be ashamed to come to him and could always count on his understanding and sympathy.

It was only when Joe was older that he found this "an excellent and friendly speech" and noted with regret: "That I never took advantage of it is the whole point of this book." In the end, Joe is left "to brood over this story of my father and myself":

> I saw it as a *stupid* story, shamefully stupid that two intelligent people, even though parent and son between whom special difficulties of communication are said to lie, should have gone along together, perfectly friendly for so many years, without ever reaching the closeness of an intimate conversation, almost totally ignorant of each other's hearts and minds.

That his father was a "mystery man" is hinted at from Joe Ackerley's beginnings: "I was born in 1896 and my parents were married in 1919." Just when and how Ackerley pieced together what he could of his parents' courtship and his father's first marriage, which shortly left him a widower with a generous annual settlement from in-laws whom he didn't want to estrange by a new marriage, were the first knots to be untied about a "strikingly handsome man" who "was a ladies' man" and was "therefore more sympathetic no doubt with female nature" than Joes was.

My Father and Myself was written over a thirty-year period, lying fallow in notebooks, diaries, and the mind; it was published in 1968, after Joe Ackerley's death. It tells the story of a family built around three children—Peter, Joe, and Nancy—during twenty-three years

without the frame of marriage, and ends with the discovery of letters left to Joe by Roger, explaining that he had a secret family (a
wife and children) and asking that they be treated fairly.

Joe had only his Aunt Bunny as a source of information about his
father's courtship of his mother and their eventual marriage vows.
His mother avoided the subject until so late in her life that she remembered little. Joe was "seldom able to take his Mother entirely
seriously." But when his aunt said that his father had a "strong streak
of coarseness . . . in his nature," he acknowledged, "Who should be
better able than she to recognize it?"

Another attempt at sorting out his father's youth takes up his
two enlistments in the army; the first ended when he paid for his
release. While in the army, he fought at the Battle of Tel-el-Kebir
(1882) and won the War Medal and Bronze Star during the Egyptian campaign. From there Joe seeks out the "transformation of
Trooper Alfred Ackerley into the cultivated, urbane, travelled and
polished young man of the world." Joe says "it is necessary" to know
that his father "had been a guardsman": "The Household Cavalry
are a fine body of men, much admired for their magnificent phy-
sique and the splendour of their accoutrements, but it will hardly
be claimed for them that they are—or at any rate were—refined in
their tastes and habits."

As a young man, before Roger entered the fruit business and became the "Banana King," he enjoyed friendships of companionship
and patronage. For four years he was secretary to Fitzroy Paley Ash-
more, a much older barrister. Of that time, the central event Joe
tries to decipher is the estrangement of his father from James Francis de Gallatin. After finding a newspaper article about a judgment
in a lawsuit between his father and Gallatin concerning £500, he
works from that, as well as shadowy and elusive recollections of family and friends, to reconstruct the motives for the falling out and the
lawsuit: "The whole matter . . . looks like one of those bitter lessons
so many of us learn when we try to buy one human heart with cash."
It is his father's heart of which he speaks, and it is Gallatin's broken
heart that he tries to understand. Underlying it all is an unfulfilled
inquiry into just what kind of relationship they had. But one sure
thing came from that friendship's end: Roger Ackerley never again
accepted the hospitality of another. And of the Household Guards,
who were courted and paid for by Joe Ackerley and other homosex-
uals, there remained the unanswered question whether for a time
Roger's sexual attentions were extended to others than "the plump
little partridges" who caught his fancy before and after marriage.

Roger Ackerley had been a soldier in battle, and one of the book's most memorable and moving parts is Joe's recollection of the First World War and of he and his brother, young officers, meeting on the front lines. Joe Ackerley wrote, "This book is not about my brother, but in connection with him my own character and story develop and his subsequent history must be briefly sketched."

> However little my father welcomed my brother when he came, he lost his favorite son when he died. Peter approximated far closer than I did to the paternal image, a chip off the old block, and was already set to fulfill my father's cherished ambitions: he would have married, and perhaps, provided grandchildren (he was already courting several girls before he died and my father was fond of children), and he would have entered the bananas business. . . . He was, in fact, all the things I was not, though we got along together perfectly well.

Joe Ackerley was wounded, but returned to the front. It was from Joe's trench that Peter was ordered to attack a gun emplacement. Again, memory flickers, but Joe recalls:

> I offered him a quick drink . . . he said, "No thanks, I'll take my rum with the men." Then, could we switch watches, his own being unreliable? He would return mine afterwards, he said. A heroic remark, and as I helped him strap on my watch, probably we saw it unbuckled from his dead wrist. But then it is impossible to speak the most commonplace word or make the most ordinary gesture without it acquiring the heavy over-emphasis of melodrama.

Peter was shot and left in no-man's-land, as was done, until he was dead or it was safe for the stretcher crews to rescue him. Joe could do nothing but wait. He later lay wounded in similar circumstances.

Peter eventually made his way back to the trench and returned home with his injuries, where he reported that Joe had "behaved splendidly." Some months later, Joe was taken prisoner of war. Peter's fate and the war's end coincide: "Just before the end of hostilities, as he was filling his pipe in the trenches and turning round to hail a friend, a whizz bang decapitated him. My father, I am told, was profoundly shaken by a grief he was too proud to share. Soon afterwards the stupid war ended and I was repatriated."

Much of the memoir is devoted to Joe's failure to reach a "nearer understanding" with his father, an understanding fuller than what was guessed at or silently understood about Joe's sexuality, which took the path of sex in a search for love, framed as the "Ideal Friend," in which hundreds of men, in his own words, passed through his hands.

Of the secret marriage and the "discovery of [his] father's duplicity," Joe wrote, "My relationship with my father in ruins; I had known nothing about him at all." Why had he learned, unlike some of his father's friends, of this other family only after his father died? That question "vaguely teased and discomfited," and though it was not the only reason for "this examining and self-examining book"—as a writer, he knew that he had "a good story to tell"— yet it strikes as the driving and uniting reason. His father's secret family was another piece of the puzzle of the secret life of love and sex never talked about between father and son. The man who "shot him into life" had done the same thing for other children with a woman not his mother. And died, if there was even the slightest need for another irony, of syphilis.

Of his father, Joe said, "His general physical effect . . . may be described by such words as 'impressive,' authoritative,' 'commanding,' but in fact, at any rate in domestic life, he exerted little authority and did not command." And so for all his father's urbanity and sway, Joe concluded "that this massive and commanding appearance really sheltered a timid, unassertive, tolerant spirit, rather child-like and secretive, often obstinate, but diffident rather than self-confident, one who preferred to stand outside of life and observe it."

Joe tells much about his own sexual life, the intrusions of physiology that began with bed-wetting and ended with incontinence, and finally says he was "impenetrable," which inferentially incorporated both the physical and psychological. For him, the road to love through sex became just the road to a "baffled sex life." And his forthrightness about that is seen in the couplings he describes and in quotations from friends and lovers who call his uncaring feelings into account.

Ackerley never speaks of his life at the BBC, his extraordinary success as the literary editor of the *Listener,* and the great admiration, gratitude, and friendship that he won from so many writers of eminence and promise.

That Ackerley chose *My Father and Myself* as the place to detail his homosexual life and practices, his adventures, preferences, and frustrations, his crossing of social lines, tied him to his father and his father's life in the matter of intimacy, appetite, and physicality, of wanting and being wanted, of loving and being loved. He alludes to his dog in the search for an "Ideal Friend," the subject of his book *My Dog Tulip.* Another dog is an essential element in his novel *We Think the World of You,* about a homosexual love affair in which one of the men is married and in jail. Both books testify to fulfillment from a quarter beyond human affection, loyalty, or companionship.

My Father and Myself prompts and presses the question of what was unfulfilled between father and son. Each lived so much in the shadows that the unresolved answer became the most enduring legacy of the relationship. Peter Parker's biography of Ackerley makes clear how brilliantly he kept his focus on the shape and consequence of the father-son relationship, holding back on matters such as his fraught relationship with his sister, and the fullness of his literary friendships and life at the BBC, all of which would have made for the broadest prism of an autobiography. Ackerley knew just where he wanted to shine the light. Parker quotes the British novelist Ivy Compton-Burnett, an Ackerley admirer, as having said the book should have been titled "Myself and My Father."

The contrasts between Gosse and Ackerley are sharp—an omnipresent, omniscient, authoritative father, an insistent presence, all too much there, set against a mysterious, laissez-faire, secretive, and deceased father. One father living too much in his son's life; the other kindly, detached. One relationship with bonds that had to broken; the other ruled by the wish that the bonds had been stronger. Both sons wanted their father's love and approval; Gosse took his chance, Ackerley missed his.

Father and Son and *My Father and Myself* meet the literary scholar A. O. J. Cockshut's test for the greatest autobiographies: "They are controlled by a leading idea, a pattern strong in its simplicity, but endlessly hospitable in receiving detail. At the same time, subjects and objects, the voice of the writer and the person described are experienced by the reader as a living unity." They are likewise distinguished by the dignity and honesty of their art and by the selves they open to us.

Spring Semester 2013

Andrew and Brian Urquhart, c. 1924. Painting by Murray Urquhart.

14

Father

BRIAN URQUHART

My father was single-minded to a fault. Painting took absolute priority in his life, and his wife and children—not to mention national events and international disasters—were all secondary. He painted during daylight hours wherever he happened to be. What he did for money remained a mystery, except that we evidently had very little of it and lived in a primitive farm cottage without electricity or running water. For my first five years, my father was a distant figure, but at least he was living with us.

In 1925, when I was six, my father, carrying his easel and paint box, rode away on his bicycle and never came home again. For years my mother never mentioned or explained this fact. Later on, my brother, Andrew, and I would spend ten excruciating days each year staying with our father in gloomy rooming houses on the outskirts of London. Those penitential visits were passed mostly on the top of London double-decker buses, the cheapest way of passing the time.

My father's father was the minister in Portpatrick, a small fishing village on the western coast of Scotland. He died four months before Murray, his only child, was born; Murray's mother died giving birth to him.

Murray grew up with doting spinster aunts in the beautiful city of Edinburgh, whose soft accent he retained. He was charming, handsome, talented, and, inevitably, spoiled. He went to art school in Edinburgh and lived in Paris for two years. He loved the French

Impressionists, and they were as far as my father would go. He was
not drawn to Braque, Picasso, or Matisse.

My father married my mother in 1911 in Bridport, an old market
town on the south coast of Dorset. As usual, he painted from dawn
to dusk every day, and my mother, who much admired his work, often accompanied him. I have on my wall in Tyringham, Massachusetts, some of the pictures he painted in the early years of their marriage. They are lively and happy.

Their first child, Andrew, was born in April 1914, four months
before the declaration of war. The Great War presented a problem
for my father, who would do anything to avoid military service. Was
he mortally afraid of violent death? Or did he consider that painting was the only thing that he had the right and obligation to do?
In any case, his obsession was such that he hid, took a false name—
anything to escape conscription.

The four years of the war must have been a nightmare for my
mother. She finally mentioned the problem to me on 4 September
1939, the second day of the Second World War, when I had to tell
her that I had joined the army. I feared she would be angry, because
I could have continued at Oxford for another year, but the memory
of her husband's performance in the First World War remained so
intense that she was positively relieved at my becoming a soldier.

My father was convinced that he would eventually become one of
the world's preeminent painters. My mother thought this immodest, but since he didn't do anything except paint, it seemed to me a
harmless, distant daydream. There was, in fact, an abortive flicker
of public interest in his paintings in the 1970s during, surprisingly,
the Lebanese civil war, when a Lebanese friend told me that a dozen
of his pictures, bought in London, were "the sensation of Beirut."

My father was a fervent spiritualist and the close friend of innumerable ghosts. He told us of his conversations with people long
dead as if he had just met them in the street. He tended to be rather
snobbish about famous people. I remember his account of his talk
with the great eighteenth-century painter Sir Joshua Reynolds. The
houses my father stayed in buzzed with psychic phenomena, and on
one occasion he hinted at a rendezvous with the Loch Ness monster. His favorite cairn terrier, Judy, jumped onto his bed and barked
each morning until his dying day in the early 1970s, although she
had died in 1936.

After he bicycled away from us, my father married his cousin,
Muriel, who swallowed without difficulty his claims to genius. My
mother never saw him again, but still loved him and admired his
painting. My brother and I never forgave him for abandoning her.

She continued to teach until she was over eighty and also somehow managed to give us both an excellent education, to which my father did not contribute.

I was so prejudiced against my father that for many years I was also prejudiced against his painting, which was stupid. He was an outstanding watercolorist in the classic British tradition, which has always suited the English climate, countryside, and character. He produced hundreds of pictures whose freshness, spontaneity, and skill remain undiminished. With two or three brushstrokes, he could summon and retain a sunny seaside or an overcast winter day in the Scottish highlands. He was also accomplished in oils, both landscapes and portraits. He drew beautifully, instantly, and without correction. He neglected, however, to make any effort to sell his pictures.

As the years pass, it seems to me more and more miraculous that one person's particular skill may defy time and decay—at least for some generations. My father had this gift, and it was the most important thing in his life. We remember, less and less, all the rest of it.

Spring Semester 2013

A version of this lecture appeared in the *New York Review of Books*, 21 February 2013.

Ivy Compton-Burnett, New York, 1965. Photograph by Irving Penn. Copyright ©
Condé Nast.

15

Ivy Compton-Burnett

RICHARD DAVENPORT-HINES

When Alan Bennett's play *Kafka's Dick* was being translated for a German production, the playwright received a list of queries from the translator. Some of the questions were macabre: "Altar: do you mean marriage or sacrifice?" was one. "Gas oven: do you mean the gas chamber of the Nazis or the kitchen stove which is used for suicide?" was another. I hope to answer a further question posed by the translator: "Ivy Compton-Burnett: who or what was that?"[1]

Ivy Compton-Burnett was born in 1884. She was the sixth of twelve children of an eminent homeopathic physician. James Compton-Burnett, who was vehement and pugnacious in his professional life, published numerous books of medical case histories written with the verve of Sherlock Holmes stories. It is fruitful to mine his medical writings, as it is those of Dr. George Auden and Dr. Adrien Proust, for influences on their children's creative output. His first wife died while giving birth to her fifth child; twelve months later he married a patient whom he described as "one of those human high-breds who will not cave in, but, if duty calls, will go on till they drop." I take that phrase from Hilary Spurling's Compton-Burnett biography, a book of surpassing critical intelligence, which reveals, in Sybille Bedford's words, both "the writer, the ruthless, truthful, devastating explorer of the evil in human nature; and the camouflaged, stone-walling, secretive *persona,* erected to protect the maimed, tumultuous human being behind it." Ivy was the eldest child of this second marriage.[2]

The politician Tom Driberg, twenty years her junior, wrote of his Edwardian boyhood that he found English family life "an institution destructive of true affection, a nexus of possessiveness, vindictiveness and jealousy." He recalled his parents' and grandparents' generations as "great haters" whose "hatred was concentrated most intensely within the family." Driberg's contemporary George Orwell similarly recalled his pre-1914 childhood: "Life was hierarchical and whatever happened was right. There were the strong, who deserved to win and always did win, and there were the weak, who deserved to lose and always did lose, everlastingly." This is the tale that Spurling's exceptional biography reconstructs and that Compton-Burnett's novels retell in parabolic versions.[3]

Ivy had an intense, conspiratorial, protective intimacy with her brother Guy, who was born soon after her first birthday. Following Guy's death in 1905, his place was taken by their brother Noel, who was later elected as a Fellow of King's College, Cambridge. Noel was killed at the Battle of the Somme in 1916 during an attack in which six hundred yards of ground were gained at the cost of nine thousand British casualties—according to that day's dispatch in *The Times,* "as brilliant a success as British arms have ever obtained." Passionate complicity and rapier-like intuition between siblings—indeed, possessive love and exclusive trust that devalue other relationships—are conspicuous in Compton-Burnett novels. Fraternal treachery or sisterly unkindness is rare. In *The Mighty and Their Fall,* a man in his twenties says he would not exist without his sister: "I get my reality from her, and always shall."

Compton-Burnett's upbringing provided several minor keys in her novels. As a child of seven, she was told by her governess about Darwinian evolution. From girlhood she always disliked Christianity for its emphasis on atonement. The underservants in her parents' home were called "squalors." The survival of the emotionally fittest, the godlessness of her protagonists, and the social segregation of their households provide recurrent themes in her fiction. Family prayers are occasions of irony, especially when the patriarch gives thanks for "the great unbreakable bond of family love." The village parson in *Men and Wives* is a cipher who chose a career in the church "because of its affinity to the stage in affording scope for dramatic gifts." Oscar Jekyll, in *A House and Its Head,* is the only intelligent Compton-Burnett clergyman; and he has lost his faith. The most religious scene in her novels is an act of pagan worship in *Elders and Betters* by two children after their mother has taken poison.

A prolonged family trauma, with a catastrophic climax, inspired her novels' emotional cannibalism. After Dr. Compton-Burnett's death in 1901, his widow wrapped herself in grieving anger and subjected her children to peevish tyranny. She practiced emotional espionage on them, smote them with tirades of rage, made life miserable and monotonous, and inflicted ceaseless verbal laceration. It was like *Who's Afraid of Virginia Woolf?* in the accents of repressed English provincial gentility. This regime persisted after Mrs. Compton-Burnett's death in 1911, for Ivy took control of her younger siblings and enforced a harsh autocracy learned from her mother. Young families, according to her character Agatha Calkin (an eldest sister who partly represents her), are "the most complex, the most significant, the most deep-rooted [things] in the world." On Christmas Day 1917, Ivy's two youngest sisters, twenty-two-year-old "Topsy" and eighteen-year-old "Baby," for whom family life seethed with aggression, nerve storms, and spite, locked themselves in a bedroom and died in each other's arms of overdoses of barbiturates. Their corpses were not found for several days. "Too much music in their lives," Ivy said in explanation of their suicides. Another brother later killed himself by leaping off a bridge. None of the eight Compton-Burnett sisters married; although two of their brothers did, neither had children to perpetuate the dynastic misery.

By November 1918, Compton-Burnett had lost everyone she had loved or needed. She had been riven with grief, had stumbled near the edge of insanity, and knew better than to waste the experience. "It is better to be drunk with loss and to beat the ground, than to let the deeper things gradually escape," she wrote at the end of her life. Fortitude was prized by her—ruthlessness too. By the time that she started writing, in the 1920s, she had developed her credo: "Life makes great demands on people's characters, and gives them, and especially used to give them, great opportunities to serve their own ends by the sacrifice of other people. Such ill-doing may meet with little retribution, may indeed be hardly recognised." The literary convention of guilty people's requital seemed nonsense to her: "The evidence tends to show that crime on the whole pays." She upheld intelligence as the highest virtue and doubted that true kindness was possible without it. Moreover, the need in people to be shown kindness precluded their getting it.[4]

By the early 1920s, Compton-Burnett was seeing almost no one connected with her past. For thirty years she shared her home with an expert on Regency furniture, Margaret Jourdain, until Miss Jourdain's death in 1951. They settled in 1934 in Braemar Mansions in a cream-stuccoed Kensington square called Cornwall Gardens. The uncompromising individuality of their life together, which it would trivialize to call eccentricity, was a source of amazement in their day. Visitors, including Francis King, James Lees-Milne, and Elizabeth Taylor, have left vivid accounts of their environment, hospitality, and conversation. King described her acolyte-guests as the "Ivy League": the novelists included Sybille Bedford, Rosamond Lehmann, Rose Macaulay, Olivia Manning, and Elizabeth Taylor; the literati, Robert Liddell, Raymond Mortimer, James Pope-Hennessy, and Edward Sackville-West. Compton-Burnett received the female equivalent of a knighthood, becoming Dame Ivy Compton-Burnett, at the recommendation of the Wilson government, in 1967 (two years before her death). The proposal to award a doctorate at Oxford was quashed by the mercenary university council, which demanded, "What has she given to the building fund?"[5]

Compton-Burnett liked women who were glamorous, well traveled, and worldly. She delighted in the company of Madge Garland, the chic lesbian professor of fashion at the Royal College of Art and former fashion editor at *Vogue.* She did not value he-men—the sort who, when carving meat, as someone says of the matricide in *Men and Wives,* "hacks the joint as if he were cutting a quarry in a cliff." One of her male favorites was the actor Ernest Thesiger, who, after war was declared in 1914, fancied himself in a kilt and applied to join a Highland regiment; but since the flamboyant Scotch accent that he assumed for the occasion proved ludicrous, he spent the war years teaching embroidery to disabled ex-servicemen. Thesiger inspired the character of feckless Mortimer Lamb, in her own favorite of her novels, *Manservant and Maidservant* (Mortimer's intrigue with his cousin's wife, was, however, against Thesiger's nature). Herman Schrijver, a Dutch-born interior decorator, was the most enduring of her male friendships. It can be objected that the alpha males in her books are not convincing: Duncan Edgeworth in *A House and Its Head* is highly sexed and meant to be dominantly masculine, but proves feline and manipulative; the bullying patriarch Miles Mowbray in *A Father and His Fate* declares of his formidable sister-in-law, "I daresay that to give a woman her head is the true manliness."

None of the Ivy League doubted that Compton-Burnett could pierce the inmost recesses of their motives, as she did her own, or that she found there impulses that were unworthy and even evil. They were equally sure that she felt neither shock nor indignation. When, as a late-middle-aged spinster, she received obscene telephone calls from strange men, she did not slam down the receiver, but listened with relish as she heard four-letter words spoken for the

first time. The notion that to understand everything about someone's motives makes one more forgiving seemed to her an inversion
of the truth: in order to be charitable, it is best to know as little as
possible about other people's inward character. Like Dulcia Bode in
A House and Its Head, she assessed people by what she knew of herself:
"It is the only sure method of judging them." Self-knowledge brings
self-obsession and selfishness in its train, she felt. To be true to oneself entails falsity to others; one's authentic inner nature should be
warded off like a scheming, needy, poor cousin. Compton-Burnett
doubted that one can know oneself without fright. "Oh, must we be
quite so honest with ourselves?" asks a character in *Elders and Betters.* "We do not know how to avoid it," comes the reply. "That is why
there is horror in every heart, and a resolve never to be honest with
anyone else."

Her Kensington flat, with its linoleum floors, startled visitors by
its starkness. They were received in a high-ceilinged drawing room,
with chairs lining its apple-green walls, which were hung with mirrors rather than pictures. The oyster-colored dining room seemed
even drearier, its narrow window opening onto the mansion block's
inner well, which sunbeams never reached. Compton-Burnett liked
chilly bedrooms but warm beds. Her famous Edwardian nursery
teas were served on a pretty Coalport tea set decorated with tiny
flowers, and comprised bread and butter, scones, honey, homemade
jam, lettuce, radishes, potted shrimp, fish and meat pastes, homemade gingerbread, chocolate cake, fruit cake, Madeira cake, walnut
cake, and weak Earl Grey tea. At her first meeting with T. S. Eliot,
they talked only of food. She had an immoderate love of expensive
chocolates. There were abundant fresh flowers in her reception
rooms. She lavished attention, but not money, on a north-facing
balcony where she grew plants from seeds and occasionally planted
petunias from Woolworths. She plied her watering can across her
balcony wearing a sou'wester, as if she were a trawlerman embarking
into the North Sea during winter storms.

In 1957, Maurice Cranston was asked by Maurice Nadeau of *Les
Lettres Nouvelles* to compile an essay on Compton-Burnett. "I was
asked to tea, and very kindly received," he recorded.

> As we sat down, she smiled at the grate—for it was a cold day—
> and said, looking at three small bits of coke glowing there: "I do
> like a good fire, don't you?" I brought up the names of Thackeray
> and Jane Austen and rather unwisely, as it turned out, Pamela
> Hansford Johnson ("I believe they live not far from here?" Ivy said
> coldly, and disapprovingly).

She ushered him toward a colossal nursery tea arrayed on the dining table.

> "Will you have beef dripping?" Ivy said. I said No, I'd rather have
> an Arrowroot biscuit. Then I said: "You have a nice big dining-
> room." Ivy said: "All the rooms are big, except the maid's room.
> That's small and very dark. Not fit to live in. A horrid room.
> Miss Jourdain had it for thirty years."[6]

Compton-Burnett loved hearing scandal. Her large, slashing handwriting resembled, according to Cranston, that of either a prison
warden or a murderer.

The novelist June Braybrooke described meeting Compton-
Burnett at the Hampstead home of the writers Kay Dick and Kathleen Farrell in 1959.

> She is an odd old thing, but very sharp and entertaining, isn't she?
> When she was leaving she called a cab that she had intended to
> take as far as Swiss Cottage and then pick up the 31 [bus]. Sud-
> denly she approached the driver, and: "My man, how much would
> it be for you to drive me to Kensington?" she asked, "*You* must
> have some idea." In the end she risked it.[7]

Compton-Burnett belonged to the generation that thought the most
shocking of class sins was to touch capital for living expenses or
personal comforts. Her novels are a reminder that until the 1960s,
scarcity, not abundance, was the common European experience.
Characters are kept on short rations, emotionally and materially.
Frustration, not satisfaction, provides the keynote of existence. One
of her stingy women waters down the children's marmalade to make
it go further.

COMPTON-BURNETT'S GRUDGE AGAINST real life, she said, was that
it did not have any plot. She planned the details of her books while
pacing in Kensington Palace Gardens. She would mutter a sentence
or two aloud over and again, balancing syllables, varying a word or
shifting a stress as she tried to perfect her trenchant dialogue. She
juggled with phrases like a logician. Her strafing of fellow writers
showed the priority she gave to disciplined structure and precise vocabulary. "The poor dear," she said of Pamela Hansford Johnson,
"writes so much and thinks so little that one fears that words have
lost all meaning for her." "I do wish," she said of Iris Murdoch, "that
she had not got involved in philosophy. If she had studied domestic
science, or trained to be a Norland nurse, I'm sure her books would
have been much better." Similarly, "Poor Olivia [Manning] has no

idea of building. The materials are good, but they're all over the place, just all over the place."[8]

Apart from pre-war juvenilia, Compton-Burnett published her first novel, *Pastors and Masters,* at the age of forty-one, in 1925, and her second, *Brothers and Sisters,* in 1929. Thereafter, with a blip at the height of the world war, she published a new novel every two years between 1929 and 1963. "She produces Compton-Burnetts as someone might produce ball bearings," said Mary McCarthy, or "Dickens produced Dickenses." Her method after finishing one book was to spend a fallow year revitalizing her imagination before starting another. Altogether she wrote nineteen novels about the atrocities of English upper-class domesticity. They are like no one else's books, although her themes of incest, usurpation, burnt wills, purloined letters, impersonation, spurious paternities, elopements, jilting, suicide, parricide, matricide, and infanticide are reminiscent of the bigamy, false identities, disappearances, arson, and murder of Mary-Elizabeth Braddon's *Lady Audley's Secret* and similar Victorian melodramas. As Elizabeth Bowen noted in 1944, Compton-Burnett created savage evocations of the disrespect for other people that underlay Victorian manners. Maurice Cranston, after questioning her, suspected that "she herself does not always understand what she is writing: she is conscious enough of the logical positivist foreground, but not, I fancy, of that violent melodramatic background."[9]

Most fiction writers suffer from the hardship of having nothing new to say; the craftiest of them, like Compton-Burnett or Alice Munro, do not try. They revisit the same households, landscapes, and emotions, finding new twists every time. Each Compton-Burnett novel after *Pastors and Masters* has a stylized late Victorian or Edwardian setting—but without a jot of nostalgia. There are railways and telegrams, but no motorcars; only once a telephone; and only once a gas fire, which is used by a sweet, loving daughter to asphyxiate her stepmother's illegitimate little son.

Compton-Burnett's sentences describing people's appearances are as terse as her father's patient notes, and just as pathologically acute. The descriptions are so lean and stiff that one can miss how informative they are. In real life, she had such poor eyesight that in railway termini she could not see from which end trains would leave platforms. Accordingly, she anticipated Henry Green in eliminating descriptive elements from her novels. Her protagonists inhabit featureless manor houses in smudged landscapes. They have inquisitive neighbors but no other visitors. The Gavestons in *A Family and a Fortune* (1939) "see no-one and go nowhere." Unlike other country gentry, her families never sit in a rose garden, attend the races, hold picnics, play cards or sports, perform charades, visit the London theatre, or repulse the overtures of new-money social climbers. No one does any work—not even the governesses. There are no pets until two cats appear in her late novel *Mother and Son*. Lust abounds, but there are few romantic kisses.

Compton-Burnett was no more interested in writing plausible novels than was Ronald Firbank. Her novels, like his, are chiefly in dialogue; they are conversation pieces comprising squabbles, rebukes, accusations, snubs, confessions, denials, and protests. To begin to read her is like learning a new language. The dialect can be mastered after the first bewildering dozen pages, but baffling snares remain. Quotation marks, which other novelists use to indicate speech by a character, do not, in Compton-Burnett novels, differentiate dialogue from internal soliloquy. Sometimes it is impossible to know which voice is speaking in a group discussion. Bernard Berenson said that if Giacometti's spindly sculptures could talk, their words would be like Compton-Burnett characters.

Compton-Burnett's introverted households resemble torture chambers. Several generations of a large family are twisted on the rack by an arbitrary, spoiled, brutal, sardonic despot. This tyrant upbraids, decries, and chastises in an amplified harangue. There is whispered defiance, subversive mimicry, and lethal eavesdropping among the despot's subjugated victims. The escalating talk is crisp, mordant, stinging, and corrosive. The servants in her novels stand in stilted postures, bearing salvers and uttering remarks like people testifying from the witness box in murder trials.

Francis King wrote that Compton-Burnett's novels were perfect to take on holiday when one does not want to pack many books. They have to be read slowly, with lynx-like vigilance. Skip a few lines, as every reader is tempted to, and one can miss a death (murders are as important in her fiction as marriages are in Jane Austen's). Incest is the theme that she can never leave alone: her handling of it has a haughty magnificence. Her novels brim with sexual predators, adulterous sneaks, and illicit passions. Wickedness is often detected but never punished. Her characters are recklessly frank in their admissions about themselves. Toadies, parasites, and hypocrites flourish. Mistrustful people invite their own betrayal.

In the first four novels, Compton-Burnett was still trying to settle her form. *Pastors and Masters* (1925) is the sole book with a contemporary setting: Cambridge in the 1920s. It opens in a boys' school run by Merry, an ill-educated, vindictive, self-pitying scold, but owned by a lazy, pretentious old charmer called Herrick. Merry and his wife, with Herrick and his half sister, are frequented by two aging dons, Masson and Bumpus, who long ago were lovers. The calm acceptance of homosexuality as integral to cultivated society is more effective for being understated. The standard Compton-Burnett theme of usurpation emerges when, sorting the papers of a dead scholar, Herrick purloins a manuscript, which he claims as his own and announces his intention of publishing. The book, though, is a piece of bright juvenilia by Bumpus, who thought he had buried the only surviving version in the coffin of a lover. Herrick proves impervious when his imposture is revealed. Despite passages of acerbic dialogue and attitudes that seem discomforting, *Pastors and Masters* is a gentle picture of the competitive vanities, comfy insularity, and erudite flippancy of a university town.

The next novel, *Brothers and Sisters,* which took four years to compose, is the most personal. Compton-Burnett imbued its protagonists with bits of her family history: a surname, personal traits, a cancer-stricken mother's creeping death, and morbid, suffocating grief. She reworked incidents, situations, and atmospheres from her girlhood, and reimagined the loving, protective trust that she experienced with her brothers, magnifying it by artistic expression until it assumed greater meaning. Apart from the central incestuous pair in *Brothers and Sisters,* there are five other brother-sister sets, all living in the same district, all in their twenties, who are so attracted to each other that they contemplate or attempt marriage. The novel begins with an archetypal Compton-Burnett sentence, hard, proud, aggressive, and exact: "Andrew Stace was accustomed to say, that no man had ever despised him, and no man had ever broken him in." Thereafter, *Brothers and Sisters* is fraught with menace and significance. Reviewers compared the originality of its prose to Hemingway's and Faulkner's. It inspired Somerset Maugham's play about a waspish patriarch's frustrated family, *For Services Rendered* (1932).

Love, or possessive passion, drives many of Compton-Burnett's protagonists to commit crimes or acts of turpitude in order to shield or benefit an adored sibling. In her third novel, *Men and Wives* (1931), Lady Haslam is a self-obsessed, querulous, and exasperating neurasthenic who confuses her imploring ambitions for her children with religious zeal. After surviving a suicide attempt, she is sent to an asylum, returns cured, tries to reassert her former dominion, and makes life so intolerable that her son poisons her. Family hatred makes him kill; love makes his siblings shield him; resentful rages are appeased.

The central protagonist of *More Women than Men* (1933) is Josephine Napier, headmistress of a girls' school, who treats her staff with silky consideration. She is fiercely possessive of her nephew Gabriel Swift, whom she has adopted and whose young bride she kills by cruel medical neglect. Mrs. Napier's brother Jonathan Swift has lived for twenty years with Felix Bacon (drawing master at the school), a younger man. Bacon brings to mind Saki's Clovis Bassington when he declares: "It is little, unnatural corners of the world that appeal to me. I am very over-civilised." This bold novel is notable for its depictions of these men's relationship and breakup, for the suppressed yearnings among the spinster schoolmistresses, and for its resolution, in which Josephine Napier becomes the business and sexual partner of a woman who witnessed the bride's manslaughter (and who is revealed to be Gabriel Swift's supposedly dead mother).

Party politics did not interest Compton-Burnett, although she upheld the social taboos of her class. She scrutinized despotism, atrocity, violence, and corruption without a tinge of political conscience. She had been oppressed by her mother. She knew herself to be the tyrant who had hounded two younger sisters to death. She had no truck with people who spoke of subconscious and unconscious motives. From the depths of her excoriating self-knowledge, and the range of her piercing observation, she decided that oppressors know exactly what cruelties they are perpetrating—despite their pretenses otherwise.

Like Driberg, Compton-Burnett thought the Victorians and Edwardians had been relentless in their disrespect for others, but that their descendants were less hate ridden and bullying. Thwarted ambition was a crippling, malicious force in her universe. She knew the damage wreaked by forceful people with no outlet for their energies. "Imagine," she said while a fugitive from the German wartime bombing of London, "a Winston Churchill, untaught and untrained . . . and then immured in an isolated life in a narrow community, and think what might have happened to his power."[10] The viperish Matilda Seaton, who, despite being a poor relation, tyrannizes the Gavestons in *A Family and a Fortune,* and Anna Donne, the avaricious conspirator in *Elders and Betters,* are power-hungry Churchills locked in provincial oubliettes. Anna Donne's verbal dueling is one of the most perfectly controlled melodramas written for a novel rather than the theatre.

Privation and cheated hopes unite Compton-Burnett characters. Longevity in her world is iniquitous. "I have been kept out of my inheritance too long," says Dudley Gaveston when, on the brink of old age, he inherits £50,000 from his ninety-six-year-old godfather. Compton-Burnett specializes in protracted, quavering deathbed scenes that often end in sudden recovery—to the chagrin of deathbed attendants. The lost or stolen testamentary wills in successive novels symbolize the enslaving human will that plots to control people even after death. Simon Challenor in *A Heritage and Its History* expresses the frustrations of an heir presumptive who is unduly set on a property that fixes his social place and the meaning of life: "I have no personal scope. My youth is escaping without giving me anything it owes me. I see it shortening before my eyes. And Uncle must leave everything to Father, before I even become the heir. It throws my life into an indefinite future . . . I am held back in everything." Simon mortifies his family and warps their outlook because of his bitter avidity. His wife says of his eventual inheritance: "It is too late. For his family, if not for him. It might not be, if he . . . had not wreaked on helpless creatures in his power the frustration he had brought on himself."

Some readers protest that Compton-Burnett's novels are absurd or "unreal." In fact, she wrote in parables intended to show truths about the worst human desires and animosities, which are impossible to put into plain language. One of her scenes of conflict (in *A Father and His Fate*) depicts the jockeying for place at the family's tea table; it may seem petty to some readers, but to others it makes sense of the power struggles in Hitler's bunker or Stalin's Kremlin. Angus Wilson said that in the epoch of Nazi and Soviet camps, "no writer did more to illumine the springs of human cruelty, suffering and bravery . . . She contrived to be the most penetrating critic of the darkness and light of her own time."[11] Compton-Burnett realized, like Rochefoucauld, that some evil traits engender great talents. She might have said, with him, that the surest promise of virtue is to be born without envy. Envy in her world outlived the good fortune of the envied. She divined the baffled misery of people caught in the clutches of egotists who have the power to satisfy their victims' hopes but prefer to frustrate them. Despite their repartee, her characters resemble chained circus beasts flailed by the lash of a pitiless ringmaster.

The books are filled with thoughts of self-murder. In *Manservant and Maidservant* (1947), the bullied brothers Marcus and Jasper Lamb do not stop their father Horace when he walks to a bridge that has been dangerously undermined. He survives, and returns to berate them for sending him to possible death. "We are afraid of you. You know we are," replies Marcus. "Nothing can alter it. You did not let us have anything; you would not let us be ourselves. If it had not been for Mother, we would rather have been dead. It was feeling like that so often, that made us think dying an ordinary thing. We had often wished to die ourselves." Elton Scrope in *The Present and the Past* (1953) reflects on life: "It is longer than anyone can realize. And it is very brave to end it. To say it is cowardly is absurd. It is only said by people who would not dare to do it."

The retorts that fifteen-year-old Aubrey Gaveston exchanges with eighty-seven-year-old Oliver Seaton in *A Family and a Fortune* are of such intensity and chill irony as to seem fantastic. Yet when the novel was published, Desmond Shawe-Taylor hailed Aubrey's characterization as "the triumph of the book . . . the little boy at once precocious and backward, alternately petted, patronised, and spurned by the family; a wizened, sensitive and unhappy creature with no defence but his sharp tongue."[12] It shows the brilliance of Compton-Burnett that such unreal dialogue can make the reader flinch with anguished recognition.

After her success with Aubrey Gaveston, Compton-Burnett began to depict observant, apprehensive, rueful children. The small brothers James and Nevill Sullivan in *Parents and Children* (1941) were described by Elizabeth Bowen as creations of imaginative genius— inviolable because they are united together in emotional isolation from those around them.[13] Next, in *Elders and Betters* (1944), there is thirteen-year-old Reuben Donne, "with coltish, uncontrolled movements, a lively nervous face, defensive, dark eyes that were sadder than his feelings warranted, and a definite lameness resulting from an early accident." Knowing, wounded children are the only protagonists whom Compton-Burnett treats with tenderness. Eleven-year-old Guy Clare in *The Present and the Past* remarks, "My life was over when I was four."

The Present and the Past (published in 1953, when Compton-Burnett was seventy) depicts a family crisis caused by the reappearance, after nine years' absence, of Guy's mother. She forms a ruthless alliance with her successor, the stepmother; their weak, silly husband, after a feeble suicidal gesture, dies. It is a rich story, told with captivating suspense and peculiar insight. Despite the nontopical milieu of her work, Compton-Burnett remained during the 1950s (like Terence Rattigan and Henry Green) more shocking than the unsubtle noise raised by the Angry Young Men.

The tautness of Compton-Burnett's prose did not slacken in old age. Death, the craving for fairness under autocracy, stealthy emotional resilience, and a Darwinian sense of natural selection remained her priorities. Compton-Burnett's most grievous victims belong in a category that other novelists seldom notice: the self-doubting late middle-aged, demoralized by their material dependence and emotional subordination to greedy, selfish, cheating parents. Perhaps the most mordant case occurs in *Mother and Son*

(1955). Its matriarch, Miranda Hume, maintains her superlative tyranny, inhibits her victims, and despoils their lives, even after death. She illustrates a truth that is conspicuous in Compton-Burnett's novels, a truth from which good people shrink and about which the rest of us feel shifty: that it may be possible to feel complete in one's life only when both of one's parents are dead, and sometimes not even then.

IN 1939, AFTER COMPARING Compton-Burnett to Kafka, the *TLS* reviewer of *A Family and a Fortune* called her the "living novelist of whom the vanguard of the elect has begun to speak with ecstatic breath."[14] She was a literary influence on writers as varied as Alan Bennett and Evelyn Waugh, and was likened by Noël Coward to Harold Pinter.[15] Her books reached the acme of their significance during the Second World War, for her preoccupations were the intimidation and crushing of the weak by totalitarian powers, and the regimes of daily fear and destruction. Elizabeth Bowen declared in 1941, at the height of the Nazi bombing of London, that "to read in these days a page of Compton-Burnett dialogue is to think of the sound of glass being swept up, one of these mornings after a blitz."[16] By 1944, Muriel Spark had such admiration for Compton-Burnett that she took a copy of *Elders and Betters* to a job interview, where she enthused about the book as a surrealist treatment of the stark doom of ancient Greek dramatists—a remark that seemed so intelligent to her interviewer that she was recruited to the Black Propaganda, or psychological warfare, department of MI6.[17]

Mary McCarthy, who once lunched with Compton-Burnett and Sonia Orwell at the Ritz, wrote the finest essay of all about her (in 1966) and here has the last word. "What flashes out of her work," declared McCarthy, "is a spirited, unpardoning sense of justice, which becomes even sharper in her later books. In her own eccentric way, Compton-Burnett is a radical thinker, one of the rare modern heretics. It is the eccentricity that has diverted attention from the fact that these small volumes are subversive packets."[18]

Fall Semester 2012

1. Alan Bennett, *Writing Home* (London, 1994), p. 158.

2. Hilary Spurling, *Ivy* (New York, 1984), p. 18; Sybille Bedford, "Ivy: An English Secret," *Guardian,* 7 June 1984.

3. Tom Driberg (Lord Bradwell), *Ruling Passions* (London, 1977), p. 29; George Orwell, "Such, Such Were the Joys," quoted in Julian Barnes, *Through the Window* (New York, 2012), p. 29.

4. Spurling, *Ivy,* p. 543; Charles Burkhart, *The Art of I. Compton-Burnett* (London, 1972), pp. 30, 42.

5. Evelyn Waugh, *The Letters of Evelyn Waugh,* ed. Mark Amory (London, 1980), p. 583.

6. Maurice Cranston to Francis King, 12 Nov. 1957, Francis King Papers (additions 1947–88), box 2, folder 4, Humanities Research Center, Austin, Texas (hereafter cited as Francis King Papers).

7. June Braybrooke to Francis King, 7 Dec. 1959, Francis King Papers, box 1, folder 4.

8. Quoted in Francis King, *Yesterday Came Suddenly* (London, 1993), p. 227.

9. Mary McCarthy, *The Writing on the Wall* (New York, 1970), p. 113; Cranston to King, 12 Nov. 1957.

10. Quoted in Burkhart, *Compton-Burnett,* pp. 28–29.

11. Angus Wilson, "Ivy Compton-Burnett," *Observer,* 31 Aug. 1969; Burkhart, *Compton-Burnett,* p. 192.

12. Desmond Shawe-Taylor, "Chateau Bornett 1939," *Spectator,* 4 Mar. 1939, p. 332.

13. Elizabeth Bowen, *Collected Impressions* (New York, 1950), p. 84.

14. Richard D. Charques, "Family Dialogue," *Times Literary Supplement,* 4 Mar. 1939, p. 133; Rosamond Lehmann, "There's Nothing Like It", *Spectator,* 19 Mar. 1937, p. 525; Barbara Pym, *A Very Private Eye* (London, 1984), p. 100.

15. Evelyn Waugh, *Scoop* (London, 1938), p. 238; Noël Coward, *The Letters of Noël Coward,* ed. Barry Day (New York, 2007), p. 243.

16. Elizabeth Sprigge, *The Life of Ivy Compton-Burnett* (New York, 1973), p. 104.

17. Muriel Spark, *Curriculum Vitae* (London, 1992), pp. 145–7.

18. McCarthy, *Writing on the Wall,* p. 143.

Dan Jacobson, 2013. Photograph © Jeremy Sutton-Hibbert.

16

Dan Jacobson

GEOFFREY V. DAVIS

I do know that everything I write has something more than its origins there.

Dan Jacobson on South Africa

Few writers exemplify the life of the successful expatriate quite as well as Dan Jacobson. While still a young man, he left his native South Africa in 1954 to pursue in England the kind of literary career that he felt would not be open to him at home. Since then he has, as fiction writer and essayist, literary critic and travel writer, autobiographer and academic, produced a body of work of impressive range and absorbing interest. Jacobson has become a novelist of real stature; working initially in the naturalistic tradition, he later turned to more experimental styles, constantly developing innovative narrative possibilities and exploring unexpected themes, ever presenting his readers with works that represented startling departures from his previous literary works.

Born in Kimberley in the Northern Cape, a place to which he retains a strong sense of attachment, Jacobson has family origins that lie in eastern Europe, a heritage he shares with South African writers such as Nadine Gordimer and Gillian Slovo. Many of his novels, essays, and autobiographical writings are thus informed not only by his identity as a South African, but also by a history of migration and, more recently, by a quest for his European roots. Although a secular Jew, Jacobson has repeatedly engaged with biblical themes, the Jewish diaspora, and the nature of religious faith.

In spite of the intellectual and literary challenges his writings pose, Jacobson's work has attracted the attention of regrettably few scholars. The late Sheila Roberts, herself a South African expatriate writer and academic, published an appreciative early monograph and followed it with a series of critical articles, proving herself to be the most consistent advocate of his work. This lecture seeks to contribute to a rediscovery of Jacobson's work.

One of the most moving moments in *Heshel's Kingdom* (1998), Jacobson's memoir of a journey to Lithuania, occurs when, with some trepidation, he finally arrives in the small town of Varniai, where his grandfather had been rabbi and his mother was born. When he meets a retired mathematics teacher, described to him as "the last Jew in Varniai," she inquires where he has come from. "For some reason," he writes, "I did not answer 'England,' as I had said to people everywhere else. South Africa, I said, *Dorem Afrika*. She repeated the two words doubtfully, as if not believing me. '*Dorem Afrika?* Then: '*F'n welche dorf?* From what town? Before I could answer, she asked, even more doubtfully, 'Kimberley?'" Jacobson, who turns out to be the first South African ever to visit the place, is understandably dumbfounded when she names what he remembers as that "small, lost, mythical town on the other side of the globe . . . which . . . I had grown up in."[1]

It is an almost epiphanic moment, that self-identification as a South African, for by the time he went to Lithuania, Jacobson had been living in Britain for over forty years. He had, for a time at least, ceased to write on South African themes. Indeed, he had on occasion spoken of his "abandonment of South Africa (as a setting) in [his] fiction" because, as he put it, "I simply felt I was too far from it, I wasn't intimate enough with it."[2] Accordingly, Roberts suggested that "it would seem that since settling permanently in London in 1954, Jacobson's career as a writer has been a drive toward ridding himself of South Africa as a place from which his imagination is fed," and she had found apparent corroboration for this view in the fact that "after *The Beginners* Jacobson was no longer to use South Africa as the setting for his novels."[3] No wonder, perhaps, that Michael Wade later posed the "crucial question . . . at what point Jacobson, who has lived in England continuously since 1955, ceased being South African."[4]

While it is indeed true that Jacobson did not write major works about South Africa for some twenty years, he has neither "rid himself" of South Africa as a source of inspiration nor ceased to be South African. While in his fiction Jacobson has sometimes ventured into unexpected territory—most recently with his novel *All for Love* (2005), which deals with the history of the Habsburg Empire—

he has throughout his career retained his interest in the country of his birth.

Among the many aspects of Jacobson's work worthy of renewed attention, the most salient is the role that South Africa plays in his writing. In the persistence with which he returns to South African themes in his work, Jacobson exemplifies the expatriate who has never wholly been able to put his emotional and intellectual origins behind him and whose consciousness remains South African. South Africa is, as he formulated it in his travelogue *The Electronic Elephant* (1994), "the territory of his imagination."[5] In Jacobson's article "A Way of Seeing," in which he responded as an expatriate to a request to consider how his "connection with the country" was reflected in his literary work, he confessed that he had not been surprised to realize "that all I had to write about, for many years after leaving South Africa, was what I had seen and learned there during my childhood and early adulthood"—to which he added significantly: "What did surprise me rather more, when I began to write on other subjects, was the extent to which the very mode of seeing and understanding which made me the person I was had been determined (forever) in South Africa. . . . That is the essential point."[6]

It is worth recalling—and Jacobson occasionally reminds us of the fact—that when he began writing, little literature had been produced in South Africa. Among his comparatively few forerunners were such writers as Olive Schreiner, Roy Campbell, William Plomer, and Alan Paton. Recording his impressions on first reading Schreiner's *The Story of an African Farm,* he notes: "I had to struggle with my own incredulity that the kopjes, *kraals* and cactus plants she mentions were of the same kind as those I was familiar with; so little experience had I had of encountering them within the pages of a book," especially since most of the literature then available to him came from England.[7] The notion that the South African landscape was largely "undescribed," Jacobson expressed frequently. His early novella *The Trap* (1953)—the only work of his "with a South African setting which was written wholly in that country"—he later described as "obsessed with the forlorn and undescribed landscapes of the veld around my home town, Kimberley."[8] Reflecting on his early work years later, he recalled the sense of obligation he felt to write about South Africa, since "it was relatively little written about thirty, forty years ago, and therefore one had a responsibility to try to render its surfaces as best one could."[9] Such attention to local detail he has retained throughout his writing career.

That does not mean, however, that Jacobson's view of the country was especially positive. In his early reflections, he repeatedly and vociferously recorded his disdain for a society with so little culture to

offer, without a challenging intellectual tradition or hardly a literature to call its own. Ever conscious of the gap between what he was
able to read from abroad and the intellectually claustrophobic local
environment, he depicted the plight of the white writer as "a member of a society which has no roots in the past, or no past at all; his
present is altogether tawdry and vulgar and thin, and morally and
culturally debased, he . . . does not and cannot write for an audience
of his own people (there are simply not enough people to support
him) . . . his future is without any certainty at all."[10] This feeling of
alienation from a society without culture or history found fictional
expression in such early novels as *The Evidence of Love* (1960) and
The Beginners (1966).

It is hardly surprising that Jacobson chose to leave. Like Olive
Schreiner, he dreamed "of an escape to a larger, freer society."[11]
Achieving his ambition to become a recognized writer seemed
to him "more plausible outside South Africa than inside it."[12] He
wanted to test himself, and he "required a certain detachment to
find out what [he] could do."[13] Although usually giving his motiva-
tion as social or intellectual—or indeed purely personal, because,
as he much later recognized, he had never been happy in South Africa—he once frankly acknowledged that he left in part because after the National Party came to power, he "disliked intensely the political dispensation which had come into existence here and which
was clearly going to be immovable for a long time."[14]

Ever since childhood, England had exercised a powerful attraction on him, sometimes for reasons that later seemed decidedly
politically incorrect. "Those who lived 'under the British crown' in
those days," he wrote,

> could think of themselves as attached to a part of a political sys-
> tem that exercised world power and was held in worldwide es-
> teem . . . the crown, the coinage, the buff envelopes marked 'On
> His Majesty's Service', the playing of 'God Save the King' at the
> end of cinema performances . . . was a source of an enlarged sense
> of selfhood, even for those who could at best claim to have been
> stepchildren of the empire.[15]

On arrival in England, Jacobson recalls, the reality proved to be
rather different, as it was for so many colonial immigrants. England
was "a cold, bleak, bombed out, seedy, unpainted, half-lit place, a
country of rationing and austerity."[16] Nevertheless, he "felt liberated" by having access to a culture that he had always experienced
"at a remove" and that opened the way to a new life.[17] Jacobson has
written much on what England meant to him, perhaps nowhere

more curiously than in *The Evidence of Love,* in an authorial excursus seeking to formulate "what it means for a South African to come to England," evoking an image of England as truth and dream, reality and vision, and calling on the "voice of England" to reveal to South Africans what the country might mean for them.[18]

Jacobson became a successful expatriate. He took up an academic career and led the life of a man of letters, writing on literary topics for the *Times Literary Supplement* and the *London Review of Books.* All his major works were written in England.

IN THE YEARS FOLLOWING HIS MOVE TO ENGLAND, Jacobson calculated that most of what he had written—"quantitatively, in numbers of words"—was "set in South Africa."[19] The country, however, gradually became a place of memory. In writing *The Evidence of Love* or *The Beginners,* for instance, he relied fairly heavily on his own experience—his family's history of migration, his childhood in the small Jewish community of Kimberley, growing into adulthood in what he later termed "proto-apartheid South Africa," working on a kibbutz in Israel, living as an expatriate in London—so much so that he confessed, "I can't distinguish now what is autobiographical and what isn't . . . The edges of real life and fiction are hopelessly blurred."[20]

Stylistically, these novels are in the naturalistic tradition, as befitted their themes. It was not until the 1970s, with *The Rape of Tamar* (1970), *The Wonder Worker* (1973), and *The Confessions of Josef Baisz* (1977), that the author "jettisoned" what he felt had become "the burden of naturalism" and embarked on the kind of thematic and stylistic experimentation that became the hallmark of his work. He characterized this transition rather well: "My own feeling . . . is that I've gone round the course twice as a novelist: first as a South African writer; then, more recently, over the last seven or eight years, writing fiction which is not only *not* about South Africa, but is also a different kind of fiction from what had gone before."[21]

Although Jacobson abandoned South Africa as the locus of his fiction, his writing as a whole continued to concern itself with the country and with his own former presence there. The autobiographical *Time and Time Again* (1985), the travelogue *The Electronic Elephant: A Southern African Journey* (1994), the memoir *Heshel's Kingdom* (1998), and numerous literary and historical essays and book reviews all bear witness to his ongoing interest in South African issues.

The Evidence of Love was temporarily embargoed from being imported to South Africa, a measure that, predictably enough, led to increased sales. The book exposes the nefarious consequences of the Immorality Act, which banned sexual contact between members of different races. In addition, the novel addresses issues of identity, questions the shortcomings of liberalism, and exposes the social and psychological predicament of the dispossessed coloreds of the Cape.

Set in Lyndhurst, Jacobson's fictional name for Kimberley, the story follows Kenneth Makeer, the son of a colored workman, and Isabel Last, the daughter of a well-to-do director of a building society. Kenneth is enabled to go to boarding school and then to study at the Inns of Court in London through the generosity of a benefactress; Isabel, having rejected the claims of a wealthy suitor, moves to London, too. While working at a barely reputable language school off Oxford Street, they begin a relationship, marry, and return to South Africa, where they are arrested, charged with contravening the Immorality Act, and sentenced to prison with hard labor.

Kenneth's search for identity serves as the unifying theme of the novel and as a means of focalizing the plight of coloreds. In a complex psychological study of the effects of dispossession and humiliation, Kenneth speaks passionately of the deprivation he suffers as a colored, barred as he is from libraries, concert halls, and galleries, unable to access knowledge, and cut off from intellectual exchange. (His frustration with South Africa often echoes Jacobson's own.) Since Kenneth's light skin color would allow him to pass for white, he is caught in a moral dilemma, for to embrace such an opportunity would be tantamount to betraying his family and isolating himself from his people. This thought does not, however, later prevent him from allowing Isabel to gain the impression that he is white.

Jacobson gives an outspokenly critical account of the oppression and constant humiliation suffered by coloreds. He notes that "in the veins of Cornelius Makeer [Kenneth's father] there flowed the blood of half the nations of Europe and of a great many of the tribes of Southern Africa," indicating the futility of any attempt to segregate the races. Kenneth's family is required to live in a colored camp, which leads to their increasing impoverishment and the consequent neglect of their sons' education. And minor political activism has disproportionate consequences: when Kenneth speaks against apartheid in a school debate, sells a "radical weekly," and distributes leaflets in a township, the Special Branch places him under surveillance and intimidates his anxious father.

When the novel was written, liberalism was a fashionable political stance adopted by whites who sought to dissociate themselves from

apartheid but stopped short of actively opposing it. The book tack-
les this head on—"What makes of someone a 'liberal' in a country
like South Africa is really a great mystery," the author notes—leading a reviewer to contend: "I do not know when I have read a more
subtle analysis of all our troubles than in the description given here
of the South African liberal's mentality."[22] Jacobson traces the genesis of such a political position in the life of Isabel Last, who becomes
involved in various good causes and is asked to start a branch of the
Liberal Party, but faced with the immensity of the distress confronting her, she becomes disillusioned with charitable activity and opts
for marriage instead.

When Kenneth and Isabel return to South Africa, knowing what
lies in store for them, they transcend the limitations of liberal philosophy, choosing action over words. As the *Guardian* reviewer perceptively noted: "The moral is that only by accepting his coloured
identity, by discovering his personal truth, can he or she make any
gesture of value in Africa or elsewhere."[23] Although the novel is not
free of structural shortcomings, it still makes an impact on readers,
for it is, in the apposite phrase of A. Alvarez, very much "a drama of
the profound difficulty of being South African."[24]

Jacobson's next novel, *The Beginners,* was conceived on a much
larger scale, running to almost five hundred pages and deploying a
cast of some forty characters. A family chronicle spanning four generations and set in four countries—Lithuania, South Africa, Israel,
and England—it seeks to encompass some of the many wanderings
and migrations of the Jewish people in the first half of the twentieth
century. The novel confronts its characters with philosophical issues, religious debates, moral choices, sexual problems, and political
options. The action spans the aftermath of the Second World War
and the major social upheavals represented by the independence of
the State of Israel and the Afrikaner Nationalists coming into power
in South Africa. Autobiographically inspired, the story recalls the
migration of Jacobson's grandmother and her children from Lithuania to South Africa; mirrors his own youthful, third-generation
restlessness in the country and his years as a student in Johannesburg; draws on the nine months he spent working on a kibbutz in
Israel; and reflects his subsequent life in England. The alienation
from South Africa felt by young people in the book seems to echo
Jacobson's own frustrations with the country.

Jacobson described the theme of this novel as "discontinuity." Recalling the First World War experiences of his father's generation,
he focuses on how, in the modern world, families are divided by

war, religious belief, political conviction, and personal choices. The Glickman family endures such disruptions, as well as those brought on by migrations; members of the younger generation seek their futures in Israel or England, where they will live as expatriates. By the end of the novel, the family's South African way of life, followed through three generations, has come to an end.

This novel of diaspora focuses on the Jewish community of Johannesburg. It articulates religious and political options facing Jews in South Africa after the Second World War, particularly their attitudes to the newly established State of Israel and on apartheid. Some members of the community immigrate to England; some advocate solidarity with Israel; others seek an alternative to the Zionism through political activism in South Africa itself. The history of the Glickmans and their community plays out against the social and political history of South Africa, particularly the underlying tensions in relations between blacks and whites as well as between Afrikaners and English speakers.

Although set largely in the white community, the novel does not overlook the condition of black Africans. They function only on the margins, within the master-servant relationship, working as houseboys, maids, and waiters and living in deplorable conditions in townships like Alexandra, which most whites are afraid to visit. They are subjected to increasingly repressive legislation: a domestic servant is prevented from sleeping in a white master's house because of the Group Areas Act, the gardener is arrested under the pass laws and sent off to a farm prison. *The Beginners* remains Jacobson's most comprehensive attempt to depict the life of South Africa in fictional form.

The Confessions of Josef Baisz (1977) represents something new in Jacobson's work. An Orwellian dystopia set in a fictional country, the novel purports to be the autobiography of one Josef Baisz, a bodyguard and self-confessed admirer of the biblical Judas. His account, which reveals his crimes, was completed just before his suicide. The novel is a study of complicity, treachery, and betrayal. Jacobson claimed that he could not have written it had he not "spent twenty-five years in Europe", describing the book as in part "a fantasy of Eastern Europe."[25]

Jacobson does not regard the novel as being about South Africa, although some of his readers may disagree. One wonders whether the censors did too, since the book was briefly embargoed from being imported. Action is set in landscapes that can hardly be other than South African in inspiration; Afrikaans-derived vocabulary abounds; and personal and place-names (Bailaburg, Smidsdriff) sound South African. There are institutions such as the Magistratuur and the Old Drostdy, holidays such as Settlement Day, and a Sixteenth of December University. Aspects of the history of the fictional country of Sarmeda match that of South Africa; for example, the ancestors of the whites set out from the south, "centuries before, to conquer the northern, tramontane province."[26] Readers familiar with South African history may find such allusions amusing. One such reader was the poet C. J. Driver, like the author an expatriate in England, who summed up his own reading experience: "I cannot help reading it as an ex-South African and my first reading of the first half of the novel was punctuated with giggles and guffaws as I spotted allusion after allusion to that crazy, hideous and fabulous country of my childhood and youth."[27] His witty renaming of Jacobson's fictional Republic of Sarmeda as "South Africa-sur-Volga" could hardly be bettered.

Jacobson may not regard the novel as being about South Africa, but he acknowledged that its themes are wholly informed by his experiences there:

> When you think of doubleness and duplicity and betrayal—topics of these kinds—I'm someone who grew up in South Africa, with all the advantages of being a white man, and all his comforts and all the privileges of being a white man, and like most South Africans—however complicated their responses to the South African situation might be—I've felt at times like a collaborator . . . The feelings of self-betrayal and of making out and of morally shady circumstances that Josef Baisz has are what white South Africans have. I know them, I've felt them.[28]

That observation seems to justify regarding *The Confessions of Josef Baisz* as one of Jacobson's South African works.

WHEN JACOBSON RETURNED TO SOUTH AFRICA in 1985 to publicize his autobiographical work *Time and Time Again,* the country was in the midst of a state of emergency. The book had been criticized in England and South Africa because reviewers found that the "rather private and domestic and intimate book" did not "answer to [their] sense of the South African situation."[29] Nevertheless Jacobson defended his freedom to write about what he called the "deep memories" of his childhood. In his literary career, the book marked an important moment, since, some twenty years after *The Beginners,* he had returned to writing about the South Africa he knew. He had, he felt, found "a way of writing about South Africa" in the form of "*tales*, real stories, narratives which would provoke the reader's curiosity" and would reflect the "erratic and fitful nature of memory."[30] The volume opens with a sketch of the history of Kimberley and of his family's presence there, perhaps a personal response to the town never having been written about. His finely drawn portraits of his neighbors in the Kimberley of his childhood, of the schoolmaster who victimized him, of the Jewish immigrant who—unusually—chose to identify with the Afrikaners rather than with the English, and of a child who drowned together provide a convincing view of the kind of social environment that shaped Jacobson's consciousness.

The Electronic Elephant (1994) represents a further departure in Jacobson's writing on South Africa. He takes the reader on a rather unusual journey along what used to be known as the Great North Road, geographically and politically important for a time in Cecil Rhodes's grand scheme of an overland Cape-to-Cairo route. The road winds its way through "one of the driest, most thinly populated, and . . . scenically least attractive regions of the subcontinent," from Kimberley through the North West province, then north through Botswana to Victoria Falls in Zimbabwe. Much of it passes through country that few would wish to visit for pleasure. But Jacobson realizes that it is "littered with the wreckage of successive ideologies . . . the imperialism of the European nations . . . Boer nationalism, the Darwinian modes of Victorian racialism, once-potent notions of economic autarky, apartheid, African nationalism, Marxism." There is hardly a shortage of things to write about.

Maintaining the dual perspective of the outsider a little unsure of his relationship to his changing country, and of the insider who has never entirely broken from his past, Jacobson questions the nature of his own memories, examining the effects of "time and absence" and exploring—fifty years on—a hinterland of the imagination inhabited by his own "forgotten self," a region "half-known, half-feared . . . on the very doorstep of the Africa I had grown up in." The book is full of chance encounters and snippets of faithfully recorded dialogue, a fund of comic and curious incident, but informed by an ever-present sense of the enormous disparities between rich and poor everywhere apparent, which induce "in resident and visitor alike, a kind of vertigo, a disbelief in the evidence of their own eyes."

The Electronic Elephant is a compendium of historical research that also becomes a meditation on historiography. Jacobson delved into the records of the London Missionary Society, the letters of Mary Moffat (wife of David Livingstone), and the writings of Livingstone himself, whom he calls "the finest writer of English prose ever to have dealt with southern African scenes and themes." Jacobson has respect for the legacy of the missionaries, who were active along his route, but notes how few converts they made, a detail memorably evoked in a scene where he and his wife, attending a service at the Kuruman Moffat Mission, find themselves the only members of the congregation.

Four years later, *Heshel's Kingdom* returned to South African themes. Characterized by an intriguing dual perspective, it is at once an account of the history of Jewish immigration to South Africa and a record of the author's journey back to Lithuania in search of his eastern European roots.

Jacobson's family origins, like those of many South African Jews, lie in Lithuania. The author recounts how his grandmother came to South Africa with her nine children (one of whom was his mother), and how all of them rejected their father's beliefs and the old ways, infatuated as they became with the opportunities offered by their new country, to which they rapidly assimilated. "In leaving Lithuania for South Africa," Jacobson concludes, "they had exchanged an anonymous death at the hands of murderers for life itself," and accordingly South Africa was for them above all "a haven of safety." Jacobson movingly describes how he, and the Jewish community generally in South Africa, gradually became aware of the dreadful fate of those who remained behind in Lithuania, and how, after the death of his mother, he felt "an obligation, even a compulsion" to visit that country.

Jacobson traces the development of his attitude to Lithuania. As a child growing up on the other side of the world, he viewed the country wholly negatively. It was a place of pogroms, the practice of orthodox religion, and poverty, all of which his mother had successfully escaped by going to South Africa—a place "where no one I knew had ever gone but whence so many of them had come," "an unimaginable region" responsible for all the problems attendant upon his family's being perceived in South Africa as different. No wonder that, as a child, he believed that his parents came from "Nowhere"—with a capital *N*.

Jacobson was finally able to go to Lithuania in the 1990s, when, after independence, it was opened to visitors from the West. His purpose was to confront the legacy of the grandfather he had never known, the rabbi Heshel Melamed (who died at the age of fifty-three and did not immigrate to South Africa): to establish "what," as he puts it, "we have in common and what we do not; how remote we are from one another and how close; in what terms it might be possible for me to put together all I already know about us both with everything I will never know." *Heshel's Kingdom* makes, as one critic emphasized, "compelling but painful reading," for in addressing his family's origins, Jacobson necessarily confronted the Holocaust.[31] His task in tracing and seeking to come to terms with his family history thus lay on the far side of "the gulf of an unspeakable history."

Throughout his life, Jacobson has been an acute observer and wise commenter on South African life and affairs, first as a resident, later, for more than fifty years, as an expatriate and occasional visitor to the country. "Like most other expatriates," he says, he has "continued to follow social and political developments in South Africa with a special degree of interest."[32] Although he did not wish to involve himself in politics and has never been an overtly political writer, he was a consistent critic of apartheid in all its manifestations. His work is distinguished by a compassion for the oppressed that he attributes to his having grown up Jewish, which "encouraged us to feel a quasi-instinctive sympathy with other despised and unjustly treated racial groups in South Africa."[33] His critique of apartheid was often incisive: the "official doctrine, which has for decades been attempting to impose by force its own versions of political and cultural separateness on the variegated groups who make up the country is false to the deepest experience even of those who invented it."[34] Over a fifty-year period, Jacobson's views on South Africa have evolved from the young man's rejection of a country that failed to fulfill his cultural and personal needs to the optimistic assessment of 2005 that "South Africa today has a democratically elected and genuinely multiracial, multicultural, multi-faith government."[35]

In the scene near the beginning of this lecture, Jacobson introduced himself to a teacher in Lithuania with the remark that he came from South Africa. Some explanation for that self-identification may perhaps be found in an earlier interview:

> In spite of all my reservations about South Africa there is [a] side of myself which is incurably involved with the country, incurably responsive to certain kinds of people, certain kinds of scenery. . . . It is very strong and I would be much deprived if I couldn't go back to visit South Africa. Whenever I go back I have an almost eerie sense of finding again what I really am. It is strange . . . All the years that passed since I left—my whole adult life in England, my family life, my children—seem like some kind of fantasy, while

there in South Africa is the part of me which remains unchanged.
It was there when I was seven, and it was there when I was 17. It is
still there.[36]

South Africa, it seems, would ever be the "territory of his imagination."

Fall Semester 2011

1. Dan Jacobson, *Heshel's Kingdom* (London, 1998), pp. 191–2.
2. "Shaun de Waal Talks to Dan Jacobson," *South African Literary Review*, 2, 1 (Mar. 1992), p. 15; Dan Jacobson, "The Private Landscape of Meaning or the Public Landscape of Politics: Stephen Gray Interviews Dan Jacobson," *Kunapipi*, 11, 2 (1989), p. 77
3. Sheila Roberts, *Dan Jacobson* (Boston, 1984), p. 35.
4. Michael Wade, "Jacobson's Realism Revisited," *Southern African Review of Books*, Oct.–Nov. 1988.
5. Dan Jacobson, *The Electronic Elephant: A Southern African Journey* (London, 1994), p. 12.
6. Dan Jacobson, "A Way of Seeing", *Times Literary Supplement*, 16 Sep. 1983, p. 996.
7. Dan Jacobson, introduction to Olive Schreiner, *The Story of an African Farm* (Harmondsworth, 1971), p. 18.
8. Dan Jacobson, preface to *The Trap and A Dance in the Sun* (Oxford, 1988), p. 1.
9. Jacobson, "Private Landscape of Meaning," p. 79.
10. Dan Jacobson, "Out of Africa," *Encounter*, Oct. 1959, p. 70.
11. Jacobson, introduction to Schreiner, *Story of an African Farm*, p. 12.
12. Jacobson, "Way of Seeing," p. 996.
13. Quoted in John Barkham, "Among Books and Authors" *Saturday Review*, 26 Feb. 1966.
14. Jacobson, "Private Landscape of Meaning," p. 78.
15. Quoted in Richard Mendelsohn and Milton Shain, *The Jews in South Africa: An Illustrated History* (Johannesburg and Cape Town, 2008), p. 118
16. Dan Jacobson, "If England Was What England Seems," *Times Literary Supplement*, 11 Mar. 2005.
17. Jacobson, "Private Landscape of Meaning," pp. 78, 77.
18. Dan Jacobson, *The Evidence of Love* (London, 1960), p. 140.
19. Dan Jacobson, interview by Ian Hamilton, *New Review*, Oct. 1977, p. 25.
20. Jacobson, "Private Landscape of Meaning," p. 81; Jacobson, quoted in Stephanie Nettell, "Continued Discontinuity," *Books and Bookmen*, June 1966.
21. Interview by Hamilton, p. 25.
22. Ibid., p. 51; Anthony Hartley, "Three Novels," *Encounter*, Sept. 1960, pp. 80–82.
23. Roy Perrott, "A Question of Identity," *Guardian*, 3 June 1960.
24. A. Alvarez, "The Difficulty of Being South African," *New Statesman*, 4 June 1960, p. 827.
25. Dan Jacobson, interview by Rochelle Furstenberg, *Jerusalem Post Magazine*, 18 May 1979.
26. Dan Jacobson, *The Confessions of Josef Baisz* (London, 1977), p. 34.
27. C. J. Driver, "A Somewhere Place," *New Review*, Oct. 1977.
28. Dan Jacobson, interview by Ronald Hayman, *Books and Bookmen*, Feb. 1980, p. 46.
29. Jacobson, "Private Landscape of Meaning," p. 75.
30. Dan Jacobson, *Time and Time Again* (London, 1985), pp. vii, viii.
31. M. J. Daymond, "Imagining the Worst," *English Academy Review*, 16 (1999), p. 81.
32. Jacobson, "Way of Seeing," p. 996.
33. Dan Jacobson, "Growing up Jewish," in *Memories, Realities, and Dreams: Aspects of the South African Jewish Experience*, ed. Milton Shain and Richard Mendelsohn (Johannesburg and Cape Town, 2000), p. 20.

34. Dan Jacobson, *Adult Pleasures: Essays on Writers and Readers* (London, 1988), p. 135.

35. Jacobson, "If England Was What England Seems."

36. Jacobson, interview by Furstenberg, p. 9.

Sherlock Holmes. Sketch by Sidney Paget, 1921.

17

The World of Sherlock Holmes

DAVID L. LEAL

Nobody writes of Holmes and Watson without love.

John Le Carré

We might imagine that to know Sherlock Holmes is to read the four novels and fifty-six short stories written by Sir Arthur Conan Doyle, but these are only the tip of the iceberg. Surrounding this work, extending this work, and to a degree supplanting this work is what might be called "the literature." The sixty stories are only the launching point for an enormous amount of creative, humorous, and fascinating writing and research. This supplementary work was started not long after the publication of the first Sherlock Holmes stories, and it developed with the encouragement of Conan Doyle. Rather than a nostalgic movement of later generations, it was an almost immediate expression of devotion by a fan base that renews itself each generation.

My lifetime interest in Sherlock Holmes, including a decade of what might be considered serious and sustained reading of the secondary literature, has not exhausted the surprisingly vast amount of writing on the subject. Anyone unfamiliar with it would be astounded by the quantity, seriousness, and generally high quality of the writing.

This literature is not hero worship of Conan Doyle. In fact, Doyle is often regarded in Holmesian circles as a somewhat careless author who treated his main character with less than ideal regard. Doyle saw himself first and foremost as an historical novelist, and the Holmes stories were a practical undertaking that launched his fame and, initially, paid the rent. He was also involved in politics and spirituality and was knighted not for creating the most famous detective in literature but for his support of the Boer War.

The secondary Holmes literature reflects a fascination with the character of Sherlock Holmes. Relatively few literary creations of the nineteenth century have had comparable staying power. Consider the following statement by a fictional Oxford don in J. C. Masterman's *To Teach The Senators Wisdom, or An Oxford Guide-Book* (1952): "Who is the best-known figure in English literature? Not Hamlet, not Mr. Pickwick, not even Robinson Crusoe, but without any shadow of a doubt Sherlock Holmes. How many millions of people know him more intimately than their own relatives!"[1]

Present-day readers are interested in the late Victorian era and the London of the period as well as in the character of Holmes. This is evoked in the 1942 poem "221B" by Vincent Starrett:

> Here dwell together still two men of note
> Who never lived and so can never die:
> How very near they seem, yet how remote
> That age before the world went all awry.
> But still the game's afoot for those with ears
> Attuned to catch the distant view-halloo:
> England is England yet, for all our fears—
> Only those things the heart believes are true.
> A yellow fog swirls past the window-pane
> As night descends upon this fabled street:
> A lonely hansom splashes through the rain,
> The ghostly gas lamps fail at twenty feet.
> Here, though the world explode, these two survive,
> And it is always eighteen ninety-five.

Consider that while some Sherlock Holmes films are set in more contemporary times, the vast majority take place during the later years of the nineteenth century. Exceptions are the fourteen Basil Rathbone and Nigel Bruce movies, which are set in London during the Second World War. The war is part of the plot of several of the films, and Holmes successfully outwits Nazis and spies. The best-known adaptation may be Granada television's thirty-six-episode *Sherlock Holmes* (1984–94), starring the late Jeremy Brett. Fans of the series appreciate the attention to detail and the careful evocation of Victorian London.

The two most recent films, *Sherlock Holmes* (2009) and *Sherlock Holmes: A Game of Shadows* (2011), star Robert Downey Jr. and Jude Law. Both are set in Victorian London, and each film earned over

$500 million. Some see the movies as too action oriented, but Holmes in the original stories was a more physical character than he was portrayed by Rathbone, Brett, and many others—a boxer, a stick fighter, and a practitioner of a hybrid martial art called, in "The Adventure of the Empty House," "Baritsu" (actually, Bartitsu).[2] Consider these lines from "The Sign of the Four," which come when a bodyguard named McMurdo denies Holmes entrance to a house.

> "I don't think you can have forgotten me. Don't you remember the amateur who fought three rounds with you at Alison's rooms on the night of your benefit four years back?"
> "Not Mr. Sherlock Holmes!" roared the prize-fighter. "God's truth! how could I have mistook you? If instead o' standin' there so quiet you had just stepped up and given me that cross-hit of yours under the jaw, I'd ha' known you without a question. Ah, you're one that has wasted your gifts, you have! You might have aimed high, if you had joined the fancy."

The popular BBC television series *Sherlock* (2010–), starring Benedict Cumberbatch and Martin Freeman, takes place in modern London. Nevertheless, it tries to stay true to features of the original stories. For instance, the modern Watson is recently returned from active duty in Afghanistan, where he was wounded, as was the original Watson in a previous century. In the first episode, Holmes makes deductions from the condition of a cell phone that exactly parallel those drawn in "The Sign of the Four" from the condition of a pocket watch.

THE ORIGINAL NAME FOR HOLMES was not Sherlock but J. Sherrinford, and the second draft name was Sherrington Hope. The name *Holmes* was in honor of the doctor and author Oliver Wendell Holmes, Sr. (not Jr., who served on the U.S. Supreme Court). Conan Doyle greatly admired him: "Never have I so known and loved a man whom I had never seen."[3] The stories written by Conan Doyle are collectively known as the "Canon." It comprises four novels and fifty-six short stories published from 1891 to 1927. Their settings range from the late Victorian era to the beginning of the First World War.

The religious dimension implied by "Canon" seems intentional. These stories are to the devoted Holmes reader what the Bible is to Christians. Yet Holmes fans are more Catholic than Protestant because they do not believe in *sola scriptura*. On the contrary, just as there is a theological and teaching tradition known as the Magisterium in the Roman Catholic tradition, so is there a vast literature surrounding the Holmesian Canon that is essential to the experience of the dedicated fan. This does not mean that the works are off-limits to criticism. On the contrary, the quality across works is variable, several stories being so poor that there is debate about whether they were in fact written by Conan Doyle. Fans have a clear sense of what Holmes would have said and done, and in a few stories the hero acts in un-Holmesian ways. For instance, he makes comments that can only be described as racist in one of the last stories, "The Adventure of the Three Gables," in stark contrast to his distinct lack of prejudice in previous stories.

Pastiche novels are modern Sherlock Holmes stories written by fans of Holmes or by mystery writers trying their hand at the Holmes genre. The typical story claims to be not a modern creation but rather the recovery of a lost, original Watson story. Such stories often begin with a sentence like the following: "On a foggy London Saturday afternoon I bought a locked steamer trunk in an antiques store on Oxford Street, and inside I found to my amazement some of the lost manuscripts of Dr. John Watson." With that convention observed, another game is afoot.

It is easy for fans to judge modern Holmes novels: either the authors have captured the voice of Watson and the spirit of Holmes, or they have not. Holmes fans largely reject pastiche novels that portray a Holmes different from the character in the Canon.

Some pastiche stories are thematic. Only one story from the Canon, "The Adventure of the Blue Carbuncle" (1892), is set during Christmas, so to the rescue is *Holmes for the Holidays* (1996), which includes stories such as "The Sleuth of Christmas Past" and "The Adventure of the Christmas Ghosts." Three years later saw the publication of *More Holmes for the Holidays,* featuring stories such as "The Christmas Conspiracy" and "The Adventure of the Christmas Bear." Others volumes fill in gaps in the Canon. *Sherlock Holmes: The Hidden Years* (2004) contains stories from the so-called Great Hiatus—the time from Holmes's disappearance at Reichenbach Falls to his reemergence in "The Adventure of the Empty House." These stories place Holmes in such varied locales as San Francisco and the Himalayas.

Some authors create stories from case titles mentioned but not described by Watson in the Canon. These number about a hundred. For instance, there is "The Giant Rat of Sumatra," which Holmes described in "The Sussex Vampire" as "a story for which the world is not yet prepared." Other frequently cited examples include "The Politician, the Lighthouse, and the Trained Cormorant" as well as "Wilson, the Notorious Canary-Trainer." Two collections of these fleshed-out stories are *Murder, My Dear Watson* (2002) and *New Sherlock Holmes Adventures* (2004).

Other authors have introduced new characters who interact with Holmes and use his methods. For example, Laurie King in *The Beekeeper's Apprentice* (1994) introduced fifteen-year-old Mary Russell, who is mentored by a retired Holmes, solves mysteries with him, and ultimately marries him. The *Washington Post Book World* called it a charming extrapolation of Holmes that would cause traditionalists to howl. While marriage may be inconsistent with the traditional image of Holmes, Conan Doyle once famously telegraphed the playwright and director William Gillette: "You may marry him or murder him or do what you want with him."[4]

In addition, Conan Doyle's son coauthored a dozen original Holmes stories that elaborate on cases mentioned in the Canon. These would seem to occupy a position between the Canon and the pastiche novels, as if perhaps some of the literary spirit of Arthur Conan Doyle had been passed down to Adrian Conan Doyle.

There have been many efforts to analyze the stories as if they were factual and to discuss interesting points, resolve contradictions, and explore the characters. This has become known as the "higher criticism." As Michael Harrison observed, by 1986 this literature amounted to "not hundreds, but thousands of books and articles."[5] To understand this writing, one essential fact must be understood: Sherlock Holmes was real. Leslie Klinger called this the "gentle fiction" of all Holmes writing. Gentle or not, experts in this literature expect aficionados to be able to answer questions like "What was Mrs. Hudson's first name"?

This "Great Game" of Holmesian higher criticism is generally thought to have been started by Ronald Knox while he was a student at Oxford. His essay "Studies in the Literature of Sherlock Holmes" (1911) notes that he is just applying Holmes's own methods to better understand the Holmes stories. His larger goal was to spoof biblical higher criticism, which sought to show, for example, that the book of Isaiah had two authors, a proto- and a deutero-Isaiah.[6] Knox argued that a close reading of the Holmes Canon revealed certain contradictions, such as that John Watson is called "James" by his wife in "The Man with the Twisted Lip." Knox therefore argued that the Holmes stories were in fact written by two Watsons, a proto- and a deutero-Watson. Perhaps to his surprise, this sort of thing found an audience, and subsequent enthusiasts included Dorothy Sayers and T. S. Eliot. Knox even received an encouraging response from Conan Doyle himself. According to Sayers, "The rule of the game is that it must be played as solemnly as a county cricket match at

Lord's: the slightest touch of extravagance or burlesque ruins the atmosphere."[7]

Another debate is whether Holmes attended Oxford or Cambridge. It is clear in the stories that he attended one or the other, since Watson refers to his university as "Camford." Records of the Oxford and Cambridge colleges have been examined for evidence of his matriculation, just as the rolls of medical associations have been combed for evidence of a Dr. Watson. Evidence can be found in one of the rare discussions, in the Canon, of Holmes' background, as in "The Adventure of the Three Students," a story that may involve a return to his (but possibly Watson's) old college. The material used in the college's long-jump pit, a key clue in the story, is described in detail. Historical research indicates that this specific material was used at Cambridge at the time but not at Oxford. In addition, as Dorothy Sayers noted, a man of Holmes's interests would have been attracted to scientific Cambridge, not humanist Oxford. But William S. Baring-Gould's creative biography of Holmes took no side in the debate, finding evidence for both universities.

In "The Gloria Scott," we read the following statement by Holmes about his university days: "Trevor was the only man I knew, and that only through the accident of his bull terrier freezing on to my ankle one morning as I went down to chapel." Fans have attempted to compare this bare scrap of vague information to the maps of real Oxbridge colleges. Since dogs were forbidden in all of them, the investigation needs to consider where a student could have lived so that a walk to chapel might have taken him outdoors.

Another conundrum concerns the number of times Watson was married. The evidence in the Canon is unclear, which has unleashed a great deal of speculation. There are other puzzling inconsistencies in the stories. For instance, why does Watson say that he keeps a bull pup when he first meets Holmes, but dogs are never mentioned again? Where did the pup go? And which part of Watson's body was wounded in Afghanistan? The stories say alternatively his shoulder and his leg. There have been creative medical efforts to reconcile this contradictory evidence—maybe a bullet went into his shoulder and was deflected downward into his leg? As Kyle Freeman noted, "The most probable [explanation] is that Conan Doyle simply misremembered where he had located the wound. In only his second Sherlock Holmes story, he hadn't foreseen that generations of sharp-eyed devotees would scan every line for inconsistencies with the fervor of medieval scholastics explicating Holy Writ."[8]

These fun investigations are made possible by numerous contradictions, fascinating hints, a lack of detail, an excess of detail, many noted but unelaborated facts, and the occasional absence of care shown by Conan Doyle in the stories. Much of this scholarly research takes the form of article-length papers, complete with extensive footnotes.

The secondary literature serves as a window on the Victorian era, and London in particular; much (but not all) of it is written by enthusiastic, well-read, intelligent amateurs. Nonfiction works dealing with the Canon include commentaries, encyclopedias, historical accounts, and writings about law, medicine, criminology, and urban geography. For example, *The Science of Sherlock Holmes* (2006), by E. J. Wagner, discusses the state of forensics in the time of the Canon. It covers such topics as fingerprinting, blood analysis, autopsies, poisons, crime scene analysis, criminal identification, ballistics, footprints, and handwriting analysis.

Michael Harrison explores the England of the time in his book *In the Footsteps of Sherlock Holmes* (1960). In "The Red Headed League," Holmes claims to have "an exact knowledge of London," and therefore many readers have sought a better understanding of the city and its environs. Harrison explores many of the urban features encountered by Holmes and Watson: streets, buildings, restaurants, neighborhoods, concert halls, modes of transportation, hospitals, and the City of London. In *The World of Sherlock Holmes* (1973), Harrison combines imaginative explorations of the life and career of Holmes with historical background material. For instance, the Canon refers to Holmes working for the pope, so Harrison discusses Pope Leo XII, the Vatican, and the Catholic Church in England.

The Bedside, Bathtub, and Armchair Companion to Sherlock Holmes (1998), by Dick Riley and Pam McAllister, includes many facts and illustrations about the Canon stories. Brief analyses of the stories are interspersed with essays on Victorian life, Victorian London, drug use in Victorian times, nobility in the nineteenth century, English money, and the British Empire, among others. Similar work can be found in the pages of academic journals. While the American Bar Association journal *Real Property, Trust, and Estate Law* is not a normal outlet for Sherlock Holmes research, a recent issue included Stephen Alton's "The Game is Afoot: The Significance of Donative Transfers in the Sherlock Holmes Canon."

Also in this category is a wide range of commentaries. The widely cited and respected *A Sherlock Holmes Commentary* (1972), by D. Martin Dakin, contains observations on many features of the Canon stories. *The New Annotated Sherlock Holmes* (2004), edited by Leslie Klinger, contains 3,560 pages in three volumes and weighs 15.5 pounds. The Canon stories are accompanied by hundreds of notes that discuss issues of plot and detail. In addition, the volumes contain essays on topics including the snakes of India, the guns used by Holmes and Watson, the Indian Mutiny, and fingerprinting. *The New Annotated Sherlock Holmes* follows by more than a generation *The Annotated Sherlock Holmes* (1967), a classic by William S. Baring-Gould. In 1993, Oxford University Press contributed the nine-volume *Oxford Sherlock Holmes,* annotated by Owen Dudley Edwards.

Baring-Gould later wrote a novel in which Nero Wolfe was presented as the son of Sherlock Holmes and Irene Adler, one of the few people to outwit Holmes. This is quite in line with the pastiche literature, which often introduces Holmes to famous people of the times. For example, *The Seven-Per-Cent Solution* (1974), by Nicholas Meyer, features a partnership between Holmes and Sigmund Freud. Meyer published two other Holmes novels: *The West End Horror* (1976), which includes characters such as Bernard Shaw, Bram Stoker, and Oscar Wilde, and *The Canary Trainer* (1993).

There is a wide array of works that are difficult to classify. *The Encyclopaedia Sherlockiana* (1977), by Jack Tracy, includes hundreds of entries about all sorts of details mentioned in the Canon. Even very minor characters are listed: "Crosby (d. 1894), a banker whose terrible death was associated in Watson's mind with a red leech (GOLD)." And in fact, the opening lines of "The Golden Pince-Nez" see Watson writing: "As I turn over the pages I see my notes upon the repulsive story of the red leech and the terrible death of Crosby the banker." And to illustrate how a detail in a Canon story can lead to a pastiche novel, in Andy Lane's *Young Sherlock Holmes: The Red Leech* (2010) a teenage Holmes in the 1860s chases John Wilkes Booth, who has escaped to England. The pursuit then leads to America, where it appears that the young Holmes foils a southern plan to invade Canada and reestablish the Confederacy there.

The literature discussed above is remarkable as a rare example of grassroots scholarship. With a few exceptions, the authors are not scholars but enthusiasts, and the books are sometimes published by little-known presses (particularly the volumes of higher criticism). Nevertheless, the quality of the writing is often very good, and the research careful and reliable.

From the beginning, the popularity of Holmes took on a life of its own, incorporating elements supplied by people whose careers were bound up with the character. Phrases that are not from the Canon are widely used nevertheless. Just as the phrase "separation of church and state" is not in the U.S. Constitution but in a letter by Thomas Jefferson, "Elementary, my dear Watson" is not in any novel written by Conan Doyle. According to the *Oxford Dictionary of Quotations* (6th ed., 2004), the line first appears in *Psmith Journalist* (1915), by P. G. Wodehouse. Holmes is not described as wearing a deerstalker in the Canon; an illustration in the *Strand* magazine showed it, and the image caught on. Holmes is never described in the Canon as smoking a curved pipe, but William Gillette used it when portraying Holmes onstage, and the depiction became required.

The Holmes stories have even inspired philosophical musings. *Sherlock Holmes Was Wrong* (2008), by Pierre Bayard, a professor of French literature at the University of Paris, claims that Holmes and Watson interpreted the evidence incorrectly in *The Hound of the Baskervilles,* and that the woman revealed as Stapleton's wife is actually the guilty party, not Stapleton himself. Bayard uses this exercise to make postmodernist points about the autonomy of fictional characters, the reliability of narrators, and the relationship between authors and their creations. He believes that characters like Holmes are alive, existing independently of their creators. Similarly, an Oxford don in Masterman's *To Teach the Senators Wisdom* asks, in reference to Holmes, "Are not some of the characters of fiction more real than historical personages?"

Is there a larger meaning behind the popularity of Holmes? The emergence of Sherlock Holmes generally tracked the rise of science in the nineteenth century. The scientific revolution was important not only for what it contributed but also for what it displaced—particularly religious belief in Britain after the publication of Charles Darwin's *On the Origin of Species* (1859). Perhaps the fascination with Holmes and his methods reflects an appreciation of—maybe even a faith in—science and the scientific method. Just as readers and viewers count on Holmes to find a logical solution to a baffling crime, they hope that science and technology will solve society's problems (even the ones caused by science and technology). The popularity of science-based police procedurals like *CSI* (in all its permutations) may likewise address the belief that rigorously applied inductive methods can be used to untangle mysteries and make sense of tragedy.

THE ONLY BRITISH CHARACTER comparable to Sherlock Holmes in longevity, popularity, and even personality traits is James Bond. Ian Fleming featured Bond in twelve novels and two volumes of short stories. This body of work has led to twenty-three movies since 1962, not including the first *Casino Royale* (1967), a spoof, and *Never Say Never Again* (1983), which was not made by the usual production team and consequently has a sort of asterisk attached to it. Although

2238 David L. Leal

the novels and, especially, the movies have proved their popularity and remained favorites for half a century, there is seemingly less to say about Bond than about Holmes. There is not a noticeable grassroots movement to write pastiche Bond stories, the series has inspired relatively little of the kind of scholarly literature described above, and there is a greater focus on the films than the original stories. Despite the continuing popularity of the films, the quasi-religious reverence lavished on Holmes is not detectable for Bond.

There have been new stories commissioned by the Ian Fleming estate, some of them very good, perhaps better than some of the originals. But for Bond fans, the focus is primarily on the films. Public interest in the Bond cars, Bond's gadgets, and what are called the Bond girls derives from the films. Books about Bond are as likely to treat the movies as the original books. The films have in some sense displaced the books.

Perhaps this is because the Bond movies are one of the few instances in popular culture in which the films are better than the source material. Consider the books *Diamonds Are Forever, Moonraker, On Her Majesty's Secret Service,* and *The Man with the Golden Gun.* In all cases, the movies have more inventive plots, the bad guys are more colorful, the exotic locales are better depicted on-screen, and some of the politically incorrect material in the books is cleaned up. The best of the novels might be *From Russia with Love* (1957), which John F. Kennedy said was one of his favorite books. It holds up well as a Cold War classic, but the Cold War is becoming ancient history to newer generations on both sides of the former Iron Curtain.

In addition, the stories sometimes come alarmingly close to portraying Bond as a not overly sophisticated assassin. By contrast, the filmic Bond varies according to the actor portraying him. Roger Moore's Bond is a more refined, although sometimes less serious, character. Timothy Dalton was a "back to basics" Bond, a tougher and more serious spy.

Is there a larger meaning (than pure entertainment) to the Holmes and Bond stories? They can be read as showing a Britain "punching above its weight." In the Bond series, when squeezed between the Americans and the Soviets, the British are portrayed as smarter than either. In the film *You Only Live Twice* (1967), it is the British who understand that a series of apparently major-power provocations are actually the work of SPECTRE, a terroristic extortion group. Whenever Bond saves the world or at least prevents a catastrophe, Britain is shown to be a crucial global actor. Similarly, Sherlock Holmes is often called on by foreign royalty and politicians, and even the pope, to solve crimes and ward off villains. Presumably the local police and consulting detectives, if any, are unable to handle these problems. Near the beginning of "The Reigate Squires," Watson notes Holmes's international reputation:

> A time when Europe was ringing with his name and when his room was literally ankle-deep with congratulatory telegrams I found him a prey to the blackest depression. Even the knowledge that he had succeeded where the police of three countries had failed, and that he had outmanoeuvred at every point the most accomplished swindler in Europe, was insufficient to rouse him from his nervous prostration.

When the Holmes stories were first published, Britain was a world power, and its empire is involved in the plots of many stories. Today, the character of Holmes continues to resonate, even if his imperial context no longer does.

Holmes and Bond remain crucial parts of contemporary British cultural capital, and politically this helps British "soft power." All nations have global images, but some are better than others. Britain should be grateful for Holmes and Bond: although they reach different audiences, both are good for the country's public relations. Poor France is stuck with Inspector Clouseau, although Belgium does better with Agatha Christie's Hercule Poirot.

In the end, readers and (mainly) viewers may have to be satisfied with enjoying the adventure of James Bond in a way that does not draw them deeply into his world. For Holmes fans, by contrast, the stories and movies are only the beginning of a rich detective adventure of their own.

Fall Semester 2012

1. J. C. Masterman, *To Teach The Senators Wisdom, or An Oxford Guide-Book* (New York, 1952), p. 127.

2. See Leslie Klinger, ed., *The New Annotated Sherlock Holmes, Volumes I and II* (New York, 2005), pp. 822–3.

3. Kyle Freeman, introduction and notes to *The Complete Sherlock Holmes, Volume I* (New York, 2003), p. 29.

4. Martin H. Greenberg, Jon L. Lellenberg, and Daniel Stashower, eds., *Murder, My Dear Watson: New Tales of Sherlock Holmes* (New York, 2002), p. viii.

5. Michael Harrison, *Immortal Sleuth: Sherlockian Musings and Memories* (Dubuque, Iowa, 1983), p. xviii.

6. On this topic generally, see Michael J. Crowe, *Ronald Knox and Sherlock Holmes: The Origins of Sherlockian Studies* (Wantage, UK, 2011).

7. Quoted in ibid.

8. Freeman, *Complete Sherlock Holmes, Volume I,* p. 870.

Johnny Weissmuller as Tarzan, 1932. Photograph by George Hurrell.

18

Tarzan

CHRISTOPHER BENFEY

Poor Tarzan. The original Tarzan of Edgar Rice Burroughs's novel *Tarzan of the Apes* is a hundred years old this year, buried under layer after suffocating layer of silent films and talkies, Johnny Weissmuller and Bo Derek, comic books and *George of the Jungle* cartoons, "Me Tarzan, you Jane," Tarzan ice cream and Tarzan bread, and untold numbers of sequels and prequels. We all know who Tarzan was even if we have never read the book. We can *see* him, raffishly clad in his lion skin, flying from vine to vine, and we can hear him ululating his two-note jungle yodel. There are very few enduring modern myths, but Tarzan, dreamed up by a Chicago-born writer who had failed at many other professions, is surely one of them. Is it possible, under such distracting circumstances, to read *Tarzan of the Apes* afresh?

The reader who makes the attempt will discover almost immediately that the original tale is far more complex than one might have believed from its many popular offspring. Time has simplified it. An outline of the plot, itself a simplification, might go something like this: an English nobleman named John Clayton, Lord Greystoke, is sent to Africa to look into European abuses of native workers, who are said to be "held in virtual slavery" in the rubber and ivory trade. A eugenicist's dream, Clayton "was the type of Englishman that one likes best to associate with the noblest monuments of historic achievement upon a thousand victorious battlefields—a strong, virile man—mentally, morally, and physically." Clayton and his pregnant wife, Alice, are marooned on a desolate but beautiful part of the African coast when the crew of their vessel mutinies, a "short and grisly" operation that Clayton witnesses "as though he had been but watching an indifferent cricket match." Clayton builds a little tree house, but an attack by a "great anthropoid ape" leaves Alice traumatized and oblivious of her surroundings.

The scene, which Lady Greystoke remembers only as "an awful dream," is suggestive of rape—"screaming with rage and pain, the ape flew at the delicate woman, who went down beneath him to merciful unconsciousness"—though Burroughs is careful to make sure that the assailant, hit by a bullet from Clayton's gun, dies just before penetration. During the night immediately following the attack, as though the marauding ape had somehow contributed to its conception, "a little son was born in the tiny cabin beside the primeval forest, while a leopard screamed before the door, and the deep notes of a lion's roar sounded from beyond the ridge." Exactly a year to the day after the child's birth, Lady Greystoke dies, and so, soon after, does her distraught husband.

The orphaned child is adopted by a grieving ape-mother named Kala, who has lost her own baby in a melee among the apes. The apes, in their ape language, call the ugly, hairless child "Tarzan," meaning "white skin." Tarzan matures slowly, according to ape expectations, but his powers of thought are superior; after solving the mechanism of the lock on his birth parents' cabin, he learns to wield a knife, to lasso his prey, and to swim; most amazingly, he teaches himself to read and write, and not just English but eventually French as well. The knife and the lasso come in handy after an attack by native warriors, whom Tarzan terrorizes and from whom he steals a bow and poisoned arrows.

Then, in the major plot twist of the tale, an exploratory party happens to show up on precisely the same stretch of shoreline: an absent-minded professor from Baltimore, accompanied by his lovely, plucky daughter, Jane Porter, and her African American mammy, "the ubiquitous Esmeralda"; the professor's assistant; and, by an extraordinary coincidence, the current Lord Greystoke, a cousin of Tarzan's, who joins the party in London "just for the adventure." Soon they encounter a group of French soldiers (another mutiny, buried treasure, a map), and there are various battles among man and beast in which Tarzan is invariably on the victorious side.

He is less victorious in the battle among Jane's suitors. At first there are only two: the usurping Greystoke and Tarzan himself, who declares his love for Jane after he has rescued her for the first time (literally "carried [her] off her feet," as Burroughs puts it) and the two have indulged in a primeval tryst. A third suitor eventually intrudes, an evil Baltimore businessman named Canler, who has funded the Porter venture and who will have Jane even if he has to buy her and—his language resembles Simon Legree's—enslave her. "Of course you are right," he tells her cheerfully. "I am buying you . . . but I thought you would prefer to pretend that it was otherwise." The novel ends in, of all places, Wisconsin, with one last rescue of a damsel in distress from, of all things, a forest fire.

Tarzan settles all debts (the buried treasure), takes Canler by the throat ("Do you wish this to live?") and sends him on his way, and nobly renounces Jane, who is having second thoughts about her primal passion and thinks that young Clayton, civilized Englishman that he is, would be a more "logical mate for such as herself": "She realized the spell that had been upon her in the depths of that faroff jungle, but there was no spell of enchantment now in prosaic Wisconsin." A sequel is promised in a closing footnote: "The further adventures of Tarzan, and what came of his noble act of self-renunciation, will be told in the next book of Tarzan."

T. S. Eliot once said that Henry James had a mind so fine that no idea could violate it. In *Tarzan of the Apes,* Edgar Rice Burroughs, by contrast, is ravished by ideas. Darwin's ideas interest him and so do the Social Darwinists. He is a proponent of both American democracy and English aristocracy. He laments the downfall of chivalry but decries colonial oppression. He loves civilization (on his way to the United States, Tarzan makes a pit stop in Paris to admire its highest manifestations) but he is also enchanted by primitivism. His idea of human origins is both tooth-and-fang primordial, rife with rape and cannibalism, and Edenic or, as he thinks of it, "Greek": no episode in the book is more idyllic than Jane and Tarzan's chaste but passionate night together in the jungle. Amid this thicket of ideas—a jungle of ideas, really—one cannot help wondering what Burroughs was after, what the ideological core of his vivid tale was meant to be.

At its narrative substratum, *Tarzan of the Apes* is perhaps nothing more complicated than a retelling of "The Ugly Duckling," that reassuring fable for all misfits. There has been some mistake: the odd bird, so out of place among the ducks, turns out to be a displaced swan. Gawkiness translates to grace. How perfectly fitted to the tribulations and final triumph of the ballet! "It does not matter in the least having been born in a duckyard," Hans Christian Andersen writes, "if only you come out of a swan's egg!" The moment of recognition for Andersen's ugly duckling comes when he bows his head at the glorious swans, as though proffering it for a beheading, and sees his reflection in the water.

When ten-year-old Tarzan glimpses his own reflection in the water, he is appalled:

> It had been bad enough to be hairless, but to own such a countenance! He wondered that the other apes could look at him at all. That tiny slit of a mouth and those puny white teeth! How they looked beside the mighty lips and powerful fangs of his more fortunate brothers! And the little pinched nose of him; so thin was it that it looked half starved . . . But when he saw his eyes; ah, that was the final blow—a brown spot, a gray circle, and then blank whiteness! Frightful! not even the snakes had such hideous eyes as he.

It will be a while before Tarzan, with Jane's tender help, learns to love his snake eyes and his blank whiteness. Predictably, Burroughs weaves some racism into his story of the ugly ape. His apes, especially Tarzan's adoptive mother, Kala, remain attractive, while the African natives are made to seem subhuman; their periodic lynching by Tarzan, gleefully wielding his lasso, is meant to be comical but will strike modern readers as horrifying.

What Burroughs mainly wanted to achieve in writing *Tarzan* was enough money on which to live. "I failed in every enterprise I attempted," he wrote. "I sold electric light bulbs to janitors, candy to drug stores, and Stoddard's Lectures from door to door." When he found himself marketing pencil sharpeners, however, it was as though one of those lightbulbs went on: he determined to take a pencil in hand and write pulp fiction.

His first attempt was *A Princess of Mars,* a fantasy of space travel that inspired the recent cinematic flop *John Carter.* Like many northerners, Burroughs had a soft spot for the defeated South as a bastion of aristocratic manners and Sir Walter Scott chivalry. The Virginian John Carter, "a splendid specimen of manhood . . . broad of shoulder and narrow of hip," is a former Confederate officer who, beamed up to Mars, helps some comely, red-skinned Martians in their own civil war. Burroughs's second book, with another castaway as its hero, was *Tarzan of the Apes.* It made his fortune, and he named his sprawling ranch outside Los Angeles Tarzana. He wrote another sixty or so books, including twenty-two works about Tarzan, none of which had anything quite like the success of the original.

Ideologically, Burroughs was attuned to his moment. Several impressive books had expressed unease that modern civilization, and American civilization in particular, had lost its manly edge, its warrior ethos—that it was, as Eliot said of Boston, "refined beyond the point of civilization." Nostalgic for the heroism of the Civil War (in which Burroughs's father had fought), many had welcomed the Spanish-American War as a testing ground for American youth; Burroughs himself tried, unsuccessfully, to join Teddy Roosevelt's Rough Riders. William James, who opposed the war, wondered whether some "moral equivalent of war" might be found to give piquancy and meaning to life. A particularly beautiful example of this literature of unease and "regeneration through violence" is Jack London's *The Call of the Wild*.

But *Tarzan of the Apes* rarely seems engaged by such questions. Burroughs's interests lie elsewhere. The emotional core of the book, its true heart of darkness, lies in the little cabin built by Tarzan's father. The apes are fascinated by this "wonderful lair," and so is Tarzan himself. It is the outpost of civilization, the little house on the prairie, the uncanny site of birth and death but also the generative site of writing and reading. It is here that young Tarzan is presented with two deeply intertwined mysteries. One is his parentage; the other is the nature of human language. These are the codes that he must crack in order to figure out who he is. The lock on the cabin door is a metaphor for these riddles.

Burroughs invests a great deal of narrative ingenuity in the adoption of baby Tarzan by his ape-mother, Kala. Rudyard Kipling made adoption by wolves believable—more of a challenge, one might think, than adoption by apes. No moment in *The Jungle Book* is more poignant than Mowgli's brief sojourn in the home of his presumed birth mother, Messua, who gives the child milk to drink. Suddenly, Mowgli feels something brush his leg. It is Mother Wolf, his adoptive mother, licking him. "I have a desire to see that woman who gave thee milk," says Mother Wolf. Then she adds, possessively, "I gave thee thy first milk."

Tarzan's adoption, like so much else in the novel, is built around coincidences. Alice dies on her infant son's first birthday. At that very moment, the unusually attractive ape Kala—the Greek word for "beautiful"—loses her own baby when the ape leader Kerchak goes mad, attacks Kala, and the baby plunges to its death. After the melee, Kerchak leads the apes toward the little cabin, while Kala, a traumatized mother like Lady Greystoke, "carried her little dead baby hugged closely to her breast."

The cabin door, always locked, unaccountably stands open. The apes enter to find a dead woman, a distraught man who rears up one last time and is killed by Kerchak, and a crying baby. Kala, who has been clutching her dead child, switches the babies. As she took up the little live baby of Alice Clayton, she dropped the dead body of her own into the empty cradle; the wail of the living had answered within her wild breast the call of universal motherhood, which the dead could not still.

Burroughs wins our assent for this adoption by insisting on Kala's beauty and her capacity for motherhood. She was, we are told, "a splendid, clean-limbed animal, with a round, high forehead, which denoted more intelligence than most of her kind possessed. So, also, she had a greater capacity for mother love and mother sorrow." Tarzan assumes, for almost the entire novel, that Kala is his birth mother, and she, with her limited means of communication, does not enlighten him about his true origins beyond hinting that his father was a great white ape of some kind. Tarzan can unlock the secret only by learning to read.

He returns to the cabin, figures out the mechanism of the lock on the door, and turns his attention to the books left there, "which seemed to exert a strange and powerful influence over him, so that he could scarce attend to aught else for the lure of the wondrous puzzle which their purpose presented to him." Fortunately, these are children's books, primers and illustrated alphabets, with pictures accompanying "the strange little bugs which covered the pages." Burroughs offers us a picture:

> Squatting upon his haunches on the table top in the cabin his father had built—his smooth, brown, naked little body bent over the book which rested in his strong slender hands, and his great shock of long, black hair falling about his well shaped head and bright, intelligent eyes—Tarzan of the apes, little primitive man, presented a picture filled, at once, with pathos and with promise—an allegorical figure of the primordial groping through the black night of ignorance toward the light of learning.

Tarzan's physical prowess in swinging through treetops is exceeded only by his linguistic genius, for, as Burroughs concedes, "it was a hard and laborious task which he had set himself without knowing it—a task which might seem to you or me impossible—learning to read without having the slightest knowledge of letters or written language, or the faintest idea that such things existed." It takes him about five years to decipher the strange little bugs and to learn to produce them himself, with a cache of lead pencils "in a hitherto undiscovered drawer beneath the table."

What we have here are really two scenes of origin: Tarzan's mysterious parentage, not to be finally resolved until fingerprints are compared at the end of the novel; and the origins of the novel we are reading, in the diary kept by Tarzan's birth father. (Burroughs's own discovery of writing through lead pencils and pencil sharpeners is probably memorialized in Tarzan's epiphany.) Burroughs further delays Tarzan's self-recognition by having Lord Greystoke keep his diary in French. We are not told why—perhaps it is what a cultivated English lord would do. So Tarzan must wait for the arrival of a Frenchman, the dashing Captain D'Arnot, to teach him French—in a couple of weeks—before he can get the full story. The first words out of Tarzan's mouth are not "Me Tarzan, you Jane" but, amazingly, "Mais, oui!"

Tarzan of the Apes presents to the twenty-first-century reader a riddle of its own: why this peculiar fixation on adoption and legitimacy? In probing Kipling's interest in adoption, Edmund Wilson, in *The Wound and the Bow,* excavated the moment in Kipling's life when, as a young child, he and his sister were farmed out, without explanation, to an abusive couple in England for a dismal six years, an experience that, in Wilson's view, left a decisive mark on Kipling's fiction. It is possible that Burroughs had some kindred private crisis, perhaps the time that he was sent away from his home in Chicago, during the flu epidemic of 1890–1891, when he was fifteen, to live on his older brother's cattle ranch in Idaho.

But the question of legitimacy feels less personal in *Tarzan of the Apes* and more, to use Burroughs's own word, allegorical. He seems to be puzzling out what Kipling called, indelicately, "the white man's burden" when he summoned the United States to enter the Spanish-American War. Is the United States, Burroughs (along with his whole generation) seems to be asking, ready to assume the burden of policing the world? Can its muscular young men, trained in the Wild West, "inherit" both the martial prowess of its mother country, Great Britain (embodied by Lord Greystoke, Tarzan's father) and the cultural flair of its occasional helper, France (represented by D'Arnot)? Can it unite its once-divided halves, figured here in the wretched images of lynching native Africans and in the humiliatingly awful linguistic inventions of Jane's maid, who fears "gorilephants" and the "hipponocerous" and is concerned that her mistress "acts sorter kinder disgranulated dis ebenin'"? Tarzan is made to stand at the cultural crossroads of all these nationalities and ethnicities as though, lost in the Wisconsin woods, he *is* America.

Amid all these mysteries of parentage and authority, the final exchange of the novel takes on an added resonance. As if channeling Sydney Carton, Tarzan has renounced his claim on Jane. Clayton, unaware that Tarzan now has proof that he, Tarzan, is the true Lord

Greystoke and could strip him of his title and his bride, expresses his gratitude.

> "I say, old man," cried Clayton, "I haven't had a chance to thank you for all you've done for us. It seems as though you had your hands full saving our lives in Africa and here.
>
> "I'm awfully glad you came on here. We must get better acquainted. I often thought about you, you know, and the remarkable circumstances of your environment.
>
> "If it's any of my business, how the devil did you ever get into that bally jungle?"
>
> "I was born there," said Tarzan, quietly. "My mother was an Ape, and of course she couldn't tell me much about it. I never knew who my father was."

On both counts, Tarzan, far more sophisticated than one might think, is telling the truth.

Fall Semester 2013

A version of this lecture appeared in the *New Republic*, 25 October 2012.

Bodleian Library, Oxford

19

Harry Potter

SUSAN NAPIER

In the summer of 1999, some friends and I went to see the musical *Cats* in London, technically accompanied by their young son, William. In actuality, William spent the entire duration of the musical glued to his seat reading *Harry Potter and the Chamber of Secrets,* the second volume of the series by J. K. Rowling, which had just come out in England the day before. To this day, I doubt that William has any idea of what happens in *Cats,* but I know for a fact that he can tell you the plot of every one of the Harry Potter novels.

Intrigued by William's obsession, I bought the first volume for my daughter, who reacted much as William had. I then slightly furtively read both books myself. I found them highly entertaining, reminiscent of some of the books I had read as a child: the *Malory Towers* series by Enid Blyton, *The Chronicles of Narnia* by C. S. Lewis, and even J. R. R. Tolkien's *Lord of the Rings.* But I was fascinated by what seemed to be the series' unprecedented hold over both boys and girls.

More than a decade later, I am still fascinated by the *Harry Potter* series, and I am not alone, even among academics. Scholarly writings on *Harry Potter* abound, including discussions by children's literature professors comparing Harry to Peter Rabbit, studies by scholars of religion looking for signs of Christianity in the series' continuing references to alchemy, and analyses by postcolonial scholars who find latent nostalgia for the British Empire lurking in the books. Many academics have embraced the *Harry Potter* series simply for its richly imaginative universe, singling out Rowling's extraordinary ability to create and sustain a fully realized magical world that surprises, delights, and terrifies across seven volumes. They mention too Rowling's skillful and unprecedented interweaving of the fantasy world with the world of the Muggles (regular humans).

One critic, Lee Siegel, describes this aspect as "realistic magicalism," noting that "Rowling has brought reality back into the literature of escape" and citing her genuinely complex and psychologically accurate portrayals of such basic human rites of passage as developing friendships, growing up, and dying.[1] Many essays note the copious amounts of character- and situation-based humor as well as the series' sheer narrative verve. Even those who can't bring themselves to praise the series from a literary viewpoint acknowledge that the books allow them to connect with students more directly and personally than, unfortunately, many of the books in the canon now seem capable of doing.

But there is also considerable contempt mixed in with the encomiums, especially in discussions written during the early years of the series. Some of these deserve to be taken seriously, not only because they are from such significant writers and scholars as A. S. Byatt and Harold Bloom, but also because a number of them are thought-provoking. At their best, they point out genuine limitations of Rowling's work and raise concerns about the social context (that is, the millennial capitalist world) in which the works appeared.

Many in the critical camp take issue with the content of the series, decrying what they see as the formulaic nature of the stories, the emphasis on plot rather than psychological focus or literate language, and Rowling's tendency to take inspiration (some call it slavish borrowing) from a host of other genres—the school story, the mystery story, the sport story, tales of adventure, fairy tales, the gothic, and previous children's fantasy series, especially those of the great British tradition. In my opinion, shared with many others, it is one of Rowling's great strengths that she can appropriate and breathe new life into a dizzying variety of genres and traditions.

Other critics have attacked the entire cultural phenomenon of *Harry Potter*'s popularity, in particular the trend of adults reading and enjoying the series. Harold Bloom, for example, sees the popularity of *Harry Potter* as yet another manifestation of the "dumbing down" of modern culture, aided by the sinister forces of cultural studies departments.[2] Even more vitriolic is A. S. Byatt, who in a much-circulated *New York Times* essay of 2003 dismisses the series as nutrient-free comfort food "written for people whose imaginative lives are confined to TV cartoons, and the exaggerated (more ex-citing, not threatening) mirror-worlds of soaps, reality TV, and celebrity gossip."[3] Another critic, Ron Charles in the *Washington Post,* combines Byatt's and Bloom's approaches, seeing *Harry Potter* as a regression to "cultural infantilism" and linking it with a detailed critique of the "mass media experience" that the *Harry Potter* phenomenon has clearly become.[4] The latter point is worth addressing, since the "mass media-ization" of the books has colored the tone of many an academic's response to the series. In Charles's view, at the height of the craze even those who didn't like the books felt forced to take a "loyalty oath" and become subject to the greedy forces of capitalism surrounding the *Harry Potter* phenomenon: an "orgy of mass marketing," enormous media hype, millions of deeply committed fans, panicky attacks from fundamentalist Christians, and numerous commercial tie-ins.

Given this swirl of outside factors, it is hardly surprising that the books themselves sometimes get lost in all the hubbub. But the books are worth returning to for their story: the story of Harry Potter and his relatives, friends, and enemies; the story of the beloved boarding school Hogwarts; and at least implicitly, a story of Britain and the industrialized world in the year 2000. For regardless of what all the learned and often valuable critiques of the series have to say, the story calls out primally to an enormous number and variety of readers. It was not the hype or statistics that kept young William glued to his seat for three hours, oblivious of the theatrical extravaganza in front of him. And it was not the lure of a *Harry Potter* book party that had my own daughter, unbeknownst to me, wake up early on the morning of her eleventh birthday and dress and comb her hair neatly in expectation of receiving her acceptance letter from Hogwarts.

So what is the allure of *Harry Potter,* and how does it tap into generational dreams, anxieties, and hopes?

In general, the series allows young readers safely to explore their identity in a fantasy world that echoes their own reality, a reality where conventional comforts such as home, security, faith, and authority can seem uncertain. In this it fulfills a primary function of fantasy: to allow its audience to examine and work through traumatic possibilities at a comfortable distance. More specifically, much of *Harry Potter*'s appeal lies in its supple reworking and updating of the tropes and conventions of fantasy, fairy tales, and, to some extent, popular children's literature in order to create genuinely meaningful works of art that confront the complexities of the twenty-first-century world. In particular, the gradually "darkening" tone of the series seems related to the study of trauma and its place in contemporary society.

Only in the last three decades or so have fantasy and the related genre of fairy tales gone from being literary modes widely derided as escapist fiction for children or "childish adults" to ones that are being taken seriously literarily, aesthetically, culturally, and psychologically. The idea of fantasy as inherently childish and faintly embarrassing still creeps into the reactions of many scholars, but in recent years, concomitant with a spate of scholarly articles and essays about fantasy, there has emerged a consensus that fantasy is a fundamental literary genre. And much of the most highly regarded and widely studied fantasy has come out of Britain.

The fantastic tradition in British literature is a long and highly influential one. As Dennis Kratz points out, fantasy formed "the mainstream of Western literature until the Renaissance."[5] In Britain, Celtic legends (notably the Arthurian cycle) and Anglo-Saxon stories such as *Beowulf* not only dominated much of premodern English literature but also inspired later British authors from Spenser to Tolkien to Rowling. Even more significant are the works of Shakespeare: *Macbeth, Hamlet, A Midsummer's Night's Dream,* and *The Tempest* contain strong elements of the supernatural and the fantastic. Given Shakespeare's position as the premier writer of English literature, it seems reasonable to suggest that his popular dramas helped make the public receptive to the fantastic as a legitimate mode of literature. Rowling's series contains echoes of the forest of Arden in its Forbidden Forest, the ghosts of Hogwarts could easily walk in Elsinore Castle, and even the grotesque Caliban, with his demonic mother, might be the forerunner of the half-giant Hagrid, whose giantess mother abandoned him as a baby.

With the rise of the realistic novel in the eighteenth and nineteenth centuries, fantasy went under wraps for a while, but still remained a major popular mode, especially in the form of the gothic, from Horace Walpole's *Castle of Otranto* (1764) to Bram Stoker's *Dracula* (1897). The gothic and supernatural gained innumerable followers in the twentieth century, becoming a major element of popular culture in books, films, and video games.

The *Harry Potter* series has strong gothic overtones: scenes set in crumbling graveyards, shadowy figures of evil, and many descriptions of the labyrinthine castle that houses Hogwarts. But the gothic is only one part of an enormous fantasy revival that swelled in the last decades of the twentieth century. Fairy tales have been almost endlessly reworked in television and film, and the "high fantasy"

Lord of the Rings blockbuster film trilogy directed by Peter Jackson grossed around $3 billion worldwide. Fantasy, fairy tales, supernatural, and gothic works have become a mainstream part of contemporary global culture.

WHAT LIES BEHIND THE DEEP HUNGER FOR FANTASY? Part of the reason is surely an increasing disaffection with technology. The middle decades of the twentieth century saw the "golden age" of science fiction, which promised a future of flying cars and space colonies. But technology today seems less and less likely to deliver utopia. Although "cool" technological products certainly exist, from robots to iPads, people are painfully aware of the environmental and perhaps even spiritual degradation that has accompanied technological progress.

It is surely no accident that the wizarding world of *Harry Potter* is a resolutely un-technological, even anti-technological one. Its denizens choose broomsticks over cars, ride old-fashioned steam trains, and ineptly attempt to use the telephone. Rowling occasionally creates a parallel consumer world, most notably in the series of finely tuned broomsticks that Harry and his friends covet. But her descriptions of Harry's dreadful Dursley relatives, sheep-like consumers of new cars, television sets, and video games, make clear that technology and material goods contribute to the dreariness of the Muggle realm. Harry's cousin Dudley, in particular, who spends the early part of the series in solitary, hypnotized contemplation of the television set, serves as a memorable contrast to Harry and the deep friendship and trust that he develops with Ron and Hermione as they engage in schoolwork, adventures, and sports.

Belief in something intangible, whether inside or outside the self, characterizes a great deal of the "magic" in *Harry Potter,* a magic that often relates to how the characters protect themselves from the dark forces massing around them. Most important is Harry's patronus, the stag-like figure of protection that he conjures out of his memories of and love for his father. But there is also the spell "riddikulus!" with its invocation of laughter and lightheartedness, which all the Hogwarts students learn in order to protect themselves from the terrifying Boggarts. Magic alone cannot help Ron when he seems to be failing in Quidditch, but magical help from Hermione helps him regain belief in his ability. On a more negative note, one of the key struggles that Harry deals with in the later books is his fellow wizards' refusal to believe him when he tells them that the evil wizard Voldemort has returned.

Besides disillusionment with technology and a desire for faith in something numinous, specific elements of the fantastic mode itself are particularly appealing to the contemporary world. To understand the special aspects of fantasy, it is helpful to go back to A. S. Byatt's comment that *Harry Potter* is "written for people whose imaginative lives are confined to . . . exaggerated . . . mirror-worlds." Leaving aside the elitist snobbery and ignorance that imbues Byatt's remark, there is a paradoxical nugget of wisdom in her characterization of fantasy and popular culture as exaggerated. In fact, fantasy is in many ways a genre of exaggeration. Fantasy exists in an uneasy, complex relationship to the real. As Eric Rabkin says, fantasy reverses the ground rules, allowing readers to explore "an unknown land, a land which is the underside of the mind of man."[6] Far from being escapist in the sense of allowing us to crawl into the nonthreatening "mirror-worlds" that Byatt excoriates, fantasy allows us to dream of alternate worlds, whether utopian or dystopian, that can critique our own. In this regard, fantasy can be seen as undermining the established order. It is subversive in the sense that Rosemary Jackson in *The Fantastic: The Literature of Subversion* describes: "characteristically attempt[ing] to compensate for a lack resulting from cultural constraints: it is a literature of desire, which seeks that which is experienced as absence and loss."[7]

Paradoxically, fantasy can be seen as conservative as well as subversive. Fantasy offers compensatory worlds that can serve as critiques of the world around us, an essentially subversive function. At the same time, these compensatory worlds, especially if they address powerful desires, can have a conservative side as well, especially by offering a glimpse of home. As Tolkien put it, "Why should a man be scorned if, finding himself in prison, he tries to get out and go home?"[8] Indeed, the quest for home is a fundamental aspect of most fantasy stories. Tom Moylan asserts, "The romance or the fantastic . . . focuses on a quest for what has been repressed or denied, for *Heimat*."[9] At the turn of the twenty-first century, where the stability, constancy, and continuity that the term *home* evokes seems increasingly threatened, it is not surprising that a work like *Harry Potter*, which shows us many versions of home, should strike a resounding chord.

The series begins with the orphaned Harry as virtually a prisoner, confined to a cupboard in the house of his dreadful Dursley relatives. While Harry's confinement and ill-treatment by the Dursleys evokes such classic fairy tales as "Cinderella," it is important to appreciate how the Dursleys' house and the village of Little Whinging are memorable satires on the numbing quality of middle-class life. Far from being a genuine home, the Dursleys' house, in its narrow-minded mediocrity and suburban sterility, strikingly encapsulates a contemporary form of prison, the straitjacket that middle-class affluence can become in a world without imagination.

Like Tolkien's prisoner, Harry longs for escape. In his case, deliverance arrives memorably and magically, first in the form of owl post, which is not only anti-technological in its use of owls rather than electronics but also prizes the ancient art of writing. Harry's liberation comes literally through letters, in this case the letters of acceptance from Hogwarts, which deluge the Dursley home and finally force them outside their suburban comfort zone.

Harry's next escape evokes both the traditional magical portal of fairy tale and its more recent iterations, such as the magic wardrobe in *The Lion, the Witch, and the Wardrobe*. In this case, the magic portal is Platform 9 and ¾, which Harry must go through at King's Cross, an act that requires belief rather than scientific proof, since he cannot see the platform and must force himself through what appears to be a brick wall. Once through, he finds another alternative to the modern world, the old-fashioned steam train that carries him to Hogwarts.

Hogwarts, in the initial part of the series, seems to be the home that Harry has been searching for, a place of security and support where his friends become a kind of family and the headmaster, Dumbledore, appears as an almost omnipotent surrogate father figure. Despite its vast size and labyrinthine features, the school gives the impression of coziness, with its welcoming fireplaces, turret bedrooms, and, in time-honored British fantasy tradition, copious amounts of delicious and wholesome food. The beautiful Scottish landscape around Hogwarts evokes the pastoral and arcadian tradition of British fantasy, even including (in an obvious nod to *The Chronicles of Narnia*) creatures from ancient myth, such as the stargazing centaurs who live in the nearby forest.

Harry finds another home in the Burrow, the house belonging to the family of his best friend, Ron Weasley. While Hogwarts, with its mysterious grandeur and hint of wildness, stands in dignified and implicitly masculine distinction to the Dursleys' suburban house, the Burrow evokes the chaotic warmth of female-nurtured family life. Presided over by the series' only true mother figure, the generous and protective Molly Weasley, the Burrow suggests an organic, all-accepting womb. In a sly bit of suburban parody, the Burrow even has its own garden gnomes, but the gnomes are alive and quite annoying.

If the series had ended early on with Harry happy at Hogwarts and the Burrow, perhaps Byatt would have had some reason to label the *Harry Potter* books as comfort food. But it turns out that even in the world of *Harry Potter,* home is not always a safe and welcoming place. As the series continues, both Hogwarts and the Burrow change from oases of comfort to places of insecurity. At Hogwarts, the change is so dramatic and disturbing that it almost shakes the series out of its positive fantasy framework, leading to the traumatic core that energizes the series. In the last book, Rowling dismantles the protective edifice that has shielded Harry and the others from early on, ending with a virtually apocalyptic vision of Hogwarts in ruins, the Burrow deserted, and many of the supporting characters dead.

This devastating conclusion, especially the destruction of Hogwarts (although it is followed by a reassuring coda), is painful for readers of the books and viewers of the films as well as for the characters. Hogwarts has been depicted as a refuge of safety, fellowship, and community. As a boarding school, it can evoke, especially for British readers, memories of the popular children's school stories by Enid Blyton, all of which end happily. Above all, Hogwarts was a magical fortress, supposedly impervious to any form of invasion. Is its destruction perhaps too disturbing, especially for children?

In fact, the magical elements of Hogwarts and of the series itself prepare readers to deal with such devastation. Like Narnia and the Shire, the two other great places of refuge in British fantasy, Hogwarts is a powerful emotional presence in the minds of readers and filmgoers. And like Narnia and the Shire, Hogwarts is a place "under perpetual threat," as Laura Miller describes Narnia.[10] Both Narnia and the Shire are invaded, and their way of life is distorted and attacked in the last volumes of their series. For child readers, accustomed to the happily-ever-after of traditional fairy tales, such scenes of devastation can be truly shocking, almost unforgivable.

Places of beauty and refuge are destroyed every day in the real world, but as the endings of all three series show, life can and must continue. By providing visions of annihilation that are not part of the day's news, fantasy writers give readers and film viewers a way of processing, at a safe remove, a fundamental human nightmare, the loss of home. Narnia, the Shire, and Hogwarts are homelike and near in our minds, but also comfortably far away in reality. And in each case, their creators take pains to offer a vision of rebirth to help allay the pain of their destruction. *The Chronicles of Narnia* promises life in an even better version of Narnia. Tolkien's promise in *The Lord of the Rings* is more down-to-earth: the gardens of the Shire flower again. Rowling's coda shows us a Hogwarts reborn and the next generation of students boarding at the magical Platform 9 and ¾.

How does the relationship between the fantastic and trauma function in the series? How does the use of trauma strengthen the appeal of *Harry Potter*? To understand the interaction of trauma and fantasy, we might return to Byatt's use of the term "exaggerated." Fantasy can take readers (or viewers) out of their normal surroundings and into another realm. But the exaggerated or defamiliarizing nature of the fantasy genre, with its outsize characters, epic situations, and supernatural activities, provides the reader a safe zone in which to experience and process traumatic events.

What is trauma? Literally, "trauma" means "wound," but as described by Freud, it specifically refers to a wound that does not heal, one that continues to cry out long after the initial wounding. More recently, the scholar Cathy Caruth has defined trauma as "a response, sometimes delayed, to an overwhelming event or set of events, which take the form of repeated intrusive hallucinations, dreams, thoughts or behaviors."[11]

Harry Potter's situation exemplifies trauma in its most fundamental form. He faced overwhelmingly traumatic events from the time he was a baby, when the evil wizard Voldemort murdered his parents. Harry's permanent forehead scar from that event embodies Freud's "wound that does not heal." It "cries out" increasingly as the story continues, in the intense bouts of pain that Harry experiences when assailed by Voldemort's feelings and memories. Perhaps even worse are the repeated hallucinations of his parents' death, obvious manifestations of post-traumatic stress. These memories and hallucinations can become completely incapacitating, as when Harry is almost killed after they cause him to fall off his broomstick during a Quidditch match in *The Prisoner of Azkaban*.

The immediate cause of Harry's emotional and literal downfall is a race of terrifying supernatural creatures known as dementors, who suck all hope and good feelings out of any person they confront. The dementors are clearly inspired Tolkien's hideous Nazgul figures, once-human kings who fell under the spell of the ring of power and became bone-chilling, cloaked, and hooded ringwraiths. But whereas the ringwraiths are reminders of the corrupting nature of power and the human potential for evil, the dementors embody the deepest form of psychological depression.

While Voldemort seems rather one-note and hackneyed in his dark deeds, the dementors brilliantly evoke a newly discovered kind

of threat. By externalizing Harry's depression into terrifying supernatural creatures, Rowling allows the reader to confront one of the
most crippling of modern ailments. Her solutions to the dementors'
threats are also brilliant, since they run the gamut from the prosaic
(eating chocolate) to the magical (creating a protective patronus).
The image of the patronus, which takes the form of a stag symboliz-
ing Harry's father, while magical, is grounded in reality. It is a solution embodying wisdom: challenge trauma by reaching into oneself
and one's memories to create an emotional force field that embodies the best aspects of home and family.

It is not an accident that Harry's patronus is a highly idealized version of his father. Much of the books' action is about Harry's search
for a compensatory father figure as well as a home. As Harry learns
more about his father, he begins to understand that unlike his idealized early vision, his father, James, was rebellious, rule breaking,
and, most disturbingly, a bully. But it is not only Harry's biological
father who is fallible. The surrogate father figures too have their
failings. In fact, a parade of inadequate, inept, or absent father figures marches through the series. The horrendous Mr. Dursley not
only brutalizes Harry but also emotionally damages his own son,
Dudley, by indulging Dudley's appetites and overlooking his failings. Mr. Weasley, while a loving father, is inept and at times amazingly ignorant of his specialty (Muggle affairs). Lupin, Harry's best
teacher in the Defense of the Dark Arts classes, is a werewolf who is
forced to leave Hogwarts because he cannot help menacing his former students. Sirius, Harry's godfather, is reckless and frustrated,
ultimately helping bring about his own brutal demise at the end of
Harry Potter and the Order of the Phoenix.

Most disturbing of all are the revelations about Dumbledore, the
great wizard headmaster of Hogwarts, who at first appears to be
the epitome of a classic mentor figure—wise, generous, and farseeing. As the series continues and darkens, however, Dumbledore becomes perplexing and problematic, a master wizard who may have
betrayed family and friends and is possibly manipulating Harry for
his own ends. He is not evil, but complex and lacking, in ways atypi-
cal of conventional mentor figures. Dumbledore is finished off in
a disturbingly violent scene, although he does return in the series'
rather mystifying ending.

Most children's books, not only fantasy ones, contain violent incidents that challenge the hero. Furthermore, Harry's orphanhood
and his adventures with his peers put him in a classic line of youthful protagonists, from fairy tales to the nineteenth-century English novel. Dickens practically developed a cottage industry about

plucky young heroes making their own way through industrializing England. At the farthest reaches of the empire, Kipling's Mowgli and Kim found their way through the jungles and cities of India. Twentieth-century British fantasy contains numerous examples of young protagonists coping more than adequately with adventure and without much adult guidance: E. Nesbit's children in books such as the time-travel fantasy *The Story of the Amulet;* the Pevensie family, who ultimately become kings and queens in *The Chronicles of Narnia;* and the young hobbits Merry and Pippin in *The Lord of the Rings,* who return home, tough and hardened from adventuring, just in time to save the Shire.

For children and young adults, the wish-fulfilling fantasy of coping on your own without parental hovering is an immensely appealing one. The crucial difference, however, between those earlier works and the *Harry Potter* series is that the protagonists in the former have mentors or authority figures whom they can turn to for guidance, such as the "learned gentleman" in *The Story of the Amulet* or Gandalf in *The Lord of the Rings.* In the twenty-first-century world of *Harry Potter,* the all-knowing and heroic Gandalf has metamorphosed into the problematic Dumbledore. What happened? This crucial absence of a mentor figure relates to the traumatic core of the series: Harry and his friends are alone in a virtually parentless world. The theme of absent or disabled authority figures recurs repeatedly: Neville Longbottom's parents are driven insane by Voldemort's torturers, and Hermione decides to wipe out her Muggle parents' memories of her, making her, in essence, another orphan.

What does it say about the *Harry Potter* generation of readers and viewers that they can accept and even embrace a world of evil, inept, or absent authority figures? Some commentators, noting Rowling's left-wing politics, find in *Harry Potter*'s world a critique of Margaret Thatcher, the authority figure under whose administration the young J. K. Rowling would have gone to school and grown up. The French philosopher Jean-Claude Milner suggests that the "occult" culture of Hogwarts is Rowling's critique of (and perhaps compensation for) a "world where the Muggles have indeed taken power."[12]

But is *Harry Potter* simply a fantasy response to the limitations of Thatcherism? If it were, it would hardly have achieved such a following outside Britain. Instead, the traumatic elements of *Harry Potter* seem to mirror, remarkably closely, certain trends in the contemporary world. The dismantling of safe structures—institutional, professional, and familial—and the increasing lack of trust in authority are not aspects only of Thatcher's Britain.

The loss of faith in authority, the concomitant need for belief in something outside the disappointing real, and the dystopian and apocalyptic elements in *Harry Potter* are echoed in contemporary popular culture. In several fantasy films released in 2012, including the gothic *Snow White and the Huntsman,* the comedic Pixar work *Brave,* and Wes Andersen's quasi fantasy *Moonrise Kingdom,* young people are forced into metaphorical and literal forests where they must survive on their own. The most compelling recent work is Suzanne Collins's blockbuster series *The Hunger Games,* which, in both book and film form, inhabits a fantasy world even darker than *Harry Potter*'s. In the dystopian realm of *The Hunger Games,* authority is not only corrupt and evil, but also specifically targeted against young people, who are forced to sacrifice themselves in a consummately violent battle for survival.

It is both depressing and significant that *Harry Potter* and *The Hunger Games* end with the protagonists retreating into domesticity once the battle has been won. Unlike the Pevensie children in the *Narnia* books, Harry and his friends do not become "kings and queens" who rule wisely and benevolently in the new order. And in contrast to Merry and Pippin at the end of *The Lord of the Rings,* they do not even seem to play much role in reviving the post-conflict world, an absence that is particularly disappointing given the many times we are told of Harry's leadership skills and Hermione's cleverness.

This is not to take away from the richness of the *Harry Potter* series. Humor, imagination, love, and hope remain major elements throughout the works. It is also possible to argue that because of their lack of mentorship, these young people were able to find stronger inner resources in their peers and in themselves. In this regard, Harry's patronus stands as a brilliant fantasy exemplar of how to work through the trauma of loss and despair. However disturbing some of Harry's real father's traits might have been, and however powerful the forces confronting him, his father's symbol of the radiant stag becomes a fantastic image of defiance and hope. It is an image that literally illuminates and helps Harry transcend the darkness of a complex and all too real world.

Spring Semester 2012

1. Lee Siegel, "Harry Potter and the Spirit of the Age: Fear of Not Flying," *New Republic,* 22 Nov. 1999.

2. Harold Bloom "Dumbing Down American Readers," *Boston Globe,* 24 Sept. 2003.

3. A. S. Byatt, "Harry Potter and the Childish Adult," *New York Times,* 7 July 2003.

4. Ron Charles "Harry Potter and the Death of Reading," *Washington Post,* 15 July 2007.

5. Dennis Kratz, "Development of the Fantastic Tradition through 1811," in Neil Barron, ed., *Fantasy Literature: A Reader's Guide* (New York, 1990), p. 3.

6. Eric Rabkin, *The Fantastic in Literature* (Princeton, 1976), p. 45.

7. Rosemary Jackson, *The Fantastic: The Literature of Subversion* (London, 1981), p. 3.

8. J.R.R. Tolkien, "On Fairy Stories," in *The Tolkien Reader* (New York, 1966).

9. Tom Moylan, *Demand the Impossible: Science Fiction and the Utopian Imagination* (New York, 1987), p. 34.

10. Laura Miller, *The Magician's Book: A Skeptic's Adventures in Narnia* (New York, 2008), p. 56.

11. Cathy Caruth, ed., *Trauma: Explorations in Memory* (Baltimore, 1995), pp. 4–5.

12. Jean-Claude Milner "Harry Potter—est-il de gauche?" *Liberation,* 26 Oct. 2007.

The Black Hole of Calcutta. Illustration from Louis Figuier, *Connais-Toi Toi-Même: Notions de Physiologie* (1879).

20

The Black Hole of Calcutta

DAVID WASHBROOK

For Britons of a certain generation, the legend of the Black Hole of Calcutta stands alongside those of the death of General Wolfe, the siege of Khartoum, and the defense of Rorke's Drift in the making of "Our Empire" story. After the fall of Calcutta in 1756 to the forces of Siraj-ud-Daulah, Nawab of Bengal, 122 British soldiers and 1 British woman were supposedly locked overnight in a confined space, where most of them suffocated to death. In response to this "outrage" and act of Oriental perversity, Robert Clive raised a military force, recaptured the British East India Company's principal citadel, overthrew Siraj-ud-Daulah, and set in motion the events leading to the rise of the British Empire in India. Imperial conquest, here, was represented as just retribution for egregious sin.

In *The Black Hole of Empire* (2012), Partha Chatterjee, a leading postcolonial critic and historian, casts a wary eye over the legend and its own history. He offers us, he says, two intertwined but distinguishable accounts: one "small," consisting of the memorialization of the event in architecture, literature, and the arts in Britain and Bengal across the imperial epoch; the second "big" (one might say huge), signaled by his subtitle, *History of a Global Practice of Power,* which is held to stretch more or less seamlessly from the fall of Tipu Sultan in 1799 to the American-led invasion of Iraq. His first perspective is highly insightful, at times quite brilliant in what it reveals. His second leaves many questions unanswered.

Whether there was a real Black Hole incident at all remains disputed among historians. The woman alleged to have died in it, for example, was still alive in Calcutta in 1801. Indeed, P. J. Marshall, in his authoritative *Bengal: The British Bridgehead* (1988), chooses to omit virtually all reference to the Black Hole. The legend appears to have been started in 1758 by John Zephania Holwell, as much for reasons internal to the politics of the East India Company as to expose Asiatic moral depravity. Moreover, because those politics failed, the alleged atrocity drew little public attention for thirty years. It was not until the 1780s that the story was revived to provide justification for the destruction of Tipu Sultan, the notorious Tiger of Mysore far away to the south, who most seriously challenged the company's interests. For the next three decades, it gained further currency as the company progressively consolidated its dominion over India, putting down a series of "cruel Oriental despots" as it went.

With victory assured, however, the needs of the day changed. As the British tried to convey the ineluctable superiority of their civilization, the legend's ambiguities became uncomfortable: it portrayed the defeat of British power at Indian hands. The next generation turned its gaze away. When the first Calcutta memorial to the Black Hole collapsed in 1821, it was not rebuilt. Yet back in England, new purposes and ambitions stirred. Resurrection of the legend for later Victorian consumption owed most to Lord Macaulay, who transformed its symbolic meaning. Rather than merely justifying the destruction of "Oriental tyranny," the Black Hole pointed to the need to bring Indians under the civilizing influence of British education, morals, and the rule of law. Liberals embraced it alongside their conservative forebears, making its "truth" incontestable. At the high noon of empire, the greatest of all Indian Viceroys (certainly in his own estimation), Lord Curzon, rebuilt the Calcutta memorial to set the legend in stone.

On the British side, parts of the story have been told before— by Kate Teltscher, Robert Travers, and Linda Colley—to which Chatterjee adds detail and depth. But where he really comes into his own is in telling the Bengali side: how Calcutta society understood and responded to the legend of its own barbarity. Chatterjee explores the resulting reappraisals, contestations, and attempted reconstructions through philosophical tracts, history textbooks, newspapers, novels, and plays written over more than a century. He examines a wide range of social practices too, from politics (Bengali "terrorists" took inspiration from Siraj-ud-Daulah's alleged misdeed) to sport (Bengali teams sought revenge for the Battle of Plassey on the football pitch). The result is a rich cultural history, especially of urban Calcutta, that strongly conveys the feeling of colonial (and incipient national) time and place. Even more, it helps explain the pervasiveness of a myth based on only the most tenuous of evidence. While the colonialists themselves may sometimes have doubted the legend of the Black Hole, the colonized were much less equivocal. Their emancipation was closely bound up with its refutation or reinterpretation.

Chatterjee's "small" history is certainly worth the price of the book. Whether the same can be said of his "big" history is more doubtful. As the portentous term "global practice of power" implies, his main concern is the discourse of imperialism down to the present. In particular, he excoriates liberalism for having promised so much and delivered so little: its early glimpses of universal liberty were subsequently compromised by applications of "the rule of colonial difference." Yet why this should have been so is never very clear, with explanation largely subsumed under the deus ex machina of capitalism and modernity, whose own character is never explored. This is the more puzzling because, from most historical perspectives, capitalism and modernity would appear closely associated with the phenomenon of liberalism in the first place.

Indeed, a major tension in Chatterjee's "big" history derives from the extent to which, while deploring the conceits of liberal theorists, he does so from unacknowledged premises that appear ultra-liberal. He expresses outrage that, in practice, universalist principles should have been sacrificed to claims of "exceptionability," in this case of colonized peoples. Yet in the real world, the accommodation of difference and exception to ideals of equality and universality must ever be the quandary of liberalism: a universal rule without flexibility is easily judged insensitive and oppressive, yet a preparedness to accommodate all difference can be deemed morally vacuous. The interesting issue is not that liberalism observes a rule of difference, but how precisely that difference comes to be defined and justified under specific sociocultural (and historical) circumstances. Unfortunately, Chatterjee's moral fervor tends to get in the way of cultural and historical precision.

This is not least because—curiously, for a student of discourse—his discursive practices give hostages to fortune. He chooses to write extensively in the first person plural. But while he claims the term is collective, he never makes clear who "we" are, and correspondingly, his rhetoric can sound less collegial than partisan: dismissive of those, both among his historical subjects and his readers, who are not "we." Also, since it can be assumed that "we" know what "we" are talking about, the strategy permits him to avoid having to define terms—be they "capitalism," "modernity," "imperialism," or even "liberalism" itself.

He also writes (after Foucault) as if "we" existed outside capitalism and modernity and could be capable of offering a distanced critique. Thomas Blum Hansen once noted how far Chatterjee's narrative strategies, in previous work, followed the trope of loss of innocence and situated him inside a "romanticist episteme" in which the alternative to the horror of contemporary modernity was taken to be either a lost "indigenous" culture or a "community-based" form of society, neither of which he was ever able to specify adequately—although the former sometimes bore an uncomfortable resemblance to upper-caste Hinduism.

In *The Black Hole of Empire*, "we" are on new terrain that, following Dipesh Chakrabarty's seminal *Provincializing Europe* (2000), at least recognizes the significance of the European Enlightenment. "Our" fall now appears to be from a global "early modernity" that offered many possibilities beyond the wretched colonial domination that ensued. Undoubtedly, history always offers unfulfilled possibilities, and the outcomes of the twentieth century can never be simply written back into the circumstances of the eighteenth. Nonetheless, there may have been compelling reasons why history turned out as it did, which Chatterjee brushes over, and his understanding of the "early modern" is highly selective and self-contradictory.

One of the rare heroes in Chatterjee's story is Rammohan Roy, who offered an early nineteenth-century vision of a multicultural society, based on principles of representative government, in East India Company–dominated Bengal. Yet Rammohan was a wealthy landlord, strongly committed to the principles of Cornwallis's Permanent Settlement, involving peasant expropriation; the strengthening of the powers of both the state and capital over social resources is an unmistakable theme of the "early modern" in India, independent even of colonial rule. What role the lowly and "non-propertied" would have played in Rammohan's ideal of government is not very clear. Moreover, if, as Chatterjee insists, a brutish mercantilism, installed by Europeans, had been part of the state system of South Asia since the sixteenth century, and if, as he no less forcefully insists, their social practices in the eighteenth century had already laid the ground for the scientific racism of the later nineteenth, it is hard to see how Rammohan's vision of multiculturalism can ever have had much chance of realization or been much more than a dream. Dreamscapes, no doubt, are useful in provoking moral reflection, but they rarely make for convincing history.

Fall Semester 2013

A version of this lecture appeared in the *Times Literary Supplement*, 5 October 2012.

School savings, Japan, 1936. Courtesy of the Communications Museum, Japan.

21

Britain and Japan

SHELDON GARON

O thers have written on the history of Anglo-Japanese diplomacy. Yet few appreciate the breadth of political and cultural relations between the two island empires. These ties
feature prominently in my book *Beyond Our Means: Why America
Spends While the World Saves* (2012). Although an historian of Japan, I
also incorporate the histories of the United States, Britain, and several other European countries in the book. It tells the modern story
of saving money not simply as a comparative history of case studies,
but as a transnational history that emphasizes interconnections over
the past two centuries. As they did in many areas of policy, nation-
states investigated how other countries encouraged popular thrift
as a key element in building stable societies and national power.

Japan is commonly portrayed as the great imitator—the plucky
nineteenth-century nation that adopted and adapted Western civilization. In actuality, transnational flows of ideas and institutions at
the time rarely moved in one direction, that is, from the West to
countries in the so-called periphery, like Japan. Indeed, during the
late nineteenth and early twentieth centuries, nations in Europe,
North America, and Australasia resembled Japan in that they systematically studied one another, and at times they would even learn
from Japan. It is within this global framework that I discuss the importance of Anglo-Japanese relations.

American scholars devote little attention to British influences on
Japan. Most highlight the role of Germany in the emergence of the

modern Japanese state following the Meiji Restoration of 1868. The new regime, writes Ian Buruma, chose to "go the German route," emulating German military discipline, mystical monarchism, and blood-and-soil propaganda.[1] Unquestionably, German learning was central to the development of Japanese science, medicine, philosophy, and universities. Moreover, the Imperial Japanese Army modeled itself self-consciously on the German army. Inspired by Helmuth von Moltke's thinking, Japanese oligarchs introduced an independent general staff directly responsible to the emperor in 1878 (interestingly, a few years before von Moltke achieved independence for the German general staff).

Nonetheless, the common view of a Germanic Japan is based largely on hindsight, colored by Japan's alliance with Nazi Germany decades later. Modern Japan was shaped by a variety of foreign influences. British models were particularly important. On the diplomatic front, Japan's closest relations until the 1930s were with Great Britain. Despite Japanese fascination with German institutions and ideas, relations between the two states were none too friendly. In 1895, following Japan's victory in the Sino-Japanese War, Germany joined Russia and France to force Japan to return the Liaodong Peninsula to China (the Russians thereupon seized Liaodong for themselves). Kaiser Wilhelm further enraged the Japanese that year by warning of the "yellow peril" (*gelbe Gefahr*). Believed to be the first to utter this phrase, he called on the white nations to unite against Japan before it could take control of China and expel Westerners from Asian markets. The British chose not to heed the Kaiser's warnings. In 1902, the two island empires concluded the Anglo-Japanese Alliance. Japan became Britain's surest military ally. Remarkably, the two nations pledged mutual support "if either signatory becomes involved in war with more than one Power." The alliance enabled Japan to isolate Russia and eventually to triumph in the Russo-Japanese War (1904–5). It also provided the basis for Japan's entry in the First World War on the side of the British and the Entente. Although both sides agreed to terminate the Anglo-Japanese Alliance in 1923, the two nations continued to cooperate as major powers in the League of Nations and at naval disarmament conferences. And while the Imperial Japanese Army long identified with the German officer corps, the navy from the start modeled itself after the Royal Navy.

Not as well known are the many stories of how Britain inspired Japanese thinking and institutions. During Japan's Meiji era (1868–1912), the Victorian penchant for character building had an enormous impact on Japanese officials as well as on members of the emerging middle class. The best-read Western author in the early Meiji period was undoubtedly the Scottish writer Samuel Smiles. His signature book, *Self-Help* (1859), related the stories of self-made men who rose from humble origins by dint of character, perseverance, honesty, diligence, thrift, and self-denial. Much as we describe Smiles as "Victorian," his books possessed an extraordinary global appeal. *Self-Help* was translated into more than twenty languages. Appearing in 1871, the Japanese translation became an instant best seller.

Why would a book focused on individual striving and the "self" prove popular in a collectivist society like Imperial Japan? As Earl Kinmonth explains, Smiles's message meshed well with the Confucian thinking of former samurai and the aspiring young men of the "New Japan."[2] Smiles likewise trumpeted self-cultivation and self-discipline. Japanese leaders appreciated his inclination to relate individual striving to national progress and a prosperous political economy. They, no less than their Western contemporaries, recognized character building and nation building as two sides of the same coin. *Self-Help* took its place as one of Japan's first officially approved "ethics" textbooks, taught in elementary schools throughout the country. The Ministry of Education later disseminated illustrations of stories from *Self-Help,* profiling those characters whose inventions contributed to the wealth of their nations.

The Japanese moreover admired Smiles's eagerness to cultivate sound habits in the populace as a whole. This eminent Victorian appealed to Japanese officials and middle-class activists who strove to improve the masses. *Self-Help* begins with tales of self-made men, but quickly moves to exhortations aimed at workers who would remain workers. Everyone, insisted Smiles, was capable of improving themselves and the nation by practicing self-reliance, diligence, and thrift. He reaffirmed that message in another best seller, *Thrift* (1875). Like his friend William Gladstone and other British Liberals, Smiles supported the establishment of national institutions that would enable the humbler classes to help themselves. These included savings banks, the Post Office Savings Bank, and thrift education in the schools. In Japan, state officials twice translated *Thrift* (1885, 1905) and frequently invoked Smiles's books in their ubiquitous savings campaigns.

In *Thrift,* the author exhorted not only men, but also women and children. To encourage the British to save, Smiles appealed to the "thrifty, cleanly woman," whom he called upon to spend the family's money "wisely" and keep household accounts fastidiously. Smiles reflected his age in this respect. Britain was awash in advice books aimed at middle-class wives, notably *Mrs. Beeton's Book of Household Management* (1861). Smiles was a friend of Isabella Mary Beeton, and his son later married her younger sister. Mrs. Beeton became famous for instructing women to write down all expenditures in a "Housekeeping Account-Book."

At the time, few such "housewives" existed in Japan, where male patriarchs usually managed household finances. Yet the Victorian ideal of the middle-class housewife would inspire Japanese women's activists and savings-campaign organizers. Over the decades, Japanese wives became associated with the act of saving within the family. Following the Second World War, the thrifty housewife emerged as the social norm in Japan. Millions read housewives' magazines and kept standardized household account books. As in nineteenth-century Britain, wives were expected to stop their men from dissipating the family's savings on women and wine. The archetypal Japanese housewife gained even greater power in the post-war years. Husbands routinely surrendered their paychecks to wives, who then doled out "pocket money" to the man while saving substantial portions of the balance. When it came to teaching children thrifty habits, Meiji-era officials were also swayed by Smiles's recommendations to expand "school savings banks." By 1906, Japan boasted one of the highest rates of school saving in the world. One-quarter of the nation's elementary school students held postal savings accounts.

Victorian influences on Meiji Japan went well beyond ideas of character building. In the realm of institutions, the new national networks of communication owed much to British models. Like contemporaries in the U.S. Post Office, Japanese officials looked to the Royal Mail for inspiration. Upon returning from a mission to London in 1871, the first supervisor of the posts—Hisoka Maejima—rapidly modernized the country's traditional postal system. He established uniform rates for mail delivery, as had Rowland Hill with the penny post in 1840, further introducing the Victorian innovation of inexpensive postal money orders. While in London, Maejima also stumbled upon the British Post Office Savings Bank (established 1861), hailed internationally as an outstanding vehicle for improving the working class. In 1875, Japan became the third independent nation to adopt postal savings. The institution proved wildly popular. The Japanese postal savings system is today the world's largest *bank* by assets. Similarly, the Japanese state built its nationwide telegraph network on the basis of the recently nationalized British system, which placed telegraph offices under the Post Office.

The Russo-Japanese War ushered in a new phase in the history of Anglo-Japanese political relations. Following its victory over the Russians, the world's only Asian power moved from being merely a taker to a *maker* of transnational knowledge. For the first but not the last time in the twentieth century, Japan emerged as a model to leading nations in the West. President Theodore Roosevelt was an open admirer of things Japanese. The cult of Japan was most pervasive in Japan's ally, Britain. In the wake of humiliating setbacks in the Boer War (1899–1900), the British of all ideological stripes called on their country to pursue "national efficiency." Observing the Russo-Japanese War, several British correspondents and volunteer nurses sent back glowing reports of Japanese "efficiency" in tactics, military hygiene, and humane treatment of prisoners. Some went further, imputing military success to the mass mobilization of the Japanese home front. The nation's strength, argued British observers, lay in the state's success in persuading all Japanese to engage in sacrifice for the good of the country.

Alfred Stead, a reporter and son of the preeminent journalist William Thomas Stead, popularized this view in his provocatively titled *Great Japan: A Study in National Efficiency* (1906). In the foreword, former Liberal prime minister Lord Rosebery gushed about what Britain might learn from Japan. While his own country "muddled through" and the "old State machine creaks on," Japan represented a "nation determined on efficiency," led by a "directing and vitalizing Government that shall do and inspire great things." In Japan, Stead elaborated, "no one Atlas is left to bear up the skies—every man, woman, and child is ready and proud to share the task." Ironically, Stead located the source of modern Japanese patriotism in the country's ancient code of bushido (the "way of the samurai"). Even poor shopkeepers and milkmen, he insisted, "retain all the instincts of the samurai."

How could the British imagine emulating Japanese success if it were based on a seemingly Oriental tradition? To understand this, we need to appreciate the transnational and circular reinvention of bushido. During the rule of the Tokugawa shoguns (1603–1868), the warrior code applied only to the samurai, whose families constituted about 5 percent of the country's households. It would have presumptuous—and illegal—for the great mass of commoners to embrace bushido as the national creed. However, in 1899, an American-trained educator named Inazo Nitobe elegantly repackaged the code in his widely read book *Bushido: The Soul of the Nation*. It is noteworthy that Nitobe wrote the book in English, and only later was it translated back into Japanese. His mission was to explain to Westerners (including his Philadelphia-born wife) how bushido

provided the Japanese with a moral code equivalent to religious instruction in Europe. Far from being the preserve of the samurai,
bushido allegedly had come to infuse the entire nation with loyalty,
patriotism, and "chivalry."

Here was a version of bushido defined by encounters with Western nationalism and ready for export back to the West. Like Nitobe,
many British commentators associated bushido with knightly chivalry—as something existing in both their own past and the Japanese present, and as something they could draw upon to make Great
Britain great again. H. G. Wells, a champion of national efficiency,
wrote *A Modern Utopia* (1905) during the Russo-Japanese War. His
utopia would be governed by honest, self-sacrificing administra-
tors, whom he pointedly called the samurai. The founder of the Boy
Scouts was another devotee of bushido. In *Scouting for Boys* (1908),
Robert Baden-Powell exhorted scouts to revive "some of the rules
of the knights of old." Unfortunately, he noted, "chivalry with us
has, to a large extent, been allowed to die out, whereas in Japan, for
instance, it is taught to the children, so that it becomes for them a
practice of their life."

The cult of national efficiency had a major impact on Britain in
the First World War. Confronting the reality of protracted war, the
traditionally liberal British state leapfrogged Japan to mobilize the
home front as few others had done. It created an array of top-down
organizations that helped channel production, labor, and the people's savings into the war effort. Influenced in part by Japan's semi-
official local associations in the Russo-Japanese War, the Treasury set
up the National War Savings Committee, which coordinated a new
nationwide network of local committees and grassroots War Savings
Associations. Several political leaders and businessmen who had
previously promoted Japanese-style national efficiency played key
roles in wartime mobilization. They urged the government to enlist
the services of "every man, woman, and child," echoing the phrase
applied earlier to Japan. Sir Robert Kindersley, investment banker
and Japanophile, directed the war savings campaign. Kindersley later related the success of the National Savings Movement to
its having been placed upon the "same foundation as that of the
Samurai—the spirit of self-sacrifice and of personal service for the
State. . . . [It] was this spirit *permeating the whole country* which won
the war for us."[3] This evocation of British bushido may have been a
bit forced, but Kindersley articulated the transnational discourses
of national efficiency circulating around the globe at the time.

And in another exhibition of this circularity, British wartime innovations in turn inspired Japanese efforts to rally civilians during

the inter-war decades. At the height of the First World War, the Japanese government dispatched teams of military and civil officials to London, capital of their closest ally. There they systematically surveyed programs of home-front mobilization, fascinated by, among other things, new propaganda techniques and nationwide savings and economizing campaigns. When the Japanese government launched a new round of peacetime savings campaigns in 1924, it chose to emulate the apparatus of the British National Savings Movement. The powerful Home Ministry set up a central committee in imitation of the National War Savings Committee and then established thousands of local volunteer committees and residential savings associations. Just as in the British Isles, officials enlisted the support of teachers, social work organizations, and religious associations. Based on their study of British and American wartime drives, campaign organizers incorporated the latest methods of mass persuasion, including advertisements, motion pictures, essay contests, posters, and radio (the last was inaugurated in Japan in 1925).

The Japanese state and society were likewise stimulated by the changing gender roles that accompanied mobilization in Britain and other belligerents. Visiting Japanese officials in 1916–18 frequently reported on wartime Britain's reliance on women to work in factories and to volunteer in savings and food campaigns. For the Japanese state, appealing directly to the nation's women was something new. In the three-generation households of the time, as noted earlier, patriarchs typically controlled the family's finances. Wives were rarely regarded as savers and consumers, nor did many assume civic roles at either the local or national level. Beginning in the 1920s, Japanese campaigns—aided by the emerging women's groups and mass-circulation housewives' magazines—targeted the "housewife" as the saver-citizen. By the late 1930s, it had become the common understanding that savings drives would focus their efforts on persuading wives. The campaigns moreover enlisted women's groups as foot soldiers in their neighborhoods.

Japan embarked on war with the Republic of China in 1937 and with the Anglo-American powers in 1941. The war must have ended Japan's decades-long fascination with Britain, one would think. Nazi institutions and strategies became the rage in the wake of the Anti-Comintern Pact of 1936 and the Rome-Berlin-Tokyo Axis of 1940. Leading intellectuals wrote enthusiastically about the Nazis' controlled economy and Fascist Italy's corporatism. And like the Nazis, the Japanese state dissolved all political parties, labor unions, and most other independent associations. Those organizations were reconstituted as units of the Imperial Rule Assistance Association in

1940. The association never achieved the level of control exercised by the Nazi party-state, although several of its architects were ardent fascists.

Surprising as it may seem, Japanese officials nonetheless continued to investigate British models throughout the war. Wartime Japan was not as isolated as is commonly thought. It was certainly much more complex than Allied propaganda's images of xenophobic, emperor-worshipping fanatics would suggest. Britain and Japan were not officially at war until December 1941. Japanese military men, diplomats, and journalists stationed in London were thus able to file detailed reports about the British home front during the first two years of the European war. Thereafter, Tokyo relied on Allied and neutral-nation journalism to gather information on British conditions.

Japanese planners embraced the doctrine of "total war," and they considered Britain one of its best practitioners. The Japanese, like the other powers, claimed to have learned the lessons of the First World War. In the next war, they agreed, the home front would be just as vital as the battlefront. To finance protracted war, civilians would have to save and economize; their food supply would have to be maintained in the face of blockades; popular morale could not be allowed to collapse; and factories and neighborhoods would need to prepare against the newest threat: aerial bombardment. Although inter-war Japanese strategists were most drawn to the total-war thinking of the German army, they recognized that Germany in the First World War had suffered famine and demoralization while the British home front held. They were also well aware of Britain's extensive preparations for the coming war, which required the unprecedented reorganization of civilian life. Neighborhoods were organized into Air Raid Precautions units, Savings Groups, and the Home Guard. When war broke out in September 1939, the British government quickly instituted a nationwide food-rationing system. It carried out the mass evacuation of children from London and other vulnerable cities. Japanese observers in London reported admiringly on the nation's ability to endure German bombardment in the Blitz.

So it was that Japanese officials continued to emulate aspects of the British war effort even as the two nations fought each other. Between 1938 and 1945, the Japanese government ran a highly interventionist savings campaign that, once again, was patterned after the British National Savings Movement of the First World War—right down to the name of the coordinating agency, the National Savings Promotion Bureau. Food rationing was introduced in 1941–42. Like the British state, the regime worked hard to encourage the production of nutritious alternatives to scarce staples. To prepare for air raids and to enforce rationing, Japanese officials organized communities into block associations and, below them, ten-household neighborhood associations. Parallels extended to the intense mobilization of women at the local level. With men away at the front or in war industries, the middle-class matron in both countries became a familiar figure, exhorting neighbors to save more. Women in both countries served as air raid wardens and in neighborhood firefighting units.

This is not to say that the Japanese primarily emulated wartime Britain. Rather, the logic of total war made the Japanese remarkably receptive to an array of models from the Axis and Allies alike. In official reports on improving Japanese civil defense or food policy at the height of the war, investigators typically referred to German practices first, British measures second, and often the programs of the Soviet Union third. Although Japanese leaders were staunchly anticommunist, Japan and the Soviet Union remained neutral toward each other until the last days of the war. Strategists expressed less interest in U.S. home-front policies because of America's weaker mobilization efforts before entering the war, as well as a history of less cordial relations between the two states.

The Second World War ended in 1945, but key aspects of the wartime experience persisted in many of the former belligerents. In post-war Japan, the state revived the savings and economizing drives just one year after surrender. Renaming them the "National Salvation Savings Campaign," officials exhorted the people to save as much as they could and to submit to "lives of austerity." This was necessary, leaders insisted, to fight galloping inflation and to finance recovery after U.S. bombers destroyed the centers of some sixty-six cities. One finance minister in 1947 recalled wistfully how the war savings campaigns had imposed "healthy discipline" on consumers, adding that "the importance of accumulating capital has not in the least changed from the wartime to the present."[4] Japan was occupied at the time by an American-led coalition of the victorious Allies. Occupation authorities voiced concern about the undemocratic, interventionist nature of the new wave of campaigns. Yet the post-war Japanese government forged ahead, mobilizing the nation's 80,000 local savings associations as if the war had never ended.

It is common to look back upon these punishing savings campaigns as just another instance of the Japanese state's historical obsession with micromanaging society. At the time, however, there was nothing peculiarly Japanese about austerity movements. Japanese

officials themselves observed that it did not matter whether countries emerged from the war "victors or vanquished." Nearly every
nation was running savings and austerity campaigns in the early
post-war years, they noted, including the French, Belgians, Dutch,
and Soviets. Like Japan, much of Europe lay in ruins. National savings drives offered one of the few means of quickly channeling the
populace's meager wealth toward reconstruction.

Japanese bureaucrats reserved their greatest praise for British statecraft. In the final months of the war, the National Savings
Committee launched a new campaign: "Keep on Saving." Citizens
were exhorted not to let up once the war ended, for continued self-
denial would build a "new and better Britain." Wartime rationing
remained in effect for milk, eggs, meat, soap, and other necessities;
the rationing of some goods persisted until 1954. Bread, which had
been freely sold in wartime, was rationed between 1946 and 1948.
National Savings campaigns remained a fixture of British life during the early post-war years. In 1950, some 300,000 savings volun-
teers and 170,000 Savings Groups operated in England and Wales.

In the immediate post-war years, unlike the time of the Russo-
Japanese War, the British evinced little interest in studying Japanese
measures. The two countries had been bitter enemies, and Japanese
expansion had hastened the end of the British Empire in Asia. Japanese officials were quicker to put aside war memories. They again
looked to Britain as the leading model of austerity. The United
States provided fewer lessons to Japan, having emerged from the war
with no damage, a manageable debt, and rising living standards. By
contrast, the British may have won the war, noted the future prime
minister Hayato Ikeda in 1947, yet they "have not chosen the easy
path."[5] They "have rationed even bread," and the British people
"have persevered, wearing extremely old and shabby clothes, and
eating small meals." In so doing, Britain had invested the "money
and material saved by lives of austerity" in economic recovery. This
may have been the first and last time that anyone admired British
popular fashion.

But in its perceived national efficiency, Britain loomed as a challenge. Japanese officials contemplated the resumption of free trade
in the near future, fearing that their recent foe was surpassing Japan in the austerity contest. The frugal British, concluded Ikeda,
"are in a hurry to establish a favorable position that allows them to
strut upon the stage of global economic competition."[6] Indeed, like
Japanese contemporaries, British leaders noted that their "island
nation" desperately needed to export manufactures to pay for imported food and raw materials. To revive its export industries, early

post-war British governments sought to boost domestic savings and investment while severely constraining consumption at home. Japanese financial officials envied Britain's success in securing an enormous loan of $3,750,000,000 from the United States in 1946, at a time when foreign investors considered Japan too risky. The British succeeded, the Japanese believed, only because their citizens saved so much while living in destitution and austerity.

Half a world apart, Britain and Japan both embraced the politics of austerity well into the 1950s. Appealing to wives in particular, campaigns exhorted households to engage in "wise spending" in Britain and "rationalized consumption" in Japan. Even as consumption levels rose rapidly in the two countries, households heard nearly identical messages to strike a "balance" between saving and spending. Although the Conservative Party was less impassioned about austerity than Labour, Conservative cabinets too tended to subordinate consumption to other priorities. The Churchill government in 1951 launched a savings campaign to reduce spending at home for the twin purposes of financing rearmament and producing more exports. As late as 1955, another Conservative government ordered a National Savings campaign, "Restraint in Spending," to diminish imports, promote exports, and improve Britain's balance of payments. In Japan, Right and Left united behind comprehensive programs of economic nationalism after the end of the Allied occupation in 1952. In what became known as "industrial policy," the state helped finance and support export industries. Protectionist policies constrained the demand for imports, and the government's Central Council for Savings Promotion ran ongoing savings and economizing campaigns. Established in 1952 and staffed by the Bank of Japan and the Ministry of Finance, the Central Council worked closely with residential women's groups, youth associations, and the nation's schools. Soaring rates of domestic saving provided the low-cost capital underpinning Japan's spectacular economic growth from the mid-1950s.

The parallels and interconnections between Britain and Japan were not to last forever. Neither country looked on the other as a model after 1960. Britain continued to decline as a military power, and it lagged behind the surging Continental economies, notably West Germany. Japan rose to become the world's second-largest economy by the early 1970s. While the Japanese state maintained an enormous role in the economy and everyday life, Britain adopted policies of neoliberalism and deregulation. By the early 1980s, Japanese confidence bordered on arrogance. Elites and the media crowed that the century of learning from the West was over. Britain became an object of derision—a nation enfeebled by the "English disease." Unlike the Japanese, it was said, the British had lost their work ethic and vitality; they fixated on redistribution and social leveling rather than expanding the economic pie.

Nonetheless, the phenomenon of transnational emulation continued, albeit with a cast of new characters. Several Asian nations arose as economic powerhouses—South Korea, Taiwan, Singapore, Malaysia, and then China. Each resembled Japan in its penchant for state-managed growth and the aggressive mobilization of society. Pundits explain these Asian success stories as the product of a unique regional heritage, labeled Confucianism or "Asian values." Consider a typical image from recent decades, that of Singaporean schoolchildren lining up to deposit money in their postal savings accounts. Such images prompted leaders such as Singapore's Prime Minister Lee Kuan Yew to boast of Asian thriftiness and discipline, which they contrasted with Western consumerism and moral degeneration. But school savings banks and other disciplinary mechanisms were hardly Singaporean innovations. Many of these practices originated in nineteenth-century Britain and other European societies. They spread around the world and profoundly influenced Japan, whose post-war "economic miracle" in turn inspired countries like Singapore. Before latching onto Asian values, Singaporean leaders in the 1970s commonly lauded Samuel Smiles and the Japanese model in the same breath. In short, we cannot fully understand any nation's history by limiting ourselves to developments and culture in that particular nation or region. Studying the Anglo-Japanese exchange of ideas and institutions sheds new light on the transnational history of an impressively interconnected world.

Spring Semester 2012

1. Ian Buruma, *Inventing Japan, 1853–1964* (New York, 2003), pp. 52–53.

2. Earl H. Kinmonth, *The Self-Made Man in Meiji Japanese Thought: From Samurai to Salary Man* (Berkeley and Los Angeles, 1981).

3. *Silver Bullet* (National War Savings Committee), 6 Aug. 1919, p. 115.

4. Takeo Kurusu, quoted in Sheldon Garon, *Beyond Our Means: Why America Spends While the World Saves* (Princeton, 2012), p. 257.

5. Quoted in Garon, *Beyond Our Means,* p. 260.

6. Ibid.

The possible breakup of Britain

22

The Breakup of Britain

LINDA COLLEY

The uneven rise of Scottish nationalism is deeply interesting, but not because it is hard to explain or because it is the only domestic fracture that matters. It has long been accepted that neither the Union of Crowns of 1603, which saw the Scottish King James VI move south to London, nor the Treaty of Union of 1707 served to cancel out Scottish distinctiveness. In educational, ecclesiastical, intellectual, and legal terms, and not only those, Scotland has always retained significant differences. Moreover, Great Britain (and still more the United Kingdom) never sought to operate as a determinedly assimilationist nation-state in the way post-Revolutionary France often tried to do. This does not mean the UK can be regarded merely as a multinational state, or (*pace* some postcolonialist commentators) as an English-constructed empire.

Instead, the UK has most closely resembled what the Columbia political scientist Alfred Stepan styles a "state-nation." Like many other state-nations—Spain, for example, Germany, or indeed India—it is a composite of countries that were once separately ruled and that remain characterized by important differences and levels of autonomy. To function and to cohere, state-nations have to operate on two levels. On the one hand, their rulers and publicists need to nurture and sustain a sense of belonging with respect to the wider political community, while, on the other, accepting and providing protection for politically salient diversities of language, religion, ethnicity, sacrosanct cultural and legal norms, or distinct territorial enclaves. It follows that the revival of separatism north of the border should be seen as more than a result of changes within Scotland itself. Rising Scottish nationalism has also been a function of a more widespread weakening in the sense of British belonging.

Some of the reasons for this weakening are well known. After 1945, a previously strong though never unanimous sense of British imperial and Protestant destiny faded; the UK became more culturally diverse; and economic and associational connections between Wales, Scotland, England, and Northern Ireland formerly sustained by common participation in trade unions and nationalized industries were substantially dismantled. Globalization too has challenged cultural as well as economic distinctiveness. Take the fate of HP sauce. This was invented in Nottingham in the 1890s, named in honor of the Houses of Parliament, and once produced in massive quantities in a celebrated factory (since demolished) in Birmingham. Now, bottles of HP sauce are manufactured in Holland by Heinz. The Palace of Westminster still features on the label, but since the revival of the Scottish Parliament in 1998, this building no longer houses the only legislature in Britain.

Westminster's altered position in the wake of devolution has contributed to something even more significant: the reduced force of a once powerful British "constitutive story" that stressed the polity's superior constitutional liberties and efficacy. Like most such narratives, this constitutive story functioned to tell people who they were, not simply to offer a version of the past; and it was propagated by such major figures as Jean-Louis de Lolme, William Blackstone, Henry Hallam, Thomas Babington Macaulay, William Stubbs, Frederic Maitland, and A. V. Dicey, and by multitudes of lesser authors such as David Lindsay Keir, the son of a Scottish Presbyterian minister. Keir's workmanlike *Constitutional History of Modern Britain since 1485,* which went through nine editions between 1938 and 1969, was both a celebration of how the British government was "conducted by . . . men sharing a common political tradition," and an affirmation of the way "institutions the world over . . . testify to the resilience and continuity of the British tradition." It is easy now to forget how pervasive constitutional histories of this sort once were in British schools, universities, and private libraries. It is also easy to overlook what they achieved. Indisputably patriotic scripture, they nonetheless offered readers some instruction in the way their central government had evolved over time and in how it was supposed to work. To that extent, these works functioned as a (limited) substitute for a written constitution. Now, such stories are rarely taught or read; and there is still no written British constitution.

A constitutive story, argues Rogers Smith, another American political scientist, is a narrative that recounts the key historical events that formed a community and describes the "priceless" character traits that community members have evolved as a result. When a state ceases to be able to direct or foster its own constitutive stories, he suggests, understandings of historical memory tend to become more localized. This is what has happened in Britain. One of the accompaniments of rising nationalism in Scotland has been a spectacular explosion of Scottish historical writing, much of it scholarly, some of it selective and imaginary. Either way, Scots are fast making their own constitutive story.

All this should seem familiar stuff to historians, since it is almost a cliché that nationalist movements characteristically seek to appropriate and rewrite the past. But present-day historians tend to be sniffy about nations and nationalism. Many now prefer to dwell on the fragmentary and the local, and on the permeability of national allegiances; or conversely, they opt for the transnational or the global past as subjects. Current Scottish nationalism is a useful reminder of just how potent and inventive nationalism continues to be.

Yet in regard to the current state of Britain, as with much else, those who stress the importance of the local, on the one hand, and the global, on the other, have a point. It is arguable, for instance, that the differences between the northern and southern sections of the island of Great Britain—imagining a line drawn roughly between Grimsby on the east coast and Gloucester to the west—have often been as important as the boundary between England and Scotland, or Wales and England. Class alignments and levels of urbanization complicate this north-south divide, but it remains significant for income, longevity, diet, cultural behavior, politics, and much more, and it has been persistent. In the late fifteenth century, English monarchs felt obliged to create a separate Council of the North, an arrangement that endured into the seventeenth century. In the late eighteenth century, Yorkshire and Lancashire were bastions of middle-class and working-class radicalism. The pattern of industrialization served to publicize the divide, as suggested by Elizabeth Gaskell's novel *North and South,* published in 1855; while in the early twenty-first century, Conservative MPs have become a scarcely less endangered species in northeastern England than they are in Scotland, and are under pressure too in the northwest.

Indeed, the fortunes of the last three Prime Ministers have been influenced by this north-south divide. It says something about the ambiguities of the Union that all three are of Scottish ancestry, as is a current Conservative pretender, Michael Gove. Gordon Brown was born in Scotland, went to university there, and has represented only Scottish constituencies; and this unalloyed Scottishness undoubtedly worked against him in sectors of the English media and electorate. Conversely, although four generations of David Cameron's paternal ancestors lived in Aberdeenshire, he was born in London, and this—along with his time at Eton and Brasenose, and a safe seat in rural Oxfordshire—makes him appear not just English, but explicitly southern English, something that does him little good in Scotland or with some in northern England. A friend at York University tells me that some of his local students would choose rule by Alex Salmond from Edinburgh over government by Cameron in London, and not just for party-political reasons. By contrast, some of Tony Blair's wide and protracted electoral success was surely due to his occupying a regional middle way. Born in Scotland, a student at Oxford, a pupil barrister at Lincoln's Inn, he was also the MP for Sedgefield in the industrial north.

The regional fractures within Britain merit attention and imaginative organizational expression. In the future, and whether the Union survives or not, there could usefully be an assembly or senate of the regions, with each being allocated the same number of representatives. This is not a new idea. Before the First World War, Winston Churchill played with the idea of dividing England into seven regions as part of a wider federal reorganization. But new modes of regional representation would not only benefit varieties of the English. The farther north one travels in Scotland, the more likely one is to encounter local councilors who choose to define themselves as Independents, as distinct from Scottish National Party or Labour. To some in the Northern Isles, Edinburgh seems as alien as London.

Thinking more inventively about regional identities would also benefit Scottish and English universities, which at present are being dragged further apart by the different funding policies of Edinburgh and London—and by politics. Students in England and Wales will soon have to pay up to £9,000 a year for a university education. But the Scottish government plans to make this increased fee apply only to English, Welsh, and Northern Irish students coming to study in Scotland. Scottish students in Scotland—along with incoming students from all other countries in the European Union—are to receive free university education. Under cover of a noble principle (free higher education as a right), a kind of nationalist academic apartheid is being constructed. In the future, students from England may well be less inclined to enter Scottish universities, out of exasperation at having to pay fees from which Scots are exempt. Conversely, many Scots are likely to be put off from studying south of the border by the prospect of heavy fees there. Yet it would surely advance the transmission and the quality of knowledge on both sides of the border, as well as wider economic development, if the top universities in northern England and lowland Scotland were actually brought into closer cooperation, assisted perhaps by some generous forced loans from the banks. That way, there might finally develop a northern-based knowledge consortium that could compete with and balance the influence and clout of the so-called Golden Triangle in the south.

For if there is to be greater recognition of regional and national differences and autonomies, there will also need to be better provision—both in Britain and throughout Europe as a whole—for bringing together the multitudinous different communities and interests. As it is, Europeans at present too often resemble the characters of Satyajit Ray's wonderful film *The Chess Players,* in which early nineteenth-century Indian nobles are shown persisting in their traditional cultural pastimes, bickering with one another, and obsessively playing chess, while all around them the British are advancing and the world is inexorably changing.

Now it is Europeans who often give the impression of wanting only to bicker with one another, play games, and look obsessively within, while—outside their continent—all is yet again changing, and not in their favor. SNP zealots and manic English Euroskeptics can sound strangely alike. Once free of London, the former insist, the world will be our oyster; once free of Brussels, the latter claim, all options will again be available to us. Such dizzy and utterly unrealistic expectations are probably a leftover of the joint Scottish and English experience of global empire. But the world is not like that anymore.

Spring Semester 2013

A version of this lecture appeared in the *London Review of Books,* 2 August 2012.

A. J. P. Taylor (c. 1962) and Hugh Trevor-Roper (1980s). Trevor-Roper photograph by Peter Lofts.

23

A. J. P. Taylor and Hugh Trevor-Roper

ADAM SISMAN

Biographers are often thought to side with their subjects—so what does it mean to have written lives of two men thought to be rivals, even enemies? I have written biographies of two British historians, Hugh Trevor-Roper and A. J .P. Taylor, and my purpose here is to consider whether one has helped me understand the other.

After giving a lecture, I was once asked about my life of Taylor, who was often considered Trevor-Roper's rival. "Now that you have studied both men in detail," my questioner began, "which do you prefer?" I replied emphatically that I didn't have a preference, and moved on to other topics. As I was signing copies of my book afterward, the same questioner cornered me. "Now that nobody else can hear us," he said, "you can tell me frankly: which do you prefer?"

In one sense the question is trivial: why should it matter one iota which one I prefer? But it does open up the wider topic of how biographers feel toward their subjects, and whether those feelings influence what they write. In writing a biography, one spends a long time alone with the person one has chosen to write about, and it is a natural to develop an attachment toward him or her in the process. Such attachments carry their own risk; the resulting books can be cloying or even embarrassing. It is not hard to think of biographers who have fallen in love with their subjects and lost their heads.

But if it is possible for biographers to admire their subjects too much, the opposite is also true. It is a common observation that

biographers who dislike those whom they have chosen to write about
tend to write unlikeable books. Biography, like marriage, is a long-
term commitment. It is not much fun to spend several years in the
company of a person one doesn't much care for. If the experience of
exploring a life is distasteful to the writer, it is likely to be so for the
reader also. This is particularly true of biographers who were en-
amored of their subjects but became disillusioned as they came to
know them more intimately. Heroes seldom survive close scrutiny.
For the hero-worshipper, the experience of disappointment is often
bitter, and such bitterness can poison the pen, staining the page.

It is natural for biographers to stress the significance of their subjects. To a large extent this is a process of self-justification: why would
one want to write about a person who wasn't important? Or, to put it
another way, the greater the significance of the subject, the greater
the significance of the biography—and perhaps, of the biographer.
To this extent, biographers are predisposed to act as their subjects'
champions. Which brings me back to Taylor and Trevor-Roper. How
can the same biographer champion two men who were professional
rivals and who took opposite sides in a heated public controversy? I
faced this potentially awkward problem when I took on the subject
of Trevor-Roper after I had written about Taylor. It was complicated
by the fact that I knew Trevor-Roper personally, while I never met
or even laid eyes upon Taylor, except on a television screen. Indeed,
though I had known him slightly for years, I came to know Trevor-
Roper well only after I had consulted him as a source for my biography of Taylor. I had approached him with some trepidation because
I shared the popular misconception that the two men had been not
just rivals but enemies.

I first met Trevor-Roper at an Oxford party in 1977. I was then
in my early twenties, and a junior editor with Oxford University
Press. I had forgotten the circumstances of this meeting until almost thirty years later, when I found in the OUP archives a letter I
wrote to him the next day. As I recalled the event—an exciting one
for me, not least because I also met Isaiah Berlin—I remembered
that I had begun the conversation cautiously, having been warned
that Trevor-Roper could be acerbic; I found him surprisingly affable. Subsequently, I invited him to lunch with two of my colleagues,
which turned out to be a stiff occasion. Only later did it occur to me
that he might have been shy, causing him to retreat behind a screen
of reserve.

We were in sporadic contact over the next dozen years as I pursued my early career in publishing. In 1990, I began work on my
first book, the biography of A. J. P. Taylor, who had died earlier in

the year. Trevor-Roper generously granted me several interviews, lent me copies of letters from Taylor and other relevant documents, and commented on a draft of my book. "I have read it with great interest and qualified pleasure," he wrote—"qualified only because it is a melancholy as well as a fascinating story." After it was published in 1994, he reviewed it favorably in the *Sunday Telegraph*. By then, we had become friendly and I was visiting him now and then at his house, the Old Rectory in Didcot. One cold winter morning I arrived to find Trevor-Roper and his wife, Xandra (both then in their eighties), in a state of agitated distress as water from a burst pipe streamed down the wall of their dining room, damaging wallpaper and pictures. Though no plumber, I climbed into the roof space and succeeded in stopping the leak.

After Xandra went into a nursing home and subsequently died, I visited Trevor-Roper more often. I drove him to his hospital appointments and dined with him at High Table in Oxford and at his home. Though almost completely blind, he was determined to continue an independent existence, and insisted on cooking me meals, refusing any offer of help. Watching him trying to light his antiquated gas stove was an alarming experience: he would turn on the gas, strike a match, and then stoop to peer at the burner until the gas caught light with a whoosh, causing the elderly historian to spring backward to avoid the jet of flame.

Trevor-Roper found it increasingly difficult, and eventually impossible, to read, so visitors would often read aloud to him, sitting in front of the gas fire in his study. I remember one occasion in particular when I read to him a piece that A. J. P. Taylor had written in the *London Review of Books,* which I had come across in the course of researching my biography. Taylor had praised Trevor-Roper as an historical essayist without rival. "When I read one of Trevor-Roper's essays," Taylor wrote, "tears of envy stand in my eyes." He continued with a personal comment: "I often read that Hugh and I are rivals or even antagonists. On my side, and I can confidently say on Hugh's, this is totally untrue. We have always been good friends and no cross word has ever passed between us." At this point I glanced at my elderly companion, who was listening intently as he leaned forward in his chair; and I hope that you will not imagine that I am embellishing when I tell you that his own eyes were moist.

At some stage the possibility arose that I might write his life. Until recently I had persuaded myself that the proposal came from him, but correspondence in his archive indicates that it originated from me. (This was a salutary reminder of the unreliability of memory.) In any case he did not actively discourage the suggestion. "There is no-one whom I would *like* as my biographer better than you," he wrote, but "I really doubt whether I merit a biography at all: what is there to say?" In another letter a year or so later, he wrote that he was frightened of what he called my "strange project." "My life has been totally conventional and uninteresting," he protested, "there is nothing to commemorate. I agree with Voltaire: 'La vie d'un écrivain sédentaire est dans ses écrits'—and my écrits are very slender. Nor am I proud of my life: on the contrary," he claimed, quoting Housman:

> When the bell justles in the tower
> The hollow night amid
> Then on my tongue the taste is sour
> Of all I ever did.

I thought he was wrong, and persisted. We talked regularly about his past, and he offered me glimpses of his dauntingly voluminous archive. He introduced me to his friend and literary executor, Blair Worden, who encouraged me to write the book. Both insisted that I should have a free rein to write whatever I liked. Trevor-Roper, who did not like being treated with too much reverence, often quoted Gibbon's preference for praise "seasoned with a reasonable admixture of acid."

I last saw him about ten days before his death in 2003. He was then in a hospice, and aware that the end was near, but he remained interested in the outside world to the last. "What news," he would often ask, "from the Republic of Letters?" I was never convinced that I was qualified to answer that question. When my biography of him was published in 2010, I thought it only honest to admit that I might have been influenced by feelings of loyalty, affection, and gratitude.

I could have had none of these feelings for Taylor, because, as I have already said, I never had any personal contact with him. But my friendship with Trevor-Roper largely postdated my book on Taylor. I was therefore interested to review my account of the relations between these two in the biographies I had written of each, published sixteen years apart. I especially wanted to see whether my friendship with Trevor-Roper had influenced my account of the episodes in which both were involved in his favor.

TAYLOR AND TREVOR-ROPER HAD FIRST been in competition in 1938, when both were interviewed for a teaching Fellowship at Magdalen College, Oxford, which Taylor eventually won. I hadn't been aware of this early rivalry when I wrote my biography of Taylor. By 1951, both men had established themselves to the extent that they were the two most obvious candidates for the post of Professor of Modern History at Oxford, the so-called Third Chair. As so often in these cases, the opposition to each of them outweighed the support, and the job was offered to a compromise candidate, one who had not even applied and who expressed considerable surprise at his appointment.

As I discovered while I was working on Taylor's biography, he and Trevor-Roper had much more in common than most people appreciated. Though Taylor leaned to the left, and Trevor-Roper to the right, more significant was that both were independent thinkers. Their temperaments too were similar. Both were sharp witted and sharp tongued. Both irreverent, they shared an impatience with the medievalists who dominated the Oxford History Faculty. Both were combative characters, unafraid to express controversial opinions in public and willing to cause offense if necessary. Both contributed articles and book reviews to the national press, and both broadcast on the BBC in a period when their stuffier colleagues felt such activities to be demeaning to a don. Both were thought to be interested in money, and both liked to drive a hard bargain. Both took a keen interest in the recent history of Germany, and in central Europe generally. Though never intimate friends, the two were on good terms in the early 1950s. They respected each other's work. They would sometimes meet for a drink or a meal. Sometimes Taylor would call on Trevor-Roper and they would take a walk together.

The contest for the Third Chair in 1951 had gone largely unnoticed outside Oxford. But in 1957, Taylor and Trevor-Roper were again candidates for an Oxford professorship, the Regius Professor of Modern History, generally regarded as the most senior post in the History Faculty but not normally an appointment that attracts much attention outside the academic world. In 1957, however, it was headline news. The coverage identified Taylor and Trevor-Roper as rivals, an image that persisted in the public imagination.

One reason for the interest in the contest was that it could be depicted as political. Unlike most professorships, Regius appointments were in the hands of the Prime Minister, acting on behalf of the monarch. The Prime Minister would consult the Chancellor of the University, who in turn consulted the Vice-Chancellor. At the same time, the Appointments Secretary (commonly known as the patronage secretary) canvassed the opinion of those whom it was thought fit to consult. In the case of the Regius Professor of Modern History at Oxford, those interested parties included members of the History Faculty and representatives from the college where the chair was based, Oriel. In the class-based politics of 1950s Britain, this system of appointment could easily be seen as a manifestation of outdated privilege.

Moreover, the fact that several of the candidates for the post were familiar to the public made the competition for the Regius Professorship news. Trevor-Roper was known as the author of the bestselling *Last Days of Hitler* and as a pundit on all matters to do with Nazidom—though in fact his interest in Hitler was a by-product of his wartime work with MI6. And Taylor was then at the height of his powers, almost certainly the most famous don in Britain. His *The Struggle for Mastery in Europe, 1848–1918* had appeared in 1954, a substantial work of old-fashioned diplomatic history, and the first volume in the series the Oxford History of Modern Europe. Early in 1957, he was asked to undertake the final volume in the Oxford History of England, which was published seven years later as *English History, 1914–1945*. Nobody else at the time could claim to have written two big Oxford histories. Taylor wrote book reviews for the *Observer* and the *New Statesman,* and columns for tabloid newspapers; broadcast talks on BBC radio; and was a regular member of the panel on *In the News,* a pioneering discussion program on British television. He was the original "tellydon."

At the end of 1956, Taylor believed he had the appointment in the bag. As an old Oriel man, he was said to be the college's preferred candidate. The Prime Minister, Sir Anthony Eden, had taken the advice of the Vice-Chancellor, Alic Smith, that Taylor should be given the post. Smith had been advised by Alan Bullock that the History Faculty backed Taylor. But though Taylor had much in his favor, he also possessed qualities that worked against him. He was prickly and a loner. His success excited envy, and his brash immodesty offended some Oxford colleagues. His epigrammatic style lent itself to uncompromising judgments. Like Trevor-Roper, he allowed his tongue to run away with him. It was typical of Taylor that when asked what he did for a living, he described himself not as an historian but as a "TV star." In politics, Taylor was a left-wing populist who enjoyed provoking people. His irreverence struck many as flippancy. His journalism seemed to some to be at odds with the values of scholarship. None of these qualities recommended him for a chair.

The press began to speculate on who would become the next Regius Professor. The *Observer* put Trevor-Rover alongside Taylor as a front-runner. Early in the New Year, the coincidental resignation of both Eden and Smith on the grounds of ill health made "the whole Regius Chair Stakes a different thing." The new Prime Minister was Trevor-Roper's publisher, Harold Macmillan, and the new

Vice-Chancellor was Trevor-Roper's former tutor and friend, J. C. Masterman, who lost no time in contacting Macmillan to emphasize that his predecessor's judgment was not to be relied upon. "The wise bookies have scrubbed the slate clear and now offer one horse only," wrote Trevor-Roper's Christ Church colleague Charles Stuart, "H. R. T-R—odds 6–4 on."

In deciding who should be the next Regius Professor, the new Prime Minister sought the advice of his old friend (and fellow Balliol man) Sir Lewis Namier. Indeed Namier might have had the chair himself had he not been too old at sixty-eight. Taylor had reason to expect Namier's favor. In the 1930s, he had worked alongside Namier in Manchester, and they had become friends. In 1956 he had been coeditor of a festschrift for Namier. Namier was fond of Taylor; he told Isaiah Berlin that some of his happiest hours had been spent at Taylor's house. But he had become stuffy in old age. He often spoke of the dignity of learning and of the need to keep scholarship pure. Namier could not understand how Taylor could lower himself to write for the popular press. In a man of learning, journalism was mere irresponsibility; and "irresponsible" was one of the most opprobrious terms in his vocabulary. Furthermore, Taylor had demonstrated his independence by writing an insufficiently respectful review of a collection of Namier's essays, and in another review had criticized the work of one of Namier's most devoted disciples, John Brooke. Namier telephoned Taylor and offered to recommend him if he would renounce journalism. Taylor refused, and the conversation ended angrily.

The chair was offered to Trevor-Roper, who accepted. Namier wrote, offering his congratulations, and Trevor-Roper replied with his thanks: "I must admit, I felt a bit of a fraud. I remain stubborn in my belief that Alan Taylor ought to have had the Chair, and that politics ought not to have excluded him; but I suppose he was *vix papabilis* [hardly the sort of person to be made pope], so I must try to wear with dignity the mantle which has been stolen from him." Taylor persuaded himself to behave graciously toward his rival. "We mustn't go on exchanging compliments (though they are deserved on both sides)," he wrote a few days after the announcement. "I am unreservedly glad at the way things have worked out. You were the only person qualified other than me; your appointment will cause quite as much pain as mine would have done; yet I'm spared all the trouble."

In fact, Taylor was hugely disappointed. Namier, he felt, had "betrayed" him. He believed that Namier not only had failed to promote his cause, but in fact had spoken against it. He wrote what was apparently a "hideous" letter to Namier, who returned it, not wanting Taylor's angry outburst to stay on the record. But Taylor broke off their friendship; they never spoke again. "The Regius Chair is a matter of unreserved pleasure to all concerned," Taylor wrote to his Oxford patron, Sir George Clark, a few days after the appointment was announced. "Everyone, including Trevor-Roper, knows my qualifications are better than his; and being vain but not ambitious, this suits me down to the ground.'

Taylor encouraged the view, widely accepted by the press, that the Regius Chair should have been his. In the preface to the volume in the Oxford History of England, he wrote that he had been "slighted in his profession." And in his autobiography, published in 1983, he gave a partisan account of the contest—so much so that Trevor-Roper wrote to him privately to correct some of his assertions. I think it is fair to claim that I was the first to attempt a dispassionate narrative of the contest for the Regius Chair. I tried to tell the story objectively while representing both Taylor's own point of view and that of his critics. At the end of my account, I attempted to assess the merits of the case. Although I understood why he had not been given the chair, and I dismissed the notion of an establishment "plot" to exclude him, my sympathies were clearly with Taylor. Trevor-Roper commented magnanimously on this passage when he read my book in typescript. "Your version is not my version," he told me, "but you have every right to tell it in the way that seems true to you."

Sixteen years later I described the same contest in my life of Trevor-Roper. I was able to add a few details as a result of my research in his archives and elsewhere: for example, that the young left-leaning historian Asa Briggs, contrary to what might have been expected, had supported Trevor-Roper's candidacy over that of Taylor, whom he deemed too irresponsible. This suggests that statements in subsequent biographies about an "intellectual consensus" in favor of Taylor were exaggerated. But the story remained essentially the same as I had written it once before. I continued to feel that Taylor was hard done by.

THE CONTEST FOR THE REGIUS PROFESSORSHIP established the notion that Taylor and Trevor-Roper were rivals, but it was the debate over the origins of the Second World War four years later, in 1961, that presented them as opponents. Taylor's book on the subject was a work of radical revisionism, the first substantial challenge to the consensus that Hitler had planned the European war that broke out in 1939. On the contrary, argued Taylor, the war had begun by accident. Hitler was a man of daring improvisation who took light-ning decisions and then presented them as the result of long-term policy. Insofar as Hitler had a foreign policy, argued Taylor, it was no different from that of his predecessors: to free Germany from the restrictions of the Treaty of Versailles, to restore a great German army, and to make Germany the greatest power in Europe from her own natural weight. Taylor discounted Hitler's talk about remak-ing the world; in his view, Hitler was a dreamer, and *Mein Kampf* a work of propaganda. He dismissed the Hossbach memorandum, a junior officer's account of Hitler's address to his generals in 1937, which had been produced by the prosecution at Nuremberg in an attempt to prove a Nazi conspiracy to commit "crimes against peace." In Taylor's view, this was evidence that Hitler was a violent and unscrupulous man, but not that he had any concrete policies, and his prophecy of events bore little resemblance to what actually happened. Taylor played down the significance of Hitler's table talk, suggesting that Hitler had merely rationalized events that had al-ready taken place.

As Trevor-Roper later pointed out, there was an element of *gamin-erie* in Taylor's makeup that led him to enjoy provoking those who unthinkingly conformed to received opinions. *The Origins of the Sec-ond World War* was praised by some reviewers as a masterpiece, but condemned by others as perverse, disgraceful, and intellectually de-plorable. One enraged critic accused Taylor of writing an apologia for the Nazis. Trevor-Roper kept his powder dry. He was one of many contributors to the correspondence generated by the review in the *Times Literary Supplement,* though only to question the logic of the anonymous reviewer, who had lauded the book as a "startlingly bril-liant performance." But it soon became known that Trevor-Roper was writing a long piece about the book. "I look forward to reading it," Taylor said in an interview with a tabloid newspaper. "He knows as much about twentieth-century history as I do about seventeenth-century history—which is not to say nothing at all." (This last sen-tence has often been misquoted, omitting the word *not.*)

Three months after the book's publication, Trevor-Roper launched a devastating polemic against it in the July issue of *Encounter.* He ac-cused Taylor of selecting, distorting, suppressing, and arranging the evidence to support his thesis, and of ignoring the program that Hitler had laid down for himself in *Mein Kampf* and elsewhere. It is hardly surprising that Trevor-Roper disliked the book. Taylor had ironically described the Munich Agreement as a "triumph for all that was best and most enlightened in British life." For Trevor-Roper, Munich had been a defining episode, the moment when he had "boiled with indignation against the appeaser." In the opening paragraphs of his piece, he recalled the passions and doubts of the 1930s. After reading the German edition of *Mein Kampf,* he had become convinced that there could be no peace with Nazi Germany, and formed the resolve that Hitler had to be stopped. To question that after all that had happened was intolerable.

Taylor responded to Trevor-Roper's *Encounter* article in a subsequent issue, comparing what he had written with what Trevor-Roper said he had written. Trevor-Roper concluded his article by saying that that the book "will do harm, perhaps serious harm, to his reputation as a serious historian"; Taylor repudiated this allegation, and alongside it wrote: "The Regius Professor's methods of quotation might also do harm to his reputation as a serious historian, if he had one."

The controversy between the two men attracted international attention, particularly in the United States, where both the *New York Times* and the *New York Herald Tribune* devoted several stories to the subject. Newspapers relished the "feud" between the "fighting dons of Oxford," particularly when Trevor-Roper agreed to take part in a televised debate with Taylor. The debate was chaired by a former pupil of Taylor's, Robert Kee. Given the sharpness of the printed exchanges, it was curiously subdued—"often lively but never bad-tempered," according to the *Oxford Mail.* Most commentators judged that Taylor won the contest, though some thought that Trevor-Roper had the better of the argument. Taylor was the more experienced television performer, and by referring to Trevor-Roper as "Hughie" while the latter addressed him as "Taylor," he succeeded in making his opponent seem stuffy. Afterward, Trevor-Roper feared that he had been "steam-rollered" by his opponent. He confessed to feeling "a bit depressed about it."

The debate on *The Origins of the Second World War* cast a long shadow. Every subsequent writer on the subject has felt obliged to respond to Taylor's thesis. There have been at least five books recapitulating and reconsidering the argument, the earliest edited by a favorite postgraduate pupil of Taylor's, Wm. Roger Louis. Three international journals have devoted whole issues to his work. In the late 1980s the American Historical Association devoted a special session to the controversy, reviewing it from the perspective of twenty-five years afterward.

My biography of Taylor devotes almost fifteen pages to the book and the debate it sparked. It explores the roots of Taylor's thinking and attempts to place his argument in a wider context, depicting it as a piece of iconoclasm, a deliberate attempt to debunk the myths bought into by British and American politicians. Trevor-Roper commented on my draft in a letter written before the book was published. "Of course I think that you have presented a one-sided account of the great controversy over *The Origins of the Second World War*," he wrote, "but then I would, wouldn't I?"

Only two pages of my Trevor-Roper biography address the argument about the origins of the Second World War. The roots of Taylor's thinking about the subject were irrelevant to Trevor-Roper's life, and his contribution to the debate, though significant, was only part of the story. But I was able to show how Taylor's portrayal of Hitler had run counter to much of what Trevor-Roper had written over the preceding decade. In "The Mind of Adolf Hitler," his introduction to *Hitler's Table-Talk*, Trevor-Roper argued that Hitler was a systematic thinker. And in 1959, Trevor-Roper had read a paper titled "Hitler's War Aims" to a conference in Germany, in which he stressed Hitler's consistency. After that essay was published, Taylor had written to him about it, warmly praising it as "a masterly production—a beautiful exercise in intellectual composition," though disagreeing with some of his conclusions—maintaining, for instance, that Hitler's acts were shaped much more by tactics than strategy. "You believe . . . you can read Hitler's mind," Taylor continued. "I hesitate: I can trace his acts (sometimes) & I'm not sure that his mind deep down was all that decisive in shaping these acts. But what you write is infinitely more interesting & stimulating than that written by others."

Both men had been offended by the Munich Agreement in 1938. For Trevor-Roper, it had been a "call to arms," while Taylor wrote an emotional letter to Duff Cooper, congratulating him on his resignation from the government over the issue. But Munich seems to have left a more lasting scar on Trevor-Roper, who was shocked by Taylor's ironic comment in his *Origins of the Second World War* that Munich "was a triumph for all that was best and most enlightened in British life." "Our generation will never escape from the 1930s," he wrote to his old friend Nicko Henderson in December 2001, only thirteen months before he died.

After the publication of my Trevor-Roper biography, I took part in a BBC radio program that revisited the famous televised debate between Taylor and Trevor-Roper, as part of a series called *Head to Head*. The format was to intersperse clips from the original debate with discussion between two guests, each of whom took the role of explaining and to some extent defending the arguments of one of the original participants. As in the Oxford Union debate sixteen years earlier, I took Taylor's part. In the opposite corner was the formidable figure of Richard Evans, Regius Professor of Modern History at Cambridge and an expert on the Nazi period. I think that I held my own, but it was a close-run thing.

To go back to the question posed at the beginning: which man do I prefer? It is probably true to say that when I first started thinking about Taylor and comparing him to Trevor-Roper, my sympathies were broadly with the former. I was then still in my thirties, and Taylor's pose as a rebel within the gates appealed to me more strongly than it does now, when I am twenty years older. Though I knew Trevor-Roper then, and liked him, I thought of him as an establishment figure, which was enough to condemn him in my eyes. I soon had cause to revise that callow judgment.

For me, the choice between the two men is loaded because I knew one personally over a considerable period of time, but never even was in the same room with the other. What is more, Trevor-Roper's archive was much fuller than Taylor's, so I had the opportunity to get to know him much better in that way too. But though I had known Trevor-Roper personally, and (so I thought) quite well, I came to know him much more intimately after his death. I recall how startled I had been when I began to research Taylor to appreciate that I was discovering things about him that not even those closest to him in his lifetime (his wives or children, for example) were aware of. I suspect that this is a universal truth: that we know far less about those close to us than we generally acknowledge.

In the archives, on the other hand, it was another matter altogether. There I could find revealing letters and other documents, including autobiographical drafts and diaries. Reading such records over a prolonged period of time left a deep impression on my mind, especially since both were such distinctive writers. In each case, their personalities were as plain to me as their handwriting. In Taylor's case, I gained a powerful sense of the character of a man whom I had never known. And Trevor-Roper's archive made me familiar with the younger Hugh, brasher and more arrogant than the self-depreciating, ironic individual I had known in old age, humbled perhaps by the chastening experience of the Hitler dairies fraud.

The embarrassing fact is that I find it exciting to rummage in an archive. While working on a biography, I become rather obsessed with my subject. Thus while working on Taylor, I am sure that I preferred him to Trevor-Roper, and vice versa. But an obsession with one's subject fades very quickly when one stops working on a biography. And it is an occupational hazard for biographers that by the time a book is published one is usually thinking about someone else.

Some years ago I read another life of A. J. P. Taylor, by an author whom I will not name. It seemed to me uninspiring, and I abandoned the book halfway through. I found myself wondering: why was I ever interested in this man? He emerged from the pages of this biography as unhappy, mean-minded, and self-serving. Why had I devoted several years of my life to him? Trying to answer these questions I pulled off the shelves a copy of my own book, which had remained unopened for some years, and started reading. At once my subject sprang to life, and I saw again what a fascinating and delightful individual he had been.

Spring Semester 2012

Four historians at British Studies: (*clockwise from top left*) Elie Kedourie, Lord Blake, José Harris, Andrew Roberts. Kedourie photograph courtesy of Sylvia Kedourie; portrait of Lord Blake by Deborah Elliott, c. 1985; Harris photograph courtesy of José Harris; Roberts photograph courtesy of Andrew Roberts.

24

Margaret Thatcher's Impact on Historical Writing

BRIAN HARRISON

Surprising to anyone for whom in the 1960s E. P. Thompson's *Making of the English Working Class* (1963) seemed in the van of progress has been the resilience and resourcefulness of historical writing about the British Conservative Party, whose mood then seemed decidedly defensive. Within British universities, especially in departments of arts and humanities, that defensive mood persisted for long after the 1960s. British universities' rapid expansion from the 1960s prompted escalation in historical research of all kinds, and in political history on the left as well as on the right. Yet whereas British labor history's dynamic seemed to stall after 1970, the history of British Conservatism went from strength to strength. In Britain today the history of Conservatism is in good health, together with lively kindred branches of history that in the 1960s seemed in decline: high political, imperial, and military. In 1955 R. T. McKenzie referred to the absence of a history of the Conservative Party since Peel as an "appalling gap."[1] No such complaint can now be made. How best to explain this change, and what did Margaret Thatcher contribute to it?

It seemed sensible to approach the inquiry directly by asking twenty-nine historians prominent since 1945 in advancing the history of modern British Conservatism and willing to discuss what prompted their research and their approach to it.[2] Andrew Roberts

firmly distances himself from the category of "Conservative historian" if it denotes a right-wing equivalent of the "socialist historians"
on the left who claim that their political allegiance generates some
special insight or even a distinctive method. He readily identifies,
though, with the category of "historian who is a Conservative"—that
is, with the historian who writes "more often about Conservatives
and Conservative governments than other kinds" and who seeks
"exactly the same rigorous level of objectivity" as any other historian.[3] For John Ramsden, writing party history was "in its very nature" partisan in the limited sense that it focuses on party activists,
not for praise or blame, but because party stands high among their
loyalties.[4] The party outlook of twenty-seven among the twenty-
nine historians in my sample is known. Eleven are "historians who
are Conservative," ten consistently support non-Conservative parties, and six are "waverers" with no firm party commitment. To the
twenty-nine, seven deceased allies must be added: Reginald Bassett, Robert Blake, George Kitson Clark, Maurice Cowling, Norman
Gash, E. H. H. Green, and John Ramsden. Five of these seven were
consistent Conservatives, with Bassett as a waverer and Green as a
non-Conservative.

The prominence of non-Conservatives among the twenty-nine is
not surprising. During Thatcher's premierships, many on the left
and in the center averted their eyes and saw her as absurd, anoma-
lous, or ephemeral, and hoped to goodness that she would soon disappear, but others felt obliged from curiosity, from self-defense, or
from a pursuit of balance to acquaint themselves with the enemy. A
similar puzzlement at the unfamiliar, not easily distinguished from
sheer scholarly inquisitiveness, may explain why the Left has so often supplied historians of the British Far Right. For Alan Sykes, for
instance, the impulse was "quite literally 'know thine enemy' and if
possible ecrasez l'infame," though no such sentiment overtly informs
his *Radical Right in Britain* (2005). G. C. Webber studied inter-war
right-wing extremism less from an inflated view of its influence in
Britain than from a belief that such studies illuminate Conservatism
in general, especially since many individuals crossed and recrossed
the dividing line between them.[5] However, Philip Williamson has recently and powerfully demonstrated the deep gulf between the Conservative Party and British fascism, together with the latter's overall
political marginality.[6] One of the two finest analyses of British inter-
war Conservatism came from Ross McKibbin, a historian well-known
for his Labour allegiance; and a centrist historian like Peter Clarke
felt no difficulty about supervising postgraduates working on Con-

servative history.[7] In *The Crisis of Conservatism* (1995), E. H. H. Green acknowledged that his "greatest debt" was to Clarke.[8]

One impulse to research for historians of Conservatism, as for others, has been its sheer fascination. For Stuart Ball, "the nature of the Conservative Party, and the difficulty in defining and capturing it, is an important factor in both drawing scholars to it and sustaining their interest—especially those who are not themselves Conservatives." The left-wing views of Bob Self, a prolific historian of Conservatism, are strongly held; yet, he says, "I always regarded the subject of my research as something completely separate and divorced from the cut and thrust of day-to-day party politics." As for Peter Marsh, a biographer of prominent Conservatives, a puzzled inquisitiveness has shaped his approach, for his Canadian Liberal and religious background led him to inquire how Conservative politicians could square their outlook with Christian social teaching.

The variety of motives prompting British Conservative historiographical advance should now be apparent. Such pluralism extends still further, inside the Conservative Party, whose success gives it the luxury of presenting a divided face to its opponents, with history deployed as a weapon in internal debate. "Historians who are Conservative" were very active in the 1970s, and the centrist Conservatives among them found a wily champion in R. A. Butler; indeed, they were sufficiently dominant in the party to argue among themselves. Butler somewhat mischievously confronted Harold Macmillan's rather grandiose six-volume autobiography (1966–73) with his short single-volume *Art of the Possible* (1971). "I have eschewed the current autobiographical fondness for multi-volume histories," says his preface, "and have preferred a single book which is not too heavy for anyone to . . . doze over in bed." In the 1970s, when Conservatives in difficulties sought guidance from history, Butler obliged by sponsoring and lightly editing the single-volume multi-author volume *The Conservatives* (1977), believing that in difficult times it might provide "a guideline for the future activities, prospects and philosophy of Conservatism."[9] More importantly, he encouraged the party's more ambitious semi-official history, which had "objective sympathy" as its declared mood. The first two of its single-author volumes appeared in 1978: Robert Stewart's *The Foundation of the Conservative Party, 1830–1867* and John Ramsden's *The Age of Balfour and Baldwin, 1902–1940*. The latter, says Ball, "showed me what could be done—and what should, and must, be done." Four volumes were planned at first, but six were the outcome by 1996. Two of these were written by R. T. Shannon, whose allegiance since the 1950s had moved from left to right and whose two-volume biography of W. E. Gladstone (1982, 1999) sought to rescue the Liberal leader from a secularized and social-democratic historiographical fate, and to restore religion, conservatism, and Conservatism to their central roles in his career.

Conservative history's vitality came from many and diverse sources, and was more spontaneous than organized, more dispersed than integrated. The direct and indirect role of Margaret Thatcher's critics was as important as that of her admirers, and in arts and humanities university circles in the 1970s and 1980s her critics were abundant. It was Thatcher's robust stance that helped produce the Social Democratic Party, which in its own way also fueled the rightward historiographical mood. David Marquand, soon to desert Labour for the SDP, published his *Ramsay MacDonald* in 1977, and his revisionist stance on the left was later reinforced by John Campbell's *Roy Jenkins* (1983) and *Nye Bevan* (1987). The vitality of Conservative history since the 1950s was pioneered long before Thatcher's became a name to conjure with. It was in the 1970s, with Sir Keith Joseph as articulator, that "bourgeois" values (self-help, thrift, self-education, foresight), which had an appeal far beyond the middle class, came out of hiding to counteract the socialist-dominated mood of public debate. Not until then was Thatcher in a position to seize her political opportunity. As for the historians, John Vincent exemplified a pre-Thatcher rightward move being made by many intellectuals in the 1970s. For him, the student revolution of the 1960s was "a Beacon of Hope," and his *Formation of the Liberal Party, 1857–1868* (1966) was imbued "with the attitude—not argument—that the Victorian Liberals were 'brave warriors in the Liberation of Mankind' in Heine's phrase." But during the 1970s, Vincent's mood grew more pessimistic and (in his own words) "became infused, not so much with Conservatism, as with Aristocratic Civilisation at its best"—so much so that he devoted years of his life thereafter to editing the diaries of aristocrats drawn from any political party.

Yet in several ways Thatcher's quest for power did indirectly foster historical inquiry. Given the failure of the Heath government (1970–4), with its pragmatic shift from free-market to interventionist policies, followed by Labour governments from 1974 to 1979, many Conservatives could find no middle ground suitable for their party: their fear of Labour hegemony and corporatist orthodoxy prompted much reaching back into Conservative history in a somewhat desperate search for a way out. Since abundant Conservative governmental experience could be drawn upon from the recent to the remote past, there was ample scope for learning from history, especially given earlier Conservative successes in propaganda and in profiting from splits on the left. These had been Ramsden's major themes in his *Age of Balfour and Baldwin*—a theme carried forward into his synoptic and ambitious history of the party since 1830 (published in 1998). There he referred to the party's "quite remarkable facility for adaptation and, closely allied to this, its appetite for power"—a facility that it was by then beginning to lose.[10]

THATCHER'S ADVENT TO POWER in 1979, consolidated by her second electoral victory in 1983, accentuated her historiographical impact. Publishers helped crystallize and firm up changed perceptions. Thatcherism "certainly helped as far as interest from publishers was concerned," Ball recalled; not only were the Conservatives back in office, but "they had become (for perhaps the first time ever) the most interesting and important subject for debate (indeed, were setting the debate)." Because her tenure was initially precarious, all weapons (including history) were deployed in a fierce battle for the party's soul. Thatcher's admirers elevated Lord Salisbury above Disraeli, and highlighted Macmillan's critics over his friends. The Conservative heroes became, for Heath, Peel the centrist; for Gash, Peel the free-marketeer; for "the wets," "one nation" Disraeli; for Thatcher's devotees, Salisbury; for Thatcher herself, Churchill overseas, though not at home. Prominent Conservatives, some still living, were demoted accordingly—most notably Butler in 1945–51, Churchill after 1951, and both Macmillan and Heath as prime ministers. For some, this outlook extended further—to repudiating whole periods of Conservative history as regrettable deviations from a norm that had ended in 1940, 1931, or even 1902. For Lord Blake, Thatcherism seemed "not a radical departure," but a reversion to the "Heathism" of 1970–2, Heathism being itself a reversion to inter-war Conservative attitudes, meaning that "the real divagation from Conservative tradition occurred in the two decades after the Second World War."[11] For Gash, Thatcherism was the third of the party's three "radical initiatives" and was only the second to succeed in government—the other two being Peel's fiscal reforms as prime minister in 1841–6 and Joseph Chamberlain's campaign in opposition for tariff reform. Gash claimed that Thatcher, like Peel, had "transformed the terms of reference for British party politics."[12]

Roberts sees history as a series of "zig-zags," and for him the Conservative Party had been "shunted into sidings . . . between 1914 and 1979." The essay on Walter Monckton in his *Eminent Churchillians* (1994) was, he wrote, "Thatcherite history . . . a straightforward polemical attack on liberal Toryism."[13] Condemnation of the centrist Conservative appeasement of organized labor at home had its overseas concomitant: the hindsighted and simplistic analysis of the National Government's appeasement of Hitler. In his *"The Holy Fox": A Life of Lord Halifax* (1991), Roberts distinguishes Halifax's more nuanced standpoint as Foreign Secretary from Neville Chamberlain's allegedly gullible variant of appeasement, and shows empathy when, for example, discussing Halifax's anti-Semitism and the impossibility of Britain's going to war in 1938 to prevent Sudeten self-determination. Yet Roberts cannot resist scrambling into the pulpit. Convinced that the roots of appeasement in the late 1930s lie in the fact that British inter-war diplomats (including Halifax) "profoundly misanalysed" the First World War's origins, he accuses Halifax of a "disastrous error" in applying to Anglo-German relations his tactics with the Congress Party in India. Chamberlain's radio reference on 27 September 1938 to the Sudeten crisis in Czechoslovakia as "a quarrel in a faraway country of whom we know nothing," Roberts dismisses as "all the more disgraceful coming from the son of the greatest imperialist of them all"; and "however stupefying this may sound," Halifax failed to apologize for Munich both during and after the war.[14]

   "The recent collapse of the post-war consensus," wrote Coleman in 1988, "may now have liberated us to ask rather different questions about the modern party's precursors." On the third page of his *Conservatism and the Conservative Party,* Coleman claimed that twentieth-century historians had hitherto redesigned the party to reflect their own centrist expectations of it, elevating those of its leaders (Liverpool, Peel, Baldwin) who could be reinvented as centrists, and showing until recently much less interest in those (Salisbury, and even the 14th Earl of Derby) who could not. From the late 1970s there was revived interest in Salisbury as exemplifying the Conservative leader who (in alliance with the Liberal Unionists after 1886) had arrested the leftward slide in British politics. Salisbury's two most vigorous champions among "historians who are Conservative," Elie Kedourie and Andrew Roberts, diverged in their view of Thatcher's pedigree. Kedourie in 1984 contrasted Salisbury's outlook with the "tender-minded Conservatism" promoted by Peel, Baldwin, and Heath, but did not liken Salisbury to Thatcher, whose pedigree he saw as Liberal rather than Conservative. Kedourie's Salisbury, "aware of the delicacy of the gradations by which right and wrong fade into each other," repudiated Gladstonian black-and-white views of politics, together with the Liberal political activism that assumed that there is a remedy for every ill.[15] The dedication of his *Salisbury: Victorian Titan* (1999) "to Margaret Thatcher thrice-elected '*illiberal* Tory,'" implies in Roberts a different political pedigree for

Thatcher, but his traditional biographical format precluded elaboration, and Salisbury's limitations receive attention so generous as to undermine the book's subtitle. In truth, no adequate discussion of Thatcher's pedigree will suffice without distinguishing between her stance in foreign and in domestic policy, and in domestic policy between two variants of Liberalism: the Victorian individualist and the twentieth-century collectivist. Whereas Thatcher's pedigree in overseas policy was predominantly Conservative, her pedigree in domestic policy was decidedly Liberal individualist.

History used for intraparty infighting is unlikely to be objective and is therefore ephemeral; less so is the longer-term impact made on historians of any color by a party's visibility in government. Success breeds success, and success demands explanation. When launching his *Ideologies of Conservatism* (2002), Green pointed out that until the 1990s "there were relatively few major surveys of the twentieth-century party," and that "the volume of work devoted to British Conservatism is far outweighed by that which has dealt with British Liberalism and Socialism."[16] By then there was felt to be a growing need for what Self calls "a corrective to a supposedly dominant and more fashionable 'Labour history' school" in interpreting Britain in the 1930s. From the late 1970s, Ball became aware of the facile tone with which historians explained away the Conservative Party's working-class supporters: the difference between Conservative and Labour was not between undemocratic and democratic, but between different ways of being democratic. In explaining Conservative success, far too much was ascribed to an irrational deference, to "false consciousness," and to the electoral impact made by the Conservative Party's superior funds and sharp practice. An outlook so lacking in nuance was, he claims, "just too determinist, and too simplistic—and, I think, very patronising in its one-dimensional view of people"; indeed, "it seemed . . . a form of snobbery."

Far more was involved here than advertising Conservatives' historical role: Conservative history's scope was being appreciably broadened. The long-standing Conservative preoccupation with biography remained secure, if only for commercial reasons, but with their growing interest in "high politics," Conservatives took new and adventurous directions. Maurice Cowling's three volumes—*1867: Disraeli, Gladstone, and Revolution; The Passing of the Second Reform Bill* (1967), *The Impact of Labour, 1920–1924: The Beginning of Modern British Politics* (1971), and *The Impact of Hitler: British Politics and British Policy, 1933–1940* (1975)—were influential. Furthermore, in their preoccupation with the social life of the elite, they opened out political history toward social history, thereby bridging the gulf between Conservative history and a Labour-permeated, working-class-preoccupied social history. Across that bridge, J. R. Vincent and others advanced into the neglected history of aristocracy. Likewise, imperial history was showing a marked capacity for self-reinvention; military history's rapid growth was subverting any notion of antithesis between soldiering and the life of the mind; E. R. Norman in his *Church and Society in England, 1770–1970* (1976) questioned how representative of their congregations and how effective in their proselytizing were the religious leaders who espoused social reform; disappointed hopes of state planning in the economy from the 1960s were helping edge economic history away from Treasury concerns and toward political economy; with encouragement from the Institute of Economic Affairs, E. G. West in his *Education and the State* (1965) and *Education and the Industrial Revolution* (1975) introduced into educational history a new rigor and a new skepticism regarding the educational impact made by the state; and the revival of the country-house ideal lent a new vitality and breadth to architectural and art history. So wide were the implications of Thatcher's retreat from the state, so arresting were her preconceptions, that the historians of Conservatism were, like her, interacting ever more widely with society as a whole.

Thatcher's preoccupation with "Victorian values" in the early 1980s exemplifies this broadened Conservative concern. Launched in a televised interview with Brian Walden on 11 January 1983, the discussion soon caught on. In a radio interview of April 1983, Thatcher described her grandmother's Victorian values: "You were taught to work jolly hard, you were taught to improve yourself, you were taught self-reliance, you were taught to live within your income, you were taught that cleanliness was next to godliness. You were taught self-respect, you were taught always to give a hand to your neighbour, you were taught tremendous pride in your country. You were taught to be a good member of your community."[17] Victorian values were not narrowly Victorian, she said: duty, responsibility to family, and self-reliance were integral to liberty and prosperity, and were "really . . . fundamental eternal truths."[18] Labour leaders competed for the moral high ground by reiterating the Dickensian critique of Victorian industrial society. In March 1983, Labour's leader, Michael Foot, in comments soon echoed by his successor, Neil Kinnock, saw Thatcher as failing to grasp even "a passing comprehension of the human suffering and indignity which the mass of our people had to endure in that predemocratic age": the labor movement had come into existence in "a fight to introduce civilized standards into the world of ruthless, devil-take-the-hindmost individualism."[19] Thatcher admitted that morality was not the monopoly of any one party, but saw morality as "the foundation of our policies . . . Enlarging choice is rooted in our Conservative tradition. Without choice, talk of morality is an idle and an empty thing."[20]

AT FIRST PROFESSIONAL HISTORIANS held aloof in their "slow-moving, restricted specialisation,"[21] but in 1986 Corelli Barnett's *The Audit of War: The Illusion and Reality of Britain as a Great Nation* located Britain's economic decline in the Attlee government's subordination of industry and commerce to the pursuit of a "new Jerusalem" through the welfare state. Despite powerful academic rebuttals of that view, the book soon persuaded Thatcher's cabinet ministers Keith Joseph and Nigel Lawson. Also influential at the time was a short book by an American historian—M. J. Weiner's *English Culture and the Decline of the Industrial Spirit, 1850–1980* (1981)—which identified the deep-rooted nineteenth-century origins of Britain's anti-industrial culture. By 1992 several reputable historians had responded more directly to Thatcher's challenge in four books with "Victorian values" in their titles, though Walvin's alone forsook professional specialization to tackle the subject as a whole in a single-author book.[22] In July 1991, a respectful article on Thatcher as "the history woman" came from an unlikely but fair-minded source: from a key figure in the History Workshop movement, Raphael Samuel. With her capacity to stir up public interest in important historical issues, and with her views unmuffled by compromise, Thatcher was, he said, "the only philosophically interesting prime minister of my adult lifetime," one who forced the British to define what it means to be British and compelled the Left to define collectivism. He regretted "that there is no longer anyone to keep us on our ideological toes."[23]

So the Thatcher governments' policies, hitherto thought politically impracticable, freed up the market in ideas as well as in commerce. Long-forgotten historical topics became interesting as subjects of historical study: philanthropy, self-help, respectability, voluntarism, privatization, and the negative variant of liberty—in short, "Victorian values." Conservatives had shied away from fully acknowledging the vitality, the self-criticism, the creativeness, the energy, and the civic responsibility of the Victorians partly because their party had never been forced to choose between its two lines of defense against the Left: championing the middle-class entrepreneurial and professional success story on the one hand and, on the other, the "Tory Democratic" vision of the benevolent landed aristocrat who defends the working man against the exploitative employer.

After Thatcher's political demise in 1990, no Conservative revisionist historian was bold enough to controvert, in a well-documented,
wide-ranging, and sharply reasoned manner, the Dickensian view
of Victorian Britain, which had lent such impetus for so long to the
British Left.

   In envisaging new policies for what we now know was a curtailed
governmental future, Thatcher and her disciples sketched out three
dimensions of a fruitful and historically based Conservative self-
defense. All three had practical purposes in mind, but also incidentally offered historians productive lines of inquiry. There was, first,
the moral case for capitalism, which in the 1970s was already being
cautiously put forward even on the left. James Callaghan as Chancellor of the Exchequer and as Prime Minister felt the need publicly
to stress the virtues of profitability; and in cabinet in October 1977,
Edmund Dell as Secretary of State for Industry deplored the fact
that a whole generation of graduates neglected such virtues: "We
have got to get them to change their attitude."[24] Conservatives after 1975 were even more robust in their arguments. Keith Joseph
complained in 1979 that "our establishment—the Church, the
educational system, the universities, the civil service, the political
parties—have broadly believed and taught that there's something
faintly discreditable about business: that business is fine, but really
it's for the tradesman's entrance."[25] By then he and Thatcher were
counteracting the post-war Conservative moral inferiority complex
when confronted by socialist egalitarian dreams. They unhesitatingly distinguished between individualism and selfishness, and emphasized the social benefits that individualism brings in its train.
The political philosopher who in 1944, with his *Road to Serfdom,* had,
in his own words, been "made to feel by most of my fellow social scientists that I had used my abilities on the wrong side," now emerged
into the limelight to challenge Bismarckian notions of the state and
to revive "the name of Gladstone," which for three decades had
been "rarely mentioned by the younger generation without a sneer
over his Victorian morality and naive utopianism."[26] Gladstonian
Liberalism was alive, socialism was doomed, and Thatcher, far from
compromising with it, was accelerating its demise.

   One consequence of this was the development of a second line
of argument: the moral case for Conservatism. Thatcher believed
that "a politician's role is a humble one": for her, the future lay
with a diminished state machine that would depend increasingly
on voluntary action. Politicians could deploy the law to set standards, they could help mold the moral environment so as "to bring
out the good in people and to fight down the bad," but ultimately

everything depended upon free choices made by the individual—the sphere of the churches rather than of governments.[27] Choice was "the essence of morality . . . the essence of religion."[28] Public welfare might be invoked from the best of motives, but if it entailed delegating personal responsibilities to impersonal structures, duties would be clumsily exercised and the diversity, resilience, and resourcefulness that grow out of individualist values would disappear. This was the context within which she uttered her famous and much-misunderstood remark that "there is no such thing as society. There are individual men and women, and there are families."[29] Collectivists might be high-minded in their aspirations for the state, but collectivism risked undermining the high mind in the individual. To quote John Stuart Mill, "the mental and moral, like the muscular powers, are improved only by being used."[30] If Thatcher often clashed with religious leaders over governmental policy in the 1980s, she struck a chord with their congregations in the priority she assigned to churches' moral functions. Asked in October 1984, when government and the churches were most at loggerheads, whether the church should take sides in political issues, 69 percent of the 983 adults polled said no, as did 73 percent of the 59 percent in the sample who were Anglicans.

A third line of Conservative self-defense, growing out of the other two, was Thatcher's championing of the voluntarist alternative to the statist option. Here she immediately lent a new emphasis to British society's long-neglected individualist Liberal and nonconformist culture. Upon her marriage she had made a familiar Methodist move into moderate high-church Anglicanism, yet her childhood religion pervaded the rest of her life. "We were Methodists," she told an early biographer, "and Methodist means method."[31] A powerful sense of duty to family, neighbors, church, community, and nation flowed naturally from that, together with plain speaking, independence of opinion, a strong work ethic, and a belief in the voluntary redistribution of wealth. Quotations from John Wesley often featured in her speeches; in 1988 she decided to read the Old Testament from end to end, reporting daily to her staff on how she was getting on. It was her nonconformist and provincial background that, for all her Conservatism, distanced her from the metropolitan establishment. Hers was, by contrast, a simplistic small-town face-to-face world where churches were integral to social life and where black could be clearly distinguished from white. In September 1984, after several years as prime minister, she could still declare, "I am in politics because of the conflict between good and evil."[32] With Thatcher as with Gladstone, whose ideas so often overlap with hers, religion buttressed an inner conviction that enabled her to achieve more in British politics than anyone initially predicted. Like him, she was a prime minister who "depended to an unusual degree on . . . search for 'rightness'. She was a woman with a low quotient of cynicism, about herself if not about her opponents."[33]

During her last years as prime minister, Thatcher was moving into areas of family policy, where she saw the role of the state and the paid social worker as small, but the role for the volunteer as large indeed. She repeatedly consulted religious leaders about how best to raise moral standards, and had high hopes for the role of philanthropy and voluntarism in public welfare and local government. Opening a new hospital wing in 1988, she emphasized "another side to the coin of economic individualism": "When you have finished as a taxpayer, you have not finished your duty as a citizen. There's more to life than just giving what you are compelled to give."[34] She regretted local government's decline, and the poll tax was her failed attempt to revive it. For urban improvement, she hoped to find twentieth-century local worthies who, like Joseph Chamberlain in mid-Victorian Birmingham, would extend their voluntarism from success in business to improving their community: "With . . . burgeoning prosperity came a burgeoning civic pride, or city fathers. There was a complete, almost a city state, a complete ideal—'This is our city'. It was a great, fundamental, personal obligation to the community."[35]

Thatcher's distress at losing power in 1990 was painful to observe but was in many ways fully deserved: she brushed aside her critics, rode roughshod over loyal colleagues, and unduly neglected the safeguards against executive delusions of grandeur that the much-maligned British constitution could (and, on this occasion, did) deploy. On the poll tax, on Britain's European alignment, and on opposition within the cabinet, she applied once too often the lonely and courageous but perilous conviction of her own rightness, which she had so often deployed successfully in the past. Somewhat paradoxically, given her political philosophy, she relished power and wept when she lost it. But perhaps her political demise was in a way a mercy, for her new lines of policy would have run into a host of difficulties. In the influential late-Victorian novel *Robert Elsmere*, Mrs. Humphry Ward presents Elsmere, founding his New Brotherhood, as declaring that only religion could provide the altruism at the national level that according to "economists and sociologists of the new type" could render the will of the individual "equal to its tasks."[36] In the rapidly secularizing Britain of the 1980s, no such religious impulse to social improvement and voluntarism existed.

Thatcher came near to acknowledging as much. When the Labour MP Frank Field asked her what was her greatest disappointment in government, she replied "as though she had thought long and hard beforehand about it," saying, "I cut taxes and I thought we would get a giving society, and we haven't." Field went on to explain that "she thought we would, by low taxation, see that extraordinary culture in America whereby people make fortunes and want, perhaps publicly, to declare what they are doing with them. That had not taken root here."[37] If she had retained power, Thatcher's aspirations would have succumbed before the fact that the Victorians failed to resolve several social and political dilemmas: how to safeguard morality without religion, how to distribute wealth more fairly but without compulsion, how to extend political participation locally and nationally amid recreational abundance, how within a mass society to preserve the values of a face-to-face community, and how within a world of large industrial and commercial structures to promote entrepreneurship and the loyalties associated with the small firm. They are dilemmas that have yet to be resolved.

Fall Semester 2011

1. R. T. McKenzie, *British Political Parties: The Distribution of Power within the Conservative and Labour Parties* (London, 1955; 2nd ed., 1963), p. v.

2. I am deeply grateful to those who replied to my initial inquiry (only one did not), for comments that greatly improved this article in draft, and for allowing me to cite material originally acquired only in confidence. All unfootnoted statements, cited only with permission, come from the correspondence and interviews that ensued. I also gratefully acknowledge helpful comments received from Kit Kowol of University College, Oxford.

3. *Conservative History Journal,* 3 (Summer 2004), p. 3.

4. J. Ramsden, *The Age of Balfour and Baldwin, 1902–1940* (London, 1978), p. xii.

5. G. C. Webber, *The Ideology of the British Right, 1918–1939* (London, 1986), pp. 3, 45.

6. "The Conservative Party, Fascism, and Anti-Fascism, 1918–1939," in N. Copsey and A. Olechnowicz, eds., *Varieties of Anti-Fascism: Britain in the Inter-War Period* (Basingstoke, 2010), pp. 73–97, esp. p. 75.

7. R. McKibbin, "Class and Conventional Wisdom: The Conservative Party and the 'Public' in Inter-War Britain," in *The Ideologies of Class: Social Relations in Britain, 1880–1950* (Oxford, paperback ed., 1991), pp. 259–93.

8. E. H. H. Green, *Ideologies of Conservatism: Conservative Political Ideas in the Twentieth Century* (Oxford, 2002), p. x.

9. R. A. Butler, ed., *The Conservatives: A History from Their Origins to 1965* (London, 1977), p. 9.

10. *An Appetite for Power: A History of the Conservative Party since 1830* (London, 1998), p. 495.

11. *The Conservative Party from Peel to Thatcher* (London, 1970; rev. paperback ed., 1985), p. 267; see also S. Ball, *Baldwin and the Conservative Party: The Crisis of 1929–1931* (New Haven, 1988), p. 218.

12. *The Radical Element in the History of the Conservative Party* (Swinton Lecture, 1989), p. 12.

13. Quotations from *Conservative History Journal,* 3 (Summer 2004), p. 4. I have silently corrected Roberts's terminal date from 1989 to 1979, as the context seems to demand; *Guardian,* 21 July 1994, p. 25.

14. A. Roberts, *"Holy Fox": A Life of Lord Halifax* (London, 1991), pp. 47–49, 120, 264.

15. Quotations from E. Kedourie, "Ld Salisbury and Politics," in his *The Crossman Confessions, and Other Essays in Politics, History, and Religion* (London, 1984), pp. 48, 52.

16. Green, *Ideologies of Conservatism,* p.1.

17. *The Times,* 16 Apr. 1983, p. 2.

18. Thatcher, comments on a BBC4 radio phone-in program, 28 Apr. 1985.

19. Foot on 29 Mar. 1983, in *The Times,* 30 Mar. 1983, p. 4. Kinnock quoted by Briggs in E. M. Sigsworth, ed., *In Search of Victorian Values: Aspects of Nineteenth-Century Thought and Society* (Manchester, 1988), p. 25.

20. M. Thatcher, *Collected Speeches,* ed. R. Harris (London, 1997), pp. 259–60.

21. J. Walvin, *Victorian Values* (London, 1987), p. 3.

22. In addition to Walvin there were G.Marsden, ed., *Victorian Values: Personalities and Perspectives in Nineteenth-Century Society* (Harlow, 1990; 2nd ed., 1998); Sigsworth, *In Search of Victorian Values. Society;* and T. C. Smout, ed., *Victorian Values: A Joint Symposium of the Royal Society of Edinburgh and the British Academy, December 1990* (British Academy, 1992).

23. R. Samuel, "The History Woman," *The Times*, 4 July 1991, p. 18.

24. For Dell, see T. Benn, *Conflicts of Interest: Diaries, 1977–1980* (London, 1990), pp. 235–56.

25. Discussion with Michael Charlton on BBC Radio 4, 30 July 1979.

26. Quotations from F. von Hayek, *The Road to Serfdom* (London, 1944; paperback ed., 1976), pp. vii, 136.

27. Quotations from Thatcher's address, 21 May 1988, to the General Assembly of the Church of Scotland, in her *Collected Speeches*, pp. 313, 311.

28. On BBC Radio's Jimmy Young show, *Independent*, 6 June 1987, p. 1.

29. *Woman's Own*, 31 Oct 1987, p. 10.

30. *Liberty* (1859), in J. S. Mill, *Collected Works*, vol. 18 (Toronto, 1977), pp. 116–17.

31. Quoted in H. Young, *One of Us: A Biography of Margaret Thatcher* (London, 1989; paperback ed., 1993), p. 6.

32. Ibid., p. 352.

33. Ibid., p. 217.

34. *Daily Telegraph*, 28 Apr. 1988, p. 1.

35. Interview with *Financial Times* reported in the *Independent*, 7 Nov. 1987, p. 2.

36. Mrs. Humphry Ward, *Robert Elsmere* (1888; World's Classics ed. 1987), p. 548.

37. *H.C.Deb.*, 10 Apr. 2013, cc.1652–3.

Tony Benn. Photograph by Phil Sharp.

25

Tony Benn

JAD ADAMS

In the 1960s, Tony Benn was compared to Willy Brandt in Germany, Pierre Trudeau in Canada, and, inevitably, Jack Kennedy in the United States. His was the forward-looking face of youthful and progressive politics. In the late 1960s, not only was he tipped for the premiership, but there seemed to be no one else in the race from the Labour side in British politics. These other comparisons were, of course, to heads of state or prime minsiters, but Tony Benn never held one of the great offices of state. He never led the Labour party, failing, in one notable election, even to become its deputy leader.

But he is not a politician who is considered noteworthy for failure of promise. He remains the most controversial figure in British politics and paradoxically, its most popular. He is the only politician who, independent of office, is still filling halls with eager audiences. It is as if his mellifluous, patrician voice talking about the issues has always been with us, and indeed, he has been performing on the national stage since 1950.

How did this man move from being a moderate social democrat and a possible future president of Europe to a class warrior, an arch-enemy of the establishment, and ultimately a national treasure? Was his bumpy ride the ill-calculated progression of a careerist? Did Benn simply "back the wrong horse" in leading the left wing in the 1970s? That certainly was a common view at the time. In the context of the rest of his life, his move to the left should be seen not as a sudden leap but as a natural working out of ideas, and as part of a long tradition of British radicalism.

Benn held cabinet-level posts in all the Labour adminsitrations in the 1960s and 1970s: Postmaster General (1964–6), Minister of Technology (1966–70), Secretary of State for Industry (1974–5), and Secretary of State for Energy (1975–9). His successful battle for a new law allowing the renunciation of peerages represented a fundamental statement about the relationship between the Lords and the Commons and the primacy of elected authority. His campaign for a referendum on membership in the Common Market (as the European Union was then called) meant a constitutional door was opened that can never again be closed. The reforms he supported in the Labour Party for the reselection of MPs and a wider franchise for the election of the party leader have had far-reaching effects in other parties and other organizations.

Benn was also one of the greatest orators of the second half of the twentieth century—admittedly a period in which the art of oratory was in decline. He has written the most extensive published political diary of his times. He has also kept what may be the best records of any politician.

Both of Benn's grandfathers were Liberal Members of Parliament; his father was a Liberal, then a Labour MP; Benn was to become the longest-serving Labour MP, holding an elected seat for more than fifty years. His son is a leading Labour MP, and his granddaughter, while still a teenager, stood for election as a Labour MP in 2011. His mother, Margaret, Lady Stansgate (1897–1991), had attended public meetings of Millicent Fawcett and Emmeline Pankhurst. She was a leader of the League of the Church Militant and campaigned for the ordination of women in the Anglican church (a cause that was won in 1992, the year after her death).

The household in which Tony Benn was born in 1925 was one in which achievement was expected, as was self-sacrifice for the common good. It was one of Gladstonian liberalism: hard work and earnestness. The children were at the table when politics and religion were the constant subject of discussion; humor was present, but it was somewhat jocose. They were teetotalers, regular churchgoers who never went to the theatre. Tony Benn lived and went to school in roads adjoining the Houses of Parliament, where his father worked. Because of his father's role as a politician and sometimes a cabinet minister, Benn met statesmen from an early age—when his father was Secretary of State for India, he met Gandhi.

William Wedgwood Benn (1877–1960) was an impressive character, a hero from the First World War. Twenty years older than his wife, he was almost fifty when Tony Benn was born, more a Victorian than a twentieth-century character. He moved from the Liberals to the rapidly expanding Labour Party in 1927 not because he had coverted to socialism, but because he could no longer stand the dishonesty of Lloyd George. He said he would just have to be a Liberal in the Labour Party, which gives an idea of quite what a broad church it was.

The Labour Party had been formed in 1900 by the trade unions, the cooperative societies, and the intellectual societies like the Fabians to give parliamentary representation to the working class. Within twenty-five years it had become the official opposition or governing party, a position it still enjoys. Its more thoughtful members knew about Marxism, but few were out-and-out Marxists. The Communist Party of Great Britian (which *was* Marxist) was formed twenty years after the Labour Party.

Tony Benn joined the Labour Party on his seventeenth birthday. He did wartime service in the home guard and then the RAF, training as a pilot. His father and older brother were air force officers. For Benn personally, the Second World War was noteworthy for two things: his father's elevation to the peerage—Winston Churchill made William Wedgwood Benn a lord; and the death of his elder brother, Michael, who was killed in his plane. That meant Tony Benn was next in line to inherit a title on his father's death.

Benn took up a place at Oxford University following his war service. He did the usual thing for a talented speaker who was ambitious: he became president of the Oxford Union. During this time he toured the United States as a guest of the American Speech Association, which invited the Union to provide three speakers to debate in the United States in October 1947. The intensive speaking experience, in which he traveled to forty-three states, was the making of Benn as a speaker. He learned how to engage an audience that knew nothing of his subject matter, and might well be hostile, and he learned how to use humor.

Soon after the U.S. trip, Benn met Caroline Middleton De Camp, who was studying at Vassar (in the company of the future Jackie Kennedy). She was from a Cincinnati family of lawyers. He proposed within ten days of meeting, they married in Ohio, and it was a long and happy marriage of more than fifty years' duration. Her influence on him was great; Benn was that rarity among his generation, a man who listened to women.

At the age of twenty-five, Benn was selected to fight the Bristol South-East seat of Sir Stafford Cripps, who was retiring because of ill health. Another socialist puritan, Cripps was far to the left of the

Labour Party. He wrote in support of Benn's candidacy, "It is splendid to see Bristol South-East has another champion in the field—
one who is as true a Socialist and who is as keen a Christian as I am
myself."[1]

Benn's speeches contained far more Christian references in the
early 1950s than they had earlier or were to do later. For example,
he told a meeting that the precept "love your neighbor" was not for
Sunday only but for every day of the week. The brotherhood of man
was a living reality in the British welfare state: "Don't you think when
you lick your insurance stamp and stick it on your card that it's got
nothing to do with the brotherhood of man; it's an example of the
community as a whole accepting responsibility for its less fortunate
members."[2]

In Parliament, he was an obedient and loyal supporter of the
Attlee government, which enjoyed national support—when Attlee
went to the country to secure a better majority in 1951, he received
more votes than Churchill, who nontheless won the election (indeed, Attlee in that election received more votes than any Labour
leader before or since).

Benn supported post-war rearmament and the Korean War but
opposed Britian's invasion of Suez—some of his finest speeches to
date were made against the Suez adventure as an illegal war of aggression. It was at this stage in his life, in the 1950s, that his colleagues in the House of Commons began to fill the chamber when
they knew Benn was due to speak.

Benn was the great communicator, the first to use television effectively in party-political broadcasts. It was largely due to him
that Labour was considered to have won the election campaign in
1959—though it didn't win the election. Afterward, he was made
a shadow cabinet minister for the first time. Also in 1959 he was
voted onto the Labour national executive as a favorite of the ordinary members, who were always his best supporters They were more
moved by his charms than those of the other two power blocs in the
party, the trade unions and the parliamentary Labour Party.

HIS FATHER'S DEATH IN 1960 meant Benn would be expelled from
the House of Commons and obliged to take up a peerage that he
did not want. A critic of such inherited privilege, he made preparations to undermine the process. He had his constituency back him
to stand again, even though, as a peer, he would be disqualified if he
won. He argued for the right of constituents to choose whom they
wished to represent them and the right of an elected MP to serve in
the House of Commons. *The Times* called it "the cause of the over-

privileged politician," not the most obvious clarion with which to summon the masses.³ But Benn was able to draw on nineteenth-century precedents: Charles Bradlaugh and Lionel Rothschild had both been elected and disbarred, and then had stood and stood again, over the issue of religious oaths. In the previous century, John Wilkes, in a similar position, stood five times until the House relented and let him take his seat.

So Benn was in a long tradition when he won a 13,000-vote majority; after he was disbarred, the Conservative candidate took the seat. This was an outrageous perversion of democracy. Benn talked about how backward-looking Britain was, how obsessed with inherited privilege. He used the campaign to invite scientists, architects, and educationalists to argue their own case for bringing Britain up to date. The government eventually agreed to do what it said it would never do: it changed the law to allow the renunciation of peerages. Benn was returned to the House of Commons, never having been Lord Stansgate. He became more than ever a nationally known figure.

Back in the Commons, Benn supported Harold Wilson in the 1963 leadership election. Wilson was the candidate aligned with the Left, though not exactly a firebrand of socialism. Benn's work was rewarded by his being made Postmaster General. His period of office was noted for two things: he treated the trade unionists as equals, having "tea and sandwiches" lunches with them; and he brought the post office into the second half of the twentieth century, updating it with satellite telecommunications and modern banking.

Wilson then made Benn technology minister in a government that wanted to be defined by its progressive attitude toward technology. At last a cabinet minister, Benn spent much of the time during his first years at the Ministry of Technology—Mintech—making speeches to rally industry and to inspire the nation with calls to training and productivity. "The battle of Britain 1966 must be won on the parking lots of America," he announced at a Ford automobile plant.⁴ His vision of technology was unabashedly utopian: "Technology serves a higher purpose than mere production. It offers us a hope for the future. It is the light at the end of the long, dark tunnel of poverty through which most of mankind has been journeying throughout the whole of human history."⁵ He was responsible for overseeing major company reorganizations involving computers, electricity, motor vehicles, and shipbuilding. He promoted the Anglo-French Concorde, a passenger jet flying at twice the speed of sound. Everything about Benn was modern. He was a supporter of Britain's entry into the European Economic Community (after

1993, the European Union), which was an issue well in keeping with those that motivated Mintech. If planning was desirable, was not planning on a continental scale even more so?

The pace of change was never fast enough for Benn. The rise of radical thought, as demonstrated by pressure groups and student demonstrations, was instinctively attractive to him. When students at Bristol University in 1968 held one of the "free university" teach-ins, an alternative form of education popular at the time, Benn paid his shilling and sat and listened to the lectures. To remain inconspicuous, he wore his spectacles and took off his jacket and tie. That night he wrote, "I realised all of a sudden that for three and a half or four years I have done absolutely no basic thinking about politics."[6]

Benn made the most dramatic speech of his career that spring, at Llandudno on 25 May 1968. The international backdrop was the assassination of Martin Luther King in the United States, the Tet offensive in Vietnam, and the Days of May in France. In a speech that defined his radicalism for the next half century he said: "It would be foolish to assume that people will be satisfied for much longer with a system which confines their national political role to the marking of a ballot paper with a single cross once every five years. People want a much greater say . . . Much of the industrial unrest—especially in unofficial strikes—stems from worker resentment and their sense of exclusion from the decision-making process, whether by their employers or, sometimes, by their union leaders."[7]

Something was being said that was different from anything said by a leading politician before. It was also, quite clearly, subversive. Benn gave six conditions that had to be met to ensure the redistribution of political power—to transfer power from institutions to the people. First, "freedom of information" legislation. Second, the government should know more about the people it was elected to serve via statistical services and the publication of more data. The third requirement would be to hold referenda on major issues. Fourth, Benn urged an opening up of the mass media to those with minority views. Fifth, "representative organizations" should be encouraged and promoted so that they could be consulted by government. For example, trade unions should be funded in order to help them perform their duties in regard to industries amply supplied with government money. Finally, there should be devolution of power to regions and localities.

These were practical objectives, and indeed, most had been realized by the end of the century. Freedom of information came in in 2000; there were referenda on staying in the European Economic Community and on devolution for Scotland and Wales (in 1975 and

1997 respectively). Minority access to the media was promoted by Channel Four television, which was launched in 1983. Data collection on individuals massively increased as a result of technological developments, but that was not seen as an advance for liberal thinking. Voluntary organizations increased their influence, and trade unions were brought in under the Trade Union and Labour Relations Act of 1974. National devolution happened for Scotland and Wales in 1998 (more regional devolution has been rejected).

Benn followed Llandudno with a series of dramatic speeches that maintained his position at the center of radical thought—for example, on industrial democracy and on the new politics, both in November 1968, in which he argued for greater participation in decision making. Also that year he became the first male politician to declare himself in favor of the women's liberation movement. Although the Wilson government lost the election of 1970, it is worth remembering its enduring achievements: equal pay for women, race relations legislation, the abolition of theatre censorship, and the reform of laws on divorce, adult homosexuality, and abortion.

Benn was increasingly aligning himself with the trade unions, the main funders and power brokers of the Labour Party. The unions, like other institutions in society, had become radicalized at the end of the 1960s. Three of the most powerful had left-wing leaders: Hugh Scanlon led the engineers, Jack Jones the transport workers, and Clive Jenkins the technicians. They gave significant help to Benn as he began to emerge through the years of opposition as the principal parliamentary voice of the unions.

The power of the unions had now become the main issue over which industrial policy was fought. The Conservative government of Edward Heath tried to control the unions with the Industrial Relations Act. It was a subject tailor-made for Benn. On one side were the unjust lawmakers with their political courts, on the other were the courageous workers standing defiantly against them. Ahead was a principle shining brightly: individual conscience has supremacy over the law. It was a principle Benn traced to the great prophets of Judaism. "Let judgement run down as waters, and righteousness as a mighty stream," he said, quoting the prophet Amos.[8]

It was at this stage that Benn began to use history more exactly to interpret the present. He had always had a fondness for historical analogies, but they tended to be drawn from general knowledge. His need for a model to interpret the confused world of early-1970s politics led him to the seventeenth century. He read the debates of the English Revolution and the Civil War, which found their parallels in the turmoil over the Industrial Relations Act. The agitators during the Revolution reflected the contemporary schismatic sects of the Left; the right wing of the Labour Party had its counterpart in the rigid, doctrinaire Presbyterians.

Benn was so aware of his own ignorance that he asked a fellow MP, the former London University lecturer Jack Mendelson, to give him a private tutorial. So in the House of Commons tea room, Benn's education was extended with an explanation of the Diggers and the Levellers and the nature of political debate in the Revolution. "I had no idea," Benn wrote in his diary, "that the Levellers had called for universal manhood suffrage, equality between the sexes, biennial Parliaments, the sovereignty of the people, recall of representatives and even an attack on property."[9] The spiritual values that informed many of the revolutionaries made them immediately attractive to Benn and led directly to his work on Christianity and socialism, published as *Arguments for Socialism* in 1979.

The last important battle between Benn and his colleagues in the opposition period was over the "twenty-five companies" proposal. This was the question whether to nationalize twenty-five of Britain's top manufacturing companies. In the event, Wilson presented a radical nationalization program involving building land, oil and gas, ports and docks, shipbuilding, aircraft production, and parts of the drug, machine-tool, construction and road-haulage industries. Benn was in the forefront of arguing for the nationalization of major British industries, seeing state direction as an answer to economic problems. But the national debate was not free market versus controlled market. The Conservatives introduced the Industry Act, which gave a high degree of control to government. The debate was not whether the state would be involved in controlling industry, but whether the state should own the industries it would control.

The Conservative Prime Minister Edward Heath's personal crusade was to take Britisn into the European Economic Community, which he achieved in 1972. Benn succeeded in making a referendum over Britain's membership into Labour Party policy. That move may well have won Labour the 1974 elections, since many people who were not Labour supporters backed the party because it offered them a chance to oppose union with Europe.

What had changed to make Benn vehemently oppose the common market? It is probable that Benn, always sensitive to the influences around him, had simply moved into a circle where the predominant feeling was against the European union. His increasing affinity with the left wing of the Labour movement meant his thinking was being influenced only by leftist trade unionists and constituency activists. He said he had been skeptical about Europe before, but was swung by his experiences as a minister. "I loathe the Common Market," he wrote after one trip. "It's bureaucratic, centralised, there is no political talk and officials control the ministers."[10] In Brussels when he proposed opening the meetings of the Energy Council to the public, every other minister found a reason why it should not be done.

Leading up to the referendum in June 1975, Benn received massive attention as the leading anti-Europe speaker. The country voted to stay in by a margin of two to one, and Benn became associated more strongly than anyone else with the losing cause. He had been made Industry Minister in the 1974 government, but Wilson, who did not trust him, demoted him to Energy Minister after the referendum. Benn never operated under his own Industry Act. All the supposedly radical things he did, for which he was viciously attacked by the press, were done under Conservative legislation. British industry was in decline under both Labour and the Conservatives, and nothing seemed able to stop it.

Benn spent more time developing his ideas of the British socialist tradition. He emphatically repudiated the right-wing accusation that it was a foreign political philosophy transplanted to Britain, always referring back to the seventeenth century: "You will find that the ideas of socialism in Britain anticipated by two centuries or more many of the things Marx said."[11] He was felt by some to have gone native in his adoration of the miners: his office was hung with mining memorabilia, helmets, and trade union banners. Lord Kearton, the chairman of the British National Oil Corporation, who worked with Benn, considered Benn's respect for the working class something of a character defect: "He was too idealistic where the unions were concerned. His Achilles' heel was that he thought anyone who was a union shop steward was a good man. Some would take advantage."[12] Benn's Parlaimentary Private Secretary, Joe Ashton (who *was* working class), put it more bluntly: "I had to turn round and tell him there were as many bastards in the working class as there were in the middle class."[13]

Benn had encouraged the movement for greater democracy in the Labour Party, and he was its most prestigious advocate, but it was by no means his show. The time had come for the people who worked to put a Labour government in power to be consulted about what it did with that power. The so-called Militant Tendency, from the name of their newspaper, were the most notable activists. They were certainly the roundheads of the Labour cause: grim, humourless, and puritanical. Benn was never a supporter of the Militant Tendency, but he opposed their explusion from the party. He was impressed by their proselytising zeal; they did not push through motions by procedural means, but wanted their issues discussed early in meetings so that they could convert people in the discussion. He had no political sympathy with them, however, and never himself used their Trotskyist analysis of society.

BENN WAS AHEAD OF THE FIELD in realizing just how radical Margaret Thatcher was. "She is opening up guerrilla raids behind our lines to try to reopen questions that were settled 25, 50 or even 100 years ago," he said in 1976.[14] Benn nonetheless admired Thatcher for her vigorous approach and her presentation of clear alternatives to the electorate.

Though Thatcher was in the ascendant after 1979 and the Left was in decline, Labour went to the country in 1983 with a more left-wing manifesto than at any previous time. For Benn, boundary redistribution meant that he lost his constituency and ended up fighting what had become an unwinnable seat in an election that was a very bad one for Labour as a whole. The breakaway Social Democratic Party split the Labour vote, and Labour received only 8,400,000 votes. Benn consoled himself that at least 8 million people had been prepared to vote for a socialist program. It may sound like a hollow consolation for a disastrous failure, but Gordon Brown's reformed Labour Party in 2010 received only 150,000 more votes than that.

Benn found a new constituency to represent, Chesterfield, a mining area, just as Thatcher was launching her assault on the unions. The miners were the backbone of the trade union movement: if they could be brought down, the Conservatives would win the battle and the unions would be brought to heel. The miners' strike bitterly divided the nation, but for many people neither of the class warriors were at all attractive: the miners' leader, Arthur Scargill, or Prime Minister Thatcher. Benn saw Scargill's hard-edged puritanism as a virtue: "I have no doubts about it at all. Arthur was one of the few trade union leaders I have ever met in my life who wasn't looking for a peerage. . . . He was a tough character, and his leadership of the miners was very strong."[15] Thatcher won. Benn's speeches over the second half of the 1980s have a revivalist air, with titles such as "Socialist Renewal," "Reviving Socialism," and "Re-establishing the Left."

In what can be described as his "late career," Benn started publishing his diaries. The transcription and editing of what was then twelve million words started in the early 1960s; the first volume, of nine, was published in 1987. He said, "The undefended frontier of the establishment is the recent past, because the historians haven't begun to distort it and the media have forgotten the arguments. You turn up with your troops where they're least expecting you."[16]

The poll tax was Thatcher's step too far to the right. To the historically minded like Benn, it brought to mind the last poll tax, in 1381, which had led to the Peasants' Revolt. Benn clearly and unequivocally said that the only correct response was civil disobedience. He would not pay the tax. He would not even register for it, which was an offense in itself. "Many of our most precious religious and political rights in this country were won by conscientious lawbreaking which compelled Parliament to make the necessary concessions to justice," he declared in March 1990.[17] The poll tax revolt affected the entire nation, across political boundaries. Unrest over the tax, along with the negative approach to Europe, formed the direct cause of Thatcher's fall in 1991. When the poll tax was abolished, immediately after Thatcher's departure, fourteen million people had not paid. It was abolished by John Major, who said it was "uncollectible."

After his retirement from the House of Commons in 2001, Benn increasingly concentrated on international issues, notably opposing wars of intervention in other countries. Two broad strands of support for his stands emerged: Labour members who felt that Benn was a remaining representative of the moral role the party should adopt; and Christians, particularly Quakers, who felt compelled to support to a man who spoke about peace with no hint of cynicism.

Benn was unperturbed about opposing all wars, regardless of their causes. He said, "I opposed the Suez war, I opposed the Falklands war, I opposed the Libyan bombing and I opposed the Gulf war and I never believed that any of those principled arguments lost a single vote—indeed, I think they gained support, though that was not why you did it. What has been lacking in Labour politics over a long period is a principled stand."[18] A large number of people who did not otherwise agree with him were pleased that someone was voicing their reservations about these wars. Benn fulfilled his function as conscience of the nation. Few agreed with him entirely, but few felt there was no truth at all in what he was saying.

In this vein, Benn supported the Stop the War Coalition, which was founded in September 2001 to oppose an attack on Afghanistan. Benn led the London demonstration that contained Quakers, druids, civil libertarians, and antiglobalizers; Muslims were to the fore, and some were active and proud supporters of the Taliban. This was a crisis for the Left. Those who had stood for modernity, sexual and racial equality, and a paternalistic state found themselves sharing a demonstration with supporters of a medieval-minded, racist, misogynistic, homophobic regime that was harboring an international terrorist organization. Something had gone badly wrong with the moral compass of the Left. That misalignment was glaringly apparent until the invasion of Iraq, which was a much easier war to oppose.

Benn appealed to the judgment of history: "When you look at the whole of this period in the Middle East over the last few years, when it takes its place in history, it will be seen as a colonial liberation movement by the Muslim world against being dominated by the big powers, by the west and Iran and so on."[19]

A theatre impresario named Clive Conway gave Benn a new platform. Conway was observing an unsuccessful show in a provincial town and asked the theatre manager what would bring the public in on a wet Wednesday in Swindon? The manager said they had packed the house when Tony Benn came on a book tour, talking about his diaries. Conway called Benn and suggested he hire theatres for a program called "An Evening with Tony Benn." Thus it was that at a time when other politicians had long since abandoned public meetings, Benn was packing audiences in: 1,700 in Sheffield, 1,800 in Bristol, 3,600 over two nights in Edinburgh. He made no attempt to dumb down his subject matter, instead offering, "Democracy, the religious war, power of multi-nationals, the role of technology, the role of empires."[20] He increasingly resorted to tradition, to his mother's teaching him to support the prophets against the kings. He remarked: "It's got me a lot of trouble in my life."[21]

What then to make of Benn and his progress in politics? Many of his colleagues would have said he was motivated by ambition, by a desire to get to the top regardless. Michael Foot believed that at some point Benn had lost interest in the present and "turned his brilliantly agile, inventive faculties to the future."[22] That he was concerned about how he would appear in the history books—he would rather be right than prime minister. There is some truth in this. Benn has a strong sense of history and, in particular, an understanding of the reverence the Labour movement has for the rebels of the past while giving position and power to the conformists of the present. But the idea that his entire life's work was dedicated to getting historical credit is too far-fetched, and too self-serving; it is the sort of thing a historian like Foot would say, putting historians at the center of the argument.

It is probably best to take Benn at face value. On the connection between politics and religion, Congregationalism, the strand of nonconformism that Benn's family followed, is distinguished by the emphasis it places on each congregation making its own decisions about its affairs, admitting of no higher temporal authority. Anyone brought up in that tradition receives the democratic message by a process of spiritual osmosis. Benn also absorbed the militancy of the religious message. He said, "Faith must be a challenge to power."

He interpreted the message literally, and perhaps overinterpreted it. It is something of a corrective to these fine thoughts of politics infused with religious fervor to think of the 1653 Parliament of the saints, the only Parliament significantly influenced by Congregationalist thought, which put political power in the hands of supposedly godly men. It was not a democratic success, to put it mildly. It was a complete disaster, and the last staging post before the dictatorship of Oliver Cromwell.

Fall Semester 2012

1. *Bristol Evening World,* 17 Nov. 1950.
2. *Western Daily Press,* 27 Nov. 1950.
3. *The Times,* 2 Mar. 1961.
4. Ford plant, Dagenham, 7 Sept. 1966, speech on the occasion of the production of the millionth Cortina.
5. European Organisation for Quality Control, 6 June 1967.
6. Benn Diaries, 14 June 1968; all references to the Benn Diaries are to the manuscript versions, which are in private hands.
7. Welsh Council of Labour conference, Llandudno 25 May 1968.
8. "Labour's Debt to Judaism," Poale Zion Dinner, 21 Oct. 1972.
9. Benn Diaries, 26 June 1973.
10. Ibid., 25 Oct. 1977.
11. LBC radio, 29 Feb. 1976.
12. Lord Kearton, interview by the author, 24 Apr. 1991.
13. Joe Ashton, interview by the author, 26 Feb. 1991.
14. *New Statesman,* 13 Aug. 1976.
15. Tony Benn, interview by the author, 12 June 1991.
16. Benn, interview by the author, 3 July 1991.
17. Memorial Lecture on Democracy and Socialism, Barkingside, 8 Mar. 1990.
18. Benn interview, 12 June 1991.
19. Benn, interview by the author, 26 May 2010.
20. Benn, interview by the author, 15 July 2004.
21. Benn interview, 26 May 2010.
22. Michael Foot, *Loyalists and Loners* (London, 1986), p. 116.

Margaret Thatcher

26

Lady Thatcher

GEOFFREY WHEATCROFT

At the British general election of 1950, the Conservative candidate for Dartford, once a Kent village but now an outer suburb of London, was a young woman named Margaret Roberts. She was an unlikely candidate at a time when there were few women in politics, a twenty-four-year-old industrial research chemist who came from a modest provincial background in Grantham, Lincolnshire, where her father was a shopkeeper and Methodist lay preacher. From there she had made her way to Oxford, also not easy for a woman then, and studied chemistry as well as becoming chairman of the Conservative Association.

Even then she was already her own woman. British politics was dominated by a collectivist spirit that was partly an inheritance from the years of total war, on which Attlee's post-war Labour government had built with the approval of "the Socialists of all parties," to whom F. A. Hayek—later one of this Miss Roberts's oracles—had ironically dedicated *The Road to Serfdom* (1944). In an article for a local paper, setting a personal tone that never changed, Miss Roberts asked, "Are YOU going to let this proud island race, who at one time would never accept charity, drift on from crisis to crisis?"

She insisted on the superiority of free enterprise over governmental intervention: "It was not a Government that built up the skill and craft of this country . . . which have made their way into the markets of the world. It was private individuals who patiently persevered, building up their businesses bit by bit." And she told the electors,

"We believe in the democratic way of life. *If we serve the ideal faithfully, with tenacity of purpose, we have nothing to fear from Russian Communism.*" Those were brave words at the moment when Senator Joseph McCarthy and other demagogic scaremongers were telling terrified Americans that they had everything to fear from communism.

As a candidate, she had to go through the routine of pressing the flesh, kissing babies, and attending local festivities. Her Methodist upbringing had left her a little unsophisticated and inhibited, so while she would meet people in the street, she could not face going into pubs, and indeed never went into one on her own all her life. All the same, she made an appearance at the fun fair in Orpington, and was persuaded to stop at the fortune-teller's booth, where the clairvoyant murmured, in words uncomfortably reminiscent of the witches in *Macbeth,* "You will be great—great as Churchill."

Although Miss Roberts failed to win her seat that year, or the next, when the Tories returned to power under the leadership of the seventy-six-year-old Winston Churchill in the rather eerie last phase of his political career, she did not forsake politics. She was snubbed by the selectors in safer Tory seats and missed the 1955 election, but was then adopted for Finchley in north London, and was elected in 1959. And so she spent five years in the House of Commons with Churchill, whose formidable though mute presence glowered from its place of honor below the gangway until he retired at last in 1964, only months before his death. It seems unlikely that, with his failing powers, he was much aware of the Member for Finchley, even when she became a junior minister.

On 17 April 2013, the funeral took place at St. Paul's Cathedral of Miss Roberts—or Margaret Thatcher, the name by which she had become world famous; more formally, Mrs. Thatcher after her marriage to an affable businessman in 1951, and then Lady Thatcher of Kesteven after she left the Commons for the Lords in 1992. Whether or not she had become as great as Churchill, there was an unmistakable echo of his funeral there nearly half a century before, on 30 January 1965. "I want lots of soldiers and bands," Churchill had said with cheerful defiance before he died. That was what he got, and so did Lady Thatcher, her body like his drawn on a gun carriage through London streets lined with soldiers. And her funeral, like his, was attended by the Queen, who has attended the funerals of no other prime ministers but those two.

During the Falklands conflict, Thatcher's resolution was called Churchillian, and she liked to invoke "Winston" (as she called him, to the private irritation of the Churchill family). However that might be, they did belong to a small group as two of the great outsiders who became prime ministers, along with Benjamin Disraeli and David Lloyd George. The unlikeliness of those latter two is obvious enough. Disraeli's very name speaks for itself, the grandson of Jewish immigrants, and Lloyd George was the first man of truly plebeian origin to reach Number 10, as well as the first, apart from Wellington and Disraeli, who had not passed through what he called the staff colleges of Oxford and Cambridge.

Although Churchill might seem an unlikely "outsider," the word is apt enough. It was not just that, as George Orwell perceptively said, although he might be have been the grandson of a duke, an Old Harrovian, and a cavalry officer, Churchill was not a gentleman, or that, as Evelyn Waugh still more sourly said, he was "always surrounded by crooks." For all his apparent status as a man born into what was then the ruling class, he was regarded for much of his adult life with deep dislike and distrust by many respectable people. Twenty years ago, apart from observing that Churchill was more revered in the United States than in his own country (as was also true of Thatcher in her later years), Michael Howard wrote, "His arrogance, his egocentricity, his flamboyance, his emotionalism, his unpredictability, his remorseless energy, not least his eccentric taste in friends and generous indulgence in drink made him an outsider to the British 'establishment' from the moment he entered politics at the beginning of the century until the day in May 1940 when they turned to him in despair because there was no one else to whom they could turn."

One word was used over and again when Lady Thatcher died. She was the most "divisive" politician of her time, we were told, as if that was a grave and obvious defect, and as if President Franklin Roosevelt had never divided his country in his day, or President Theodore Roosevelt for that matter. As to those three earlier prime ministers, they not only divided opinion, but were actively hated as well. One shortcoming of Robert Blake's splendid biography of Disraeli, as Blake later acknowledged, was that it paid too little attention to the sheer envenomed anti-Semitic bigotry he inspired. Lloyd George became another object of peculiar loathing in his radical days, as a "pro-Boer" and then as a Chancellor who wanted to pay for public welfare with higher taxes. Churchill was his comrade then, and was execrated even more by the rich as a class traitor. If anything, Disraeli was the most collegiate prime minister of the quartet. The others relied on kitchen cabinets, and with some pretty dubious denizens at that; the "crooks" surrounding Churchill were scarcely more egregious than Mrs. Thatcher's entourage of wizards, mountebanks, and plain frauds.

In one respect, it was she who seemingly differed from the others, in that she only ever served one party. "Every little boy and every girl / That's born into the world alive / Is either a little Liberal / Or else a little Conservative!" or so sings Private Willis in *Iolanthe*, but affiliation in English political history has really been much more fluid. Disraeli entered politics in the 1830s as a Radical, and he could not possibly have been accepted by the aristocratic Whigs; the haughty Lady Holland even thought that the brilliant and educated Thomas Babington Macaulay's "want of pedigree" was a handicap in a patrician House of Commons. Only the quirks of fortune turned Dizzy into a Tory and the hired gun of "the gentlemen of England."

It was Macaulay who called W. E. Gladstone, at the start of his career, "the rising hope of those stern and unbending Tories," little guessing that Gladstone would end as Disraeli's bitter rival, "the people's William," adored by the masses and execrated by the upper classes—and Queen Victoria—as a subversive radical demagogue. Lloyd George, by contrast, moved to the right as prime minister of a predominantly Conservative coalition from 1916, personally concerned by the threat of socialism and the need for party realignment, Tory and Liberal joining to combat Labour. Churchill's fickle flight between parties is notorious, elected as Tory in 1900, bolting to the Liberals in 1904 not long before their landslide election victory, and then twenty years later, when the Liberals had begun their long decline, sheepishly returning to the Tory ranks. Although he genially said that anyone can rat, but it takes someone special to rerat, it is scarcely surprising that he acquired a reputation for both for inconstancy and opportunism.

By contrast, Thatcher was a Tory throughout, from Oxford to the House of Lords. But perhaps the label "Conservative" is misleading. It was a very telling complaint against her in the 1980s that she never seemed to conserve anything. The truth may have been that she was less conservative than partly reactionary and partly radical, something else that might have been true of Churchill if one takes snapshots of his career at different junctures. "Winston has become a legend," his wife observed almost in puzzlement some years before his death; like him, Thatcher became a creature of myth. And in both cases, the words from *The Man Who Shot Liberty Valance* apply: "When the legend becomes fact, print the legend."

WITH THATCHER AS MUCH AS WITH CHURCHILL, disentangling fact from fiction is no easy task, and some legends about her now seem incorrigible. She was "Mrs. Thatcher milk snatcher," the Education Secretary in Edward Heath's government who took away the free half-pint of milk that schoolchildren had daily enjoyed—or some-times had been forced to drink—since the post-war Labour gov-ernment. She was the wicked witch who made devastating cuts in welfare spending, and whose protestation that the National Health Service was "safe in our hands" was hypocritical falsehood; she will-fully destroyed the mining industry by closing pits and ruining whole communities; she was viscerally hostile to the European com-munity and everything to do with it; or so the legend goes.

By now it seems almost futile to interject any corrective, but per-haps one should try. Mrs. Thatcher was the sole voice in the Heath Cabinet opposed to ending the free-milk program. State spending as a proportion of gross domestic product was almost unchanged when she left Downing Street in 1990 from what it had been when she arrived there in 1979, and spending on the Health Service had increased by some 60 percent in real terms. More pits were closed during the rather less than eight years of Harold Wilson's two pre-mierships than in the rather more than eleven years of Margaret Thatcher's.

While Thatcher was a member of his Cabinet, Heath successfully applied for Britain to join what was then the European Economic Community. When Wilson returned to office, he ostensibly renegoti-ated the terms of membership before holding a referendum on con-tinued membership in 1975 to placate his divided party—a maneu-ver that David Cameron hopes to imitate. Leading figures from both parties campaigned on either side, and one of the most prominent Tory speakers in the camp for continued membership was Marga-ret Thatcher. She sometimes appeared wearing a pullover patterned with the flags of the European member states, in photographs now difficult to locate and, for all one knows, formally suppressed.

Then there is the comforting narrative of Thatcher as the ardent supporter of the United States and close ally of President Ronald Reagan, whose eight years in the White House coincided with her prime ministership, allowing them to dominate the 1980s arm in arm. Or as the journalist Harold Evans put it at the time of Reagan's death, "The relationship between Thatcher and President Reagan was closer even than Churchill and Roosevelt." Then again, the self-proclaimed "very right-wing" historian Andrew Roberts wrote in the *Wall Street Journal* after Lady Thatcher's death that "her support for Israel was lifelong and unwavering." It is almost tempting to leave these legends alone, so much bigger than the facts have they be-come, but let us take a closer look.

Of course Thatcher was an anticommunist who strongly sup-ported NATO and the Atlantic alliance. But it is quite wrong to mistake that for uncritical adherence to all that Washington did, and although she did on occasion use that dubious phrase "special relationship," she refuted it in practice. As Richard Aldous observes in *Reagan and Thatcher: The Difficult Relationship* (2012), the 1980s were the very time when historians were unraveling the wartime alliance and showing how bitter Anglo-American rivalry and hostility often were, and how public displays of amity concealed mutual suspicion or even dislike between Churchill and Roosevelt. And as Walter Russell Mead has written, Roosevelt was the most Anglophobic U.S. president of the twentieth century, one of whose great achievements was, in John Maynard Keynes's phrase, to "pick out the eyes of the British Empire" economically during the war while supplanting British supremacy with American.

There were likewise sharp differences between Thatcher and Reagan. She was appalled by shillyshallying in Washington when the Argentines invaded the Falkland Islands in 1982. One prominent member of Reagan's administration was Jeane Kirkpatrick, who saw Buenos Aires as an important ally, and in any case as an "authoritarian" as opposed to a totalitarian regime (in the sense that the junta of Generals Galtieri and Videla merely tortured and "disappeared" opponents in authoritarian fashion). The British ambassador in Washington at the time was the able and amiable Sir Nicholas Henderson, whom Thatcher had shrewdly recalled after his official retirement. On the night of the invasion, Kirkpatrick dined at the Argentine embassy, which Henderson said was if he had taken tea with the Iranians on the day the American hostages were captured in Tehran. As the Argentines were routed, Henderson recalled, Reagan lectured the prime minister about the need for magnanimity, a word he "kept trying to put in Mrs. Thatcher's vocabulary, quite unsuccessfully."

She was again enraged by the somewhat opera buffa American invasion of Grenada without even a word of warning to her, although the island was technically under British sovereignty. To a degree her American devotees never appreciated, Thatcher genuinely believed in international law and said that great powers cannot just "walk into independent sovereign territories." If the United States was going to claim a new right to invade countries whose regimes it disliked, then "we are going to have really terrible wars in the world," words that sound remarkably prescient today. She privately thought the Reagan administration clueless and inept in the Middle East, and she was incensed by what she saw as Reagan's truckling to Mikhail Gorbachev at Reykjavik in October 1986. It only confirmed what she already thought of the president. Her first Foreign Secretary was

Lord Carrington, who resigned penitently after the Foreign Office failed to foresee the Falklands invasion. One day while they were discussing Reagan, she pointed to her head and said, "Peter, there's nothing there." And ten years later, when all concerned had left office, "Nico" Henderson said in private conversation, "If I reported to you what Mrs. Thatcher really thought about President Reagan, it would damage Anglo-American relations."

As to her "lifelong and unwavering" support for Israel, Roberts may be telling readers what they want to hear, but that does not make it accurate history. Thatcher was elected leader of the Conservative party in February 1975. When Menachem Begin became prime minister of Israel in June 1977, breaking the Labour monopoly that had lasted since the creation of the state, the leader of the opposition told her colleagues that she would never shake hands with a man she understandably considered a bloodstained terrorist. In early 1986, when she had been prime minister for nearly seven years, she went to Washington, where she met George Shultz, Reagan's Secretary of State, and gave him the kind of tongue-lashing that her cabinet ministers knew all too well. Were the Israelis ever going to leave the West Bank, she asked, or did they regard it as part of their historic territory? And she added that peace would never come to the Middle East until justice was done for the Palestinians, which itself would not happen as long as Washington gave uncritical endorsement to every Israeli action. She has a devout conservative claque in America; they might be disconcerted if they knew more about the real Thatcher.

This was only part of the broader way in which the woman was misunderstood by both friend and foe, although the enemies were the more obtuse. She drove some people not only into frenzies of impotent rage but almost out of their senses, to the point that they lost touch with reality, then and even now. A small example: shortly after her death, a commentator in the *Guardian* mentioned the reasons "why she was so unpopular across Britain when she was in power." In what esoteric or arcane sense is the word *unpopular* being used here? Thatcher was the most electorally successful politician of her age, much more so than Tony Blair, who followed her lead in so many ways. A few figures speak for themselves.

In her three general elections of 1979, 1983, and 1987, the Tories under Thatcher's leadership achieved large parliamentary majorities, a huge majority in 1983, 397 out of 650 parliamentary seats (61 percent). Her popular vote in those elections was 13.7 million, 13 million, and 13.8 million, or as percentages, 43.9, 42.4, and 42.3. The equivalent figures for the three elections that Blair and Labour "won" in 1997, 2001, and 2005 were 13.5 million, 10.7 million, and 9.5 million, or 43.2, 40.7, and 35.2 percent, and the derisive quotation marks around "won" are used deliberately: it is hard to justify any system of voting that gives a clear majority of parliamentary seats to a party garnering little more than a third of the vote.

ALL THIS TAKES US BACK TO one of the more amusing subplots of those years, "Mrs. Thatcher and the chattering classes," the name that someone coined for the literary, artistic, and academic intelligentsia, although perhaps lumpenintelligentsia might be better. They not only loathed "Mrs. T," but also spoke and wrote as though England in the 1980s were an occupied country, groaning under the iron heel of a junta that could have been imposed only by military force, since that woman could not possibly have won by popular vote. In June 1983, the *New Statesman* published an article by the late Angela Carter, the fashionable novelist. With all her "her patent absurdity," Thatcher was "a voice from the past," she wrote contemptuously: "It's a wonder her perorations aren't drowned with peals of mirth every time she opens her mouth . . . Her contract is up for negotiation again, and it is, perhaps, characteristic of the overweening upper servant that she appears to believe there is no chance it will not be renewed." Well, "the overweening upper servant" was quite right. In a matter of days after this was published, the "contract" was indeed renewed when Thatcher was reelected with an enormous majority and a lead of almost 15 percentage points over Labour in the popular vote.

It got worse. By the time of the 1987 election, the chatterers were being polled for their views. Some were at least candid about their own interest in the matter. "As an artist," the composer Michael Tippett said, "I'm impelled to vote Labour, since it's the only party committed to doubling the arts budget," and the actor Antony Sher said, "As a member of the arts I am heartened by [Labour's] pledge to double the arts budget." Those responses were comparatively restrained. More and more, the language about Thatcher from "members of the arts" was marked by its sheer extravagance. Michael Frayn looked for "the best hope of getting the present barbarians out," while Julian Barnes longed "to turn out Mrs Thatcher and her spayed cabinet, whose main achievement in the last eight years has been the legitimisation of self-interest as a public and private virtue." The playwright Dennis Potter was blunter still. He thought that the most appropriate response to the election "would be to hawk up a gobbet of contemptuous spittle onto the ballot paper," but he felt it necessary to brace himself and vote, since "Mrs Thatcher is the most obviously repellent manifestation of the most obviously arrogant, dishonest, divisive, and dangerous British government since the war. All that really counts is getting these yobs and louts away from the swill bucket."

But the louts stayed at the bucket, and the barbarians weren't turned out. Mrs. Thatcher and her spayed government won almost exactly the same percentage of the vote as four years earlier and, on a higher turnout, won more popular votes than any party had before. How could the British people possibly have paid so little attention to members of the arts, university common rooms, and literary North London? What was so wrong with the masses that they seemed not to share the instinctive personal revulsion toward Thatcher felt by so many *belles âmes*? There was an echo here of Pauline Kael saying in 1972 that she simply couldn't understand how Richard Nixon could have been reelected: "Nobody I know voted for him." It is quite possible that Sher, Barnes, and Potter did not know socially anybody who voted for Thatcher. But very many people did.

After that third victory, her chattering foes showed even less sense of proportion. One left-liberal group was begun with the name Charter '88, and an anti-Thatcherite magazine was launched called *Samizdat*. But both names deliberately echoed the resistance in Eastern Europe: there had been a Charter '77 in Czechoslovakia, and *samizdat* in Russian refers to dissident underground publications. Most of these Chartists were comfortable professional men and women; the magazine was edited by the late Ben Pimlott, a charming man, an excellent political historian, and a salaried professor at London University. He might perhaps have thought twice before comparing himself and his colleagues to persecuted Russian writers or Czech professors who had been reduced to working as janitors.

Best of all was the 20 June Group, which might have been exactly what Engels had in mind when he derided Oscar Wilde and "a form of socialism which has actually donned evening dress and lounges on sofas." Its prime movers were the playwright Harold Pinter and his wife Antonia Fraser, and members of this underground resistance cell met at Lady Antonia's large house in Holland Park. They included Margaret Drabble, Fay Weldon, and Salman Rushdie, before a threat from a different regime forced him into hiding. Pinter scented persecution everywhere, and said, "We have a precise agenda and we are going to meet again and again until they break down the windows and drag us out."

Others words were still more revealing. Jonathan Miller, the opera director and writer, hated the prime minister's "odious suburban gentility" and the way she appealed to "the worst elements in commuter idiocy." She was "loathsome, repulsive in almost every way," and the question why the bulk of the cultural establishment was so hostile to her was silly: "It's the same as why the bulk of the human race is hostile to typhoid." Mary Warnock, the philosopher and head of Girton College, Cambridge, was likewise repelled by the way that Thatcher shouted at people in a manner that was unmistakably lower middle class; her clothes and hair were intolerable, "packaged together in a way that's not exactly vulgar, just *low*."

Behind the impotent rage and self-importance lay something that did indeed offer a key to Thatcher's success. Much of the Old Left still evinced a horror of consumerism and the acquisitive society, or to put it another way, of allowing the poor to enjoy some of the choices and pleasures formerly confined to the rich. That was what the novelist John Fowles meant when he complained about the "selfward tendency in most of the electorate since the 1950s," which was made much worse by "the ethos of the grocer's daughter." In still more bizarre words, the poetaster Adrian Mitchell screamed, "Thatcher's vision is a little plastic credit card . . . unisex aerobic centres, sado-video centres and plonk bars. And it was under Thatcher that you were first offered Filofaxes, mangetout peas, jacuzzis and compact bloody discs."

Two more novelists responded to the death of Thatcher in the same terms. Martin Amis said, "Margaret Thatcher rubbed me up the wrong way[,] something rotten as a human being[,] and I didn't like her emphasis on market-state acquisitiveness." Ian McEwan chimed in, "What bound all opposition to Margaret Thatcher's programme was a suspicion that the grocer's daughter"—note the same sneer—"was intent on monetising human value." It might be unkind to wonder whether those two have ever shown any interest in acquisition or monetary value in the course of their careers, or indeed to wonder what is wrong with compact bloody discs.

Those effusions said far more about the critics than about Thatcher, but they also unintentionally helped explain Thatcherism. The veteran Marxist historian E. J. Hobsbawm recognized, a little late in the day, that "Labour's long march" had ended with the decline of the industrial working class and the eclipse of socialism, but he was still repelled by Thatcherism, or the "anarchism of the lower middle classes." As Tony Judt pointed out, that aversion neatly combined two bugbears of the Old Left: a loathing of anarchism, or the idea that people could live together through cooperation and mutual aid without a vanguard party (or secret police and labour camps) to keep them in order, and a contempt for the petite bourgeoisie, a class that has a tendency to think for itself and try to control its own life.

That hatred of Thatcher from superior persons was a mixture of snobbery—blatant in the case of Miller, Warnock, and even Hobsbawm—and a distaste for the economic emancipation of the masses, which has been a strong theme among the intelligentsia for more than a century. Added to this was sheer contempt for those masses and the incomprehensible electoral support they gave Thatcher, in the process letting down their intellectual and cultural betters. Altogether, there was a flavor of Algernon Moncrieff in *The Importance of Being Earnest:* "Really, if the lower classes don't set us a good example, what on earth is the use of them?"

Not everyone on the Left was so obtuse. The late Raphael Samuel was a gifted social historian, once one of the younger members of the well-known Communist Party Historians Group, along with Hobsbawm, E. P. Thompson, and others. Only months after her own party deposed her, Samuel saluted Margaret Thatcher and her innate if untutored sense of history: "She showed an intuitive capacity to seize on what was new and developing—perhaps the first condition of the historical imagination—and she clearly cares passionately about the past, or at least her version of it." He instanced her "excited intervention" in the debate over how history was taught in schools; her superbly tactless lecture at the time of the bicentennial of the French Revolution in 1989, telling the French that it was the English who had invented liberty (a good Whig sentiment rather than a Tory one); and her invocation of "Victorian values."

In all that, he found that "one of the unnerving things about Mrs Thatcher for anyone on the Left was that she spoke our language, or at any rate addressed our traditions, far more convincingly than she did those of her own party." Her strength and weakness within that party had been her outsider status, which was just what Samuel admired her for. And his remarkably generous and astute tribute went on to say that she

> had no feelings for the traditions of the British ruling class or—despite her invocations of Churchill—for the imperial dimensions of British history, whence her impatience with the Commonwealth and her indifference to royalty. A lifetime of active politics seems to have insulated her from, rather than drawn her into, the mystique of Westminster and Whitehall.
>
> She reached out instead to the provincial England of her childhood, constructing an alternative national epic in which there was a merchant-adventurer in every counting house, a village Hampden in every store . . . She spoke in accents not of church

but of chapel, and in her radical contempt for paternalism it is not difficult to find echoes of her Northamptonshire shoemaker forebears. Her version of Victorian values was of a piece with this, invoking the plebeian virtues of self-reliance and self-help rather than the more patrician ones of chivalry and *noblesse oblige*.

This lecture has not attempted any assessment of Margaret Thatcher's political achievements, balancing success and failure, or even of her personality. One comparison with Churchill is worth making. He was "a brilliant but wayward child," Neville Chamberlain wrote in 1928 in a perceptive private letter about his then Cabinet colleague, "and he has *les défauts de ses qualités*." That last was just as true of Thatcher, and it was poignant that her defects grew so salient that in the end they contributed to her political demise. Nevertheless, and while "the verdict of history" is never easy to deliver with confidence, it seems fair to say, without any partisanship or exaggeration, that just two British governments since the Second World War changed the country and changed the political landscape. One was Attlee's Labour government of 1945 to 1951, and the other was Margaret Thatcher's of 1979 to 1990. And there was one undeniable triumph: the woman who had said in 1950 that if we served the democratic ideal with tenacity, "we have nothing to fear from Russian Communism" was in office nearly forty years later to see the Berlin Wall torn down.

Another historian on the Left might provide a last word. *The New Old World* (2009) by the neo-Marxist Perry Anderson comprises a series of long essays on contemporary France, Germany, and Italy. In his foreword, he says that he would have liked the opportunity to look at some other countries, such as Spain, but did not "not regret the omission of Britain, whose history since the fall of Thatcher has been of little moment." As a roundabout compliment, and a verdict for the time being, that will do very well.

Spring Semester 2013

The Queen

27

Elizabeth II

MAX HASTINGS

Queen Elizabeth's diamond jubilee, celebrating her sixty years on Britain's throne, roused much more public enthusiasm than skeptics had predicted. There were thousands of village and street parties up and down England, albeit few in Scotland, where enthusiasm for the Crown has become tepid. Despite the uncooperative weather, there was widespread real excitement about the grand Thames procession of boats, which was reviewed by the Queen.

In the 1990s, both before and after the death of Diana, Princess of Wales, the monarchy went through an extremely rocky patch, when sympathy for the institution waned. Today, however, personal respect for the Queen has never been higher. There is a recognition that she has trodden with skill an extraordinarily difficult path, as a hereditary incumbent in an age of democratic populism. She never auditioned for the role on a game show like *Britain's Got Talent,* nor passed a competitive examination nor attended an interview for the job; but she has turned out to be jolly good at it.

Her reign has been an unflagging display of discipline, discretion, and dutifulness. If the reverse of those qualities is a certain dullness, so be it. She is exactly what she seems, a typical upper-class countrywoman of her generation: uneducated and philistine, but honest and decent through and through. She is roused to visible excitement only when watching racehorses run. But she has seldom said a word or made a gesture that might alienate any faction among her subjects except the opponents of country sports.

Her conservatism, social and political, is assumed; but there is not a shred of evidence linking her to any unwelcome enthusiasm except for those horrible corgi dogs. She combines common sense and opacity, her supremely cautious conversation leavened by flashes of dry wit. Dignity is at a discount in the twenty-first century, but retains its uses in public life. Hers is compromised never by her own actions, and only infrequently by other people's.

Some recall with a shudder the night of New Year's Eve 2000, when her Prime Minister, Tony Blair, discarded protocol to clutch her hand for the singing of "Auld Lang Syne" at the opening of his disastrous Greenwich Millennium Dome. The Lord's anointed do not willingly do intimacy with lesser mortals, least of all politicians, and her subjects sympathized with her.

The Queen's success seems the more remarkable because she has reigned through a period of relative national decline. Victoria, the last monarch to celebrate a diamond jubilee, had the huge advantage of presiding when Britain's fortunes were at their zenith. Indeed, Victoria's popularity seemed chiefly attributable to the British people's self-congratulation about what their country became during her reign, rather than to anything she herself did. Her conduct as Queen was selfish and petulant. There was little in her character to admire, especially after the early death of her splendid consort, Prince Albert, in 1861.

Queen Elizabeth has behaved much better, displaying wisdom by responding to changing times. Always financially prudent, she has swallowed economy measures at her palaces, together with the scrapping of the royal yacht without replacement, and has agreed to pay income tax on her private fortune. Her disappointments as a parent have prompted plenty of unwelcome media attention. Princess Anne is the only one of her four children who behaves relatively normally, displays sensitivity about keeping appropriate company, and keeps off the front pages. But seldom throughout history have even successful monarchs contrived to rear satisfactory offspring.

If anything, public sympathy for the Queen is increased by her family troubles, which make her seem not much different from many of her subjects. A bow is in order to her husband, Prince Philip. For all his famous crustiness and outbursts of political incorrectness, he has been an outstanding consort. A lonely figure, of a penurious Greek-German background, who once said "the trouble is, I don't belong anywhere," he is a gifted and thoughtful man who has been an ornament to British life and a wonderful support to his wife.

"Philip is the only one who can tell the Queen things she might not want to hear," in the words of a courtier, and so he sometimes does.

Most of Queen Elizabeth's subjects want her to reign forever, partly because they cherish the continuity she represents in a turbulent age and partly because of unease about what might follow if her son succeeds her. The Prince of Wales conspicuously lacks his mother's discipline and discretion; he pursues eccentric causes with messianic zeal. Courtiers assert soothingly that if he assumes the crown he will relapse into Trappist silence, accepting its constraints. But there seem grounds for doubt whether, as a sexagenarian, he will suddenly acquire the prudence that characterizes his mother.

If he attempted to change the character of the monarchy, to make himself more assertive, trouble could quickly follow. It seems mistaken to confuse widespread public respect for the Queen with inalienable support for dynastic rule. History shows how suddenly and dramatically hostility to the royal family can erupt if its members behave unwisely. The imperialist Cecil Rhodes once visited Kaiser Wilhelm II of Germany, who asked what he could do to make himself more popular in Britain. Rhodes said: "You might try doing nothing." There was a tense pause; then the Kaiser exploded into uneasy laughter.

Queen Elizabeth has done nothing ungracefully and endured a public life of stultifying boredom in a fashion that has done much service to her country. A few intellectual snobs mock her resistance to culture and her anodyne conversation. But she has understood the most important thing about modern constitutional monarchs: that they are judged for what they are, rather than for what they do.

This is something that the Prince of Wales, forever eager to tackle huge issues beyond his intellectual capacity, has never grasped. While it is true that he sometimes puts himself on the virtuous side of public controversies, the proper function of the royal family in a constitutional monarchy is to stay out of controversy altogether. Not that this implies that Britain is threatened with a republic any time soon: few people hanker for radical constitutional change. They tremble at the notion of Mr. Blair, or for that matter David Beckham, occupying a presidential palace. But the Queen's successor will do well to consider her conduct a template for his own, rather than indulge perilous notions about creating a "new style" monarchy.

The Queen and Prince Philip have worn extraordinarily well, but given their advanced ages, it is inevitable they are now set in their ways and want no unwelcome surprises. She is said to have much warmer relations with her grandchildren than ever she did with her children. Prince William, especially, is the object of much warmth and many hopes. Her happiest hours are passed at Sandringham or Balmoral with her horses and dogs, and who can grudge them to her? The jubilee was a quintessential Old Britain affair. Much of New Britain, including the young and immigrant population, took scant notice. No matter. Given how hard it is to preserve traditional institutions in every society amid the storm-tossed billows of the twenty-first century, what seems remarkable is the strength of real enthusiasm for the Queen. A host of British people say to each other: hasn't she done well, then? The jubilee celebrations enabled the nation to say as much to her.

Spring Semester 2012

A version of this lecture appeared in the *Financial Times,* 1 June 2012.

28

British Studies at the University of Texas, 1975–2013

Paul Scott (Novelist, London), 'The *Raj Quartet*'

Ian Donaldson (Australian National University), 'Humanistic Studies in Australia'

Fritz Fellner (Salzburg University), 'Britain and the Origins of the First World War'

Roger Louis (History), 'Churchill, Roosevelt, and the Future of Dependent Peoples during the Second World War'

Michael Holroyd (Biographer, Dublin), 'Two Biographies: Lytton Strachey and Augustus John'

Max Beloff (Buckingham College), 'Imperial Sunset'

Robin Winks (Yale University), 'British Empire-Commonwealth Studies'

Warren Roberts (HRHRC) and David Farmer (HRHRC), 'The D. H. Lawrence Editorial Project'

Harvey C. Webster (University of Louisville), 'C. P. Snow as Novelist and Philosopher'

Anthony Kirk-Greene (Oxford University), 'The Origins and Aftermath of the Nigerian Civil War'

Spring Semester 1976

Joseph Jones (English), 'World English'

William S. Livingston (Government), 'The British Legacy in Contemporary Indian Politics'

John Higley (Sociology), 'The Recent Political Crisis in Australia'

Round Table Discussion, 'Reassessments of Evelyn Waugh': Elspeth Rostow (Dean, General and Comparative Studies), Standish Meacham (History), and Alain Blayac (University of Paris)

Jo Grimond (former Leader of the Liberal Party), 'Liberal Democracy in Britain'

Round Table Discussion, 'The Impact of Hitler on British Politics': Gaines Post (History), Malcolm Macdonald (Government), and Roger Louis (History)

Round Table Discussion, 'Kipling and India': Robert Hardgrave (Government), Gail Minault (History), and Chihiro Hosoya (University of Tokyo)

Kenneth Kirkwood (Oxford University), 'The Future of Southern Africa'

C. P. Snow, 'Elite Education in England'

Hans-Peter Schwarz (Cologne University), 'The Impact of Britain on German Politics and Society since the Second World War'

B. K. Nehru (Indian High Commissioner, London), 'The Political Crisis in India'

Round Table Discussion, 'Declassification of Secret Documents: The British and American Experiences Compared': Robert A. Divine (History), Harry J. Middleton (LBJ Library), and Roger Louis (History)

Fall Semester 1976

John Farrell (English), 'Revolution and Tragedy in Victorian England'

Anthony Honoré (Oxford University), 'British Attitudes to Legal Regulation of Sex'

Alan Hill (English), 'Wordsworth and America'

Ian Nish (London School of Economics), 'Anglo-American Naval Rivalry and the End of the Anglo-Japanese Alliance'

Norman Sherry (University of Lancaster), 'Joseph Conrad and the British Empire'

Peter Edwards (Australian National University), 'Australia through American Eyes: The Second World War and the Rise of Australia as a Regional Power'

Round Table Discussion, 'Britain and the Future of Europe': David Edwards (Government), Steven Baker (Government), Malcolm Macdonald (Government), William S. Livingston (Government), and Roger Louis (History)

Michael Hurst (Oxford University), 'The British Empire in Historical Perspective: The Case of Joseph Chamberlain'

Ronald Grierson (English Banker and former Public Official), 'The Evolution of the British Economy since 1945'

Marian Kent (University of New South Wales), 'British Oil Policy between the World Wars'

Constance Babington-Smith (Cambridge University), 'The World of Rose Macaulay'

Round Table Discussion, 'Adam Smith after 200 Years': William Todd (History), Walt Rostow (History and Economics), and James McKie (Dean, Social and Behavioral Sciences)

Spring Semester 1977

Carin Green (Novelist) and Elspeth Rostow (American Studies), 'The Achievement of Virginia Woolf'

Samuel H. Beer (Professor of Government, Harvard University), 'Reflections on British Politics'

David Fieldhouse (Oxford University), 'Decolonization and the Multinational Corporations'

Gordon Craig (Stanford University), 'England and Europe on the Eve of the Second World War'

John Lehmann (British Publisher and Writer), 'Publishing under the Bombs— The Hogarth Press during World War II'

Round Table Discussion, 'The Author, His Editor, and Publisher': Philip Jones (University of Texas Press), William S. Livingston (Government), Michael

Mewshaw (English), David Farmer (HRC), Roger Louis (History), and William Todd (History),

Dick Taverne (former Member of Parliament), 'The Mood of Britain: Misplaced Gloom or Blind Complacency?'

Round Table Discussion, 'The Origins of World War II in the Pacific': James B. Crowley (Yale University), Lloyd C. Gardner (Rutgers University), Akira Iriye (University of Chicago), and Roger Louis (History)

Rosemary Murray (Cambridge University), 'Higher Education in England'

Burke Judd (Zoology) and Robert Wagner (Zoology), 'Sir Cyril Burt and the Controversy over the Heritability of IQ'

Round Table Discussion, 'The Wartime Reputations of Churchill and Roosevelt: Overrated or Underrated?': Alessandra Lippucci (Government), Roger Louis (History), William S. Livingston (Government), and Walt Rostow (Economics)

Fall Semester 1977

Donald L. Weismann (Art and Art History), 'British Art in the Nineteenth Century: Turner and Constable—Precursors of French Impressionism'

Standish Meacham (History), 'Social Reform in England'

Joseph Jones, 'Recent Commonwealth Literature'

Lewis Hoffacker (former US Ambassador), 'The Katanga Crisis: British and Other Connections'

Round Table Discussion, 'The Copyright Law of 1976': James M. Treece (Law), Roger Louis (History), Warren Roberts, and Bill Todd (History)

Round Table Discussion, 'Freedom at Midnight: A Reassessment of Britain and the Partition of India Thirty Years After': Charles Heimsath (Visiting Professor of Indian History), Bob Hardgrave (Government), Thomasson Jannuzi, (Center for Asian Studies), C. P. Andrade (Comparative Studies), and William S. Livingston (Government),

Lord Fraser of Kilmorack (Conservative Party Organization), 'The Tory Tradition of British Politics'

Bernth Lindfors (English), 'Charles Dickens and the Hottentots and Zulus'

Albert Hourani (Oxford University), 'The Myth of T. E. Lawrence'

Mark Kinkead-Weekes (University of Kent) and Mara Kalnins (British Writer), 'D. H. Lawrence: Censorship and the Expression of Ideas'

J. D. B. Miller (Australian National University), 'The Collapse of the British Empire'

Round Table Discussion, 'The Best and Worst Books of 1977': Peter Green (Classics), Robert King (Dean, Social and Behavioral Sciences), William S. Livingston (Government), Bob Hardgrave (Government), Roger Louis (History), and Warren Roberts (HRHRC)

Spring Semester 1978

Round Table Discussion, 'British Decadence in the Interwar Years': Peter Green (Classics), Malcolm Macdonald (Government), and Robert Crunden (American Studies),

Round Table Discussion, R. Emmet Tyrrell's *Social Democracy's Failure in Britain:* Terry Quist (UT Undergraduate), Steve Baker (Government), and Roger Louis (History),

Stephen Koss (Columbia University), 'The British Press: Press Lords, Politicians, and Principles'

John House (Oxford University), 'The Rhodesian Crisis'
T. S. Dorsch (Durham University), 'Oxford in the 1930s'
Stephen Spender (English Poet and Writer), 'Britain and the Spanish Civil War'
Okot p'Bitek (Ugandan Poet), 'Idi Amin's Uganda'
David C. Goss (Australian Consul General), 'Wombats and Wivveroos'
Leon Epstein (University of Wisconsin), 'Britain and the Suez Crisis of 1956'
David Schoonover (Library Science), 'British and American Expatriates in Paris in the 1920s'
Peter Stansky (Stanford University), 'George Orwell and the Spanish Civil War'
Alexander Parker (Spanish and Portuguese), 'Reflections on the Spanish Civil War'
Norman Sherry (Lancaster University), 'Graham Greene and Latin America'
Martin Blumenson (Department of the Army), 'The Ultra Secret'

Fall Semester 1978

W. H. Morris-Jones (University of London), 'Power and Inequality in Southeast Asia'
Round Table Discussion, 'The British and the Shaping of the American Critical Mind: Edmund Wilson's *Letters on Literature and Politics*': Hartley Grattan (History), Gilbert Chase (American Studies), Bob Crunden (American Studies), and Roger Louis (History),
James Roach (Government), 'The Indian Emergency and its Aftermath'
Bill Todd (History), 'The Lives of Samuel Johnson'
Lord Hatch (British Labour Politician), 'The Labour Party and Africa'
John Kirkpatrick (HRHRC), 'Max Beerbohm'
Brian Levack (History), 'Witchcraft in England and Scotland'
M. R. Masani (Indian Writer), 'Gandhi and Gandhism'
A. W. Coates (Economics), 'The Professionalization of the British Civil Service'
John Clive (Harvard University), 'Great Historians of the Nineteenth Century'
Geoffrey Best (University of Sussex), 'Flight Path to Dresden: British Strategic Bombing in the Second World War'
Kurth Sprague (English), 'T. H. White's *Once and Future King*'
Gilbert Chase (American Studies), 'The British Musical Invasion of America'

Spring Semester 1979

Round Table Discussion, 'P. N. Furbanks's Biography of E. M. Forster': Peter Green (Classics), Alessandra Lippucci (Government), and Elspeth Rostow (LBJ School)
Round Table Discussion, 'E. M. Forster and India': Roger Louis (History), Bob Hardgrave (Government), Gail Minault (Professor of History), Peter Gran (History), and Bob King (Dean of Liberal Arts)
Paul M. Kennedy (University of East Anglia), 'The Contradiction between British Strategic Policy and Economic Policy in the Twentieth Century'
Richard Rive (Visiting Fulbright Research Fellow from South Africa), 'Olive Schreiner and the South African Nation'
Charles P. Kindleberger (Massachusetts Institute of Technology), 'Lord Zuckerman and the Second World War'
John Press (English Poet), 'English Poets and Postwar Society'
Richard Ellmann (Oxford University), 'Writing a Biography of Joyce'
Michael Finlayson (Scottish Dramatist), 'Contemporary British Theater'

Lawrence Stone (Institute for Advanced Study, Princeton), 'Family, Sex, and Marriage in England'

C. P. Snow, 'Reflections on the Two Cultures'

Theodore Zeldin (Oxford University), 'Are the British More or Less European than the French?'

David Edwards (Government), 'How United the Kingdom: Greater or Lesser Britain?'

Michael Holroyd (British Biographer), 'George Bernard Shaw'

John Wickman (Eisenhower Library), 'Eisenhower and the British'

Fall Semester 1979

Robert Palter (Philosophy), 'Reflections on British Philosophers: Locke, Hume, and the Utilitarians'

Alfred Gollin (University of California, Santa Barbara), 'Political Biography as Political History: Garvin, Milner, and Balfour'

Edward Steinhart (History), 'The Consequences of British Rule in Uganda'

Paul Sturges (Loughborough University, UK), and Dolores Donnelly (Toronto University), 'History of the National Library of Canada'

Sir Michael Tippett (British Composer), 'Moving into Aquarius'

Steven Baker (Government), 'Britain and United Nations Emergency Operations'

Maria Okila Dias (University of São Paulo), 'Intellectual Roots of Informal Imperialism: Britain and Brazil'

Alexander Parker (Spanish and Portuguese), 'Reflections on *Brideshead Revisited*'

Barry C. Higman (University of the West Indies), 'West Indian Emigrés and the British Empire'

Gaines Post (History), 'Britain and the Outbreak of the Second World War'

Karen Gould (Art and Art History), 'Medieval Manuscript Fragments and English Seventeenth-Century Collections: New Perspectives from *Fragmenta Manuscripta*'

Round Table Discussion of Jeanne MacKenzie's *Dickens: A Life:* John Farrell (English), Eric Poole (HRHRC) and James Bieri (English):

Joseph O. Baylen (Georgia State University), 'British Journalism in the Late Victorian and Edwardian Eras'

Peter T. Flawn (President, University of Texas), 'An Appreciation of Charles Dickens'

Spring Semester 1980

Annette Weiner (Anthropology), 'Anthropologists in New Guinea: British Interpretations and Cultural Relativism'

Bernard Richards (Oxford University), 'Conservation in the Nineteenth Century'

Thomas McGann (History), 'Britain and Argentina: An Informal Dominion?'

Mohammad Ali Jazayery (Center for Middle Eastern Studies), 'The Persian Tradition in English Literature'

C. Hartley Grattan (History) 'Twentieth-Century British Novels and the American Critical Mind'

Katherine Whitehorn (London *Observer*), 'An Insider's View of the *Observer*'

Guy Lytle (History), 'The Oxford University Press's *History of Oxford*'

C. P. Snow, 'Reflections on *The Masters*'

Harvey Webster, '*The Masters* and the Two Cultures'

Brian Blakeley (Texas Tech University), 'Women and the British Empire'

Stephen Koss (Columbia University), 'Asquith, Balfour, Milner, and the First World War'
Tony Smith (Tufts University), 'The Expansion of England: New Ideas on Controversial Themes in British Imperialism'
Stanley Ross (History), 'Britain and the Mexican Revolution'
Rowland Smith (Dalhousie University), 'The British Intellectual Left and the War, 1939–1945'
Richard Ellmann (Oxford University), 'Oscar Wilde: A Reconsideration and Problems of the Literary Biographer'
James Bill (Government), 'The United States, Britain, and the Iranian Crisis of 1953'

Fall Semester 1980

Decherd Turner (HRHRC), 'The First 1000 Days'
Roger Louis (History), 'Britain and Egypt after the Second World War'
Alistair Horne (Woodrow Wilson Center), 'Britain and the Fall of France'
Round Table Discussion, 'Literary Fraud: H. R. Trevor-Roper and the Hermit of Peking': Edward Rhodes (History), Peter Green (Classics), William Todd (History), and Roger Louis (History),
Mark Kinkead-Weekes (Kent University), 'D. H. Lawrence's *Rainbow:* Its Sense of History'
Sir John Crawford (Australian National University), 'Hartley Grattan: In Memoriam'
John Stubbs (University of Waterloo), 'The Tory View of Politics and Journalism in the Interwar Years'
Donald L. Weismann (Art and Art History), 'British Art in the Nineteenth Century'
Fran Hill (Government), 'The Legacy of British Colonialism in Tanzania'
R. W. B. Lewis (Yale University), 'What's Wrong with the Teaching of English?'
Charlene Gerry (British Publisher), 'The Revival of Fine Printing in Britain'
Peter Gran (History), 'The Islamic Response to British Capitalism'
Tina Poole (HRHRC) 'Gilbert and Sullivan's Christmas'

Spring Semester 1981

Bernard N. Darbyshire (Visiting Professor of Government and Economics), 'North Sea Oil and the British Future'
Christopher Hill (Oxford University), 'The English Civil War'
Elizabeth Heine (UT San Antonio), and Roger Louis (History), 'A Reassessment of Leonard Woolf'
Bernard Richards (Oxford University), 'D. H. Lawrence and Painting'
Miguel Gonzalez-Gerth (Spanish and Portuguese), 'Poetry Once Removed: The Resonance of English as a Second Language'
John Putnam Chalmers (HRHRC), 'English Bookbinding from Caedmon to Le Carré'
Peter Coltman (Architecture), 'The Cultural Landscapes of Britain: 2,000 Years of Blood, Sweat, Toil & Tears to Wrest a Living from this Bloody Mud'
Thomas H. Law (former Regent, University of Texas), 'The Gold Coins of the English Sovereigns'
Round Table Discussion, 'Canadian-American Economic Relations': Sidney Wein-

traub (LBJ School), James W. McKie (Economics), and Mary Williams (Canadian Consulate, Dallas)

Amedée Turner (European Parliament), 'Integrating Britain into the European Community'

Muriel C. Bradbrook (Cambridge University), 'Two Poets: Kathleen Raine and Seamus Heaney'

Ronald Sampson (Industrial Development Department, Aberdeen), 'Scotland—Somewhat of a British Texas?'

Fall Semester 1981

Jerome Bump (English), 'From Texas to England: The Ancestry of Our Victorian Architecture'

Lord Fraser of Kilmorack, 'Leadership Styles of Tory Prime Ministers since the Second World War'

William Carr (University of Sheffield), 'A British Interpretation of American, German, and Japanese Foreign Policy 1936–1941'

Iqbal Narain (Rajasthan University, Jaipur), 'The Ups and Downs of Indian Academic Life'

Don Etherington (HRHRC), 'The Florence Flood, 1966: The British Effort—or: Up to our Necks in Mud and Books'

E. V. K. Fitzgerald (Visiting Professor of Economics), 'The British University: Crisis, Confusion, and Stagnation'

Robert Crunden (American Studies), 'A Joshua for Historians: Mordecai Richter and Canadian Cultural Identity'

Bernth Lindfors (English), 'The Hottentot Venus and Other African Attractions in Nineteenth-Century England'

Chris Brookeman (London Polytechnic), 'The British Arts and Society'

Nicholas Pickwood (Freelance Book Conservator), 'The Libraries of the National Trust'

Kurth Sprague (English), 'John Steinbeck, Chase Horton, and the Matter of Britain'

Martin J. Wiener (Rice University), 'Cultural Values and Socio-Economic Behavior in Britain'

Werner Habicht (University of Würzburg), 'Shakespeare in Nineteenth-Century Germany'

Spring Semester 1982

Stevie Bezencenet (London College of Printing), 'Contemporary Photography in Britain'

Jane Marcus (English), 'Shakespeare's Sister, Beethoven's Brother: Dame Ethel Smyth and Virginia Woolf'

Wilson Harris (English) and Raja Rao (Philosophy), 'The Quest for Form: Britain and Commonwealth Perspectives'

Al Crosby (American Studies), 'The British Empire as a Product of Continental Drift'

Lord St. Brides (Visiting Scholar), 'The White House and Whitehall: Washington and Westminster'

Elizabeth Fernea (English and Middle East Studies), 'British Colonial Literature of the Middle East'

Maurice Evans (Actor and Producer), 'My Early Years in the Theater'

Joan Bassin (Kansas City Art Institute), 'Art and Industry in Nineteenth-Century England'

Eugene N. Borza (Pennsylvania State University), 'Sentimental British Philhellenism: Images of Greece'

Ralph Willett (University of Hull), 'The Style and Structure of British Television News'

Roger Louis (History), 'Britain and the Creation of the State of Israel'

Peter Russell (Oxford University), 'A British Historian Looks at Portuguese Historiography of the Fifteenth Century'

Rory Coker (Physics), 'Frauds, Hoaxes and Blunders in Science—a British Tradition?'

Ellen DuBois (State University of New York, Buffalo), 'Anglo-American Perspectives on the Suffragette Movement'

Donald G. Davis, Jr. (Library Science), 'Great Expectations—and a Few Illusions: Reflections on an Exchange Teaching Year in England'

Anthony Rota (Bertram Rota Ltd.), 'The Changing World of the Bookdealer'

Eisig Silberschlag (Visiting Professor of Judaic Studies), 'The Bible as the Most Popular Book in English'

Fall Semester 1982

Woodruff Smith (UT San Antonio), 'British Overseas Expansion'

The Rt. Hon. George Thomas (Speaker of the House of Commons), 'Parliamentary Democracy'

Nigel Nicolson (English Historian and Biographer), 'The English Country House as an Historical Document'

Lord St. Brides (Visiting Scholar), 'A Late Leaf of Laurel for Evelyn Waugh'

Lt. Col. Jack McNamara, USMC (Ret.), 'The Libel of Evelyn Waugh by the *Daily Express*'

James Wimsatt (English), 'Chaucer and Medieval French Manuscripts'

Christopher Whelan (Visiting Professor, UT Law School), 'Recent Developments in British Labour Law'

Brian Wearing (University of Canterbury, Christchurch), 'New Zealand: In the Pacific, but of It?'

Robert Hardgrave (Government), 'The United States and India'

James McBath (University of Southern California), 'The Evolution of *Hansard*'

Paul Fromm (University of Toronto), 'Canadian–United States Relations: Two Solitudes'

John Velz (English), 'When in Disgrace: Ganzel's Attempt to Exculpate John Payne Collier'

Roger Louis (History), 'British Origins of the Iranian Revolution'

Spring Semester 1983

Sir Ellis Waterhouse (Oxford University), 'A Comparison of British and French Painting in the Late Eighteenth Century'

E. J. L. Ride (Australian Consul General), 'Australia's Place in the World and Her Relationship with the United States'

Edward Bell (Royal Botanic Gardens, Kew), 'Kew Gardens in World History'

The Very Rev. Oliver Fiennes (Dean of Lincoln), 'The Care and Feeding of Magna Carta'

C. V. Narasimhan (former Under-Secretary of the United Nations), 'Last Days of the British Raj: A Civil Servant's View'

Warren G. Osmond, 'Sir Frederic Eggleston and the Development of Pacific Consciousness'

Richard Ellmann (Oxford University), 'Henry James among the Aesthetes'

Janet Caulkins (University of Wisconsin–Madison), 'The Poor Reputation of Cornish Knights in Medieval Literature'

Werner Habicht (University of Würzburg), 'Shakespeare and the Third Reich'

Gillian Peele (Oxford University), 'The Changing British Party System'

John Farrell (English), 'Scarlet Ribbons: Memories of Youth and Childhood in Victorian Authors'

Peter Russell (Oxford University), 'A Not So Bashful Stranger: *Don Quixote* in England, 1612–1781'

Sir Zelman Cowen (Oxford University), 'Contemporary Problems in Medicine, Law, and Ethics'

Dennis V. Lindley (Visiting Professor of Mathematics), 'Scientific Thinking in an Unscientific World'

Martin Blumenson (Department of the Army), 'General Mark Clark and the British in the Italian Campaign of World War II'

Fall Semester 1983

Anthony King (University of Essex), 'Margaret Thatcher and the Future of British Politics'

Alistair Gillespie (Canadian Minister of Energy, Mines, and Resources), 'Canadian-British Relations: Best and Worst'

Charles A. Owen, Jr. (University of Connecticut), 'The Pre-1400 Manuscripts of the *Canterbury Tales*'

Major-General (Ret.) Richard Clutterbuck (University of Exeter), 'Terrorism in Malaya'

Wayne A. Wiegand (University of Kentucky), 'British Propaganda in American Public Libraries during World War I'

Stuart Macintyre (Australian National University, Canberra), 'Australian Trade Unionism between the Wars'

Ram Joshi (Visiting Professor of History), 'Is Gandhi Relevant Today?'

Sir Denis Wright (former British Ambassador to Iran), 'Britain and the Iranian Revolution'

Andrew Horn (University of Lesotho), 'Theater and Politics in South Africa'

Philip Davies (University of Manchester), 'British Reaction to American Politics: Overt Rejection, Covert Assimilation'

H. K. Singh (Embassy of India), 'United States-Indian Relations'

Round Table Discussion, 'Two Cheers for Mountbatten: A Reassessment of Lord and Lady Mountbatten and the Partition of India': Roger Louis (History), Ram Joshi (Visiting Professor of History), and J. S. Mehta (LBJ School)

Spring Semester 1984

M. S. Venkataramani (Jawaharlal Nehru University), 'Winston Churchill and Indian Freedom'

Sir John Thompson (British Ambassador to the United Nations), 'The Falklands and Grenada in the United Nations'

Robert Farrell (Cornell University), 'Medieval Archaeology'

Allon White (University of Sussex), 'The Fiction of Early Modernism'

Round Table Discussion, 'Orwell's *Nineteen Eighty-Four*': Peter Green (Classics), Roger Louis (History), Miguel Gonzalez-Gerth (Spanish and Portuguese), Standish Meacham (History), and Sid Monas (Slavic Languages and History)

Uriel Dann (University of Tel Aviv), 'Hanover and Britain in the Time of George II'

José Ferrater-Mora (Bryn Mawr College), 'A. M. Turing and his "Universal Turing Machine"'

Rüdiger Ahrens (University of Würzburg), 'Teaching Shakespeare in German Universities'

Michael Brock (Oxford University), 'H. H. Asquith and Venetia Stanley'

Herbert Spiro (Free University of Berlin), 'What Makes the British and Americans Different from Everybody Else: The Adversary Process of the Common Law'

Nigel Bowles (University of Edinburgh), 'Reflections on Recent Developments in British Politics'

Harold Perkin (Rice University), 'The Evolution of Citizenship in Modern Britain'

Christopher Heywood (Sheffield University), '*Jane Eyre* and *Wuthering Heights*'

Dave Powers (Kennedy Library), 'JFK's Trip to Ireland, 1963'

R. W. Coats (Visiting Professor of Economics), 'John Maynard Keynes'

Elie Kedourie (LSE), 'Conservative Politics in the Late Nineteenth Century'

David Evans (Astronomy), 'Astronomy as a British Cultural Export'

Fall Semester 1984

John Henry Faulk, 'Reflections on My Sojourns in the British Middle East'

Lord Fraser of Kilmorack, 'The Thatcher Years—and Beyond'

Michael Phillips (University of Edinburgh), 'William Blake and the Rise of the Hot Air Balloon'

Erik Stocker (HRHRC), 'A Bibliographical Detective Story: Reconstructing James Joyce's Library'

Amedée Turner (European Parliament), 'Recent Developments in the European Parliament'

Michael Hurst (Oxford University), 'Scholars versus Journalists on the English Social Classes'

Charles Alan Wright (Law), 'Reflections on Cambridge'

J. M. Winter (Cambridge University), 'Fear of Decline in Population in Britain after World War I'

Henk Wesseling (University of Leiden), 'Dutch Colonialism and the Impact on British Imperialism'

Celia Morris Eckhardt (Biographer and author of *Fannie Wright*), 'Frances Wright and *England as the Civilizer*'

Sir Oliver Wright (British Ambassador to the United States), 'British Foreign Policy—1984'

Leonard Thompson (Yale University), 'Political Mythology and the Racial Order in South Africa'

Flora Nwapa (Nigerian Novelist), 'Women in Civilian and Military Rule in Nigeria'

Richard Rose (University of Strathclyde), 'The Capacity of the Presidency in Comparative Perspective'

Spring Semester 1985

Bernard Hickey (University of Venice), 'Australian Literary Culture: Short Stories, Novels, and "Literary Journalism"'

Kenneth Hafertepe (American Studies), 'The British Foundations of the Smithsonian Castle: The Gothic Revival in Britain and America'

Rajeev Dhavan (Visiting Professor, LBJ School and Center for Asian Studies), 'Race Relations in England: Trapped Minorities and their Future'

Sir John Thompson (British Ambassador to the United Nations), 'British Techniques of Statecraft'

Philip Bobbitt (Law), 'Britain, the United States, and Reduction in Strategic Arms'

David Bevington (Drama Critic and Theater Historian), 'Maimed Rites: Interrupted Ceremony in *Hamlet*'

Standish Meacham (History), 'The Impact of the New Left History on British and American Historiography'

Iris Murdoch (Novelist and Philosopher), and John O. Bayley (Oxford University), 'Themes in English Literature and Philosophy'

John P. Chalmers (HRHRC), 'Malory Illustrated'

Thomas Metcalf (University of California, Berkeley), 'The Architecture of Empire: The British Raj in India'

Robert H. Wilson (English), 'Malory and His Readers'

Lord St. Brides, '*A Passage to India:* Better Film than Novel?'

Derek Pearsall (York University), 'Fire, Flood, and Slaughter: The Tribulations of the Medieval City of York'

E. S. Atieno Odhiambo (University of Nairobi), 'Britain and Kenya: The Mau Mau, the "Colonial State," and Dependency'

Francis Robinson (University of London), 'Indian Muslim Religious Leadership and Colonial Rule'

Charles B. MacDonald (U.S. Army), 'The British in the Battle of the Bulge'

Brian Levack (History), 'The Battle of Bosworth Field'

Kurth Sprague (English), 'The Mirrors of Malory'

Fall Semester 1985

A. P. Thornton (University of Toronto), 'Whatever Happened to the British Commonwealth?'

Michael Garibaldi Hall (History), and Elizabeth Hall (LBJ School), 'Views of Pakistan'

Ronald Steel (Visiting Professor of History), 'Walter Lippmann and the British'

Douglas H. M. Branion (Canadian Consul General), 'Political Controversy and Economic Development in Canada'

Decherd Turner and Dave Oliphant (HRHRC), 'The History of the Publications of the HRHRC'

Robert Fernea (Anthropology), 'The Controversy over Sex and Orientalism: Charles Doughty's *Arabia Deserta*'

Desley Deacon (Government), 'Her Brilliant Career: The Context of Nineteenth-Century Australian Feminism'

John Lamphear (History), 'The British Colonial "Pacification" of Kenya: A View from the Other Side'

Kingsley de Silva (University of Peradeniya, Sri Lanka), 'British Colonialism and Sri Lankan Independence'

Thomas Hatfield (Continuing Education), 'Colorado on the Cam, 1986: From "Ultra" to Archaeology, from Mr. Micawber to Mrs. Thatcher'

Carol Hanbery MacKay (English), 'The Dickens Theater'

Round Table Discussion, 'The Art of Biography: Philip Ziegler's *Mountbatten*': Ronald Brown, Jo Anne Christian, Roger Louis (History), Harry Middleton (LBJ Library), and Ronald Steel

Spring Semester 1986

Round Table Discussion, '*Out of Africa:* The Book, the Biography, and the Movie': B. J. Fernea (English and Middle Eastern Studies), Bernth Lindfors (English), and Roger Louis (History)

Robert Litwak (Woodrow Wilson Center), 'The Great Game: Russian, British, and American Strategies in Asia'

Gillian Adams Barnes (English), and Jane Manaster (Geography), 'Humphrey Carpenter's *Secret Gardens* and the Golden Age of Children's Literature'

Laurie Hergenhan (University of Queensland), 'A Yankee in Australia: The Literary and Historical Adventures of C. Hartley Grattan'

Brian Matthews (Flinders University, Adelaide), 'Australian Utopianism of the 1880s'

Richard Langhorne (Cambridge University), 'Apostles and Spies: The Generation of Treason at Cambridge between the Wars'

Ronald Robinson (Oxford University), 'The Decline and Fall of the British Empire'

William Rodgers (Social Democratic Party), 'Britain's New Three-Party System: A Permanent or Passing Phenomenon?'

John Coetzee (University of Cape Town), 'The Farm Novel in South Africa'

Ayesha Jalal, (Cambridge University), 'Jinnah and the Partition of India'

Andrew Blane (City College of New York), 'Amnesty International: From a British to an International Movement'

Anthony Rota (Antiquarian Bookseller and Publisher), 'London Pride: 1986'

Elspeth Rostow (LBJ School), 'The Withering Away of Whose State? Colonel Qaddafi's? Reflections on Nationalism at Home and Abroad, in Britain and in the Middle East'

Ray Daum (HRHRC), 'Broadway—Piccadilly!'

Fall Semester 1986

Round Table Discussion: Dean Robert King and Members of the '"Unrequired Reading List" Committee—The British Component'

Paul Sturges (Loughborough University, UK), 'Popular Libraries in Eighteenth-Century Britain'

Ian Bickerton (University of Missouri), 'Eisenhower's Middle East Policy and the End of the British Empire'

Marc Ferro (Visiting Professor of History), 'Churchill and Pétain'

David Fitzpatrick (Visiting Professor of History, Queen's University, Ontario), 'Religion and Politics in Ireland'

Adam Watson (University of Virginia), 'Our Man in Havana—or: Britain, Cuba, and the Caribbean'

Norman Rose (Hebrew University), 'Chaim Weizmann, the British, and the Creation of the State of Israel'

Elaine Thompson (American University), 'Legislatures in Canberra and Washington'

Roger Louis (History), 'Suez Thirty Years After'

Antonia Gransden (University of Nottingham), 'The Writing of Chronicles in Medieval England'

Hilary Spurling (British Biographer and Critic), 'Paul Scott's *Raj Quartet:* The Novelist as Historian'

J. D. B. Miller (Australian National University), 'A Special and Puzzling Relationship: Australia and the United States'

Janet Meisel (History), 'The Domesday Book'

Spring Semester 1987

Round Table Discussion, 'Contemporary Perspectives on Evolution': Miguel Gonzalez-Gerth (Spanish and Portuguese), Robert Fernea (Anthropology), Joe Horn (Psychology), Bruce Hunt (History), and Delbert Thiessen (Psychology)

Alistair Campbell-Dick (Strategic Technology), 'Scottish Nationalism'

Anthony Mockler (British Freelance Historian and Biographer), 'Graham Greene: The Interweaving of His Life and Fiction'

Michael Crowder (Visiting Professor of African History, Amherst College), 'The Legacy of British Colonialism in Africa'

Carin Green (Classics), 'Lovers and Defectors: Autobiography and *The Perfect Spy*'

Lord St. Brides, 'The Modern British Monarchy'

Victor Szebehely (Aerospace Engineering), 'Sir Isaac Newton'

Patrick McCaughey (National Gallery of Victoria, Melbourne), 'The Persistence of Landscape in Australian Art'

Adolf Wood (*Times Literary Supplement*), 'An Informal History of the *TLS*'

Nissan Oren (Hebrew University), 'Churchill, Truman, and Stalin: The End of the Second World War'

Sir Michael Howard (Oxford University), 'Britain and the First World War'

Sir John Graham (former British Ambassador to NATO), 'NATO: British Origins, American Security, and the Future Outlook'

Daniel Mosser (Virginia Polytechnic Institute and State University), 'The Chaucer Cardigan Manuscript'

Sir Raymond Carr (Oxford University), 'British Intellectuals and the Spanish Civil War'

Michael Wilding (University of Sydney), 'The Fatal Shore? The Convict Period in Australian Literature'

Fall Semester 1987

Round Table Discussion, 'Anthony Burgess: The Autobiography': Peter Green (Classics), Winfred Lehmann (Linguistics), Roger Louis (History), and Paul Woodruff (Philosophy)

Robert Crunden (History and American Studies), 'Ezra Pound in London'

Carol MacKay (English), and John Henry Faulk (Austin), 'J. Frank Dobie and Thackeray's Great-Granddaughter: Another Side of *A Texan in England*'

Sarvepalli Gopal (Jawaharlal Nehru University and Oxford University), 'Nehru and the British'

Robert D. King (Dean of Liberal Arts), 'T. S. Eliot'

Lord Blake (Visiting Professor of English History and Literature), 'Disraeli: Problems of the Biographer'

Alain Blayac (University of Montpellier), 'Art as Revelation: Gerard Manley Hopkins's Poetry and James Joyce's *Portrait of the Artist*'

Mary Bull (Oxford University), 'Margery Perham and Africa'

R. J. Moore (Flinders University, Adelaide), 'Paul Scott: The Novelist as Historian, and the *Raj Quartet* as History'

Ian Willison (British Library), 'New Trends in Humanities Research: The *History of the Book in Britain* Project'

The Duke of Norfolk, 'The Lion and the Unicorn: Ceremonial and the Crown'

Hans Mark (Chancellor, UT System), 'The Royal Society, the Royal Observatory, and the Development of Modern Research Laboratories'

Henry Dietz (Government), 'Sherlock Holmes: A Centennial Celebration'

Spring Semester 1988

Lord Jenkins (Oxford University), 'Changing Patterns of British Government from Asquith via Baldwin and Attlee to Mrs. Thatcher'

Lord Thomas (author of *The Spanish Civil War* and *Cuba, or the Pursuit of Freedom),* 'Britain, Spain, and Latin America'

Round Table Discussion, 'Chinua Achebe: The Man and His Works': Barbara Harlow (English), Bernth Lindfors (English), Wahneema Lubiano (English), and Robert Wren (University of Houston)

Charles Townshend (Keele University, UK), 'Britain, Ireland, and Palestine, 1918–1947'

Richard Morse (Woodrow Wilson Center), 'T. S. Eliot and Latin America'

Chinua Achebe (Nigerian Novelist), 'Anthills of the Savannah'

Tapan Raychaudhuri (Oxford University), 'The English in Bengali Eyes in the Nineteenth Century'

Lord Chitnis (Rowntree Trust and the British Refugee Council), 'British Perceptions of U.S. Policy in Central America'

Kurth Sprague (English), 'Constance White: Sex, Womanhood, and Marriage in British India'

George McGhee (former US Ambassador to Turkey and Germany), 'The Turning Point in the Cold War: Britain, the United States, and Turkey's Entry into NATO'

Robert Palter (Trinity College), 'New Light on Newton's Natural Philosophy'

J. Kenneth McDonald (CIA), 'The Decline of British Naval Power, 1918–1922'

Yvonne Cripps (Visiting Professor of Law), '"Peter and the Boys Who Cry Wolf": *Spycatcher*'

Emmanuel Ngara (University of Zimbabwe), 'African Poetry: Nationalism and Cultural Domination'

Kate Frost (English), 'Frat Rats of the Invisible College: The Wizard Earl of Northumberland and His Pre-Rosicrucian Pals'

B. Ramesh Babu (Visiting Professor of Government), 'American Foreign Policy: An Indian Dissent'

Sir Antony Ackland (British Ambassador to the United States), 'From Dubai to Madrid: Adventures in the British Foreign Service'

In the Spring Semester 1988, British Studies helped sponsor four lectures by Sir Brian Urquhart (former Under-Secretary of the United Nations) under the general title 'World Order in the Era of Decolonization.'

Fall Semester 1988

Round Table Discussion on Richard Ellman's *Oscar Wilde:* Peter Green (Classics), Diana Hobby (Rice University), Roger Louis (History), and Elspeth Rostow (American Studies),

Hugh Cecil (University of Leeds), 'The British First World War Novel of Experience'

Alan Knight (History), 'Britain and the Mexican Revolution'

Prosser Gifford (Former Deputy Director, Woodrow Wilson Center, Washington, DC), and Robert Frykenberg (University of Wisconsin–Madison), 'Stability in Post-Colonial British Africa: The Indian Perspective'

Joseph Dobrinski (Université Paul-Valéry), 'The Symbolism of the Artist Theme in *Lord Jim*'

Martin Stannard (University of Leicester), 'Evelyn Waugh and North America'

Lawrence Cranberg (Fellow, American Physical Society), 'The Engels-Marx Relationship and the Origins of Marxism'

N. G. L. Hammond (Bristol University), 'The British Military Mission to Greece, 1943–1944'

Barbara Harlow (English), 'A Legacy of the British Era in Egypt: Women, Writing, and Political Detention'

Sidney Monas (Slavic Languages and History), 'Thanks for the Mummery: *Finnegans Wake*, Rabelais, Bakhtin, and Verbal Carnival'

Robert Bowie (Central Intelligence Agency), 'Britain's Decision to Join the European Community'

Shirley Williams (Social Democratic Party), 'Labour Weakness and Tory Strength—or, The Strange Death of Labour England'

Bernard Richards (Oxford University), 'Ruskin's View of Turner'

John R. Clarke (Art History), 'Australian Art of the 1960s'

Round Table Discussion on Paul Kennedy's *The Rise and Fall of the Great Powers:* Alessandra Lipucci (Government), Roger Louis (History), Jagat Mehta (LBJ School), Sidney Monas (Slavic Languages and History), and Walt Rostow (Economics and History)

Spring Semester 1989

Brian Levack (History), 'The English Bill of Rights, 1689'

Hilary Spurling (Critic and Biographer), 'Paul Scott as Novelist: His Sense of History and the British Era in India'

Larry Carver (Humanities Program), 'Lord Rochester: The Profane Wit and the Restoration's Major Minor Poet'

Atieno Odhiambo (Rice University), 'Re-Interpreting Mau Mau'

Trevor Hartley (London School of Economics), 'The British Constitution and the European Community'

Archie Brown (Oxford University), 'Political Leadership in Britain, the Soviet Union, and the United States'

Lord Blake (Editor, *Dictionary of National Biography*), 'Churchill as Historian'

Weirui Hou (Shanghai University), 'British Literature in China'

Norman Daniel (British Council), 'Britain and the Iraqi Revolution of 1958'

Alistair Horne (Oxford University), 'The Writing of the Biography of Harold Macmillan'

M. R. D. Foot (Editor, *Gladstone Diaries*), 'The Open and Secret War, 1939–1945'

Ian Willison (former Head of the Rare Books Division, British Library), 'Editorial Theory and Practice in The History of the Book'

Neville Meaney (University of Sydney), 'The "Yellow Peril": Invasion, Scare Novels, and Australian Political Culture'

Round Table Discussion on *The Satanic Verses:* Kurth Sprague (American Studies), Peter Green (Classics), Robert A. Fernea (Anthropology), Roger Louis (History), and Gail Minault (History and Asian Studies)

Kate Frost (English), 'John Donne, Sunspots, and the British Empire'

Lee Patterson (Duke University), 'Chaucerian Commerce'

Edmund Weiner and John Simpson (Editors of the new *OED*), 'Return to the Web of Words'

Ray Daum (HRHRC), 'Noel Coward and Cole Porter'

William B. Todd (History), 'Edmund Burke on the French Revolution'

Fall Semester 1989

D. Cameron Watt (London School of Economics), 'Britain and the Origins of the Second World War: Personalities and Politics of Appeasement'

Gary Freeman (Government), 'On the Awfulness of the English: The View from Comparative Studies'

Hans Mark (Chancellor, UT System), 'British Naval Tactics in the Second World War: The Japanese Lessons'

T. B. Millar (Menzies Centre for Australian Studies, London), 'Australia, Britain, and the United States in Historical Perspective'

Dudley Fishburn (Member of Parliament and former Editor of *The Economist*), '*The Economist*'

Lord Franks (former Ambassador in Washington), 'The "Special Relationship"'

Herbert L. Jacobson (Drama Critic and friend of Orson Welles), 'Three Score Years of Transatlantic Acting and Staging of Shakespeare'

Roy Macleod (University of Sydney) 'The "Practical Man": Myth and Metaphor in Anglo-Australian Science'

David Murray (Open University), 'Hong Kong: The Historical Context for the Transfer of Power'

Susan Napier (UT Assistant Professor of Japanese Language and Literature), 'Japanese Intellectuals Discover the British'

Dr. Karan Singh (Ambassador of India to the United States), 'Four Decades of Indian Democracy'

Paul Woodruff (Philosophy), 'George Grote and the Radical Tradition in British Scholarship'

Herbert J. Spiro (Government), 'Britain, the United States, and the Future of Germany'

Robert Lowe (*Austin American-Statesman*), '"God Rest You Merry, Gentlemen": The Curious British Cult of Sherry'

Spring Semester 1990

Thomas F. Staley (HRHRC), 'Harry Ransom, the Humanities Research Center, and the Development of Twentieth-Century Literary Research Collections'

Thomas Cable (English), 'The Rise and Decline of the English Language'

D. J. Wenden (Oxford University), 'Sir Alexander Korda and the British Film Industry'

Roger Owen (Oxford University), 'Reflections on the First Ten Years of Thatcherism'

Robert Hardgrave (Government), 'Celebrating Calcutta: The Solvyns Portraits'

Donatus Nwoga (University of Nigeria, Nsukka), 'The Intellectual Legacy of British Decolonization in Africa'

Francis Sitwell (Etonian, Seaman, and Literary Executor), 'Edith Sitwell: A Reappraisal'

Robert Vitalis (Government), 'The "New Deal" in Egypt: Britain, the United States, and the Egyptian Economy during World War II'

James Coote (Architecture), 'Prince Charles and Architecture'

Harry Eckstein (University of California, Irvine), 'British Politics and the National Health Service'

Alfred David (Indiana University), 'Chaucer and King Arthur'

Ola Rotimi (African Playwright and Theater Director), 'African Literature and the British Tongue'

Derek Brewer (Cambridge University), 'An Anthropological Study of Literature'

Neil MacCormick (University of Edinburgh), 'Stands Scotland Where She Should?'

Janice Rossen (Senior Research Fellow, HRHRC), 'Toads and Melancholy: The Poetry of Philip Larkin'

Ronald Robinson (Oxford University), 'The Decolonization of British Imperialism'

Fall Semester 1990

Round Table Discussion on 'The Crisis in the Persian Gulf': Hafez Farmayan (History), Robert Fernea (Anthropology), Roger Louis (History), and Robert Stookey (Center for Middle Eastern Studies)

John Velz (English), 'Shakespeare and Some Surrogates: An Account of the Anti-Stratfordian Heresy'

Michael H. Codd (Department of the Prime Minister and Cabinet, Government of Australia), 'The Future of the Commonwealth: An Australian View'

John Dawick (Massey University, New Zealand), 'The Perils of Paula: Young Women and Older Men in Pinero's Plays'

Gloria Fromm (University of Illinios, Chicago), 'New Windows on Modernism: The Letters of Dorothy Richardson'

David Braybrooke (Government), 'The Canadian Constitutional Crisis'

Sidney Monas (Slavic Languages and History), 'Paul Fussell and World War II'

James Fishkin (Government), 'Thought Experiments in Recent Oxford Philosophy'

Joseph Hamburger (Yale University), 'How Liberal Was John Stuart Mill?'

Richard W. Clement (University of Kansas), 'Thomas James and the Bodleian Library: The Foundations of Scholarship'

Michael Yeats (Former Chairman of the Irish Senate and only son of the poet William Butler Yeats), 'Ireland and Europe'

Round Table Discussion on 'William H. McNeill's *Arnold J. Toynbee: A Life*': Standish Meacham (Dean, Liberal Arts), Peter Green (Classics), Roger Louis (History), and Sidney Monas (Slavic Languages and History)

Jeffrey Meyers (Biographer and Professor of English, University of Colorado), 'Conrad and Jane Anderson'

Alan Frost (La Trobe University, Melbourne), 'The Explorations of Captain Cook'

Sarvepalli Gopal (Jawaharlal Nehru University), 'The First Ten Years of Indian Independence'

Round Table Discussion on 'The Best and Worst Books of 1990': Alessandra Lippucci (Government), Roger Louis (History), Tom Staley (HRHRC), Steve Weinberg (Physics), and Paul Woodruff (Philosophy)

Spring Semester 1991

David Hollway (Prime Minister's Office, Government of Australia), 'Australia and the Gulf Crisis'

Diane Kunz (Yale University), 'British Post-War Sterling Crises'

Miguel Gonzalez-Gerth (Spanish Literature and the HRHRC), 'T. E. Lawrence, Richard Aldington, and the Death of Heroes'

Robert Twombly (English), 'Religious Encounters with the Flesh in English Literature'

Alan Ryan (Princeton University), 'Bertrand Russell's Politics'

Hugh Kenner (Johns Hopkins University), 'The State of English Poetry'

Patricia Burnham (American Studies), 'Anglo-American Art and the Struggle for Artistic Independence'

Round Table Discussion on 'The Churchill Tradition': Lord Blake (former Provost of Queen's College, Oxford), Lord Jenkins (Chancellor, Oxford University), Field Marshal Lord Carver (former Chief of the Defence Staff), Sir Michael Howard (former Regius Professor, Oxford, present Lovett Professor of Military and Naval History, Yale University), with a concluding comment by Winston S. Churchill, M.P.

Woodruff Smith (UT San Antonio), 'Why Do the British Put Sugar in Their Tea?'

Peter Firchow (University of Minnesota), 'Aldous Huxley: The Poet as Centaur'

Irene Gendzier (Boston University), 'British and American Middle Eastern Policies in the 1950s: Lebanon and Kuwait; Reflections on Past Experience and the Post-War Crisis in the Gulf'

John Train (*Harvard* Magazine and *Wall Street Journal*), 'Remarkable Catchwords in the City of London and on Wall Street'

Adam Sisman (Independent Writer, London), 'A. J. P. Taylor'

Roger Louis (History), 'The Young Winston'

Adrian Mitchell (Melbourne University), 'Claiming a Voice: Recent Non-Fiction Writing in Australia'

Bruce Hevly (University of Washington), 'Stretching Things Out versus Letting Them Slide: The Natural Philosophy of Ice in Edinburgh and Cambridge in the Nineteenth Century'

Henry Dietz (Government), 'Foibles and Follies in Sherlock's Great Game: Some Excesses of Holmesian Research'

Summer 1991

Roger Louis (History), and Ronald Robinson (Oxford University), 'Harold Macmillan and the Dissolution of the British Empire'

Robert Treu (University of Wisconsin–Lacrosse), 'D. H. Lawrence and Graham Greene in Mexico'

Thomas Pinney (Pomona College), 'Kipling, India, and Imperialism'

Ronald Heiferman (Quinnipiac College), 'The Odd Couple: Winston Churchill and Chiang Kai-shek'

John Harty (Alice Lloyd College, Kentucky), 'The Movie and the Book: J. G. Ballard's *Empire of the Sun*'

A. B. Assensoh (Southern University, Baton Rouge), 'Nkrumah'

Victoria Carchidi (Emory and Henry College), 'Lawrence of Arabia on a Camel, Thank God!'

James Gump (University of California, San Diego), 'The Zulu and the Sioux: The British and American Comparative Experience with the "Noble Savage"'

Fall Semester 1991

Round Table Discussion on Noel Annan's *Our Age:* Peter Green (Classics), Robert D. King (Dean, Liberal Arts), Roger Louis (History), and Thomas F. Staley (HRHRC)

Christopher Heywood (Okayama University), 'Slavery, Imagination, and the Brontës'

Harold L. Smith (University of Houston, Victoria), 'Winston Churchill and Women'

Krystyna Kujawinska-Courtney (University of Lodz), 'Shakespeare and Poland'

Ewell E. Murphy, Jr. (Baker Botts, Houston), 'Cecil Rhodes and the Rhodes Scholarships'

I. N. Kimambo (University of Dar es Salaam), 'The District Officer in Tanganyika'

Hans Mark (Chancellor, UT System), 'The Pax Britannica and the Inevitable Comparison: Is There a Pax Americana? Conclusions from the Gulf War'

Richard Clutterbuck (Major-General, British Army, Ret.), 'British and American Hostages in the Middle East: Negotiating with Terrorists'

Elizabeth Hedrick (English), 'Samuel Johnson and Linguistic Propriety'

The Hon. Denis McLean (New Zealand Ambassador to the United States), 'Australia and New Zealand: The Nuisance of Nationalism'

Elizabeth Richmond (English), 'Submitting a Trifle for a Degree: Dramatic Productions at Oxford and Cambridge in the Age of Shakespeare'

Kenneth Warren, M.D. (Director for Science, Maxwell Macmillan), 'Tropical Medicine: A British Invention'

Adolf Wood (*Times Literary Supplement*), 'The Golden Age of the *Times Literary Supplement*'

Eugene Walter (Poet and Novelist), 'Unofficial Poetry: Literary London in the 1940s and 1950s'

Sidney Monas (Slavic Languages and History), 'Images of Britain in the Poetry of World War II'

St. Stephen's Madrigal Choir, 'Celebrating an English Christmas'

Spring Semester 1992

Jeremy Treglown (Critic and Author), 'Wartime Censorship and the Novel'

Toyin Falola (History), 'Nigerian Independence, 1960'

Donald S. Lamm (W.W. Norton and Company), 'Publishing English History in America'

Colin Franklin (Publisher and Historian of the Book), 'The Pleasures of Eighteenth-Century Shakespeare'

Thomas F. Staley (HRHRC), '*Fin de Siècle* Joyce: A Perspective on One Hundred Years'

Sarvepalli Gopal (Jawaharlal Nehru University), '"Drinking Tea with Treason": Halifax and Gandhi'

Michael Winship (English), 'The History of the Book: Britain's Foreign Trade in Books in the Nineteenth Century'

Richard Lariviere (Sanskrit and Asian Studies), 'British Law and Lawyers in India'

Round Table Discussion on A. S. Byatt's *Possession:* Janice Rossen (Visiting Scholar, HRHRC), John P. Farrell (English), and Roger Louis (History)

William H. McNeill (University of Chicago), 'Arnold Toynbee's Vision of World History'

Derek Brewer (Cambridge University), 'The Interpretation of Fairy Tales: The Implications for English Literature, Anthropology, and History'

David Bradshaw (Oxford University), 'Aldous Huxley: Eugenics and the Rational State'

Steven Weinberg (Physics), 'The British Style in Physics'

Sir David Williams (Cambridge University), 'Northern Ireland'

Summer 1992

R. A. C. Parker (Oxford University), 'Neville Chamberlain and Appeasement'

Adrian Wooldridge (Oxford University and *The Economist*), 'Reforming British Education: How It Happened and What America Can Learn'

Chris Wrigley (Nottingham University), 'A. J. P. Taylor: An English Radical and Modern Europe'

Fall Semester 1992

Round Table Discussion on E. M. Forster's *Howards End:* The Movie and the Book, Robert D. King (Linguistics), Roger Louis (History), Alessandra Lippucci (Government), and Thomas F. Staley (HRHRC)

Lord Skidelsky (Warwick University), 'Keynes and the Origins of the "Special Relationship"'

Sir Samuel Falle (former British Ambassador), 'Britain and the Middle East in the 1950s'

Ian MacKillop (University of Sheffield), 'We Were That Cambridge: F. R. Leavis and *Scrutiny*'

Walter Dean Burnham (Government), 'The 1992 British Elections: Four-or-Five-More Tory Years?'

Don Graham (English), 'Modern Australian Literature and the Image of America'

Richard Woolcott (former Secretary of the Australian Department of Foreign Affairs), 'Australia and the Question of Cooperation or Contention in the Pacific'

Ian Willison (1992 Wiggins Lecturer, American Antiquarian Society), 'The History of the Book in Twentieth-Century Britain and America'

Iain Sproat, (Member of Parliament), 'P. G. Wodehouse and the War'

Standish Meacham (History), 'The Crystal Palace'

Field Marshal Lord Carver (former Chief of the British Defence Staff), 'Wavell: A Reassessment'

Lesley Hall (Wellcome Institute for the History of Medicine, London), 'For Fear of Frightening the Horses: Sexology in Britain since William Acton'

Michael Fry (University of Southern California), 'Britain, the United Nations, and the Lebanon Crisis of 1958'

Brian Holden Reid (King's College, London), 'J. F. C. Fuller and the Revolution in British Military Thought'

Neil Parsons (University of London), '"Clicko," or Franz Taaibosch: A Bushman Entertainer in Britain, Jamaica, and the United States *c.* 1919–40'

John Hargreaves (Aberdeen University), 'God's Advocate: Lewis Namier and the History of Modern Europe'

Round Table Discussion on Robert Harris's *Fatherland:* Henry Dietz (Government), Robert D. King (Linguistics), Roger Louis (History), and Walter Wetzels (Germanic Languages)

Kevin Tierney (University of California), 'Robert Graves: An Outsider Looking In, or An Insider Who Escaped?'

Spring Semester 1993

Round Table Discussion on 'The Trollope Mystique': Janice Rossen (author of *Philip Larkin* and *The University in Modern Fiction*), Louise Weinberg (Law School), and Paul Woodruff (Plan II Honors Program and Philosophy)

Bruce Hunt (History), 'To Rule the Waves: Cable Telegraphy and British Physics in the Nineteenth Century'

Martin Wiener (Rice University), 'The Unloved State: Contemporary Political Attitudes in the Writing of Modern British History'

Elizabeth Dunn (HRHRC), 'Ralph Waldo Emerson and Ireland'

Jason Thompson (Western Kentucky University), 'Edward William Lane's "Description of Egypt"'

Sir Michael Howard (Yale University), 'Strategic Deception in the Second World War'

Gordon A. Craig (Stanford University), 'Churchill'

Round Table Discussion on the Indian Mathematician Ramanujan: Robert D. King (Linguistics), James W. Vick (Mathematics), and Steven Weinberg (Physics)

Martha Merritt (Government), 'From Commonwealth to Commonwealth, and from Vauxhall to *Vokzal:* Russian Borrowing from Britain'

Sidney Monas (Slavic Languages and History), 'James Joyce and Russia'

Peter Marshall (King's College, London), 'Imperial Britain and the Question of National Identity'

Michael Wheeler (Lancaster University), 'Ruskin and Gladstone'

Anthony Low (Cambridge University), 'Britain and India in the Early 1930s: The British, American, French, and Dutch Empires Compared'

Summer 1993

Alexander Pettit (University of North Texas), 'Lord Bolingbroke's *Remarks on the History of England*'

Rose Marie Burwell (Northern Illinois University), 'The British Novel and Ernest Hemingway'

Richard Patteson (Mississippi State University), 'New Writing in the West Indies'

Richard Greene (Memorial University, Newfoundland), 'The Moral Authority of Edith Sitwell'

Fall Semester 1993

Round Table Discussion on 'The British and the Shaping of the American Critical Mind—Edmund Wilson, Part II': Roger Louis (History), Elspeth Rostow (American Studies), Tom Staley (HRHRC), and Robert Crunden (History and American Studies)

Roseanne Camacho (University of Rhode Island), 'Evelyn Scott: Towards an Intellectual Biography'
Christopher Heywood (Okayama University), 'The Brontës and Slavery'
Peter Gay (Yale University), 'The Cultivation of Hatred in England'
Linda Ferreira-Buckley (English) 'England's First English Department: Rhetoric and More Rhetoric'
Janice Rossen (HRHRC), 'British University Novels'
Ian Hancock (O Yanko Le Redzosko) (Linguistics and English), 'The Gypsy Image in British Literature'
James Davies (University College of Swansea), 'Dylan Thomas'
Jeremy Lewis (London Writer and Editor), 'Who Cares about Cyril Connolly?'
Sam Jamot Brown (British Studies) and Robert D. King (Linguistics), 'Scott and the Antarctic'
Martin Trump (University of South Africa), 'Nadine Gordimer's Social and Political Vision'
Richard Clogg (University of London), 'Britain and the Origins of the Greek Civil War'
Herbert J. Spiro (United States Ambassador, Ret.), 'The Warburgs: Anglo-American and German-Jewish Bankers'
Colin Franklin (Publisher and Antiquarian Bookseller), 'Lord Chesterfield: Stylist, Connoisseur of Manners, and Specialist in Worldly Advice'
Jeffrey Segall (Charles University, Prague), 'The Making of James Joyce's Reputation'
Rhodri Jeffreys-Jones (University of Edinburgh), 'The Myth of the Iron Lady: Margaret Thatcher and World Stateswomen'
John Rumrich (English), 'Milton and Science: Gravity and the Fall'
J. D. Alsop (McMaster University), 'British Propaganda, Espionage, and Political Intrigue'
Round Table Discussion on 'The Best and the Worst Books of 1993': David Edwards (Government), Creekmore Fath (Liberal Arts Foundation), Betty Sue Flowers (English), and Sidney Monas (Slavic Languages and History)

Spring Semester 1994

Thomas F. Staley (HRHRC), 'John Rodker: Poet and Publisher of Modernism'
Martha Fehsenfeld, and Lois More Overbeck (Emory University), 'The Correspondence of Samuel Beckett'
M. R. D. Foot (Historian and Editor), 'Lessons of War on War: The Influence of 1914–1918 on 1939–1945'
Round Table Discussion on 'Requiem for Canada?' David Braybrooke (Government), Walter Dean Burnham (Government), and Robert Crunden (American Studies)
Ross Terrill (Harvard University), 'Australia and Asia in Historical Perspective'
Sir Samuel Falle (British Ambassador and High Commissioner), 'The Morning after Independence: The Legacy of the British Empire'
Deborah Lavin (University of Durham), 'Lionel Curtis: Prophet of the British Empire'
Robin W. Doughty (Geography), 'Eucalyptus: And Not a Koala in Sight'
Al Crosby (American Studies and History), 'Captain Cook and the Biological Impact on the Hawaiian Islands'

Gillian Adams (Editor, *Children's Literature Association Quarterly*), 'Beatrix Potter and Her Recent Critics'

Lord Amery, 'Churchill's Legacy'

Christa Jansohn (University of Bonn), and Peter Green (Classics), '*Lady Chatterley's Lover*'

R. A. C. Parker (Oxford University), 'Neville Chamberlain and the Coming of the Second World War'

John Velz (English), 'King Lear in Iowa: Jane Smiley's *A Thousand Acres*'

Jan Schall (University of Florida), 'British Spirit Photography'

Daniel Woolf (Dalhousie University), 'The Revolution in Historical Consciousness in England'

Fall Semester 1994

Kenneth O. Morgan (University of Wales), 'Welsh Nationalism'

Round Table Discussion on Michael Shelden's *Graham Greene: The Man Within:* Peter Green (Classics), Roger Louis (History), and Thomas F. Staley (HRHRC)

Robert D. King (Linguistics), 'The Secret War, 1939–1945'

Brian Boyd (University of Auckland), 'The Evolution of Shakespearean Dramatic Structure'

Lord Weatherill (former Speaker of the House of Commons), 'Thirty Years in Parliament'

Hans Mark (Aerospace Engineering), 'Churchill's Scientists'

Steven Weinberg (Physics), 'The Test of War: British Strengths and Weaknesses in World War II'

Dennis Welland (University of East Anglia), 'Wilfred Owen and the Poetry of War'

Alan Frost (La Trobe University), 'The *Bounty* Mutiny and the British Romantic Poets'

W. O. S. Sutherland (English), 'Sir Walter Scott'

Hazel Rowley (Deakin University, Melbourne), 'Christina Stead's "Other Country"'

Herman Bakvis (Dalhousie University), 'The Future of Democracy in Canada and Australia'

Peter Stansky (Stanford University), 'George Orwell and the Writing of *Nineteen Eighty-Four*'

Henry Dietz (Government), 'Sherlock Homes and Jack the Ripper'

James Coote (Architecture), 'Techniques of Illusion in British Architecture'

Round Table Discussion on 'The Best and Worst Books of 1994': Dean Burnham (Government), Alessandra Lippucci (Government), Roger Louis (History), Sidney Monas (Slavic Languages and History), and Janice Rossen (HRHRC)

Spring Semester 1995

Elizabeth Butler Cullingford (English), 'Anti-Colonial Metaphors in Contemporary Irish Literature'

Thomas M. Hatfield (Continuing Education), 'British and American Deception of the Germans in Normandy'

Gary P. Freeman (Government), 'The Politics of Race and Immigration in Britain'

Donald G. Davis, Jr. (Library and Information Science), 'The Printed Word in Sunday Schools in Nineteenth-Century England and the United States'

Brian Bremen (English), "Healing Words: The Literature of Medicine and the Medicine of Literature'

Frances Karttunen (Linguistic Research Center), and Alfred W. Crosby (American Studies and History), 'British Imperialism and Creole Languages'

Paul Lovejoy (York University, Canada), 'British Rule in Africa: A Reassessment of Nineteenth-Century Colonialism'

Carol MacKay (English), 'Creative Negativity in the Life and Work of Elizabeth Robins'

John Brokaw (Theatre and Dance), 'The Changing Stage in London, 1790–1832'

Linda Colley (Yale University), 'The Frontier in British History'

Iwan Morus (University of California, San Diego), 'Manufacturing Nature: Science, Technology, and Victorian Consumer Culture'

Brian Parker (University of Toronto), 'Jacobean Law: The Dueling Code and "A Faire Quarrel" (1617)'

Kate Frost (English), '"Jack Donne the Rake": Fooling around in the 1590s'

Mark Kinkead-Weekes (University of Kent), 'Beyond Gossip: D. H. Lawrence's Writing Life'

Summer 1995

S. P. Rosenbaum (University of Toronto), 'Leonard and Virginia Woolf at the Hogarth Press'

Maria X. Wells (HRHRC), 'A Delicate Balance: Trieste, 1945'

Kevin Tierney (University of California, Berkeley), 'Personae in Twentieth Century British Autobiography'

Fall Semester 1995

Brian Levack (History), 'Witchcraft, Possession, and the Law in Jacobean England'

Janice Rossen (HRHRC), 'The Home Front: Anglo-American Women Novelists and World War II'

Dorothy Driver (University of Cape Town), 'Olive Schreiner's Novel *From Man to Man*'

Philip Ziegler (London), 'Mountbatten Revisited'

Joanna Hitchcock (Director, University of Texas Press), 'British and American University Presses'

Samuel H. Beer (Harvard University), 'The Rise and Fall of Party Government in Britain and the United States, 1945–1995'

Richard Broinowski (Australian Ambassador to Mexico and Central America), 'Australia and Latin America'

John Grigg (London), 'Myths about the Approach to Indian Independence'

Round Table Discussion on *Measuring the Mind* (Adrian Wooldridge) and *The Bell Curve* (Richard J. Herrnstein and Charles Murray): David Edwards (Government), Sheldon Ekland-Olson (Dean of Liberal Arts), Joseph Horn (Psychology), and Robert D. King (Linguistics)

Paul Addison (University of Edinburgh), 'British Politics in the Second World War'

John Sibley Butler (Sociology), 'Emigrants of the British Empire'

Round Table Discussion on the Movie *Carrington:* Peter Green (Classics), Robin

Kilson (History), Roger Louis (History), Sidney Monas (Slavic Languages and History), and Elizabeth Richmond-Garza (English)

Spring Semester 1996

Kevin Kenny (History), 'Making Sense of the Molly Maguires'
Brigadier Michael Harbottle (British Army), 'British and American Security in the Post-Cold War'
Carol MacKay (English), 'The Singular Double Vision of Photographer Julia Margaret Cameron'
John Ramsden (University of London), '"That Will Depend on Who Writes the History": Winston Churchill as His Own Historian'
Jack P. Greene (Johns Hopkins University), 'The *British* Revolution in America'
Walter D. Wetzels (German), 'The Ideological Fallout in Germany of Two British Expeditions to Test Einstein's General Theory of Relativity'
Thomas Pinney (Pomona College), 'In Praise of Kipling'
Michael Charlesworth (Art History), 'The English Landscape Garden'
Stephen Gray (South African Novelist), 'The Dilemma of Colonial Writers with Dual Identities'
Jeremy Black (University of Durham), 'Could the British Have Won the War of American Independence?'
Dagmar Hamilton (LBJ School), 'Justice William O. Douglas and British Colonialism'
Gordon Peacock and Laura Worthen (Theatre and Dance), 'Not Always a Green and Pleasant Land: Tom Stoppard's *Arcadia*'
Bernard Crick (University of London), 'Orwell and the Business of Biography'
Geoffrey Hartman (Yale University), 'The Sympathy Paradox: Poetry, Feeling, and Modern Cultural Morality'
Dave Oliphant (HRHRC), 'Jazz and Its British Acolytes'
R. W. B. Lewis (Yale University), 'Henry James: The Victorian Scene'
Alan Spencer (Ford Motor Company), 'Balliol, Big Business, and Mad Cows'
Peter Quinn: A Discussion of His Novel, *Banished Children of Eve*

Summer 1996

Martin Stannard (Leicester University), 'Biography and Textual Criticism'
Diane Kunz (Yale University), 'British Withdrawal East of Suez'
John Cell (Duke University), 'Who Ran the British Empire?'
Mark Jacobsen (U.S. Marine Corps Command and Staff College), 'The North-West Frontier'
Theodore Vestal (Oklahoma State University), 'Britain and Ethiopia'
Warren F. Kimball (Rutgers University), 'A Victorian Tory: Churchill, the Americans, and Self-Determination'
Louise B. Williams (Lehman College, City University of New York), 'British Modernism and Fascism'

Fall Semester 1996

Elizabeth Richmond-Garza (English and Comparative Literature), 'The New Gothic: Decadents for the 1990s'
Robin Kilson (History), 'The Politics of Captivity: The British State and Prisoners of War in World War I'

Sir Brian Fall (Oxford University), 'What Does Britain Expect from the European Community, the United States, and the Commonwealth?'
Roger Louis (History), 'Harold Macmillan and the Middle East Crisis of 1958'
Ian Willison (Editor, *The Cambridge History of the Book in Britain*), 'The History of the Book and the Cultural and Literary History of the English-Speaking World'
Walter L. Arnstein (University of Illinois), 'Queen Victoria's Other Island'
Noel Annan (London), '*Our Age* Revisited'
Michael Cohen (Bar-Ilan University, Tel Aviv), 'The Middle East and the Cold War: Britain, the United States, and the Soviet Union'
Reba Soffer (California State University, Northridge), 'Catholicism in England: Was it Possible to Be a Good Catholic, a Good Englishman, and a Good Historian?'
Wilson Harris (Poet and Novelist), 'The Mystery of Consciousness: Cross-Cultural Influences in the Caribbean, Britain, and the United States'
H. S. Barlow (Singapore), 'British Malaya in the late Nineteenth Century'
Donald G. Davis, Jr. (Library and Information Science), 'British Destruction of Chinese Books in the Peking Siege of 1900'
Round Table Discussion on the Film *Michael Collins:* Elizabeth Cullingford (English), Kevin Kenny (History), Robin Kilson (History), and Roger Louis (History)
A. G. Hopkins (Cambridge University), 'From Africa to Empire'
Austin Chapter of the Society for the Preservation and Encouragement of Barber Shop Quartet Singing in America

Spring Semester 1997

Round Table Discussion on 'T. S. Eliot and Anti-Semitism': Robert D. King (Jewish Studies), Sidney Monas (Slavic Languages and History), and Thomas F. Staley (HRHRC)
Phillip Herring (University of Wisconsin–Madison), 'Djuna Barnes and T. S. Eliot: The Story of a Friendship'
Bryan Roberts (Sociology), 'British Sociology and British Society'
Andrew Roberts (London), 'The Captains and the Kings Depart: Lord Salisbury's Skeptical Imperialism'
Colin Franklin (London), 'In a Golden Age of Publishing, 1950–1970'
Susan Pedersen (Harvard University), 'Virginia Woolf, Eleanor Rathbone, and the Problem of Appeasement'
Andrew Seaman (Saint Mary's University, Halifax, Nova Scotia), 'Thomas Raddall: A Novelist's View of Nova Scotia during the American Revolution'
Gordon Peacock (Theatre and Dance), 'Noel Coward: A Master Playwright, a Talented Actor, a Novelist and Diarist: Or a Peter Pan for the Twentieth Century?'
Roland Oliver (University of London), 'The Battle for African History, 1947–1966'
Alistair Horne (Oxford University), 'Harold Macmillan's Fading Reputation'
Richard Begam (University of Wisconsin–Madison), 'Samuel Beckett and the Debate on Humanism'
Christopher Waters (Williams College), 'Delinquents, Perverts, and the State: Psychiatry and the Homosexual Desire in the 1930s'
Sami Zubaida (University of London), 'Ernest Gellner and Islam'

Walter Dean Burnham (Government), 'Britain Votes: The 1997 General Election and Its Implications'

Fall Semester 1997

Judith Brown (Oxford University), 'Gandhi: A Victorian Gentleman'
Thomas Cable (English), 'Hearing and Revising the History of the English Language'
Round Table Discussion on 'The Death of Princess Diana': Judith Brown (Oxford), David Edwards (Government), Elizabeth Richmond-Garza (English), Anne Baade (British Studies), Alessandra Lippucci (Government), and Kevin Kenny (History)
David Hunter (Music Librarian, Fine Arts Library), 'Handel and His Patrons'
Anne Kane (Sociology), 'The Current Situation in Ireland'
James S. Fishkin (Government), 'Power and the People: The Televised Deliberative Poll in the 1997 British General Election'
Howard D. Weinbrot (University of Wisconsin–Madison), 'Jacobitism in Eighteenth-Century Britain'
J. C. Baldwin, M.D. (Houston), 'The Abdication of King Edward VIII'
Kenneth E. Carpenter (Harvard University), 'Library Revolutions Past and Present'
Akira Iriye (Harvard University), 'Britain, Japan, and the International Order after World War I'
Anthony Hobson (London), 'Reminiscences of British Authors and the Collecting of Contemporary Manuscripts'
David Killingray (University of London), 'The British in the West Indies'
Alan Knight (Oxford University), 'British Imperialism in Latin America'
Round Table Discussion on King Lear in Iowa: The Movie '*A Thousand Acres*': Linda Ferreira-Buckley (English), Elizabeth Richmond-Garza (English), Helena Woodard (English), and John Velz (English)
Timothy Lovelace (Music) and the Talisman Trio

Spring Semester 1998

Richard Ollard (Biographer and Publisher), 'A. L. Rowse: Epitome of the Twentieth Century'
Round Table Discussion of Arundhati Roy's *The God of Small Things:* Phillip Herring (HRHRC), Brian Trinque (Economics), Kamala Visweswaran (Anthropology), and Robert Hardgrave (Government)
Jonathan Schneer (Georgia Institute of Technology), 'London in 1900: The Imperial Metropolis'
Trevor Burnard (University of Canterbury, New Zealand), 'Rioting in Goatish Embraces: Marriage and the Failure of White Settlement in British Jamaica'
Felipe Fernández-Armesto (Oxford University), 'British Traditions in Comparative Perspective'
Michael Mann (University of California, Los Angeles), 'The Broader Significance of Labour's Landslide Victory of 1997'
Dane Kennedy (University of Nebraska), 'White Settlers in Colonial Kenya and Rhodesia'
Round Table Discussion on 'Noel Annan, Keynes, and Bloomsbury': Jamie Galbraith (LBJ School), Elspeth Rostow (LBJ School), and Walt Rostow (Economics and History)

Lisa Moore (English), 'British Studies—Lesbian Studies: A Dangerous Intimacy?'

James Gibbs (University of the West of England), 'Wole Soyinka: The Making of a Playwright'

Marilyn Butler (Oxford University), 'About the House: Jane Austen's Anthropological Eye'

R. J. Q. Adams (Texas A&M University), 'Britain and Ireland, 1912–1922'

John M. Carroll (Asian Studies), 'Nationalism and Identity in pre-1949 Hong Kong'

Round Table Discussion on the Irish Referendum: Anne Kane (Sociology), Kevin Kenny (History), Roger Louis (History), and Jennifer O'Conner (History)

Fall Semester 1998

Louise Hodgden Thompson (Government), 'Origins of the First World War: The Anglo-German Naval Armaments Race'

John P. Farrell (English), 'Thomas Hardy in Love'

Carol MacKay (English), 'The Multiple Conversions of Annie Besant'

Roy Foster (Oxford University), 'Yeats and Politics, 1898–1921'

Robert Olwell (History), 'British Magic Kingdoms: Imagination, Speculation, and Empire in Florida'

Sara H. Sohmer (Texas Christian University), 'The British in the South Seas: Exploitation and Trusteeship in Fiji'

Helena Woodard (English), 'Politics of Race in the Eighteenth Century: Pope and the Humanism of the Enlightenment'

D. A. Smith (Grinnell College), 'Impeachment? Parliamentary Government in Britain and France in the Nineteenth Century'

Round Table Discussion on the Irish Insurrection of 1798: Robert Olwell (History), Lisa Moore (English), and Kevin Kenny (History)

Robert D. King (Jewish Studies), 'The Accomplishments of Raja Rao: The Triumph of the English Language in India'

Donald G. Davis, Jr. (Library and Information Science and History), 'Religion and Empire'

A. D. Roberts (University of London), 'The Awkward Squad: African Students in American Universities before 1940'

Chaganti Vijayasree (Osmania University, Hyderabad), 'The Empire and Victorian Poetry'

Martha Deatherage (Music), 'Christmas Celebration: Vauxhall Gardens'

Spring Semester 1999

Round Table Discussion on *Regeneration,* Pat Barker's Trilogy on the First World War: Betty Sue Flowers (English), Roger Louis (History), and Paul Woodruff (Humanities)

Alistair Campbell-Dick (Cybertime Corporation), 'The Immortal Memory of Robert Burns'

Hugh Macrae Richmond (University of California, Berkeley), 'Why Rebuild Shakespeare's Globe Theatre?'

Ralph Austen (University of Chicago), 'Britain and the Global Economy: A Post-Colonial Perspective'

Jerome Meckier (University of Kentucky), 'Aldous Huxley's American Experience'

Peter Marsh (Syracuse University), 'Joseph Chamberlain as an Entrepreneur in Politics: Writing the Life of a Businessman Turned Statesman'

Roger Adelson (Arizona State University), 'Winston Churchill and the Middle East'
Margot Finn (Emory University), 'Law, Debt, and Empire: The Calcutta Court of Conscience'
Fred M. Leventhal (Boston University), 'The Projection of Britain in America before the Second World War'
Larry Siedentop (Oxford University), 'Reassessing the Life of Isaiah Berlin'
Ross Terrill (Harvard University), 'R. H. Tawney's Vision of Fellowship'
Juliet Fleming (Cambridge University), 'The Ladies' Shakespeare'
Elizabeth Fernea (English and Middle Eastern Studies), 'The Victorian Lady Abroad: In Egypt with Sophia Poole and in Texas with Mrs. E. M. Houstoun'
Richard Schoch (University of London), 'The Respectable and the Vulgar: British Theater in the Mid-Nineteenth Century'
Ferdinand Mount (Editor, *TLS*), 'Politics and the *Times Literary Supplement*'

Fall Semester 1999

Round Table Discussion on the Boer War, 1899–1902: Barbara Harlow (English), John Lamphear (History), and Roger Louis (History)
Sharon Arnoult (Southwest Texas State University), 'Charles I: His Life after Death'
Kenneth O. Morgan (Oxford University), 'Lloyd George, Keir Hardie, and the Importance of the "Pro-Boers"'
Richard Cleary (Architecture), 'Walking the Walk to Talk the Talk: The Promenade in Eighteenth-Century France and England'
Keith Kyle (Journalist and Historian), 'From Suez to Kenya as Journalist and as Historian'
Malcolm Hacksley (National English Literary Museum, Grahamstown, South Africa), 'Planting a Museum, Cultivating a Literature'
Ben Pimlott (University of London), 'The Art of Writing Political Biography'
Geraldine Heng (English), 'Cannibalism, the First Crusade, and the Genesis of Medieval Romance'
A. P. Martinich (Philosophy), 'Thomas Hobbes: Lifelong and Enduring Controversies'
Round Table Discussion on Lyndall Gordon, *T. S. Eliot: An Imperfect Life:* Brian Bremen (English), Thomas Cable (English), Elizabeth Richmond-Garza (Comparative Literature), and Thomas F. Staley (HRHRC)
Shula Marks (University of London), 'Smuts, Race, and the Boer War'
Round Table Discussion on the Library of the British Museum: William B. Todd (English), Irene Owens (Library and
Information Science), and Don Davis (Library and Information Science and Department of History).
Henry Dietz (Government), '*The Hound of the Baskervilles*'

Spring Semester 2000

Susan Napier (Asian Studies), 'The Cultural Phenomenon of the Harry Potter Fantasy Novels'
Round Table Discussion on *Dutch: A Memoir of Ronald Reagan:* A Chapter in the 'Special Relationship?': Roger Louis (History), Harry Middleton (LBJ Library), and Elspeth Rostow (LBJ School)
Norman Rose (Hebrew University, Jerusalem), 'Harold Nicolson: A Curious and Colorful Life'

Charlotte Canning (Theatre and Dance), 'Feminists Perform Their Past'

John Ripley (McGill University), 'The Sound of Sociology: H. B. Tree's *Merchant of Venice*'

Sergei Horuji (Russian Academy of Sciences), 'James Joyce in Russia'

Janice Rossen (Biographer and Independent Scholar), 'Philip Toynbee'

Max Egremont (Novelist and Biographer), 'Siegfried Sassoon's War'

Paul Taylor (London School of Economics and Political Science), 'Britain and Europe'

Lord Selborne (Royal Geographical Society), 'The Royal Geographical Society: Exploration since 1830'

Craig MacKenzie (Rand Afrikaans University, Johannesburg), 'The Mythology of the Boer War: Herman Charles Bosman and the Challenge to Afrikaner Romanticism'

Peter Catterall (Institute of Contemporary British History, London), 'Reform of the House of Lords'

Bernard Porter (University of Newcastle), 'Pompous and Circumstantial: Sir Edward Elgar and the British Empire'

Craufurd D. Goodwin (Duke University), 'Roger Fry and the Debate on "Myth" in the Bloomsbury Group'

Jamie Belich (University of Auckland), 'Neo-Britains? The "West" in Nineteenth-Century Australia, New Zealand, and America'

Round Table Discussion on Norman Davies, *The Isles:* Sharon Arnoult (Midwestern State University, Wichita Falls), Raymond Douglas (Colgate University), Walter Johnson (Northwestern Oklahoma State University), David Leaver (Raymond Walters College, Cincinnati), and John Cell (Duke University)

Fall Semester 2000

Round Table discussion on Paul Scott, the Raj Quartet, and the Beginning of British Studies at UT—Peter Green (Classics), Robert Hardgrave (Government and Asian Studies), and Roger Louis (History)

Suman Gupta (Open University), 'T. S. Eliot as Publisher'

Jeffrey Cox (University of Iowa), 'Going Native: Missionaries in India'

Kevin Kenny (Boston College), 'Irish Nationalism: The American Dimension'

Joseph Kestner (University of Tulsa), 'Victorian Battle Art'

James E. Cronin (Boston College), 'From Old to New Labour: Politics and Society in the Forging of the "Third" Way'

Gerald Moore (Mellon Visiting Research Fellow, HRHRC), 'When Caliban Crossed the Atlantic'

Richard Howard (Shakespearean Actor, London), '"Health and Long Life to You": A Program of Irish Poetry and Prose Presented by an Englishman, with Anecdotes'

Stephen Foster (Northern Illinois University), 'Prognosis Guarded: The Probable Decolonization of the British Era in American History'

Frank Prochaska (University of London), 'Of Crowned and Uncrowned Republics: George V and the Socialists'

Robert H. Abzug (History and American Studies), 'Britain, South Africa, and the American Civil Rights Movement'

Paula Bartley (Visiting Research Fellow, HRHRC), 'Emmeline Pankhurst'

Thomas Jesus Garza (Slavic Languages), 'A British Vampire's Christmas'

Spring Semester 2001

Betty Sue Flowers (UT Distinguished Teaching Professor), 'From Robert Browning to James Bond'

Larry Carver (English), 'Feliks Topolski at the Ransom Center'

Oscar Brockett (Theatre and Dance), 'Lilian Baylis and England's National Theatres'

Linda Levy Peck (George Washington University), 'Luxury and War'

R. James Coote (Architecture), 'Architectural Revival in Britain'

Adam Roberts (Oxford University), 'Britain and the Creation of the United Nations'

Mark Southern (Germanic Studies), 'Words over Swords: Language and Tradition in Celtic Civilization'

Round Table discussion on Ben Rogers, *A Life of A. J. Ayer:* David Braybrooke (Government and Philosophy), Al Martinich (History and Philosophy), David Sosa (Philosophy), and Paul Woodruff (Plan II and Philosophy)

Bartholomew Sparrow (Government), 'British and American Expansion: The Political Foundations'

Jose Harris (Oxford University), 'Writing History during the Second World War'

Charles Loft (Westminster College), 'Off the Rails? The Historic Junctions in Britain's Railway Problem'

Dan Jacobson (University of London), 'David Irving and Holocaust Denial'—Special Lecture

Dan Jacobson (University of London), 'Self-Redemption in the Victorian Novel'

George S. Christian (British Studies), 'The Comic Basis of the Victorian Novel'

Paul Taylor (London *Independent*), 'Rediscovering a Master Dramatist: J. B. Priestley'

Fall Semester 2001

Round Table Discussion on Ray Monk's Biography of Bertrand Russell, *The Ghost of Madness*—Al Martinich (History and Philosophy), David Sosa (Philosophy and British Studies), and Paul Woodruff (Plan II and Philosophy)

Alex Danchev (Keele University), 'The Alanbrooke Diaries'

Robert M. Worcester (LSE and Market Opinion Research International), 'Britain and the European Union'

Martha Ann Selby (Asian Studies), 'The Cultural Legacy of British Clubs: Manners, Memory, and Identity among the New Club-Wallahs in Madras'

Roger Owen (Harvard University), 'Lord Cromer and Wilfrid Blunt in Egypt'

James Loehlin (English), 'A Midsummer Night's Dream'

Jeffrey Meyers (Biographer), 'Somerset Maugham'

Elspeth Rostow (LBJ School), 'From American Studies to British Studies—And Beyond'

Nicholas Westcott (British Embassy), 'The Groundnut Scheme: Socialist Imperialism at Work in Africa'

Round Table Discussion on 'The Anglo-American Special Relationship': Gary Freeman (Government), Roger Louis (History), Elspeth Rostow (American Studies), and Michael Stoff (History)

Christopher Heywood (Sheffield University), 'The Brontës: A Personal History of Discovery and Interpretation'

James Bolger (New Zealand Ambassador and former Prime Minister), 'Whither New Zealand? Constitutional, Political, and International Quandaries'

R. J. Q. Adams (Texas A&M), 'Arthur James Balfour and Andrew Bonar Law: A Study in Contrasts'

Ferdinand Mount (Editor, *Times Literary Supplement*), 'British Culture since the Eighteenth Century: An Open Society?'

James Loehlin (English), 'A Child's Christmas in Wales'

Spring Semester 2002

Round Table Discussion on Adam Sisman, *Boswell's Presumptuous Task:* Samuel Baker (English), Linda Ferreira-Buckley (English), Julie Hardwick (History), and Helena Woodward (English)

A. G. Hopkins (History), 'Globalization: The British Case'

Susan Napier (Asian Studies), 'J. R. R. Tolkein and *The Lord of the Rings:* Fantasy as Retreat or Fantasy as Engagement?'

Wilfrid Prest (Adelaide University), 'South Australia's Paradise of Dissent'

Tom Palaima (Classics), 'Terence Rattigan's *Browning Version*'

Alan H. Nelson (University of California, Berkeley), 'Thoughts on Elizabethan Authorship'

Penelope Lively (London), 'Changing Perceptions of British and English Identity'

Hans Mark (Aerospace Engineering), 'The Falklands War'

David Butler (Oxford University), 'Psephology—or, the Study of British Elections'

Robert L. Hardgrave (Government), 'From West Texas to South India and British Studies'

Geoffrey Wheatcroft (London), 'The Englishness of English Sport'

Eileen Cleere (Southwestern University), 'Dirty Pictures: John Ruskin and the Victorian Sanitation of Fine Art'

Jamie Belich (Auckland University), 'A Comparison of Empire Cities: New York and London, Chicago and Melbourne'

Churchill Conference—Geoffrey Best (Oxford University), Sir Michael Howard (Oxford University), Warren Kimball (Rutgers University), Philip Ziegler (London), Roger Louis (History)

Catherine Maxwell (University of London), 'Swinburne's Poetry and Criticism'

Round Table Discussion on Churchill and the Churchill Conference: Rodrigo Gutierrez (History), Adrian Howkins (History), Heidi Juel (English), David McCoy (Government), Joe Moser (English), Jeff Rutherford (History), William S. Livingston (UT Senior Vice President), and Roger Louis (History)

Fall Semester 2002

James K. Galbraith (LBJ School of Public Affairs), 'The Enduring Importance of John Maynard Keynes'

Michael Green (University of Natal), 'Agatha Christie in South Africa'

Sumit Ganguly (Asian Studies), 'Kashmir: Origins and Consequences of Conflict'

Margaret MacMillan (University of Toronto), 'At the Height of His Power: Lloyd George in 1919'

Douglas Bruster (English), 'Why We Fight: *Much Ado About Nothing* and the West'

John Darwin (Oxford University), 'The Decline and Rise of the British Empire: John Gallagher as an Historian of Imperialism'

Kevin Kenny (Boston College), 'The Irish in the British Empire'

David Wallace (University of Pennsylvania), 'A Chaucerian's Tale of Surinam'

Peter Bowler (Queen's University, Belfast), 'Scientists and the Popularization of Science in Early Twentieth-Century Britain'

Bernardine Evaristo (London), 'A Feisty, Funky Girl in Roman England'

Frank Moorhouse (Australia), 'Dark Places and Grand Days'

David Cannadine (University of London), 'C. P. Snow and the Two Cultures'

Round Table Discussion on 'Edmund S. Morgan's Biography of Benjamin Franklin'—Carolyn Eastman (History), Bruce Hunt (History), Roger Louis (History), Alan Tully (History)

Mark Lawrence (History), 'The Strange Silence of Cold War England: Britain and the Vietnam War'

Tom Cable (English), 'The Pleasures of Remembering Poetry'

Spring Semester 2003

Round Table Discussion on 'W. G. Sebald—*Rings of Saturn*': Brigitte Bauer (French and Italian), Sidney Monas (History and Slavic Languages), Elizabeth Richmond-Garza (English and Comparative Literature), Walter Wetzels (Germanic Studies)

Diana Davis (Geography), 'Brutes, Beasts, and Empire: A Comparative Study of the British and French Experience'

Colin Franklin (Publisher), 'Rosalind Franklin—Variously Described as "The Dark Lady of DNA" and "The Sylvia Plath of Molecular Biology"'

Sidney Monas (History and Slavic Languages), 'A Life of Irish Literature and Russian Poetry, Soviet Politics and International History'

Neville Hoad (English), 'Oscar Wilde in America'

Selina Hastings (London), 'Rosamond Lehman: Eternal Exile'

Bernard Wasserstein (Glasgow University), 'The British in Palestine: Reconsiderations'

Anne Chisholm (London), 'Frances Partridge: Last of the Bloomsberries'

Philip Morgan (Johns Hopkins University), 'The Black Experience and the British Empire'

Jeremy duQuesnay Adams (Southern Methodist University), 'Joan of Arc and the English'

Didier Lancien (University of Toulouse), 'Churchill and de Gaulle'

Avi Shlaim (Oxford University), 'The Balfour Declaration and Its Consequences'

Martin J. Wiener (Rice University), 'Murder and the Modern British Historian'

Winthrop Wetherbee (Cornell University), 'The Jewish Impact on Medieval Literature: Chaucer, Boccaccio, and Dante'

Philippa Levine (University of Southern California), 'Sex and the British Empire'

Summer 2003

Donald G. Davis, Jr. (History and the School of Information), 'Life without British Studies Is Like . . .'

Kurth Sprague (English and American Studies), 'Literature, Horses, and Scandal at UT'

David Evans (Astronomy), 'An Astronomer's Life in South Africa and Texas'

Tom Hatfield (Continuing Education), 'Not Long Enough! Half a Century at UT'

Fall Semester 2003

Richard Oram (HRHRC), 'Evelyn Waugh: Collector and Annotator'

Round Table Discussion on 'Booker Prize Winner James Kelman: Adapting a Glasgow Novel for the Texas Stage': James Kelman (Glasgow), Mia Carter (English), Kirk Lynn, and Dikran Utidjian

Simon Green (All Souls College, Oxford University), 'The Strange Death of Puritan England, 1914–1945'

Elizabeth Richmond-Garza (English and Comparative Literature), *'Measure for Measure'*

Lewis Hoffacker (U.S. Ambassador), 'From the Congo to British Studies'

A. P. Thornton (University of Toronto), 'Wars Remembered, Revisited, and Reinvented'

Deryck Schreuder (University of Western Australia), 'The Burden of the British Past in Australia'

Robert Mettlen (Finance), 'From Birmingham to British Studies'

Paul Schroeder (University of Illinois), 'The Pax Britannica and the Pax Americana: Empire, Hegemony, and the International System'

Ferdinand Mount (London), 'A Time to Dance: Anthony Powell's *Dance to the Music of Time* and the Twentieth Century in Britain'

Brian Bond (University of London), '*Oh! What a Lovely War:* History and Popular Myth in Late-Twentieth Century Britain'

Wendy Frith (Bradford College, England), 'The Speckled Monster: Lady Mary Wortley Montagu and the Battle against Smallpox'

Harry Middleton (LBJ Library), 'The Road to the White House'

Jeremy Lewis (London), 'Tobias Smollett'

Christian Smith (Austin, Texas), 'Christmas Readings'

Spring Semester 2004

Round Table Discussion on 'The Pleasures of Reading Thackeray': Carol Mackay (English), Judith Fisher (Trinity University), George Christian (British Studies)

Thomas F. Staley (HRHRC), '"Corso e Recorso:" A Journey through Academe'

Patrick O'Brien (London School of Economics), 'The Pax Britannica, American Hegemony, and the International Order, 1793–2004'

Michael Wheeler (former Director of Chawton House Library), 'England Drawn and Quartered: Cultural Crisis in the Mid-Nineteenth Century'

Walter Wetzels (Germanic Studies), 'Growing Up in Nazi Germany, and later American Adventures'

Kathleen Wilson (State University of New York, Stony Brook), 'The Colonial State and Governance in the Eighteenth Century'

Elizabeth Fernea (English and Middle Eastern Studies), 'Encounters with Imperialism'

Chris Dunton (National University of Lesotho), 'Newspapers and Colonial Rule in Africa'

Miguel Gonzalez-Gerth (Spanish and Portuguese), 'Crossing Geographical and Cultural Borders—and Finally Arriving at British Studies'

Peter Stansky (Stanford University), 'Bloomsbury in Ceylon'

Round Table Discussion on *The Crimson Petal and the White:* John Farrell (English), Betty Sue Flowers (LBJ Library), Roger Louis (History), Paul Neimann (English)

Ann Curthoys (Australian National University), 'The Australian History Wars'

Martha Ann Selby (Asian Studies), 'Against the Grain: On Finding My Voice in India'

Steven Isenberg (UT Visiting Professor of Humanities), 'A Life in Our Times'

Summer 2004

Carol Mackay (English), 'My Own Velvet Revolution'
Erez Manela (Harvard University), 'The "Wilsonian Moment" in India and the Crisis of Empire in 1919'
Scott Lucas (Birmingham University), '"A Bright Shining Mecca": British Culture and Political Warfare in the Cold War and Beyond'
Monica Belmonte (U.S. Department of State), 'Before Things Fell Apart: The British Design for the Nigerian State'
Dan Jacobson (London), 'Philip Larkin's "Elements"'
Bernard Porter (University of Newcastle), 'Oo Let 'Em In? Asylum Seekers and Terrorists in Britain, 1850–1914'

Fall Semester 2004

Richard Drayton (Cambridge University), 'Anglo-American "Liberal" Imperialism, British Guiana, 1953–64, and the World Since September 11'
David Washbrook (Oxford University), 'Living on the Edge: Anxiety and Identity in "British" Calcutta, 1780–1930'
Joanna Hitchcock (University of Texas Press), 'An Accidental Publisher'
Alan Friedman (English), '*A Midsummer Night's Dream*'
Antony Best (London School of Economics), 'British Intellectuals and East Asia in the Inter-war Years'
John Farrell (English), 'Beating a Path from Brooklyn to Austin'
Christopher Middleton (Liberal Arts), 'Relevant to England—A Reading of Poems'
Gail Minault (History and Asian Studies), 'Growing Up Bilingual and Other (Mis)adventures in Negotiating Cultures'
Roger Louis (History), 'Escape from Oklahoma'
John Trimble (English), 'Writing with Style'
Niall Ferguson (Harvard University), 'Origins of the First World War'
James Hopkins (Southern Methodist University), 'George Orwell and the Spanish Civil War: The Case of Nikos Kazantzakis'
James Currey (London), 'Africa Writes Back: Publishing the African Writers Series at Heinemann'
Sidney Monas (History and Slavic Languages), 'A Jew's Christmas'
Geoffrey Wheatcroft (London), '"In the Advance Guard": Evelyn Waugh's Reputation'

Spring Semester 2005

Katharine Whitehorn (London), 'It Didn't *All* Start in the Sixties'
Gertrude Himmelfarb (Graduate School, City University of New York), The Whig Interpretation of History'
Kurt Heinzelman (English and HRHRC), 'Lord Byron and the Invention of Celebrity'
Brian Levack (History), 'Jesuits, Lawyers, and Witches'
Richard Cleary (Architecture), 'When Taste Mattered: W. J. Battle and the Architecture of the Forty Acres'
Edward I. Steinhart (Texas Tech University), 'White Hunters in British East Africa, 1895–1914'
Don Graham (English), 'The Drover's Wife: An Australian Archetype'

A. C. H. Smith, (London) 'Literary Friendship: The 40-Year Story of Tom Stoppard, B. S. Johnson, and Zulfikar Ghose'
Paul Woodruff (Philosophy and Plan II), 'A Case of Anglophilia—And Partial Re-
covery: Being an Account of My Life, with Special Attention to the Influence
of England upon My Education'
Toyin Falola (History), 'Footprints of the Ancestors'
Robert Abzug (History) 'Confessions of an Intellectual Omnivore: The Conse-
quences on Scholarship and Career'
Deirdre McMahon (Mary Immaculate College, University of Limerick), 'Ireland
and the Empire-Commonwealth, 1918–1972'
James Coote (Architecture), 'Building with Wit: Sir Edwin Lutyens and British
Architecture'
Jay Clayton (Vanderbilt University), 'The Dickens Tape: Lost and Found Sound
before Recording'
Christopher Ricks (Oxford University), 'The Force of Poetry: Shakespeare and
Beckett'

Summer 2005

Blair Worden (Oxford University), 'Poetry and History of the English Renais-
sance'
Robert Bruce Osborn (British Studies), 'The Four Lives of Robert Osborn'
Alessandra Lippucci (Government), 'Perseverance Furthers: A Self-Consuming
Artifact'
William H. Cunningham (former President of the University of Texas), 'Money,
Power, Politics, and Ambition'
David V. Edwards (Government), 'Friendly Persuasion in the Academy'
Elizabeth Richmond-Garza (English), 'A Punk Rocker with Eight Languages'
Richard Lariviere (Liberal Arts), 'Confessions of a Sanskritist Dean'

Fall Semester 2005

Celebration of 30th Anniversary and Publication of *Yet More Adventures with
Britannia*
Robert D. King (Jewish Studies), 'T.S. Eliot Reconsidered'
Round Table Discussion on 'The London Bombings': James Galbraith (LBJ
School), Elizabeth Cullingford (English),
Clement Henry (Government), Roger Louis (History)
Dolora Chapelle Wojciehowski (English), 'The Erotic Uncanny in Shakespeare's
Twelfth Night'
Karl Hagstrom Miller (History), 'Playing Pensativa: History and Music in
Counterpoint'
James D. Garrison (English), 'Translating Gray's *Elegy*'
Miguel Gonzalez-Gerth (Spanish and Portuguese), 'Another Look at Orwell: The
Origins of *1984*'
Round Table Discussion on 'The Imperial Closet: Gordon of Khartoum, Hector
McDonald of the Boer War, and Roger Casement of Ireland': Barbara Harlow
(English), Neville Hoad (English), John Thomas (HRHRC)
Guy Ortolano (Washington University in St. Louis), 'From *The Two Cultures* to
Breaking Ranks: C.P. Snow and the
Interpretation of the 1960s'
Catherine Robson (University of California, Davis), 'Poetry and Memorialization'

Round Table Discussion on 'Britain and the Jewish Century': Lauren Apter (History), Robert D. King (Jewish Studies),
Sidney Monas (History and Slavic Languages)
Hans Mark (Aerospace Engineering), 'Churchill, the Anglo-Persian Oil Company, and the Origins of the Energy Crisis: From the Early 20th Century to the Present'
Randall Woods (University of Arkansas), 'LBJ and the British'

Spring Semester 2006

Richard Gray (London), 'Movie Palaces of Britain'
Samuel Baker (English), 'The Lake Poets and the War in the Mediterranean Sea'
Thomas F. Staley (HRHRC), 'Graham Greene and Evelyn Waugh'
Gary Stringer (Texas A&M), 'Love's Long Labors Coming to Fruition: The John Donne Variorum Donne'
Caroline Elkins (Harvard University), 'From Malaya to Kenya: British Colonial Violence and the End of Empire'
Grigory Kaganov (St. Petersburg), 'London in the Mouth of the Neva'
Graham Greene (London), 'A Life in Publishing'
John Davis (Oxford University), 'Evans-Pritchard: Nonetheless A Great Englishman'
Barry Gough (Wilfrid Laurier University), 'Arthur Marder and the Battles over the History of the Royal Navy'
Ivan Kreilkamp (Indiana University), '"Bags of Meat": Pet-Keeping and the Justice to Animals in Thomas Hardy'
James Wilson (History), 'Historical Memory and the Mau Mau Uprising in Colonial Kenya'
Anne Deighton (Oxford University), 'Britain after the Second World War: Losing an Empire and Finding a Place in a World of Superpowers'
Steve Isenberg (Liberal Arts), 'Auden, Forster, Larkin, and Empson'
Harriet Ritvo (MIT), 'Animals on the Edge'
Peter Quinn (New York), 'Eugenics and the Hour of the Cat'
Dan Jacobson (London), 'Kipling and South Africa'

Fall Semester 2006

Michael Charlesworth (Art and Art History) and Kurt Heinzelman (English), 'Tony Harrison's "v."'
Peter Stanley (Australian War Memorial), 'All Imaginable Excuses: Australian Deserters and the Fall of Singapore'
Selina Hastings (London), 'Somerset Maugham and "Englishness"'
James W. Vick (Mathematics), 'A Golden Century of English Mathematics'
John O. Voll (Georgetown University), 'Defining the Middle East and the Clash of Civilizations'
James Loehlin (English), 'The Afterlife of Hamlet'
Daniel Topolski (London), 'The Life and Art of Feliks Topolski'
John Darwin (Oxford University), 'The British Empire and the British World'
David Cannadine (University of London), 'Andrew Mellon and Plutocracy Across the Atlantic'
John Lonsdale (Cambridge University), 'White Settlers and Black Mau Mau in Kenya'
Kate Gartner Frost (English), 'So What's Been Done about John Donne Lately?'

John Summers (Harvard University), 'The Power Elite: C. Wright Mills and the British'

Marrack Goulding (Oxford University), 'Has it been a Success? Britain in the United Nations'

Priya Satia (Stanford University), 'The Defence of Inhumanity: British Military and Cultural Power in the Middle East'

Don Graham (English), 'Burnt Orange Britannia: A Missing Contributor!'

Spring Semester 2007

Bernard Porter (Newcastle University), 'Empire and British Culture'

Paul Sullivan (Liberal Arts Honors Program), 'The Headmaster's Shakespeare: John Garrett and British Education'

Round Table Discussion on 'The Queen': Elizabeth Cullingford (English), Karen King (American Studies), Roger Louis
(History), Bryan Roberts (Sociology)

Martin Francis (University of Cincinnati), 'Cecil Beaton's Romantic Toryism and the Symbolism of Wartime Britain'

Susan Crane (Columbia University), 'Animal Feelings and Feelings for Animals in Chaucer'

Michael Charlesworth (Art History), 'The Earl of Strafford and Wentworth Castle'

Adam Sisman (London), 'Wordsworth and Coleridge'

Jenny Mann (Cornell University), 'Shakespeare's English Rhetoric: Mingling Heroes and Hobgoblins in *A Midsummer Night's Dream*'

David Atkinson (Member of Parliament), 'Britain and World Peace in the 21st Century'

Bertram Wyatt-Brown (University of Florida), 'T. E. Lawrence, Reputation, and Honor's Decline'

Roger Louis (History), 'All Souls and Oxford in 1956: Reassessing the Meaning of the Suez Crisis'

Indivar Kamtekar (Jawaharlal Nehru University), 'India and Britain during the Second World War'

Cassandra Pybus (University of Sydney), 'William Wilberforce and the Emancipation of Slaves'

Stephen Howe (University of Bristol), 'Empire in the 21st Century English Imagination'

Geoffrey Wheatcroft (London), 'The Myth of Malicious Partition: The Cases of Ireland, India, and Palestine'

Charles Rossman (English), 'D. H. Lawrence and the "Spirit" of Mexico'

Kenneth O. Morgan (House of Lords), 'Lloyd George, the French, and the Germans'

Fall Semester 2007

R. J. Q. Adams (Texas A&M), 'A. J. Balfour's Achievement and Legacy'

Robin Doughty (Geography), 'Saving Coleridge's Endangered Albatross'

Caroline Williams (University of Texas), 'A Victorian Orientalist: John Frederick Lewis and the Artist's Discovery of Cairo'

Susan Pedersen (Columbia University), 'The Story of Frances Stevenson and David Lloyd George'

Eric S. Mallin (English), 'Macbeth and the Simple Truth'

Mark Oaten, M.P., 'How "Special" Is the Special Relationship?'
Dan Birkholz (English), 'Playboys of the West of England: Medieval Cosmopolitanism and Familial Love'
Jeremy Lewis (London), 'The Secret History of Penguin Books'
Matthew Jones (Nottingham University), 'Britain and the End of Empire in South East Asia in the Era of the Vietnam War'
Martin Wiener (Rice University), '"Who knows the Empire whom only the Empire knows?": Reconnecting British and Empire History'
Book Launch: *Penultimate Adventures with Britannia* (Follett's Intellectual Property)
Hermione Lee and Christopher Ricks (Oxford), 'The Elusive Brian Moore: His Stature in Modern Literature'
Gabriel Gorodetsky (Tel Aviv University), 'The Challenge to Churchill's Wartime Leadership by Sir Stafford Cripps (the "Red Squire")'
Helena Woodard (English), 'Black and White Christmas: The Deep South in the Eighteenth Century'

Spring Semester 2008

Round Table Discussion on Tim Jeal's new biography, *Stanley: The Impossible Life of Africa's Greatest Explorer,* Diana Davis
(Geography), A. G. Hopkins (History), Roger Louis (History)
Elizabeth Richmond-Garza (English and Comparative Literature), 'New Year's Eve 1900: Oscar Wilde and the Masquerade of Victorian Culture'
Robert Hardgrave (Government), 'The Search for Balthazar Solvyns and an Indian Past: The Anatomy of a Research Project'
Lucy Chester (University of Colorado), 'Zionists, Indian Nationalism, and British Schizophrenia in Palestine'
Michael Brenner (University of Pittsburgh), 'Strategic and Cultural Triangulation: Britain, the United States, and Europe'
Roger Morgan (European University, Florence), 'The British "Establishment" and the Chatham House Version of World Affairs'
Jason Parker (Texas A&M), 'Wilson's Curse: Self-Determination, the Cold War, and the Challenge of Modernity in the "Third World"'
Stephen Foster (Northern Illinois University), 'The American Colonies and the Atlantic World'
A. G. Hopkins (History), 'Comparing British and American "Empires"'
James Turner (Notre Dame University), 'The Emergence of Academic Disciplines'
Dror Wahrman (Indiana University), 'Invisible Hands in the Eighteenth Century'
Narendra Singh Sarila (Prince of Sarila), 'Mountbatten and the Partition of India'
Pillarisetti Sudhir (American Historical Association), 'The Retreat of the Raj: Radicals and Reactionaries in Britain'
Keith Francis (Baylor University), 'What Did Darwin Mean in *On the Origin of Species*? An Englishman and a Frenchman Debate Evolution'

Fall Semester 2008

'Ted and Sylvia'—Round Table Discussion, (UT English), Judith Kroll, Kurt Heinzelman, Betty Sue Flowers, Tom Cable
Roby Barrett (Middle East Institute), 'The Question of Intervention in Iraq, 1958–59'
John Kerr (San Antonio), 'Cardigan Bay'

Sue Onslow (London School of Economics), 'Julian Amery: A Nineteenth-Century Relic in a Twentieth-Century World?'

John Rumrich (English), 'Reconciliation in *The Winter's Tale:* The Literary Friendship of Robert Greene and William Shakespeare'

Richard Jenkyns (Oxford), 'Conan Doyle: An Assessment beyond Sherlock Holmes'

Theresa Kelley (University of Wisconsin), 'Romantic British Culture and Botany in India'

Sir Adam Roberts (Oxford), 'After the Cold War'

Geoffrey Wheatcroft (London), 'Churchill and the Jews'

Sir Brian Harrison (Oxford), 'Prelude to the Sixties'

Eric Kaufmann (London School of Economics), 'The Orange Order in Northern Ireland'

Robert McMahon (Ohio State University), 'Dean Acheson: The Creation of a New World Order and the Problem of the British'

Mark Metzler (History), 'Eye of the Storm: London's Place in the First Great Depression, 1872–96'

James Loehlin (English), Christmas Party at the New Campus Club, reading passages from Charles Dickens, *A Christmas Carol*

Spring Semester 2009

Margaret MacMillan (Oxford University), 'The Jewel in the Crown'

Bernard Wasserstein (University of Chicago), 'Glasgow in the 1950s'

Dominic Sandbrook (London), 'The Swinging Sixties in Britain'

Karl Meyer and Shareen Brysac (New York Times and CBS), 'Inventing Iran, Inventing Iraq: The British and Americans in the Middle East'

Albert Lewis (R. L. Moore Project), 'The Bertrand Russell Collection: The One That Got Away from the HRC'

Sir David Cannadine (Institute of Historical Research, London), 'Colonial Independence'; Linda Colley (CBE, Princeton University), 'Philip Francis and the Challenge to the British Empire'

George Scott Christian (English and History), 'Origins of Scottish Nationalism: The Trial of Thomas Muir'

Discussion led by Brian Levack and Roger Louis (History), 'Trevor-Roper and Scotland'

Warren Kimball (Rutgers University), 'Churchill, Roosevelt, and Ireland'

Ferdinand Mount (London) and R. J. Q. Adams (Texas A&M), 'A. J. Balfour and his Critics'

Dan Jacobson (London), Betty Sue Flowers (LBJ Library), and Tom Staley (HRHRC), Tribute to Betty Sue Flowers—'Hardy and Eliot'

John Darwin (Nuffield College, Oxford), 'Britain's Global Empire'

Saul Dubow (Sussex University), 'Sir Keith Hancock and the Question of Race'

Weslie Janeway (Cambridge), 'Darwin's Cookbook'

Julian Barnes, Barbara Harlow, Miguel Gonzalez-Gerth, 'Such, Such Was Eric Blair'

Cassandra Pybus (Visiting Fellow, UT Institute of Historical Studies), 'If you were regular black . . .': Slavery, Miscegenation, and Racial Anxiety in Britain'

Fall Semester 2009

Peter Green (Classics), 'The Devil in Kingsley Amis'

John Farrell (English), 'Forgiving Emily Brontë'

Samuel Baker (English), 'Wedgwood Gothic'

Louise Weinberg (Law), 'Gilbert and Sullivan: The Curios Persistence of Savoyards'

Elizabeth Richmond-Garza (English), 'Love in a Time of Terror: King Lear and the Potential for Consolation'

John Rumrich (English), 'John Milton and the Embodied Word'

Round Table Discussion on Effective Teaching: Tom Cable (English), David Leal (Government), Lisa Moore (English), Bob Woodberry (Sociology)

James M. Vaughn (History and British Studies), 'The Decline and Fall of Whig Imperialism, 1756–1783'

Round Table Discussion on Bloomsbury: Betty Sue Flowers (English), Roger Louis (History), Lisa Moore (English), David Sosa (Philosophy)

Sir Harold Evans, 'Murder Most Foul'

Peter Cain (Sheffield Hallam University), 'The Radical Critique of Colonialism'

John Gooch (Leeds University), 'Pyrrhic Victory? England and the Great War'

Maya Jasanoff (Harvard University), 'The British Side of the American Revolution'

Maeve Cooney (British Studies), Christmas Party at the Littlefield Home, reading O. Henry's 'The Gift of the Magi'

Spring Semester 2010

Thomas Jesus Garza (UT Language Center), 'The British Vampire's Slavic Roots'

Marilyn Young (New York University), 'The British and Vietnam'

Daniel Howe (University of California at Los Angeles), 'What Hath God Wrought'

Roberta Rubenstein (American University), 'Virginia Woolf and the Russians'

Samuel R. Williamson (University of the South at Sewanee), 'The Possibility of Civil War over Ireland in 1914'

Steve Pincus (Yale), 'The First Modern Revolution: Reappraising the Glorious Events of 1688'

Selina Hastings (London), 'Somerset Maugham: A Life Under Cover'

Eugene Rogan (Oxford), 'Modern History through Arab Eyes'

T. M. Devine (University of Edinburgh), 'Did Slavery Make Scotland Great?'

Phillip Herring (University of Wisconsin–Madison), 'A Journey through James Joyce's *Ulysses*'

Alison Bashford (Harvard), 'Australia and the World Population Problem, 1918–1954'

Berny Sèbe (Birmingham University), 'French and British Colonial Heroes in Africa'

J. L. Berry (Austin, Texas), 'The Post-Twilight of the British Empire on the Zambian Copper Belt'

Bernard Porter (University of Newcastle), 'The Myth of Goths and Vandals in British Architecture'

Fall Semester 2010

Jonathan Schneer (Georgia Institute of Technology), 'The Balfour Declaration'

Larry Carver (Liberal Arts Honors Program), 'Reacting to the Past: How I Came to Love Teaching Edmund Burke'

Thomas Pinney (Pomona College), 'Kipling and America'

Donna Kornhaber (English), 'Accident and Artistry in *The Third Man*'

Doug Bruster (English), 'Rating *A Midsummer Night's Dream*'

Peter Stansky (Stanford University), 'Julian Bell: From Bloomsbury to Spain'

Crawford Young (University of Wisconsin, Madison), 'The British Empire and Comparative Decolonization'

Jeffrey Cox (University of Iowa), 'From the Kingdom of God to the Third World'

Roberta Rubenstein (American University), 'Approaching the Golden Anniversary: Dorris Lessing's *The Golden Notebook*'

Kenneth O. Morgan (House of Lords), 'Aneurin Bevan: Pragmatist and Prophet of the Old Left'

Robert Vitalis (University of Pennsylvania), 'From the Persian Gulf to the Gulf of Mexico: What We Know About BP'

James Curran (Sydney University), 'The Great Age of Confusion: Australia in the Wake of Empire'

Archie Brown (St Antony's College, Oxford), 'Margaret Thatcher and the End of the Cold War'

Phyllis Lassner (Northwestern University), 'The End of Empire in the Middle East and the Literary Imagination'

Spring Semester 2011

Tillman Nechtman (Skidmore College), 'Nabobs: Empire and the Politics of National Identity in Eighteenth-Century Britain'

Brian Levak (History), 'Demonic Possession in Early Modern Britain'

David Kornhaber (English), 'George Bernard Shaw: Modernist'

Lisa L. Moore (English), 'Sister Arts: The Erotics of Lesbian Landscape'

Bartholomew Sparrow (Government), 'Brent Scowcroft, Mrs. Thatcher, and National Security'

Philip Bobbitt (Law School and LBJ School), 'The Special Relationship'

Deborah Harkness (UCLA), 'Fiction and the Archives: The Art and Craft of the Historian'

Peter Clarke (Trinity Hall, Cambridge), 'The English-Speaking Peoples'

A. G. Hopkins (History), 'The United States, 1783–1861: Britain's Honorary Dominion?'

Reba Soffer (California State University at Northridge), 'Intellectual History, Life, and Fiction'

Joanna Lewis (London School of Economics), 'Harold Macmillan and the Wind of Change'

Andrew Lycett (London), 'Arthur Conan Doyle and Rudyard Kipling'

Geoffrey Wheatcroft (London), 'The Grand Illusion: Britain and the United States'

Priscilla Roberts (University of Hong Kong), 'Henry James and the Erosion of British Power'

John Higley (Government), 'Degeneration of Ruling Elites? Recent American and British Elites'

Fall Semester 2011

Paul Woodruff (Philosophy), Roger Louis (History), and David Leal (Government), 'The Oxford of Maurice Bowra and Hugh Trevor-Roper'

Marian Barber (UT Austin), 'The Scots, Irish, English, and Welsh in the Making of Texas'

Geoffrey Davis (University of Aachen), 'The Territory of My Imagination: Rediscovering Dan Jacobson's South Africa'

Nadja Durbach (University of Utah), 'Poverty, Politics, and Roast Beef: Poor Relief and the Nation in Early Nineteenth-Century Britain'

Max Hastings (*Financial Times*), 'The Queen'
Leonard Barkan (Princeton University), 'What's for Dinner on a Desert Island: Feast and Famine in The Tempest'
Lindsey Schell (University Libraries), 'The Royal Wedding and the Making of a Modern Princess'
Laurence Raw (Baskent University), 'Shakespeare and the Home Front during World War II'
Sir Brian Harrison (Oxford University), 'Surprising Resilience: Historians of British Conservatism since 1945'
Troy Bickham (Texas A&M), 'A New Grand Transatlantic Drama: Britain and the Anglo-American War of 1812'
Eli P. Cox III (Marketing), 'The Betrayal of Adam Smith'
Nicholas Rogers (York University), 'Crime, Punishment, and Governance in Eighteenth-Century Britain'
Donald Lamm (W. W. Norton and Company), 'The History of Oxford University Press'
Al Martinich (History and Government), 'Locke and the Limits of Toleration'

Spring Semester 2012

Philippa Levine (Chair), John Berry (Austin), Donna Kornhaber (English), Roger Louis (History), Elizabeth Richmond-Garza (English), 'The Iron Lady'
Brian Cowan (McGill University), 'Henry Sacheverell and the Cult of Eighteenth-Century Personalities'
Ronald Heiferman (Quinnipiac University), 'Churchill, Roosevelt, and China'
Jeremi Suri (History and LBJ School), 'British Imperialism and American Nation-Building'
Susan Napier (Tufts University), 'Harry Potter and the Fantastic Journey'
Andrew Roberts (School of Oriental and African Studies), 'Poetry, Anthology, and Criticism: Michael Roberts and the BBC'
Michael Charlesworth (Art History), 'Derek Jarman and British Films: Paintings, Poetry, and Prose'
John Voll (Georgetown University), 'Britain and Islam in the Twentieth Century'
Sheldon Garon (Princeton University), 'Anglo-Japanese Cultural Relations, 1868–1950'
Anand Yang (University of Washington, Seattle), 'Convicts in British India'
George Bernard (University of Southhampton), 'Editing the *English Historical Review*'
Selina Todd (St. Hilda's College, Oxford), 'The Problem Family in Postwar Britain'
Christine Krueger (Marquette University), 'The Victorian Historian Mary Anne Everett Green'
Jeremy Lewis (London), 'David Astor and the *Observer*'
Michael Winship (English), 'Napoleon Comes to America: The Publishing of Sir Walter Scott's *Life of Napoleon Buonaparte* (1827)'
Adam Sisman (London), 'Writing the Biographies of A. J. P. Taylor and Hugh Trevor-Roper'

Fall Semester 2012

Donna Kornhaber (English), 'Charlie Chaplin's Forgotten Feature: A Countess from Hong Kong'
Tom Palaima (Classics), 'The War Poems of Robert Graves'

Rosemary Hill (All Souls College, Oxford), 'Prince Albert'
David Washbrook (Cambridge University), 'The Black Hole of Calcutta'
Ferdinand Mount (London), 'John Keats and Insults of Drug-Inspired Poetry'
Sucheta Mahajan (Jawaharlal Nehru University), 'Independence and Partition of
     India Reassessed'
Richard Davenport-Hines (London), 'Ivy Compton-Burnett'
Albert Beveridge III (Johns Hopkins), 'The Rise, Fall, and Revival of Anthony
     Trollope'
Philip Stern (Duke University), 'The Evolution of the City of Bombay'
Betty Smocovitis (University of Florida), 'Rhapsody on a Darwinian Theme'
Jad Adams (University of London), 'Tony Benn: The Making of a British Radical'
Paul Levy (*Wall Street Journal*), 'Lytton Strachey'
William Janeway (New York), 'Beyond Keynesianism: Maynard Keynes and the
     Good Life'
Daniel Raff (Wharton School of Business), 'The Ancient University Presses Make
     Up Their Minds'
David Leal (Government), 'Method and Irrationality in the Traditions of Sherlock
     Holmes'

Spring Semester 2013

Kariann Yokata (University of Colorado, Denver), 'Unbecoming British? The Place
     of Post-Colonial Americans in the British Empire'
Brian Levack (History), 'The British Imperial State in the Eighteenth Century'
Anne Chisholm (London), 'Dora Carrington and the Bloomsbury Circle'
James Banner (Washington, D.C.), 'Academics, Intellectuals, and Popular History'
Selina Hastings (London), 'The Red Earl'
John Spurling (London), 'Sir Edmund Gibson and the British Raj'
Hilary Spurling (London), 'Pearl Buck and China'
Steven Isenberg (Quondam Executive Director of PEN), 'Fathers and Sons:
     Edmund Gosse and J. R. Ackerley'
Janine Barchas (English), 'Jane Austen between the Covers'
Wm. Roger Louis (History and British Studies), 'The History of Oxford University
     Press, 1896–1970'
Sir Christopher Bayly (Cambridge), 'Distant Connections: India and Australia in
     the Colonial Era'
Philip Waller (Oxford), 'Writers, Readers, and Reputations'
Jordanna Bailkin (University of Washington), 'Unsettled: Refugee Camps in
     Britain'
Geoffrey Wheatcroft (London), 'Assessing Margaret Thatcher'
Daniel Baugh (Cornell University), 'France and the British State and Empire,
     1680–1940'
Richard Carwardine (Oxford), 'Lincoln and Emancipation: The British and Inter-
     national Consequences'
Linda Colley (Princeton University), 'The Breakup of Britain'
Brian Urquhart (New York), 'My Father: Watercolorist'